DEEP
BLUE

Twenty Years Behind The Badge

by

Sgt. Michael Miller (ret.)

We few, we happy few, we band of brothers...

All the events in this book are true to the best of my knowledge and memory. In some cases, names have been changed to protect the innocent, the guilty, and all those in between. You know who you are.

This book would not have been possible without the support and encouragement of my family and friends. I first want to thank all those men and women in blue, my brothers and sisters in this crazy adventure we call "the Job". I particularly want to thank Mitch Lovett, for bringing me into it; Beth Ondrak, my first partner with whom I started police work all those years ago; John Reynolds - don't worry JR, I still won't tell all the things you've done and gotten away with; Jody Sansing, for still not telling all the things we did and got away with; John Bayman, who was my mentor and guiding hand when I was a baby sergeant; John Defelice, for his humor and wisdom; Angel Cross, for bringing a little humanity to it all; Suzanne Rogers, for the encouragement to strike out in a new direction; Matt Cisneros - my old partner. I couldn't have done all this without you, and I wouldn't have wanted to. And finally and most important, my wife Carolyn, my daughter Alex, and my son Nick, who gave meaning to it all.

MONSTERS

*"Beware that when battling monsters, you do not
become a monster, for when you gaze long into the abyss,
the abyss also gazes into you."*
                                            - Friedrich Nietzsche

Every veteran cop, no matter how thick the protective
shell that you try to build around yourself, has cases they
will never forget, no matter how hard you try. I have a few
that creep back into my mind when I least expect it and don't
want it, faces from the past that come to me, usually just as I
am lying in bed and drifting off to sleep. One of them began
for me on a bitter cold morning in the dead of winter. I was
driving my patrol car southbound on Interstate 25 on a day
shift that started like any other, when the voice of the police
dispatcher came over the radio to me; *"Car 129, copy a call of
shots fired."* I picked up the mike and answered, and dispatch
reported that someone in the parking garage of an apartment
complex had heard what they thought sounded like a gunshot.
We get these now and then, and very rarely is it an actual
gunshot. It is usually a car backfiring, or a pneumatic nail
gun at a construction site, or something innocuous like that.
I exited the highway and started heading back in the direction
of the apartment complex when dispatch radioed me again and
said they were now getting more calls of shots fired at the same
location, fourth floor of the parking garage. I picked up the
mike again and said I was responding Code 3 and flipped on

the patrol car lights and siren and kicked up my speed as other units started to converge.

I was the first to arrive, driving between the two wings of the apartment complex to the big central parking garage. The entrance to the parking garage required a key card and the apartment managers would not give them to the police, so we were unable to drive up to the fourth floor. I parked my car and headed on foot for the bank of elevators and was joined en route by a buddy of mine named Dave. Dave and I rode the elevator up and emerged onto the fourth floor. We drew our guns and halted by the elevator, listening for any more shots or sounds of movement. It was quiet, with no sounds other than the distant traffic below us.

We began to search the parking garage, alert for any sound or movement, and as we did so I saw some papers strewn on the concrete floor, then what looked like a lunchbox, then a scarf, and we followed the trail of debris around a corner. It was looking like a struggle had taken place here, and my heart was starting to sink in my chest. Suddenly a female officer ahead of us called out. It was a call that sent a chill down my spine. We ran over to where she was standing, staring down at the ground between two cars. We looked where she was pointing, and then we saw her there. A young woman, a pretty young woman with long brown hair lying motionless on the cold gray floor.

We immediately picked her up and carried her out from between the cars and laid her on the concrete and checked her vital signs. No pulse, no breathing. We started doing rescue breathing and chest compressions to try to keep her heart going and blood circulating to her brain. She was already going cold to the touch. As we were pulling her out from between the cars and checking her over, we saw that she had a pair of gunshot entrance wounds in her upper back. One of the officers came running up with a trauma kit to stop the bleeding, but I knew already that it was too late for that, too late for us to do anything to save her. She was already gone.

We sealed off the area with crime scene tape and started a careful grid search of the entire garage, while we waited for the detectives and Crime Lab technicians to arrive. They would photograph her body, take fingerprints, measure the wounds, try to recover the bullets to do ballistics. I looked down at this young woman, her face pale and beautiful even in death, a person in the prime of life, and I wondered what kind of animal could do such a thing to another human being. Whatever this woman was or could have been; a wife, a mother, somebody's child, somebody's sweetheart, had ended suddenly and violently here in this parking garage. We knew next to nothing at this point, but I made a silent vow – we all did - that we would find this bastard and make him pay for what he had done.

We began knocking on doors and interviewing the residents of the apartment complex, while other officers checked to see if there were cameras in the parking garage or at the complex entrance. This is how police work is done, how crimes get solved. Grunt work. Talking to people, looking at security camera videos, trying to find somebody who saw something. You do it right and you do it thorough. As our investigation progressed a picture began to emerge. I knocked on a door and talked to an older woman who said her friend Elizabeth was supposed to go to work this morning, but her car was still right there in the parking garage, not a hundred feet from us. *Elizabeth was okay, wasn't she?* the lady asked me. What do you say to people in that situation? We got her information and worked that angle, her employment, along with a couple of other leads we were checking. Our first job was to identify the victim, find out who she was and hopefully that would lead us to who had a reason to kill her, and we were able to do that quickly.

Elizabeth was a beautiful young woman, athletic, smart, and well-liked by her coworkers, beloved by her family and her fiancé. They were to be married that summer. Out of respect for the privacy of the family I will not use her real name here. She was also being stalked by one of her coworkers who was obsessed with her. This coworker had been fired for his relentless harassment of her, and he was determined to take his revenge.

Because of subsequent events we will never know what he really had in mind, but this is what I believe. I believe he wanted to make her suffer, that he intended to abduct her in that parking garage right outside of her apartment. He would know when she was leaving for work. My gut instinct tells me he was going to use the gun to overpower her, force her into the car, and then rape her, to satisfy his twisted fantasies and pay her back for his getting fired. But she didn't go along with his plan, maybe she *knew* what he intended to do. So she fought, she struggled with him, and tried to run and he shot her in the back then pulled her body between the cars to hide it. He took her cell phone, for reasons unknown, and kept it with him in his car and later took it to his apartment. It is not uncommon for murderers to take something, some trophy, from their victim. The detectives pinged her phone, and the signal was moving as he drove around seemingly aimlessly. I believe he was contemplating the monstrosity of what he had just done. Sometimes people get so fixated on an idea; revenge, money, bloodlust, sexual fantasies, whatever, but they never think *what do I do after it's done? How do I live with it?*

After spending weary hours at the crime scene, I had just returned to the station and was walking in the back door when one of our sergeants came flying down the hall at a run. I asked Dustin what was up and he said "We just found the bastard!" I said I was coming with him, and we jumped in his car and roared off with tires squealing. We drove the several miles to where the suspect was holed up, arriving at the apartment complex where he lived. It was a very large complex, with many buildings that all looked maddeningly identical, and we drove around looking for the right building. I suddenly spotted it and said *"There it is!"* Dustin cranked the wheel over and stopped on the side of the building. We jumped out and made our way cautiously down the side of the building until we located the right apartment. We took up positions on either side of the door with guns drawn.

We briefly debated whether to attempt contact at the door, but decided to hold our positions until other officers began to arrive. We didn't know anything about the layout of the apartment or where the suspect might be. We radioed our position to dispatch, then began assessing the situation. The front door was in a kind of recessed alcove, with a peephole viewer in the door and no sidelight windows. It was a multi-story building, and to my left was a garage and immediately above us was a large balcony, probably for the second-floor apartment. We needed a map of the layout of these apartments, the floor plans, and whether there were stairs or a back door, so we called for the next responding officer to get maps from the leasing office.

As it turned out, unbeknownst to us at the time, the suspect had begun texting his ex-wife after the murder. He told her what he had done, and he told her that now he knew he would die. She called the police immediately, and one of our detectives met her and struck up a conversation with the suspect. He said to the detective that he would never surrender and spend the rest of his life in prison, and that he knew we had his apartment surrounded. Ominously, he also said he had a fully loaded AR-15 and that he intended to die in a shootout with the police, to die in a blaze of gunfire.

It was still just me and Dustin at the door, and we had by no means surrounded his apartment. What the public doesn't realize is that when critical incidents like this happen, those first few minutes we are often flying by the seat of our pants, usually having little information and making decisions on the go. We had radioed in our location, but we were out of our own city now and no one else knew exactly where we were. It was a big complex where all the buildings looked the same, and we were tucked away in a corner of the complex, almost completely hidden from view. To make it worse my department was a small agency and we had only a handful of officers on duty at any given time, so there would be no cavalry to come riding over the hill.

One of our Commanders came up on the radio and said he was taking overall Incident Command, and Denver PD SWAT would be taking Tactical Command. He had established his Command Post in the apartment leasing office, and he got on the radio and ordered all sergeants to respond immediately to the CP for a briefing. I looked over at Dustin, and he looked back at me. *It's just you and me, bud.* Dustin was a cop's cop, true blue, and he got on the radio and said "Negative sir, I can't leave this position." The Commander got back on the radio and ordered him to respond *immediately* to the Command Post. We looked at each other again, and I wouldn't have blamed him a bit if he had peeled off and left me there all by my lonesome. But he keyed his radio mike and said "That's a *negative*, sir! I cannot leave this post."

After about ten minutes another cop buddy of mine named Bryan arrived. He had been driving all over the complex looking for us. He took Dustin's position and only then did Dustin leave to go to the Command Post. In the Commander's defense, I don't think he was aware that he had just two guys on the suspect's apartment. When Dustin left it was me and Bryan. He was one of our SWAT guys, and he was also a K-9 Officer and he brought his dog out with him. Tag was a big black-faced Belgian Malinois, and what I liked about Tag was that he was as friendly to everyone as your family pet - until it was time to go to work. Then the switch in his head flipped and he was all fur and teeth. Dogs are wonderful assets, who love to work and will literally give their lives to save their handlers. Depending on how the situation played out, we had to be ready to send Tag in to get the bad guy. Tag knew it, too, and he was ready to go. As I was talking to Bryan, I realized for the first time that someone was actually in contact with the suspect and talking to him, and his dire warning about shooting it out with the police.

I had now been on this post for about twenty minutes, and I was looking around wondering where the hell the Denver guys were. Did they not even know we were here and what we were doing? This place should have been swarming with cops. As it turns out, in the fog of war the Denver SWAT Team had been notified but the Denver patrol officers had not. They had no idea we were even out here. Before coming to my current department I had been an officer with Denver PD, on patrol in the public housing projects of District Six, the roughest part of the city. I knew these guys, and I knew that if they were aware of the situation we had here, there would have been a hundred cops here in five minutes. Those guys were tough and eager, and they would have come in on their day off for a call like this.

It was bitter cold outside, a chill winter day, and when I had run out the door with Dustin I didn't have my gloves, a hat, or a coat. Once the initial adrenaline dump wore off and I settled in covering the door, I started to notice the cold. I started shivering, then my ears went completely numb. Soon I couldn't feel my hands. They were like wooden blocks, and every now and then I would have to physically look down at my hands to make sure I was still holding my gun. I couldn't feel a thing. I honestly didn't know if I could even pull the trigger if the bad guy came charging out.

I heard a noise behind me and turned around to see who was coming up. Gerry Whitman was walking up behind me. Gerry was Captain of the DPD SWAT Team, and when I worked for Denver he was the Chief of Police. I liked Gerry, and he liked me. I gave him a quick sitrep and he told me some of his operators would be coming up soon to join us. Seeing him brought back a memory. When I was at DPD my partner and I were involved in a fatal shooting; a bad man had been prowling our area late at night pulling armed robberies and pistol-whipping people, and all of us cops in the District were looking for him. My partner and I found him one night and he ran, and during the foot chase he pulled a .357 Magnum revolver from his waistband and turned on us with it. He did not survive the encounter.

After the shooting I was sitting on a couch all alone in Internal Affairs, waiting to be interviewed, and my head was spinning with a million questions, as you can imagine; *What was going to happen to us? How am I going to tell my wife about this? Could we have done anything different?* These were the thoughts going through my head, when in walks Chief Whitman. He sits down next to me on the couch and says not to worry, we've got your back, and is there anything at all I can do for you? I really appreciated that, because sometimes the police brass are real quick to throw officers to the wolves for political reasons, especially when the cops are white and the dead suspect is black, as it was with us.

A few minutes later some of the Denver SWAT guys started arriving, moving into position with me and Bryan. They had a medic to treat any officers or bystanders who might be injured, or the suspect. That was the rule; officers first, civilians second, and the suspect last. SWAT pulled up a big black Bearcat armored vehicle on the side of the apartment opposite from us and started shouting to the suspect by using a bullhorn, telling him to drop his rifle and come out. Then we settled in for the negotiation phase. If you can keep a situation from blowing up at the beginning, there is an excellent chance we can bring a case to an end without bloodshed. When tempers are hot and people are desperate to escape and the situation is fluid and dynamic, you never can tell what is going to happen. It's totally unpredictable. That's why we try to contain people, to get everything and everyone to just *settle down*. And it usually works.

The problem with the negotiation phase is that it usually takes time. A long time. A long, long time. Now the cold was so intense that I had stopped shivering. When you stop shivering, you are in trouble. Your body is starting to shut down the blood flow to the surface and extremities, to conserve its energy for core life-sustaining functions. The SWAT medic looked at me and said "You're going hypothermic. You need to get out of here." I started to turn away when we heard a muffled *POP!* from inside the apartment. All of our guns instantly came up. It was a single gunshot. The suspect could have committed suicide, offed himself as they so often do when cornered and surrounded. Or it could have been an accidental discharge, from a guy walking around with his finger on the trigger coupled with a high stress level. Or it could have been an attempt to lure us in, to make entry so he could engage us, to commit suicide-by-cop and take some of us with him.

We had a brief discussion and decided not to make entry. Somebody said "Get the'bot." So we brought up the robot, a slick little vehicle with tracks like a baby tank and an extendable arm that could hold a video camera. Or a shotgun. We brought up a battering ram and the breacher rammed the door, knocking it backwards off its hinges while the rest of us covered. I let out a low whistle. I had assumed that the interior of the apartment would be right behind the door. You open the door, you go in. But we had never got the floor plan we had been asking for, and directly in front of us was a staircase going up. The suspect's apartment was actually on the *second* floor, and his balcony was right over our heads. Thank God we had the tactical sense to always stay under cover, or he could have leisurely taken aim and shot us from that balcony. Believe me, that's the kind of stuff that sends a chill up your spine.

We sent the robot in, and it crawled up the stairs. There was a small handheld television screen so the operators could see what the robot saw, and as it moved through the apartment it found the suspect in the bedroom. He was dead. He had shot himself, committed suicide. He murders this woman, takes a beautiful life full of promise, then takes the coward's way out.

Afterward I went and found a patrol car, I don't even know whose patrol car it was. I just climbed in and turned on the heater. I had never been so cold in my life. I couldn't feel anything. When I opened the door handle, I had to look at it and concentrate on what I was doing. I just dropped my body into the driver's seat, mentally and physically exhausted. I turned on the heat full blast and just soaked in the warmth. After ten minutes the interior of the car was like a furnace, and I was still shaking. After another ten minutes I began to feel better, to feel my fingers and face again.

While I was sitting there, watching through the windshield the other cops, the press with their cameras and microphones, the paramedics, all moving in front of me like a silent movie, I thought about all that had happened that day, what a tragic waste it had all been. That poor girl, all the things she could have and should have been. I thought about her fiancé, planning their wedding, their marriage, their children, growing old together. There are those who say there really isn't such a thing as evil. They usually say this from the comfort and safety of a philosophy class or the padded chairs of a coffee shop. Those people are wrong. I know. I've seen it.

PART ONE

ONE

"There's a lot of law at the end of a policeman's night stick."
Grover Whalen, New York police commissioner, 1928

IF YOU ARE EVER A VISITOR TO THE MILE HIGH CITY and should find yourself in the bustle and hurry of Interstate 25, look above your head at the big green and white street signs and when you come to the one that says Exit 210 - Colfax Avenue, take it if you want a break from the bumper to bumper traffic and wish to see the beating heart of Denver. As you head east you will be approaching downtown, with its glittering Capitol Dome, towering glass and steel skyscrapers, and the turrets and spires of the beautiful Cathedral of the Immaculate Conception. But before you get quite there, when you cross the Colfax bridge and get back onto solid ground, turn to the right and leave the main road behind and you will find yourself in the Lincoln Park neighborhood. Precinct 617. My beat.

I had been with the Denver Police Department for about a year when I was newly assigned to my precinct in District Six, but I was no rookie, fresh-faced and young and eager. I had already been a police officer for more than a decade, and while I was no longer young or fresh-faced, I still had a small spark of eagerness left in me. The city of Denver had always been divided into five police districts, but the city fathers carved District Six out of the worst parts of three other districts and it now encompassed the downtown area, several of the most crime-ridden neighborhoods in the city, and Capitol Hill with its government offices, courthouses, and broad sidewalks which swarmed with lawyers and government officials and business execs by day, and with drug dealers, drug addicts, and hookers by night.

When you come off the Colfax bridge, start looking to your right and soon you will see a little gas station, nestled there near the corner of Colfax and Osage. This particular gas station looks sleepy and innocuous in the daytime, like a thousand other gas stations on a thousand other corners, but by way of introduction to the neighborhood I will tell you a story that took place here. You might even still be able to see the bullet holes in the wall. During the day commuters pass through this station, buying gas and sodas and lottery tickets, hoping to strike it rich and leave the rat race behind, before moving off on their daily errands, but at night this little place transforms. The parking lot fills to capacity with motorcycles, low riders, groups of 'bangers rolling their eyes and flashing gang signs in challenge to each other, hoods and bikers gathered here and there in pockets, with their scantily dressed, frizzy haired ladies wearing too much makeup hanging on them. Locals know not to come here after dark, and the occasional traveler passing through soon learns.

I was working the graveyard shift on this particular night, and a friend of mine named Manuel worked the same precinct but on the swing shift. The swing shift, Detail 3, stayed on until 2 a.m. while I and my teammates on Detail 1 worked from nine at night until seven in the morning. On this warm summer evening Manny got a call of a drive by shooting at this gas station. The dispatcher didn't sound overly excited, so Manny asked if there were any casualties. "Negative, no reports of injury" she droned back. He acknowledged and said he was en route and would advise on cover. I was still in the locker room getting suited up, but I had turned my radio on and was listening to it as was my habit, so I could get an idea of what was going on in the city before I took the elevator up from the basement to the third floor for roll call. I heard the call, and decided if we didn't get anything hot right out of the chute I would go over there to help him with a neighborhood canvass or with the paperwork.

Now Manny was on his way to the gas station, but something intervened to change his direction. Two somethings, actually. Two somethings that were young and cute and flirty. Another officer called Manny on his cell phone and told him he was up on the Sixteenth Street Mall, and just happened to be talking to two hotties who knew Manny and were asking where he was. The Mall was a long and colorful strip of shops, restaurants, movie theaters, and street vendors right in the middle of downtown, where Sixteenth Street had been closed to all vehicle traffic except the RTD city buses. Manuel was a handsome single guy, so he had a decision to make; go to this call, which was probably nothing because there were no injuries reported and the shooter was undoubtedly long gone, or head downtown to chat with some honeys and maybe set something up for later. He had a quick mental debate, then made a sudden right turn and accelerated, headed for the bright lights and warm bodies of The Mall. Girls 1, Duty 0.

I had finished with roll call and was picking up my war bag to go out to my car when dispatch called Manny again. *"Car 667, what's the status on that drive by shooting report?"* The radio gave only static in reply, so she called him again. On the third try, Manny came across and said hurriedly "Oh that was nothing. UTL!" (Unable to Locate the shooters). Dispatch acknowledged, but the exchange caught the attention of Sergeant Johnson. Sergeant Johnson was one of the District Six sergeants, and he was big, black, and mean. He stalked around the station with a permanent glowering scowl on his face, and between that pit bull gaze and his bulging muscles he was one scary man, even to us. He was also Manny's sergeant, and he didn't like

Manny very much. Sergeant Johnson thought Manuel was a womanizing screw-off... *I can't imagine why*... and would have loved to nail him for misconduct or violating policy, any policy.

Ten minutes later, dispatch called me and said the owner of the gas station was still waiting for an officer to respond. I was a little perplexed because Manny had already checked and said there was nothing to it. But by this time I was on the road and in the precinct, so I spun the patrol car around and headed that direction. I pulled into the parking lot and saw nothing out of the ordinary. Lights were on, cars were at the pumps, people going in and out. I figured the owner must be one of those good citizens who just wants to say his piece, to voice his outrage and be heard, so I pulled up, got out, and walked in.

When I opened the door, I stopped dead in my tracks. The place looked like Hurricane Katrina had stopped by for a visit, and she was angry. The glass doors that line one wall of every convenience store, where they keep all the beer and bottled water and sandwiches, were all shattered out and glass and pools of liquids were everywhere. The soda fountain had been shot up and was spewing caramel colored fluids. The drive-through window on the north side of the station was shot out, and the cash register had a bullet hole in it. It looked like a squad of Marines and a band of Taliban had done battle inside the gas station. *"Holy Shit!"* was all I could think to say.

The turbaned Indian gas station attendant came over to me and said in that peculiar Indian-accented English "My Gott! Where have you been!? *Look* at this place! I have been waiting for half an hour for you!" He continued berating me while gesturing excitedly at the carnage in the store for a few more minutes, but I was able to confirm that no one was hit. I walked around examining the crime scene inside and out, and judging by the row of shiny brass 7.62 x 39 shell casings on the street outside, it seemed that a carload of shooters had driven by on Colfax and unloaded a full magazine on the north side of the gas station with at least one AK-47 and maybe more, probably aiming at some rivals inside or in the parking lot. The bullets had gone right through the brick wall of the station and wreaked havoc inside. It was amazing that no one was killed.

I got on my portable radio and said I needed the Crime Lab. Dispatch asked what for, and I replied that there was some property damage inside the gas station. Sergeant Johnson's voice immediately came over the radio, full of suspicion. He wanted to know if there had been shots fired into the gas station. I said yes, then immediately grabbed my Department-issued cell phone and called Manny, who was so busy talking to the pretty young things that he hadn't heard a single word of what was going on over the radio. I told him if he valued his job he'd better say goodbye to the honeys and get his ass down here to the gas station, *Pronto!* He didn't have a clue what I was talking about, so I told him that drive by shooting that he said was nothing looked like The Battle of Fallujah. He still sounded confused, but when I told him Sergeant Johnson was probably on his way down here at this very moment he said *"I'm on my way!"* and disconnected.

He must have burned rubber and run every red light in the District, because he was there in just a couple of minutes. I already had my camera out and was shooting pictures, and as soon as he walked in the front door I shoved the camera into his hands and said "Start taking pictures!" He said "Of what?" and I said "Anything! The floor, the soda fountain, the Indian guy standing at the register! Just start shooting!" He took the camera and lifted it to his eye to take a picture of the morose Indian clerk, and at that very second Sergeant Johnson's big form filled the doorway. He looked like Darth Vader standing there. He was so sure he was going to bust Manny, yet there he was dutifully snapping pictures and investigating the crime scene. The scowl on his face got even deeper, and he turned around and stalked away without saying a word. At DPD they drilled it into us

from Day One in the Police Academy; *We take care of our own.*
Even if that means protecting a screw-off playboy from his own
sergeant's righteous wrath.

* * *

Like most American kids I watched cop shows growing
up. *Dragnet,* with "Just the facts, Ma'am" Joe Friday and Bill
Gannon was a little before my time, so I grew up on *Miami
Vice* and *Starsky and Hutch* and even the old *Mannix* series. I
also liked *Magnum P.I.,* which technically was not a cop show
but he did get to live in Hawaii and drive a red Ferrari. Still, I
had never consciously wanted to be a cop, and I stumbled into
it quite by accident, sort of like when you're walking one way
but looking behind you and run into something you didn't see
coming.

The road that would lead me to wearing a badge and a
gun began several years earlier, with a chance meeting with an
old friend. First of all you have to know that I am one of those
unfortunate cursed people for whom everything comes the hard
way. Have you seen the movie *Just My Luck?* The male lead
gets splashed by cars in his new suit, his clothes catch on fire, he
steps in dog poop, burns himself with his coffee, and that's just
one morning on the way to work. That guy is me. I grew up in
Cheyenne, Wyoming and when me and my buddies graduated
from high school I didn't have the money to pay for college, so I
stood sadly by and watched as my best friends since kindergarten
loaded up their U-Haul, talking eagerly and excitedly about
college and college parties and college girls, and drove away
without so much as a backward glance at me.

No one from my family had ever gone to college, and both
of my parents felt that the right thing to do was get a decent
working man's job and stick with it. My dad had a buddy, old
Mr. Potter, who lived in our trailer court and was a plumber. My

dad wanted me to go on as his apprentice and learn the trade. I should point out that my dad also tried to fix me up with the very homely daughter of one of his other friends.

Now we were all blue-collar country boys, my whole family – my cousins and kinfolk back there in Alabama and Arkansas, or up here in Wyoming, it made no difference - we were sons of the soil. We spent our childhood in overalls and no shoes, with chickens and dogs running around our bare feet. But I always felt a little different. I knew early on I was born with the smarts to do something more, to be something different. My parents saw it too, and they pegged my active imagination as laziness and a wandering mind, that had to be whipped out of me so I could put my nose to the grindstone and work hard. Well, I got whipped plenty, and it seemed like my nose was on the grindstone all the time, but my mind kept right on wandering. I knew all along I had no intention of being a plumber's apprentice. I had bigger dreams for myself, and I knew college was the only way for me to escape the trailer court where I grew up and the life of a laborer that beckoned as my future.

The next day I had to go back to work at the furniture store where I was a delivery and warehouse guy, working and scrimping and saving, trying to get enough money together to take me over the hill to Laramie, fifty miles and another world away. The following August found me with a few thousand dollars in my pocket; I was lucky, because the furniture store went out of business at about that time. I would like to think I played no part in that, but considering that two other places I had worked at also went out of business I wasn't so sure that my bad karma wasn't rubbing off on my employers. But whether I bore any responsibility for their financial misfortunes or not I walked away from it with a light and happy heart. I loaded up my little red 1983 Nissan Sentra with my meager belongings and sang all the way over the hill the fifty miles to Laramie and the University of Wyoming.

I enrolled in school, Business Administration, and was reunited with my old boyhood pals Johnnie and Brad. We rented a four-bedroom apartment, along with Sonny, the boyfriend of Brad's knockout older sister Debbie. I got a job, I had an apartment, classes were starting, and for the first time in a long time things looked like they were finally going my way. So naturally disaster struck. The disaster was called 1987. Not just one disaster, but an entire disastrous year where the punches kept coming until I was down and out. The worst year of my life began with a bang. Literally. I was driving my Nissan on the twisty mountain highway between Laramie and Cheyenne when I heard a rattle coming from the engine bay, which quickly grew in volume and intensity while I looked frantically for a place to pull over on the narrow, steep-sided road. The rattle reached a crescendo and suddenly ended in a bang, after which there was dead silence, and I lost all power.

I coasted the car to a stop on a little paved turnout and popped the hood. Oil was everywhere in the engine compartment and on the underside of the hood, and I noticed with a sinking heart that the oil filler cap, a cheap slip-on type, was nowhere to be seen. My little car had fried its engine. I walked the ten miles remaining to get to Cheyenne, sticking my thumb out every time a car came up behind me, but no one stopped. It was January, it was cold, and where was all this famed "friendly Western hospitality" I always heard about? Finally, an old man in a beat-up pickup stopped and carried me the last half-mile into town.

Just as I suspected, the mechanic said my engine had seized up when the oil filler cap popped off and the oil had all come out. It would be six hundred bucks to fix it. At the time I was working at a local Wendy's for minimum wage and could barely cover my rent, so it might as well have been six million. I didn't even have money for a bicycle, so having no other choice I walked to school in the morning, walked to work in the evening, and walked home again at midnight. In the dead of winter. In Laramie, Wyoming. I felt like an Eskimo, closing my eyes against the driving snow and wind and plodding along, just placing one foot in front of the other the whole three miles home. I would come home with my face and hands and feet so cold I couldn't feel any of them. I would crawl into bed shivering so bad just trying to warm up enough to fall asleep. Then I would get up and do it again the next day. It was a hell of a way to make minimum wage.

I had too much stubborn pride to ask my parents for help, and I'm not real sure they would have given it in any case. Finally, Spring arrived and the weather began to get warmer. My walks home actually became pleasant. I wanted to get a bicycle, but I still didn't have two quarters to rub together to go buy one anyway. I was doing okay in school, but it was becoming too much for me to handle with work and my other difficulties, and I ended up withdrawing from my classes halfway through the Spring semester. Now I wasn't even going to school. I was just working and marking time, for what purpose I did not know. I was spinning my wheels and going nowhere in this one-horse town. I knew it and I wanted to get out of it, but I didn't know how. I didn't know what to do or where to turn.

The final straw, the unseen uppercut that knocked me out, was when the semester ended and Brad and Johnnie and Sonny announced they were moving back to Cheyenne for the summer. I had thought they were going to stay in Laramie, and when they didn't I was left with a four-bedroom apartment in which I could barely afford one bedroom. When the day came that the lease ended and we had to be out, I packed up my meager belongings and moved them outside into the parking lot and sat on the steps to take stock of the situation: I had no car, I had no money, I had dropped out of school, and I was homeless. If adversity is good for the soul, at least I was in good shape in the spiritual world even if I was not doing so hot in the physical one.

I spent the next few weeks alternately staying with friends or either of my two brothers, like a drifter who blows in for a few days and then is gone, not wanting to be an unwelcome burden on any of them any longer than I had to. When I had to sell some of my old schoolbooks to buy Top Ramen noodles, I knew I had reached rock bottom. Curiously, even though nothing was turning out the way I had planned and I didn't see any prospects of things improving, I felt strangely optimistic, even if it was only because I knew there was nowhere to go from here but up.

Then one day in early June I was walking along thinking about how to get out of this mess I found myself in when I bumped into an old friend of mine. I had known Wayne since we were just kids, and I used to go to his house to watch movies and eat pizza while his dad, an Air Force colonel nearing retirement, would shuffle about in his slippers muttering and grumbling to himself under his breath. In contrast to me Wayne was looking fit as a fiddle, well fed, and happy as a jay bird. We got to talking, but I didn't tell him any of my troubles. Too much pride, again. As he talked I got interested. *Real* interested. He said he had joined the Navy and they were going to pay for his school; books, tuition, spending money, the whole nine yards. It was a program called the Sea/College Fund; you would do just two years on active duty and four in the Reserves, and they would give you nineteen thousand dollars for college. *Nineteen thousand dollars!* I hadn't had more than forty bucks cash at one time in a whole year. I couldn't believe my ears. I wanted to run down to the recruiter right that second. Except the recruiter was fifty miles away. Since I didn't have a car I had to ask Wayne to get his truck and drive me to Cheyenne that day. I walked into the Armed Forces Recruiting Center in the mall and went right in and signed up before the Navy changed their mind. When I signed on that line, I felt like a giant weight had just been lifted off my shoulders. It was June 2, 1987, and I had joined the Navy.

* * *

I didn't ship out right away, there was a delay of a few months, and in the meantime I still needed a job and a place to live. I went around town picking up job applications, and I was standing in the parking lot of the Mini Mart on Third Street, just wondering where I should apply next, when I saw a fellow standing there looking at me. He was a middle- aged guy with brown hair and glasses and a kindly face, and he said to me "Are you looking for a job?" *An angel from Heaven!* "I sure am!" I said to him, and he said "Good, cause I've got one for you!" How my luck had changed!

My new job turned out to be a great one. My boss's name was Joe, and he was the owner of the Diamond Horseshoe Bar. The Diamond was a wild, riotous joint out north of town, safely beyond the city limits and the reach of the local police. It was known for fist fights and hard drinking and wild nights. I imagine it would have been right at home in Dodge City or Tombstone or someplace at the end of the tracks back in the Wild West. My job there was to do whatever needed to be done. I was a barbacker, fetching beer and whiskey from the cellar, I helped the bouncers break up fights and throw people out, and I washed the dishes and swept the floors when the place closed up. Back then the legal drinking age was only nineteen in Wyoming, and I was having a hell of a good time at my new gig.

With a job in hand, the other problem I had was finding a place to settle in and live until my shipping out date came up in November. I didn't want to be a burden on my brothers, but just like the job that problem soon worked itself out, too.

My brother Dan was a big, strapping boy and he was on the University of Wyoming football team. He was also a track star, finishing third in the nation in the 400-meter dash, so I guess we got some good genetics somewhere along the line. He was having a football party one weekend when I happened to be staying over, flopping on his couch. I'm not much for parties, and although I was decent looking I was painfully shy around girls when I was young. If a girl ever flirted with me I would get red in the face and get all tongue-tied and embarrassed. Most of the girls thought it was funny, but they would soon leave to go find other boys to flirt with.

At this party there was one girl that came up to talk to me, only she didn't leave like all the others had. She stayed and talked to me, or rather she talked and I just sat there and listened for most of the night. In fact she invited me over to her apartment the next day, and before you know it I had a place to hang my hat for a few months until I shipped out. She knew right from the start that I was leaving soon, and I was honest with her and never tried to lead her on. I was never in love with her, but I liked her and I appreciated what she did for me. I was not proud to take what felt like charity, but it was either that or sleep under a bridge. Some might think I took advantage of her, but moral judgments are easy to make from the comfort and security of your living room chair, and it looks a whole lot different from the other side.

* * *

November 9, 1987. I do not remember the date I lost my virginity, I sometimes forget anniversaries and birthdays, but the day I shipped out for Basic Training is permanently stamped in my mind. My dad drove me to the Greyhound bus terminal to see me off. My father was a career military man, serving first in the Army and then retiring out of the Air Force. He did two tours in Vietnam, one of them on an aircraft crash rescue team, helicoptering out to rescue downed pilots - or recover the bodies for a proper burial. Little did I know it at the time, but I would also serve on an aircraft crash rescue team. He was a stern man, not given to showing a lot of affection. When I was growing up I saw my father as John Wayne, Gary Cooper, one of a long line of tough, lean, stern men. I also remember that when I was a kid we would kiss him good night before bed, and I remember feeling the stubble on his cheek if he had not shaved that day. When my dad dropped me off he gave me a hug, and he was not the hugging type of man so it filled my heart to know that my dad was proud of me.

I can't point to one specific reason I enlisted, but I imagine it was a combination of patriotism, looking for adventure, and a chance to prove myself. The same reasons that American boys have been enlisting since the 1700's, I expect. My whole family was military; my Dad was in the Army and the Air Force, both of my older brothers had served in the Army, and I had an uncle in the Marines. I was proud to follow in their footsteps, to carry on a proud family tradition. I thought too, of all those who had gone before me, people marching through the history books I had read, men that I admired, from George Washington to Audie Murphy to Carlos Hathcock. Now I was serving just the way they had, and I felt it was a way of stepping up beside them, doing my duty to my country, too.

I reported for basic training, the infamous Boot Camp, at Recruit Training Center San Diego. *Ahhh...San Diego...* The sun, the sand, the beaches, the ocean waves, the beautiful weather, girls in bikinis...Yeah, I didn't see any of that. Every military veteran, from every branch, remembers boot camp like it was yesterday. Ask a Korean War vet if he remembers Basic Training and I'll bet you he can describe it in detail. He may not remember where he left his car keys or to wear the same color socks, but he will remember boot camp.

The first three days at RTC was spent in "R & O", Receiving and Outfitting. We had to hurry everywhere we went. To the chow line, to the barracks, to the various buildings where we got uniform and gear issue, and we even had to hurry over to the barber where we got our heads shaved bald as a cue-ball. *Double-time it Recruit!!* No one ever explained to us exactly why we had to hurry all the time, but I figured it was best not to ask. We also had no more names. We were all just "Recruit."

On the fourth day we were formed up into companies, each with about 90 men. I was in Company 946, a Drill Company. You have no doubt seen military drill, with crisp dress uniforms and silver sabers and parade rifles, ranks of men moving with silent precision through the Manual of Arms. That was us. I was the Adjutant, the guy standing at the front of the ranks bawling out orders to the troops and waving a shiny sword around. There were about ninety of us in the company to start, but there would be fewer in the end, as people dropped out along the way. They drilled us all right, day and night, hour after hour. I can't remember the names of half of the people I've ever worked with, but I remember my Company Commander's name. Pain has a way of ingraining things into your memory, doesn't it?

Senior Chief T.A. Salazar was a fireplug of a man, compact and muscular, with an immaculate uniform with every button polished, creases standing out sharp, and every one of the many ribbons on his thick chest exactly in place. This man radiated physical presence. He never told us what the T.A. stood for, so we made up our own which I cannot print here. He was a Filipino, and his nickname around the base was "Shogun", an ancient and revered name for samurai warlords. He was in phenomenal physical condition, and he loved to PT. That would be physical training. He told us that when he died make sure we bury him with his running shoes on, so he can run in Heaven.

Since he loved to PT, that meant we also had to PT, whether we loved it or not. We ran in the sand on the beach, we ran on the streets of the base, we ran in the pouring rain, we even ran in our sleep, I am pretty sure. You ever see a dog having a dream and twitching his feet in his sleep? That was us. We did pushups by the thousands, calisthenics, flutter kicks, jumping jacks, and 8-count bodybuilders until our muscles ached and our lungs burned. Our company flag had a blue background with a grinning pirate skull wearing a sailor cap and with crossed bones centered beneath it. Under the bones it said PT TO THE GRAVE! After a while we came to believe that it was not merely a slogan, but an achievable objective.

Some guys couldn't take it and dropped out, which was unacceptable to The Shogun. When someone would drop out of the PT, Salazar would halt the whole company. He would stand the weaker soul at attention in the center of the group, and scream *"DROP!!!"* and the rest of us would drop and crank out pushups while sending daggers and quiet curses toward the guy who was responsible for us having to do this.

I did not see it at the time, but what Salazar was doing was not unfairly punishing the group for the sins of the individual. He was weeding out those who did not have the mental toughness to push through the pain, because in combat you could not count on those people, so it was better to get rid of them early. For the rest of us, he was molding us into a unit, using peer pressure, shame, and group encouragement to forge us all into being something more than the sum of our parts. You learned to push through the pain, not because of fear of punishment, but because you did not want your shipmates to suffer because of you. Not letting them down became more important than your discomfort.

The base was right next to the MCRD, the Marine Corps Recruit Depot, and at times as we would be out on our company runs we would pass Marines running the other direction. When this happened Salazar would always pick up our pace and change our "Jodies", our running songs, to challenge the Marines. The Marines would naturally respond in kind, and the lyrics of our running songs were a little too colorful to print in a book intended for a broad audience. We had a black recruit in the company from down South who had a rich, fine voice and he always led us in our jodies.

The running songs were usually about some bastard named Jody who was always trying to steal your girl back home while you were bravely serving your country in exotic places afar, if the songs be true. I kid you not when I say to you that to this very day sometimes as I lay in bed at night and my mind is drifting into unconsciousness, I still hear the drum of a hundred pairs of boots running in cadence and the words *"I wanna be a com-bat sailor! I wanna go to a foreign land!"* still lullaby me to sleep.

* * *

When we screwed up or were not working hard enough to satisfy the Shogun, we got punished. And brother we failed often to live up to his standards! When we got punished it was called "getting mashed", as in what happened to potatoes, or bugs. When we got mashed we often had to do rifle drills. Since we were a drill company, we naturally had drill rifles. These were non-firing replicas of the Model 1903 Springfield .30-06 caliber bolt-action rifle that had served our boys so well in World Wars I and II. You think a 9 pound rifle is heavy when you hump it through the woods and over the hills looking for deer? Try this; we had to put on our coats and run in place, while hoisting and lowering that damned rifle over our heads, or forward in front of us, for what seemed like hundreds of repetitions. A 9 pound rifle feels like 9 tons when you've been holding it at arm's length in front of you for five minutes, or raising it above your head for the two hundredth time. Salazar was a Vietnam vet, and he did not want us to miss out on what he had experienced, so sometimes we would play "Vietnam", a fun game where we had to do rifle drills in the steaming shower with the hot water on. In full uniform.

One day we really pissed Salazar off. We were all being lazy on a run; it was a warm drowsy day and we were dogging it. His face got dark and stormy, and he ordered us all to go into the barracks and form up in the bay. He barked at us to grab the rifles, and we knew we were in for it. He was mashing us indoors these days, because the base commander had seen him mashing us on "the grinder", that big outdoor asphalt area next to the barracks that all veterans remember with mixed feelings of loathing and fondness, and thought he was being too hard on us. So Salazar just moved us indoors.

He started in on us, jogging us in place, hoisting the rifles up and down, and the mashing went on and on it seemed. And God help you if you dropped a rifle! These were parade rifles, polished mahogany wood and gleaming silver bayonets, and if you put so much as a scratch on one of those, even breathed hard on it, you would pay until you were begging for him to stop. All of us had muscles burning, sweat pouring off us, and Salazar was pacing up and down the squad bay with a scowl on his face. He stopped right in front of me and turned to face the other row of recruits. His back was to me, just four tantalizing feet away, and all I could think about was swinging that rifle butt around and cracking him over the head. But my next thought was *Yeah, but then he'll spin around and kill me with his pinky finger.*

In addition to our regular PT, if a guy really screwed up or was a disciplinary problem, he got sent to "marching party" at the end of our regular training day. Guys would get worked out extra special then. He would also send you to marching party if he found out it was your birthday, as I discovered on my 21st birthday. I protested to him that I had done nothing wrong, but Salazar told me that no one should have a birthday without a party.

We knew nothing about Salazar's background, and frankly we never asked, but he was an older guy, I'd say mid-forties, with over twenty years in the Navy. One day we were having a pushup contest in the squad room bay, and one of the guys topped us all with 75 pushups. Salazar walked in and asked what we were doing, well actually he asked what the hell we were doing, and when we explained it and proudly said the record was 75, Salazar immediately dropped and cranked out 80, like a piston. He popped up and walked out without saying another word. We all looked at each other thinking *Who the hell is this guy?*

Sometimes SEALs would come over from nearby Coronado and hang out in the office with Salazar, probably joking and laughing about the old days, or about what he was doing to us now. To us recruits, these SEALs were like gods, with their super levels of fitness and confidence and that gold Trident pinned to their shirts. Once in awhile there would be "SEAL Night" at a marching party, for the biggest screw-offs and attitude problems in the Company. I was squared away and never had to go to one, but these guys would come back dragging into the squad room supported on the shoulders of their shipmates, looking like shell-shocked zombies.

The SEAL recruiter came around to our company one day and asked if any of us pieces of whale shit thought they had what it takes to be a SEAL. A group of us were young and fit and feeling pretty cocky, so we said *Hell yes, we've got what it takes!* Turns out all of us were wrong, except for one guy named Bube. To be a SEAL you first had to go to BUD/S, Basic Underwater Demolition / SEAL training. But to even get into BUD/S you had to take a series of physical fitness tests. I had played football, ran track, and was confident I could pass whatever they threw at us. What I hadn't counted on was that the first test was a swim test. As it turns out, I swim like a rock. I'm from Wyoming, land of mountains and prairies. We don't swim.

As boot camp progressed we got more used to the routine, and moved into training sessions like shipboard and aircraft firefighting, small arms, and classroom work, and I was starting to really enjoy my time at boot camp. There were still times that I hated Senior Chief Salazar, but I loved the guy too. The military guys know what I'm talking about. He pushed us so hard we thought we would break, and some guys did break. But those who made it didn't break. We grew stronger, tougher, harder. When I came in I thought I was fit, I thought I was tough, but by the end of nine weeks under the gentle hand of the Shogun I was hard as nails. I had a six-pack that bodybuilders would envy, I was lean and mean and cut. Runs and PT that killed me in the first week were a breeze now. And we felt different. I wouldn't say I was cocky; let's just say I suffered from an excess of self-confidence.

As the weeks went on we saw less and less of Salazar, as we moved into classroom work with other instructors. At the end of the day we took orders from our RCPO, our Recruit Chief Petty Officer selected from our own company. This was a way of grooming promising young men for leadership positions. It was a difficult and stressful position that could drive a person crazy, and one night while I was on fire watch in the barracks and everyone was asleep, our RCPO sat bolt upright in bed and shouted out EVERYBODY SHUT THE FUCK UP! then dropped back to his pillow. I've heard of people sleepwalking, but until then I'd never heard of anybody sleep-cursing. RCPO Thomas, if you're out there, you did a good job brother.

Another reason that we saw less of Salazar was that he was also the WSI, the Water Survival Instructor, for the entire Naval Training Center. One day I was sent to find him to relay a message, and I went to the huge indoor pool complex where we did our water survival training and swim tests. I first looked in the pool area. No dice. I went into the office and asked some NCO's if they had seen Senior Chief Salazar. They looked at me, as they are fond of saying in the Navy, like I was lower than whale shit and said "He's in the pool" and dismissed me. I went back out, thinking maybe I had missed him. Nope, no dice. Nobody out there. I hesitantly walked back into the office and started to say "Sir I'm sorry to bother you..." when one of them barked at me *"Are you hard of hearing, Recruit!? Do you have a problem with following instructions!!?"* I said "NO SIR!" and ran out of the room. I was standing out there looking at the surface of the water and wondering what to do, when my eyes fell upon something in the pool. I stepped closer and peered down to see. There was Salazar, calmly sitting on the bottom of the pool. All he needed was a damn newspaper and a cup of coffee. I stepped back to wait. A minute passed. Then two. Then three. Suddenly he came bubbling up to the surface, took a deep breath, and swam over to the edge. I popped to attention and relayed the message, wondering all the time *who the hell is this guy?* I was expecting to be brusquely dismissed, but alone like this he was suddenly like a regular guy, talking to me like I was a human being. He told me he had been watching me and that I was doing well and to keep it up. He told me that when I left boot camp and entered the Fleet to stay sharp, don't let yourself get fat and lazy.

In our society we have been taught to admire movie stars, professional athletes, business tycoons, and musicians. We have been told we should aspire to be rich and famous, that to have a big house and fancy cars and your name on a magazine cover is what life is all about. In the twelve years I spent in the military, and twenty years in law enforcement after that, I met the finest people I have ever known. Dedicated, hard-working, patriotic, competent men and women who care deeply about this country and who would without hesitation give their lives to save a teammate if they had to. I was honored simply to be among them.

When the day came for graduation I stood at the front of the company, in my dress blues with a sword flashing, and shouted out commands to the company to pass in review. It was a colorful, grand show for all the assembled officers and enlisted, and especially for the parents of the proud young men. I had excelled in basic training and finished at the top of my class, and because of that I received my first promotion. In the military, I felt like I was home.

* * *

After I left boot camp I went to more schools and more training, and I was ultimately assigned to the aircraft carrier USS *Coral Sea*, CV-43. The *Coral Sea* was an old boat, built to take the fight to Imperial Japan, but she was not completed until 1947, just a bit too late to see action in World War II. At first I was disappointed to be on an old slow hulk, because I wanted to be on a brand new shiny nuclear carrier, with speed and firepower and panache. But I soon found out how lucky I was to be on that old boat. *Why was that,* you ask? Because the nuclear carriers also have awesome powerful nuclear reactors that provide all the electrical power and fresh water the boat needs. Which means the boat never needs to hit port, while my rusty old boat with its rusty old boilers needed to port plenty and often. We did a Caribbean Cruise and a Mediterranean Cruise, and we hit port twice as often as my buddy on CVN-69, the USS *Eisenhower,* "The Mighty Ike".

Sailors from time immemorial have dreamed of the exotic foreign ports they will visit, the adventures they will have, and the beautiful foreign girls with alluring accents and come-hither looks they will meet. In World War II our boys met dusky-eyed native island girls in sarongs in the Pacific Theater or took evening walks hand in hand with mademoiselles and frauleins in the European Theater, and you could almost hear Bing Crosby or The Andrews Sisters crooning love songs in the background. We modern sailors of course were bound by tradition and the honor of the US Navy to do our part.

The first overseas port my ship visited was St. Thomas, US Virgin Islands. We were all excited to go ashore on this island paradise, but before anyone left on liberty the fire watches and work details had to be assigned. After all, we couldn't just all rush ashore and leave the ship empty, bobbing gently in the surf. I was crestfallen when Petty Officer First Class Maynard mustered us in ranks and called out my name to stand flight deck watch. I started to protest, but the bullet-headed, no-nonsense petty officer shot me a dire look that made me shut my mouth. Maynard had a shiny bald head, with steely eyes and a ramrod for a backbone. He was a man with no sense of humor, an impressive bristling mustache, and tattooed forearms like hams. In short, he was the perfect NCO. So I reluctantly accepted my fate, and stood forlornly on the bow staring out at the beckoning white sand beaches and the palm trees swaying gently in that delicious Caribbean breeze, while my shipmates boarded the launch and motored toward paradise, gaily shouting farewells and catcalls at me.

We were only in the Virgin Islands for one night, so I never got to go ashore. My so-called friends and shipmates started staggering in by ones and twos around midnight. They were drunk, broke, and deliriously happy. They told stories of meeting American college girls, tourists from the mainland, dancing at the night clubs with Mexican and Puerto Rican beauties, and walking on the beach in the moonlight with giggling, firm young women. All their stories, of course, only made me even more unhappy. I finally left the berthing space in disgust and went back up on the flight deck. I'd rather be around jet fuel and F-18's than listen to their stories anymore. But I had my revenge, and oh but it was sweet!

Our very next port was Santo Domingo, in the Dominican Republic. The weather was getting up and the swells were looking dark and angry, and the skipper was considering cancelling all shore leave. I couldn't believe it! Because I stayed behind on watch last time, Petty Officer Maynard (God bless him!) made sure I was on the first boat to run into shore. Now it looked like I was going to get stiffed again. Finally the skipper relented and started sending the motor launches ashore. The ride in was scary. The wave crests would push the boat so high we could no longer see the shore, then we would plunge down into the troughs with a spray of seawater. The boat pilot said he was turning back, but the hue and cry we raised made him quickly change his mind, lest we toss him overboard. So we at last made the shore, and I have to admit that when we tossed lines to the hands on the pier and they tied us off to the bollards, I said a little prayer of thanks to Poseidon for bringing us ashore safely.

After our boat arrived, the pilot (who was a Dominican) radioed back to the *Coral Sea* that he wasn't coming back to the ship. Not until the sea state calmed down, at any rate. So as it turns out ours was the only boat that made it, and the sea state didn't calm down for three days. *Three days ashore!* The Navy put us up in a hotel called the La Jaragua. The officers who authorized it never saw the hotel, because they were back on board the ship getting seasick riding the swells in the harbor. If they saw it they would never have approved.

The hotel was beautiful, spacious, quite expensive, and oozing with island charm. It had a piano bar downstairs, and I went there to have a look around and pass some time. There was a gent in a tux playing the piano and a lovely Latina in a shiny dress was singing songs I didn't understand but it didn't really matter. I had never seen a piano bar before, or any kind of bar where there wasn't sawdust on the floor and country music twanging from the jukebox. I caught a pretty young girl on the other side of the bar stealing glances at me. It was probably the tropical whites uniform, but I was feeling like Maverick in *Top Gun* so I sauntered over and introduced myself. Again, the excess of self-confidence.

The girl was from Chile, and she had that wonderful light brown skin, and green eyes and long straight black hair. It was love at first sight. Or something like it, anyway. She was well-dressed like everyone else in that place, and as it turned out her father was a diplomat, some kind of ambassador from Chile to the Dominican Republic. We hung around together for the entire three days I was on the island; it was dark and squalling but we went for walks on the beach in the rain anyway, or got a secluded table in the piano bar and sometimes we had lunch or dinner with her father and his friends and diplomatic guests.

This was the first time I had ever been around people and places like this. Everyone was formal, polite, and gracious. They drank wine and ate on china plates and wore dinner jackets and ties. Where I came from dressing up meant wearing shoes and putting on a shirt, and at the dinner table it was every man for himself and if you weren't fast the biscuits and fried chicken would be gone. In my full household there were two kinds of people; the quick and the hungry. Where they talked politely about politics and the world events of the day, we talked about whether a Ford or a Chevy would win the Winston Cup in NASCAR this year. I was introduced to a whole new world, and to my own surprise I didn't hate it. The day did finally come when the storm passed and the sea calmed down, and the skipper was ordering us to return to the ship at once because we were already behind schedule. I said goodbye to the girl at the pier (and the other sailors watching were green with envy, I might add), and she gave me her phone number and address to write to her. I promised I would and got back in the boat and motored away. I never did write to her; I thought that I'd meet a girl like that in every port, and I threw her address away.

* * *

After leaving Santo Domingo we headed across the Atlantic, for the real purpose of our deployment. We would spend several months in the Mediterranean as part of the Sixth Fleet, showing the flag, conducting war games with our allies, and shadowboxing with our old adversaries the Russians. I worked on the flight deck, as a Plane Captain. Now that may sound important but what it really meant was that I was a glorified grease monkey, one step above the bottom rung of flight deck society. The bottom rung were the "grapes", the purple shirted guys who tugged the massive fuel hoses around, gassing up all the airplanes. We had the blue shirts, the "chocks and chains" guys who kept all the airplanes securely tied down to the rolling deck. The green shirts were the airframers, the red shirts were the ordnance guys, affectionately called "BB stackers", who loaded the right bombs and missiles on the right aircraft, and the yellow shirts were at the top of the food chain, the plane directors who moved the aircraft around the deck like giant chess pieces in an afterburner-fueled symphony. All the pieces moved seamlessly together to keep 'em flying, with "cat shots" off the front end and "traps" at the back end as planes landed.

I was a brown shirt, and I lovingly washed and cleaned and greased "my" plane, Seabat 602, an E-2C Hawkeye airborne early warning aircraft. The Hawkeye is pretty distinctive looking because it has a big rotating dome containing antennas on top, plus it was the only plane that had propellers instead of jet engines. Everyone called it the Hummer because it sounded like a giant bumblebee when the engines were turning.

I also did pre-flight and post-flight inspections to make sure nothing important had fallen off the airplane in the last flight. I liked working on the flight deck even if I was just a glorified grease monkey, and I took pride in my plane. It made me feel good that I was serving my country, and I liked the action and danger of working "on the roof" instead of down belowdecks. And it was dangerous. We had 66 aircraft in the airwing, the CAG 13 Guardians. We had F-18 Hornets because our carrier was too small for the F-14 Tomcats. That was disappointing to me because the big 'Cat was my favorite airplane. We also had our Hawkeyes, squadrons of A-6 Intruder attack jets, EA-6

Prowler electronic warfare birds, and H-3 Sea King helicopters to hoist out anyone who went into the drink, if the ever-present sharks following the boat didn't get them first.

With all those airplanes turning and moving on the deck you couldn't afford to relax even for a second. You could get cooked by jet engines, as I found out when I nearly got roasted when an A-6 turned behind me. The powerful jet blast knocked me off my feet, and I desperately grabbed one of the metal pad-eyes on the deck to keep from being blown across the deck. The problem was the terrific heat from the engines was literally cooking my bare hand as I held on. Just when I couldn't take it anymore and had to let go, the Intruder turned away and I was saved. Aside from that, you could get chopped up by props and rotors, run over by tractors, or just get blown overboard, where once again the sharks would be waiting for you, if the giant screws of the ship didn't suck you under and puree your hapless body first.

We lost people on our cruise. All my buddies from boot camp that I stayed in touch with lost people on their cruises, too. We lost one shipmate who walked right into the turning props of the Hawkeye. It was nighttime, everyone was tired, and when the props are spinning you can't even see them. We lost one of our Marine brothers to the tail rotor of a helicopter, and a Hornet pilot was lost at sea. No one ever knew what happened to him, but we found some wreckage of his plane, and the investigation board concluded he had probably become disoriented on the night flight, and inadvertently put his plane into the water.

We also had one sailor killed in a motorcycle accident in port. Even in peacetime being a sailor or Marine, a soldier or airman, is a dangerous profession in a dangerous world, and we mourned our comrades lost to the perils of the sea, because we knew that but for the grace of God it might have been us.

* * *

When I look back across the years at the time I spent in the Navy, it sure fills me with some warm good feelings for those days. Me and my friends - Tom McCoy, Rich Goedel, Jonathan Burgess Edwards, Jeff Goble - we were all just a bunch of handsome, carefree young rascals. We'd spend our nights cruising Virginia Beach in a convertible Mustang with the top down, or doubled up on Tom's motorcycle, or go strolling down the Boardwalk on the beach, trading smiles with all the pretty girls walking past us. Sometimes we'd pick them up and hang out with them, or we'd make out on the beach. Or we'd go shoot pool and drink beer, whatever we felt like doing after work.

I liked those days, but I don't miss them. Everything has its time and place, and I don't want to go back there. I have a good life, a beautiful and caring wife, a career I love, and great kids, and I still have those same good friends. What more could I ask for?

* * *

I had a lot of adventures during my time in the Navy, which are stories for another day and perhaps another book, and I did a lot of growing up in that time. When I finished my active duty hitch in the Navy, I stayed in the Reserves for ten more years, and switched over to being what the Navy called a Master-At-Arms. Now I know that sounds really cool, and it might conjure up visions of a black-clad ninja whirling a sword around, but it wasn't quite that exciting. It is an old British Royal Navy term from the days of sail, for the military police, and that's what I became. It was there that I met a fellow named Mitch.

He was older than me, and muscular with dark hair and a really cool Tom Selleck-style mustache, and he seemed like a pretty good guy. After he gave me the tour of the Naval Reserve Center he led me back to a little group of people and introduced me around, where we sat and talked making acquaintances. I found out Mitch was a cop, a Lieutenant and a SWAT team commander, no less. In fact, the whole group was cops. There was Harry, who was a sergeant at the Arapahoe County Sheriff's Office, and Mark, who was a deputy sheriff for Jefferson County, and Danny O'Shea, a good-natured hulking Irishman who was a patrolman at Denver PD. Growing up, I didn't know any cops and had never hung around them before, but I took an instant liking to these guys. Their war stories were interesting and funny, and their easy camaraderie appealed to me. They showed off their "shields", their badges, and listening to them it seemed that though they were all from different departments they were all members of the same exclusive club. I got the impression that a cop from L.A. and a cop from New York could meet in a bar in Miami and be instant friends.

After that first meeting I hung out with them each drill weekend, and though they were always friendly to me I never felt like I was in the club, I was always an outsider. Mitch suggested one drill weekend that I come out and do a ride-along with him some night. I thought *What the hell? This could be fun,* so I went out on a Friday night with him, and that was it. One night and I was hooked. It was as though I wasn't really sure of what I wanted to be when I grew up and suddenly the clear answer was laid out in front of me. The law enforcement bug sank its sharp little teeth into me and right then I decided I wanted more than anything to be a cop. I went to Mitch and told him I wanted to join the police force, and he just smiled and said he knew I would. He announced it to the group at the next drill weekend and all the guys were patting me on the back and congratulating me, and it felt good. I felt for the first time that I at least got my foot into the door of the clubhouse.

I was living with my girlfriend at her mother's house while we were looking for a place of our own, and when I came home and told them I wanted to go to the police academy they both thought I had lost my mind. Why do you want to be a *cop?* they asked in unison. Police work is dangerous, you have to deal with criminals all the time, you have to work shifts, and on and on. In the near future I was to find that a common response, but I was undeterred. I think they were secretly hoping this was just a phase, like boys wanting to be an astronaut or a race car driver.

The first thing I had to do was go to a police academy. As a cost-saving measure the state of Colorado stopped running CLETA, the Colorado Law Enforcement Training Academy, for all the new hires statewide, and private academies started springing up at community colleges and as private enterprises. Now you had to pay your money and go to the academy just like any trade school, and when you graduated the Peace Officer Standards and Training Board assigned you a state certification number and you went out job hunting like any other schmo, poring over the Help Wanted ads, mailing out resumes, putting on the suit and tie and nervously going to interviews.

But the academy had to come first, so I started looking around at academies and settled, mostly because of the price, on one called the Colorado Institute of Law Enforcement Training, which was up in Fort Collins and about fifty miles from where I lived at the time. I sent in my application and kept my fingers crossed, rushing to the mailbox every day to see if I had been accepted. At last the day came when I opened the mailbox and there was an envelope with the pink and green CILET logo in the upper left corner. I turned it over in my hands for a moment, afraid to open it. At last I opened it and extracted the folded letter. I opened it up and read that after a rigorous selection process I had been accepted to the Police Academy. I was in the club!

* * *

I was to quickly find out that I needn't have worried so much about getting in. This was a business after all, and they wanted customers. You pay your money and you're in, and the rigorous selection process consisted of whether or not your check cleared. I had to move out of the house in Denver, which to tell you the truth I was glad to do - a guy just doesn't want to live with his girlfriend's mom. I felt like a freeloader, plus I had to be on my best behavior all the time. I couldn't walk around in my underwear, I couldn't just lay on the couch and watch football while downing a pizza, I couldn't even break wind when I needed to. That kind of pressure is hard to live with day in and day out.

I answered a Roommate Wanted ad in the paper, checked the place out, and moved in. My main criteria was that I needed a place that would let me have my dog, Tiki, a white husky puppy I rescued from the animal shelter. He was so cute sitting there in a cage all by himself barking happily at me, and my heart just went out to the little guy, so I took him home. My roommate seemed like a typical single yuppie, trying to climb the corporate ladder, driving a Porsche, the house filled with modern art and sculptures of half-naked women, but as it turns out he was mostly just an alcoholic. Every day I would come home from the Academy and he'd be sitting on the couch staring at the blank TV screen with empty beer cans strewn around his feet. I would usually just turn the TV on so he would at least have something to look at, and then go to my own room to study. One day he decided to paint the porch - red - but had a few beers while he was thinking about it, then had a few more after he got started, then a couple more to quench his thirst over lunch. When I came home the back yard was littered with beer cans, the porch was red, the walls of the house next to the porch were red, the glass patio door was red, and my white dog had a big red stripe on his back. I moved out the next day.

The director of the academy was a blonde-haired, portly woman with very pale skin, who claimed to be a Lakota Indian. She would be having a conversation in the hall with you about school or the weather or whatever and she would suddenly stare into space and break into anguished streams of Lakota speech and start talking about "My People", like those faithful in church who suddenly fall into the aisle and start speaking in tongues, or Moses demanding that Pharaoh free the Israelites. She was a nice lady, if a little touched, but I thought to myself *if this green-eyed, white skinned, platinum blonde is an Indian maiden then I'm Denzel Washington*. That was my first clue that the world of law enforcement draws a few kooks to it.

My academy lasted 12 weeks, the minimum the state would allow for certification, and there were 29 of us in my class. All the instructors were police officers from local departments, and they all knew their business but my favorite instructors were a guy named Pat Cillo, who taught us Accident Investigation, and a huge, hulking black deputy sheriff named Riley Gant who taught us firearms. I grew up hunting and shooting since I was old enough to steady a rifle and excelled at the firearms training. This was thanks to my solidly redneck roots, as my whole family hailed from the backwoods of Arkansas and Alabama. For our clan, toting a gun was as natural as kids carrying cell phones nowadays. I remember padding through the woods as a boy with my old Winchester thirty-thirty lever action deer rifle in my hands, staring at the back of my father's plaid shirt on the trail ahead of me. I would like to point out that most of the country's great snipers like Carlos Hathcock and Chris Kyle also started out as redneck Southern deer hunters, too. Don't mess with them Southern country boys; they'll part your hair at three hundred yards.

When I would visit my cousins and aunts and uncles and other kinfolk down South, we had to leave the paved main road and drive down gravel side roads, which eventually turned into dirt tracks through the pine woods. You could practically smell the moonshine and hear the banjo music from *Deliverance* when you got close to the house. They talked about The War Between The States like it had happened yesterday, or as they called it The War of Northern Aggression, and I had many ancestors who had fought for the Confederacy. We had only arrived in Wyoming when my dad, a career Air Force man, got transferred there. I grew up in rural Wyoming, and I spent many a pleasant day on the back of my horse. I loved the wide open spaces, the mountains and the rivers, and the people. They still had plenty of rednecks here, they just tended to be on horseback, but they could still part your hair at three hundred yards. In any case, I did my family heritage proud by winning most of the shooting competitions in the Academy. Graduation day came at last, and with my Peace Officer Standards and Training Board certification in hand I said goodbye to my friends and went back to Denver in search of my first real police job.

* * *

I found out that police jobs were not that easy to get. For every opening at a cop shop there were about a hundred applicants, and although I had a college degree and military service, both pluses, I was having a hard time finding gainful employment. At the time I had no money, I was driving a crappy car, and I needed a job. Like many recent academy graduates I turned to private security work to make a living while I waited for my break. I hired on with a company with the comical name of Wackenhut, which generated many predictable nicknames like Wack-a-nut.

Now let's just acknowledge from the outset that being a security guard has got to rank as one of the top ten Least Respected Jobs in America. Ask anyone what they picture when they think of a security guard and they will conjure up an image

---

of either a doddering old retiree who can barely see past his glasses, shuffling around with a belt full of keys working as the night watchman, or a fat cop-wannabe pimply faced teenager patrolling the local shopping mall like a glorified hall monitor. In truth, that covers most of them but Wackenhut had the contract for several courthouses and tried to put their best people on them. The group of people I worked with were mostly like me, trying to find police jobs but working here to pay the bills, and a lot of them were pretty sharp. But first we had to pass the training course.

There were about a dozen of us in the week-long class, and I noticed one very quiet Hispanic guy sat in the back of the room and never said a word. Come to find out about halfway through the class that he didn't speak a lick of English. He hadn't understood a word that had been said. When this was brought to the instructor's attention he just shrugged his shoulders and kept teaching. What this poor Hispanic guy was thinking I'll never know, but I have to wonder what was going through his mind when at the end of the course the big white man who has been talking to him for a week in a language he doesn't understand takes him to a building, hands him a gun, and motions him to go inside. For all he knew he was being ordered to go stick the place up. To be perfectly honest, the instructor was sincere and was giving out good information, but it wasn't his call to decide who got in and who didn't.

At the end of the week we had to go to the range to qualify and be issued our weapons. At the indoor range we all lined up and one at a time we would walk up to the line, pick up the ancient .38 caliber revolver lying there, point it at the human silhouette target ten feet away and squeeze off five shots. If any of them hit the paper, you passed. After the range day, we were given our guns, five rounds of ammunition, and a black leather holster. My issued weapon was a battered and worn old Smith and Wesson .38 that I'm pretty sure saw service in the trenches

33

of Verdun or on the beaches at Iwo Jima. The holsters were just as ancient but I dug through the box and found one that fit, though it was too short so the barrel of my revolver stuck out about two inches at the bottom. Now well equipped, I went to my post.

I was assigned to the Adams County Courthouse. We worked the entrances, checking people for weapons and contraband, waving through the DA's and judges, and scowling at the defense attorneys. I often worked inside the courtrooms during trials, even though the Adams County Sheriff's Office deputies were technically responsible for security inside the courtrooms. Between the needs of the jail and the Transport Platoon they were always short-handed so we would provide extra bodies.

This was my first exposure to the inner sanctums of the criminal justice system, and I found it fascinating. The duel of wits and wills between the prosecutors and defense attorneys, the stern oversight of the judges, the utter unpredictability of juries, the lives hanging in the balance, the stories of human tragedy and heroism that played out, all of it was far more exciting than any movie or television drama could replicate. I was in the courtroom for the final appeal of Gary Lee Davis, who was sentenced to death for the extraordinarily brutal kidnapping, rape, and murder of Virginia May. He confessed to raping some fifteen other women. Looking at such a monster in the courtroom sent an involuntary chill down your spine, like looking at Hannibal Lecter. Davis would become the first person to be executed in Colorado in thirty years. If ever a man earned it, he did. I also worked the sensational trial of Robert Harlan, who kidnapped and raped casino cocktail waitress Rhonda Maloney. Maloney escaped and flagged down a passing motorist, beginning a high speed car chase that ended with Harlan literally shooting her to death almost on the front steps of the Thornton Police Department.

My scariest moment came when I worked the murder trial of a Mexican national who hacked his wife to death. He was facing a possible death penalty if convicted, and the courtroom pews were packed with his family members. They were openly hostile and the threat of violence was thick in the air. The tension was near the breaking point as the jury shuffled back in from deliberations. The foreman handed the bailiff a slip of paper, and the judge read out the verdict. *On the charge of Murder in the First Degree...Guilty.* As soon as the verdict was read the courtroom exploded with shouts and threats of violence, and the courtroom was ordered to be cleared immediately. We got the family members out with much pushing and shoving and threatening, and they all spilled out into the parking lot. Now we had to bring the prisoner out.

In those days, before the new courthouse was built, the Transport van from the jail was simply parked in the public parking lot and the prisoners were walked into and out of the courthouse. The deputies from the Transport Platoon had to walk the condemned man back out through the parking lot, and we went along to provide extra security. The west parking lot of the courthouse was filled with his family members, and we had to walk right through them to get him into the van. That was the longest thirty yards of my life.

As soon as we came out with him in shackles, they closed in around us. There were curses and shouts in both Spanish and English, and as we were shoving and pushing our way through the crowd I heard shouts to "Take him back!" I walked through with my right hand on my gun and my left shoving people. There were no metal detectors out here, we had no body armor vests, and I was sure there were weapons in some of those cars. At any moment I expected to feel a knife in my back, and I decided if I was stabbed I was just going to pull my gun and start shooting. *This was sooo not worth six dollars and thirty five cents an hour!* I was also angry; there had to be a better way to do this than to expose us to this kind of needless danger. That was my first exposure to the hard fact that when money butts up against officer safety, money usually wins. We finally got him into the van and the deputies piled in and hurriedly drove away, and we went back to business.

* * *

It wasn't always danger and excitement, of course. Sometimes I had to pull night court bailiff duty. Everybody hated night court, partly because the cases were generally nothing more than petty squabbles, and partly because we were all used to working the day shift and getting off at five, but everybody had to take their turn in the barrel. Night court was all small stuff; traffic tickets, animal control citations, and small claims civil court. It really was just like you see on TV, with Judge Judy or Judge Joe Brown presiding, and the antagonists would stand at their podiums apart from each other and air their dirty laundry for all the world to hear. She'd say *"Yes I broke his cell phone but only because I found out he been sleepin' with my best friend!"* And he would fire back *"I only did that 'cause you was with my best friend the week before!"* and the audience would watch the volleys go back and forth like we were at a tennis match, with an occasional *"oooh!"* from the audience thrown in at some especially juicy tidbit.

On one occasion a woman in a wheelchair came into the courtroom and with much hustling and bustling and complaining got herself past the crowd and up to the defendant's table. Across from her was her landlord, who was suing her for unpaid rent and damage to the apartment. The landlord complained that she had not paid rent for three months and had knocked holes in the walls of the apartment.

The woman in the wheelchair, a middle-aged pleasant looking woman with brown hair and a plain dress, did not deny she was behind in the rent, but begged the judge to show mercy to her because after the accident that put her in her wheelchair she couldn't work anymore, so she lost her job and hadn't been able to find work since. Everyone in the courtroom now turned with some very hard and unfriendly eyes to the landlord. The landlord, a tall bony white man, said that he sympathized with her but he had bills to pay, too, and if he listened to every sob story a tenant told him he'd never collect any money. All eyes went back to the woman to return the volley. She pleaded with the judge to just give her more time, and as she wrung her hands and begged him her eyes started to tear up. The judge considered for a moment, then made his ruling. He was very sympathetic to the woman, but the law was the law. If she wanted leniency, she had to ask the landlord, not him. Everyone looked at the landlord. He shook his head. *No, no leniency.*

The people in the courtroom scowled at him, and there were mutterings of *asshole!* and *what a jerk!* going through the room. The judge ordered silence, and also ordered the woman in the wheelchair to pay up or be evicted. Everyone felt sorry for her, but she was in no mood for that. "You're just going to throw a woman in a wheelchair out on the street?!" she demanded. "Where am I supposed to live? What am I supposed to do?!" The judge suggested that the county had assistance programs for people in need and she should go see them on Monday. The judge finished by telling me to escort her out of the courtroom and see that she got safely to her car. With that, he called the next case. The woman whipped her wheelchair around and drove fuming out of the courtroom.

It was quiet and empty out in the hallway, and she was so mad she was pushing furiously on the wheels of the chair, and I was practically jogging to keep up with her. The whole time I could hear the echoes of her voice faintly floating back to me as she was muttering to herself and cursing the judge and the landlord and me and the whole damn system. We got to the doors and I reached over and pushed the automatic door opener button. "I can do it myself!" she snapped at me and half turning in her chair gave me a look that would have curdled new milk. The door swung silently open, and she started wheeling herself across the parking lot. She turned back to me and snarled "I don't need you to babysit me! Run along back to your courtroom, Barney Fife!" I told her "Ma'am, the judge said to see you safely to your vehicle, so I'm going to do that. Besides, this can be a bad neighborhood at night, so let's just get you to your car, okay?" She was being a bitch, but I did feel sorry for her so I just let her insults roll off my back. She looked like she was getting ready to say something really nasty, but then thought better of it and just wheeled herself across the lot.

Now that we were outside I didn't know if I should offer to push her, or if she would get offended by that, or what the protocol was here. I had never really been around people in wheelchairs, but I thought if it was me pushing myself around all the time I'd be happy to let someone else do the pushing for awhile. With this woman, though, I thought I'd better not even ask. We got to her car, and right away I didn't know again what I should do. Was I supposed to help her get out of the chair and into the car? I pictured myself leaning down and putting my arms under hers and pulling her up out of the chair and having her knee me in the groin.

She saw me hesitating and said "Get the hell out of my way!" I took a step back and up she jumps out of the chair. She grabbed the chair, whipped it around, and folded it up in a jiffy. She tossed it in the trunk of her car, and looked back at me and said "Well what the hell are you looking at, asshole?!" and walked around to the driver's door and hopped in. She gunned the engine to life, then dropped it into gear and laid rubber going out of the lot.

* * *

Sometimes we had to work over in Division B. Division B was Family Court, where a couple could go to either begin a marriage or to end one. Marriages, divorces, adoptions, child custody, child support, it was a one-stop shop for all things domestic. The courtroom was very small, so small in fact that the guard's desk was outside in the hall. If I heard shouting or yelling inside the courtroom, I would get up and go in to see who was getting upset about what. My primary duty, however, seemed to consist of being a witness for Justice of the Peace marriages. Come in, witness the ceremony, say *"Congratulations!"* to the happy couple, and sign on the line. The couples who opted for the J.O.P. wedding rather than the traditional white dress, church, and cake were generally either very young people who didn't have the money to buy cupcakes much less a wedding cake, or older couples on their second or third or even fourth marriages, who had already done the traditional marriage at least once and could no longer stomach the pomp and expense and drama.

Working in the courthouse I became friends with a deputy named Tony Martinez. Tony was a little shorter than me, a tough guy with biceps that stretched out his shirt sleeves and a passion for custom motorcycles. He worked in the Transport Platoon, and as it turned out his father-in-law was a Deputy Chief at Denver PD. Tony knew I was looking for a real cop job and said he would put in a good word for me at the Sheriff's Department. He was true to his word, and when an opening came up for a position in the jail I put in for it, and I got the job.

TWO

THE JOB wasn't a commissioned officer position, but was what they called a Community Service Officer, a civilian position, but I was at least officially working for the Sheriff's Department now and it was a step in the right direction. I was so excited because I was going to be making $17,000 a year. Like kids everywhere I had worked all the usual menial jobs in high school; fast food joints, a stint as a furniture delivery guy, a cashier at a grocery store, and in college I delivered pizza in my faithful AMC Gremlin. Now I was going to be paid an actual *salary*, not just a pittance per hour. This was important to me because I had finally decided to ask my girlfriend to marry me, after five years of dating, but I wouldn't ask her until I had a real job and could support us.

My job in the jail was to sit up in an elevated pod, protected by wire mesh and plexiglass from the occasional hurled object, frequently hurled cups of body fluids, and the constantly hurled curses of the inmates down below, while in front of me I had a panel with buttons to control every cell door in the pod. I would open all the doors precisely at 7:00 a.m. and close them up again at 9:00 p.m., when (hopefully) all the inmates would be safely inside. Then the deputies could do their bed checks. I was disappointed that I would not be issued a weapon, because even though I had been forced to surrender my old .38 when I left Wackenhut I was already finding I felt sort of naked without the comforting heft of a sidearm. Granted, the heavy old steel revolver was a better weapon as a club than as a gun, but I missed it just the same. I worked the 7 pm to 7 am shift, 12 hours on and 12 hours off, with three days on followed by three days off. During most of my shift the inmates were locked into their cells and asleep, so I didn't have much to do in the quiet darkness except read books. As one month blended into another I began to grow bored with it all, thinking this kind of high-tech babysitting is not really what I had in mind for my law enforcement career. Crockett and Tubbs didn't do this, Starsky and Hutch didn't do this, and Riggs and Murtaugh *certainly* didn't do this!

Soon after I arrived some well-meaning but misguided person in the state legislature thought the inmates would benefit from some new exercise equipment, so the state budgeted what must have been a year's salary for a dozen deputies on a truckload of new weight equipment for the prisoners. We watched the new equipment being unloaded and we were all thinking *how about some decent food and equipment for the deputies?* Our equipment was old and decrepit and we never had enough of it, but in the minds of the pity-the-poor-prisoners crowd every inmate in there was just a miscarriage of justice and *we* were the real bad guys for keeping them in there. This equipment wasn't the standard barbells and dumbbells but rather was shiny, fancy machines set up in the yard, with cables and pulleys and weight plates, everything but the curvy women from the commercials in tight leotards demonstrating how to use it.

The inmates showed their appreciation for the kind gesture by stealing the pins and all the metal parts from the machines that weren't welded down to make shanks with, and finally a group of them just decided the hell with it and lined up on either side of a hefty machine and picked it up and used it as a battering ram to batter down the door to the outer yard. The door gave way and inmates began running for the tall perimeter fences. The alarm was sounded and deputies rushed in from everywhere. I believe that three inmates actually made it over the fence, and the town of Brighton went on a virtual lockdown while police dogs and SWAT teams and deputies went door to door searching for the escapees. They were eventually all recovered, and the weight machines disappeared. There's a lesson in there for those who allow their soft hearts to give them soft heads, but I doubt they'll listen to it.

The ingenuity of the prisoners was at times amazing. While doing a cell check one of the deputies found a rope hidden under a bed. This rope was made from toilet paper and bedsheet strands, and it was a work of art. The prisoner had taken long pieces of toilet paper and thin strips of bed sheet and rolled them into tight strands, and then weaved the many individual strands into a rope about an inch thick. We laughed at the idea of a toilet paper rope, but when we pulled on it we found it was amazingly strong. If only they could funnel such ingenuity and industry into something productive and useful, something *not* against the law, they would all be millionaires.

* * *

I was still doing my weekend drills in the Navy Reserve, and still hanging around with the little group of cops. I felt more like one of the guys now, but technically I wasn't because I was still a civilian even though I worked for the Sheriff's Department. I would listen to them tell stories of muggings and foot chases and SWAT callouts, and I'd tell them I finished another chapter of *Old Yeller*. I was not satisfied, and I was looking around for something more. Mitch knew I was restless and eager to get a commissioned officer job and suggested it might pump up my resume if I got some experience as a Reserve Police Officer over at his cop shop, Federal Heights PD. It was a volunteer position so I wouldn't get paid, and it would cut into my days off but at least it was street work and would get me some hands-on experience. I jumped at the chance, and he set it up for me.

He took me down to the station and fitted me for a uniform, issued me some old basketweave leather gear he found in a cardboard box in the bottom of a closet, and handed me my badge. I held the badge in my hand, turning it over and looking at it. It was heavy, not like my cheap tin security guard badge. I liked it. That night when I got home I put on my uniform and all my gear, pinned on my badge, picked out a favorite pistol to carry, and stood in front of the mirror looking at myself. Yep, there was no doubt about it...I looked damn good!

When I arrived for roll call that first night, I wasn't sure what to expect. I walked in and everyone looked at me with a detached, curious expression like *"Who the hell let that guy in here?"* Some of the guys just ignored me like I wasn't even there, while others were a little more friendly in that they grunted a sort-of greeting at me before turning away. When you join a cop shop, just because you're there wearing a badge doesn't mean you're one of them. You gotta prove yourself first, before they'll accept you. I had been in the military so I knew the drill, and just kept my mouth shut figuring the time would come when I could show these guys I was a straight shooter and could be counted on in a scrap.

I had a blue mini-Maglite flashlight stuck in my belt, and one of the guys zeroed in on it right away and started giving me crap about my pretty blue flashlight. The other guys picked up on it immediately and joined in. *Damn!* My first day on the Job and they're all laughing at me. Not only was I an unknown quantity to them, but now I had a strike against me before I ever went on my first call!

As a Reserve Officer I was not allowed to be on my own yet. I was too new and so I would partner up with somebody for the shift. I had been with Federal Heights for about three months, coming in once or twice a week and working different shifts, getting to know the teams. One day I came into the station and the sergeant says I need to go down to the Denver City Jail to pick up a prisoner and bring him back for court. I asked who I was riding with and he said "You're solo now" and tosses me the keys. *Solo? Wow!* I figured they must really be starting to trust me now, to turn me loose on my own. I went out to the car and sat down behind the wheel. This was the first time I had ever been in the squad car by myself. If the shit hit the fan, there would be no experienced officer beside me to take charge, to tell me what to do. Whatever happened today, whether it be a simple fender bender or Charles Manson on the loose, it was all on me. Suddenly my mouth was dry, and all the controls inside the car for the lights, the radio, the siren, the switch for the shotgun rack, all looked strange and foreboding.

Still, as I pulled out of the lot I thought they were showing me they trusted me now, and I was determined not to let them down. I headed out onto I-25 south, and it was very cool the way cars would slow down around me and the drivers ahead of me kept nervously checking their rearview mirrors. I had driven this stretch of I-25 a thousand times, but never in the cruiser. I was the shark in the tuna pod, and all the tuna kept a wary eye on me. I liked it. I liked it right up until I got to downtown Denver, that is. When I made the exit onto Colfax Avenue, I suddenly remembered how much I *hated* driving downtown.

Denver is an old city, founded back in the Old West mining and gambling and cowboy days, long before Colorado became a state. The downtown area was designed a long time ago and developed piecemeal as the city grew, with no plan or design. It is a maze of narrow one-way streets, diagonals, turn-only lanes, a giant jigsaw puzzle that couldn't have been more confusing if they started out to make it that way. I think the Greater Denver Chamber of Commerce designed it that way on purpose, to trap out-of-towners and keep them endlessly circling downtown, trying in vain to find their way out until they just give up and get a hotel. There were plenty of locals who wouldn't go downtown if they didn't have to, and I was one of them. After all, I had recently moved from Laramie, Wyoming, population 25,000 and that may have included the antelope and the coyotes.

I did manage to find the Denver City Jail. Technically, it was the Pre-Arraignment Detention Facility, or PADF, and not the actual jail. I spotted it at last, a big grey building across the plaza from Police Headquarters that looked more like a stormtrooper outpost than a jail. I saw it, but I had to circle the block three times before I could figure out how to actually get in there. When I did finally get in and parked my police car, I just stood there in amazement when I got out. Denver Police Headquarters was huge, a big imposing multi-story building with a swirl of cops, perps, wits, and detectives going in and out of its glass doors. It had a huge cobblestone plaza with a flag-bedecked memorial in the center. Together with PADF it covered an entire city block. Our quaint little station in Federal Heights would have fit in the lobby with room to spare.

My eyes were popping, and I thought to myself "Wow! Now there's a *real* police station! I gotta get here someday!" I shook myself out of my reverie and went into the jail. The intake deputy behind the counter looked up at me and said "Whaddaya got?" I stuttered and stammered and said I was here to pick up a prisoner. It must have been really obvious that I was a boot and didn't know a perp from a pizza because he started talking very slowly and explained how the process worked when you took a prisoner out. *Sign here. Give me this form. Take that form. Now go stand over there.*

They brought the prisoner up and the deputy said "Okay, here's your guy!" and promptly turned back to his paperwork and ignored me. I wasn't sure what to do next, but it was okay because apparently my prisoner had been through this routine before, because he knew exactly what to do. He was a cocky young Hispanic guy, with slicked back hair and a self-assured look on his face. I tried to act like I was an old hand and led him out to the car and put him in the back. He was a talkative fellow and kept up a steady chatter from the back. I didn't mind him talking but I wanted him to shut up right now because I had to get back into the mass of traffic without sideswiping anyone or cutting anyone off. I started to make a turn and the prisoner said "No No man, don't go that way! You gotta get over to 13th, man, and then go up to Speer! Hey, you're new at this aren't you!?" I tried to play it off like *of course* I knew we had to go up to Speer, but after a while of circling around downtown pretending I knew what I was doing I finally just said the hell with it and gave up and let my prisoner direct me around, turning when he said to turn, going where he said to go. I was really hoping he wasn't jacking me around just for fun, but before long we popped out onto I-25 northbound. It was thoroughly humiliating.

* * *

I got my undergraduate degree in Physical Education. I could have become a P.E. teacher, but the idea of trying to corral a bunch of screaming running six-year olds and teach them to skip rope and play kickball somehow just didn't appeal to me. Not that I didn't like kids, I just didn't have the patience to deal with them. I became a personal trainer instead, where I only had to corral a few clients, none of whom were running or screaming. Just some mild grunting and sweating. My first job out of college was at a very posh south Denver health club called the Greenwood Athletic Club. It was an absolutely state of the art club, with the latest and most advanced new equipment coming in all the time, stuff from Germany and Sweden that looked like high-tech shiny torture racks that I didn't have the foggiest idea how to use because I couldn't read the bad translation for the directions.

The club also had a café that served trendy food like wheatgrass shakes that cost eight dollars a glass and tasted truly awful. But the patrons ordered and drank them because everybody else did, and they would take a drink and smile at each other and say "Mmmmm! This wheatgrass is *soooo* delicious!" then wipe the brownish-green milk moustache off their lips. I always imagined they went through the Wendy's drive-thru on their way home for a Big Bacon Classic with fries.

There were about a dozen of us personal trainers working there, and among ourselves we called the place "Silicon Hills". There were enough fake boobs in that one building to keep Dow Corning in business for years. Back then gravity boots were still a fad. If you don't remember them, they looked kind of like ski boots, with a big hook on the back. You'd strap them on, then grab onto a metal bar overhead and do a sort of hanging somersault movement to get the hooks over the bar, then you would hang upside down. I know, it sounds crazy now, but the idea was to decompress your spine and your joints. It was very popular then, and you'd walk into the gym and all along the walls you'd see people hanging upside down like bats roosting in a cave. They'd be flipping through an upside down Vogue or Cosmo, listening to Walkmans upside down with their hair hanging to the floor and bobbing their heads to the music. But their boobs would be standing straight out at attention, no droop in them at all.

My clients were an interesting group. I quickly found out that you're not just a trainer to your clients; you're also a confidant, shade-tree psychologist, and relationship counselor. They tell you everything, and I do mean everything. I got to hear about extra-marital affairs, money troubles, work troubles, the whole ball of drama of society's upper crust. I felt like I was living in an episode of *Real Housewives of Beverly Hills*. I had one client, a successful stockbroker who had poured everything into her career with no time for love, who came to me and said "I'm forty years old and I need a man! Make me look good!" You gotta give her points for directness; she knew exactly what she wanted. I got her looking good, and she got her man, a doctor no less. Nothing like a satisfied client.

Sometimes clients start to get a little *too* attached to their trainers. I was training a couple, a man and a wife, he was fifty'ish and she was ten years younger, and like most men who've spent a career at a desk job he was a little soft and paunchy, and here I was twenty-something and buff, and the wife all too frequently commented on the differences between me and her husband. She'd rub my arm and say things like *"oooh* feel that *definition!"* Then her tone would change abruptly and she would say "Harold is so flabby!" casting a disdainful look at Harold, sweating and puffing on one of the machines. Then she would say "Being a personal trainer must be so *exciting!"* Then the voice change and "Harold sells doorknobs!" Her comparisons and her attentions made me very uncomfortable, not least since Harold was the one paying me. Also, I thought it was pretty unfair and downright crappy of her to have such a low opinion and obvious disdain for her husband. They lived in Greenwood Village and she didn't work, so no doubt he was providing her with a very nice lifestyle. I couldn't even get in the front door of this place if I didn't work here. I couldn't even afford one of those twigs and grass milkshakes from the café. Not surprisingly, Harold decided not to continue our professional relationship, in the interests of saving his personal relationship with Mrs. Harold.

I quickly grew tired of being a personal trainer. After a while the clients all start to blend in with each other and the encouragement you give them starts to become mechanical; *"That's it. You're doing good. One more rep"* and trying to force some excitement into your voice. When I got the job at the Adams County Sheriff's Department I turned in my resignation at the athletic club. Four years of college, six months of work. However, I did meet a lovely young woman named Jessica Urban who was preparing for the Miss Colorado pageant, and I worked with her some giving her training and dieting advice.

Definitely more interesting than Harold the doorknob salesman. She looked lean and toned and tan on stage and won the crown that year, so it was really nice to see something good come out of my work besides catching husbands for stockbrokers.

It was about the beginning of April when I got an unexpected phone call. The guy on the other end said "Hi. I'm Detective Chris Hazlett from the Cherry Hills Police Department. Would you be interested in coming down to interview for a job with us?" It was the call I had been waiting a year for.

THREE

Detective Hazlett came to my house for our first meeting. We had moved out of my girlfriend's mom's house and into a little rundown duplex on a short street. We had the upper floor, and a trucker and his wife had the downstairs. When the doorbell rang I answered and let Chris in. He was a blonde-haired congenial guy with glasses and had an easy way about him. We sat in the living room and had a long talk while he asked me about my background, my military service, my family, and more while my girlfriend played the gracious hostess and made some appetizers and iced tea for us. After a while I could see that underneath the detective's relaxed, easygoing manner he was actually carefully evaluating me, drawing me out with innocuous questions, taking note of my home surroundings, even the books on my bookshelf, taking in the whole picture of who I was. He was good.

After a couple of hours he got up and thanked us for our hospitality, and said "I'll need to talk to your neighbors. That won't be a problem, will it?" I said "No, not at all!" but at the same moment I thought to myself "Oh, great! The *neighbors!*" Just the week before, my neighbor's dog, a big Rottweiler mix, and my dog Tiki had gotten into a big furball of a fight when their dog jumped the fence into my back yard. I had of course pitched in to help my dog and given the Rottie a blast of pepper spray in the face (which I noted had very little effect on it) and called Animal Control on them, and the Animal Control Officer had written out a citation to them for harboring a vicious dog. So, I was pretty sure I would not get a good report from that neighbor.

Nonetheless I kept my fingers crossed for the next few days, and when Chris called me back and said I would be moving forward in the hiring process, I breathed a huge sigh of relief.

Over the next few months I had to go down to the police station or meet with Detective Hazlett several times, as we scheduled polygraph tests, did background investigations, a physical exam, and filled out paperwork. I was nervous over the polygraph test. Not that I had committed any serious crimes, mind you, but like everyone I had committed a few minor infractions. As the polygraph examiner attached the leads to my chest and my finger my heart began to beat faster. Just to my right and fully in my view was a moving chart, with several needles tracing different colored lines across the paper. That made me even more nervous, which I am sure it was intended to do, as with every answer I gave the needles jumped and scrawled their squiggly lines which had meaning only to those who knew how to read their secret messages.

The examiner told me that if I had done something wrong I had better just tell him about it now, because if it was minor they could work with it, but if I concealed *anything* from them, anything at all, I was done for in this process, the end of the line. So I figured I had better come clean with him; *forgive me Father with the black box, for I have indeed sinned...* when I was working my way through college as a Pizza Hut delivery driver the boss let us take a small pizza home once a week, but I always made myself a large. With extra toppings. And sometimes a side salad. When I finished telling the examiner I waited cringing for him to throw me out, but he just looked at me for a minute without speaking, then sat back in his chair and said "The guy in here before you told me he used to deal crack down in Five Points. I think you're okay with the pizza."

At last the day came when Detective Hazlett told me to come down to the station one more time. It had taken months, but all the paperwork was done, the background investigation was over, and I was meeting the Chief of Police. I came down to the station and Chris pulled me aside and told me to just relax and be myself, then led me down the hall. The Chief of Police at Cherry Hills was Les Langford, a balding soft-spoken man in his fifties who bore a passing resemblance to Captain Picard from *Star Trek*. He appeared to be very physically fit and wore his gun like he knew how to handle it. After introductions we sat down and he asked me some general questions about myself, then he got down to business; "Why do you want to come work for Cherry Hills?" This was the part where I was supposed to say something nice about the Department, like "Because you have such a strong community policing program" or "You're such a progressive, modern agency" but instead I went with brutal honesty; "I never heard of Cherry Hills until Detective Hazlett called me six months ago." The Chief considered this for a moment, silently nodding his head slowly while looking me over with a pondering eye. He then said "What do you think is the most important quality a police officer can possess?" I searched my brain, thinking about knowledge of the law, tactical skill, physical fitness, but looking at him I made a character guess that those were not the kinds of things he was looking for, and I said simply "Honesty." He broke into a big smile and extended his hand and said "Welcome aboard!"

The Chief told me after the interview to go upstairs and see the police secretary. I went down the hall, up the stairs, and through the door to the main office and found her. She looked up from her desk strewn with flotsam and jetsam and said "Oh there you are! I've been waiting for you!" She reached into a desk drawer and pulled out a badge and handed it to me, then told me to raise my right hand and repeat after her. I took the badge and raised my right hand, then she pulled a piece of paper out of the drawer and read off the oath of office. I was feeling a little confused but did as I was told. When I was finished she said "Okay, you're a police officer now! Be at work at 6:30

tomorrow morning." I walked away, feeling happy but also a bit disappointed. *That was it?* Wasn't there supposed to be a big ceremony, with American flags and speeches and solemn oaths? I wasn't even in uniform; I was in a t-shirt and jeans. After all, the NYPD gets a big ceremony in Times Square with the mayor and dignitaries giving speeches, and white gloves thrown in the air, and although we weren't NYPD you'd think I could at least get someone besides the secretary. She didn't even get out of her chair to give me the oath. But it was May 16, 1995, and I had at long last become a police officer.

* * *

The first step for a new police officer is Field Training. A rookie gets assigned to a seasoned veteran to learn the ropes, get to know the city and how things are done in the department, everything from procedures for transporting a prisoner to filling out all the myriad reports to where to go to get the car washed when a drunk pukes in it. At the same time the Field Training Officer is carefully evaluating the new guy, making sure he's moving along with the program. Can he find his way around the city? Is he picking things up and responding to training? Does he know what paperwork goes with what call? And most of all, how is his officer safety? If a new guy lets a suspect get too close to his weapon, or he doesn't take charge on a scene, or if he crosses the tube in front of another officer's gun, then maybe this guy should think about a nice desk job somewhere before he gets himself or another officer killed. It takes a certain type of mentality to be a police officer, and you just never know with people. We had a bright young kid who gave a great interview, looked real good on paper, but he freaked out just directing traffic. He actually ran out of the intersection and back to his FTO crying *"They're not listening to me!"* What's he going to do when not only are they not listening to him but they're actively trying to ventilate him with a shotgun? Nice kid, but we had to let him go.

My first Field Training Officer was a guy named Mike Schaffer. Mike was an old guy, almost thirty years on the Job and literally knocking on the door of retirement. I was his last hurrah, his last trainee, and when he finished with me in four weeks he was hanging up his badge and gun for good. Mike worked the graveyard shift, and he was always complaining about the cold. He would drive around at night with the heater on, his coat on and buttoned up, and the windows rolled up. I was thinking *It's June for crying out loud! What is this guy, a reptile?* but I wisely kept such thoughts to myself. To make matters worse he had this droning, dry low sand-papery monotone voice that never varied in pitch or tone, and as we drove around in the dark city the combination of the warm car, his monotonous voice telling me about the old days, and the deep night would have me nodding off just a couple of hours into the shift. I would be doing head bobs off the passenger side dashboard, fighting to stay awake and Mike would suddenly stop the car and look over at me and say "Where are we?" *Where are we?* Are you kidding me? We could be in New Jersey for all I knew.

I spent four weeks with Schaffer, all on the night shift, and one night as we drove past the quaint little St. George's Church I spotted an open door on the side of the building. I excitedly turned to Mike and said "Did you see that? That door was open on the west side! We gotta go check it out! There could be a burglar in there!" He just grunted "I didn't see nothin'" and kept driving. A week later we were sitting at the stoplight at Colorado Boulevard and Hampden Avenue. A car came speeding eastbound on Hampden, blew right through the red light and made a squealing left turn up Colorado. I turned to Mike and said "Did you see that?! Let's go get him!" Mike said "Looked like it was green to me." Plainly, Mike was done with police work. He was just riding it out, ticking off the days until it was over. After nearly thirty years I can't say I blame him. Cops get real superstitious when they're close to retirement. Too many cops have bought the farm checking that one last open door or contacting that one last suspicious person.

On our last night together he pulled the car into the alley by the back door. He reached over and picked up the microphone and said "332 end of watch." The dispatcher's voice came back "End of watch for Mike Schaffer after 27 years in law enforcement. Goodbye and good luck Mike." The way fellow officers honor the service and say goodbye is with simple radio clicks, and as the clicks continued sounding for several minutes Mike broke down and started crying. I turned away because it just didn't seem right to intrude on him at a time like that. After retirement he and his wife moved to Laughlin, Nevada. At least he'll be warm out there. Godspeed, brother. You earned it.

My second phase of FTO was with a female officer named Kate. She was a pretty, petite blonde-haired woman who was a little past her prime but still attractive, and very nice and soft-spoken. We hit it off immediately and ended up mostly just driving around the city having long, deep conversations about life, careers, relationships, the whole range of weighty issues that trouble all people everywhere. One day I was driving and listening to her as she talked and I ran right through a stop sign without even noticing. She could have dinged me on my daily evaluation, but she said it had been so long since a man had paid that much attention to what she was saying that she was flattered enough to let it slide.

Kate and I responded to a silent alarm at a residence early one morning, and while checking around the outside we found a patio door partly open. Our Policy and Procedures Manual said before entering a house we were to loudly announce our presence a minimum of three times before entering. This was a controversial policy among the officers, because while it prevented accidental shootouts between police and homeowners it also allowed the burglars to either run away, hide, or find cover and get ready for us. In any case, we properly and loudly announced our presence and, receiving no response, we entered the house and began to search.

Contrary to what you see on TV and in the movies, when you search a house you don't rapidly move through with guns up and shouting "CLEAR!" at every room and stairway like the high-speed low-drag special ops teams. It looks cool when Jason Bourne or James Bond does it, but for us ordinary cops you do it *slow*, slow and methodical. You watch your noise and light discipline and cover each other's backs. Kate and I had searched most of the first floor and seen and heard nothing, and now we began to move down a wood-floored hallway toward the kitchen, guns at the Low Ready position.

As we moved down the hall I heard the faintest creak of a loose floorboard from around the corner up ahead. We both stopped, and my pistol came up on target with my finger caressing the smooth cool metal of the trigger. Someone was there, quiet and just out of sight. Suddenly he came around the corner fast and into the hallway and my finger began to reflexively tighten. It was a kid, a little boy about seven years old, still in his pajamas and carrying a glass of milk. He looked up at me and said "Hi Mister Policeman!" and just pitter-pattered right past us on his way back to his bedroom, just like we belonged there. *God bless kids* I thought as I breathed a huge sigh of relief.

My next FTO was also a woman, but she was not quite so easy going. She was a tough little sergeant named Pat who sometimes used me as bait for her police dog. She would tell me to go hide in a church or in the Public Works garage, and then she'd go to the truck and get Artie, her big black and tan German Shepherd. She would rough up his face and ears to get him excited, saying "You want to go *get him*, don'tcha boy!" and the dog would start barking and straining at his leash, and she'd say "GO GET HIM! FIND HIM!" and turn him loose. It was nerve wracking to be hiding in a closet in the dark and hear the dog's snuffling and growling as he got closer and closer, inexorably tracking me down like a furry guided missile. Then he would find me and go ballistic barking and snarling and pawing at the door I was hiding behind, while I was crouching on the other side praying the door would hold. I started looking heavenward to find places to climb up to so he wouldn't bite me if he ever got through. I liked Pat and respected her, but between being dog bait and her being a tough evaluator, that was not such a fun phase.

I was on day shift now, and that was something new. I had not really had a chance to see the city before, so I drove around taking in the place that would be my new home. Cherry Hills Village was a beautiful little city, an oasis in an urban blight. To the west of us was Englewood, a white ghetto where meth could be bought anytime, anywhere and where the locals had more tattoos than teeth. To the north and east were the outlying neighborhoods of Denver. But in The Village most of the homes were sprawling mansions on meticulously landscaped acreage. It had a lot of wild open space with nature trails and woodsy fields, and a large irrigation ditch called the Highline Canal ran a twisting course through the entire city from north to south, flanked like a river by a belt of trees on either side. Cherry Hills was like a transplanted and scaled down Beverly Hills. Several professional athletes like John Elway of the Denver Broncos and Joe Sakic of the Colorado Avalanche lived here, as well as billionaire businessmen and millionaire doctors, lawyers, and socialites. There were two posh country clubs, one in the gated and guarded Glenmoor neighborhood and the other the more well-known Cherry Hills Country Club, where rumor had it that the price of admission was more than I made in a year, and you still had to pay for your rounds of golf and *hors d'oeuvres* in the clubhouse.

The Field Training Officers had a mean little trick they pulled on each new recruit. They would tell the new guy "Hey, let's go to dinner at Perkins tonight" and the new guy would say sure, whatever you say sir, and a group of officers would all meet there and sit down at the big table in the corner, next to the windows overlooking the parking lot. As it turns out, there was a reason for this panoramic view. Meanwhile, Eric Nielsen would ghost up there and sneak across the lot, and since the cars were fleet-keyed he would silently open the door of the recruit's car and climb into the driver's seat. Eric was not very tall, he was about five foot six and slender, but he was one mischievous little elf. He would hunker down below the dashboard, then shift the car into neutral so it would start rolling down the sloped lot, picking up speed as it rolled right past the corner window. Then the officers inside would say to the new trainee "Hey, isn't that your car rolling away?" The recruits' eyes would get as big around as saucers and they would drop their food and run for the door at top speed, with horrible visions of their patrol car and their short careers careening right out onto Colorado Boulevard and causing a wreck, while the officers inside were howling with laughter, and when they saw the recruit sprinting across the lot after their runaway car they were practically rolling in the aisle. I didn't think it was very funny when they did it to me, but it sure was a lot funnier when we did it to the other recruits.

My last FTO was Pat Weathers, and I was only with him for my final two-week "checkout ride" before I would be turned loose on my own. Pat's nickname at the PD was "Wild Man Weathers", and he was a legend around the Department. On the night of his high school senior prom he rode his motorcycle through the halls of the school, and he'd been raising hell ever since. The brass hated him, the younger cops idolized him, and the local criminals feared him. During my phase with him we got a call one morning of a mugging. Two males rolled a woman down at the Southglenn Mall and ran off with her purse, then they jumped on the #24 RTD city bus heading north up

University Boulevard into Cherry Hills. We went looking for the bus and found it just south of Belleview Avenue.

Weathers was driving and just cut the bus off, pulling the squad car in front of it with lights and sirens going. He was a good bit older than me, but he was out the door and gone before I even had my seat belt off. He didn't bother with lengthy explanations to the bus driver, just moved down the aisle until he saw the two perps hiding in the back. "YOU TWO!" he barked "GET OUT HERE!" They hesitated and looked at each other for support, and Weathers pulled his stainless pistol from his holster and said "Don't make me shoot you right here boys, 'cause I will!" The passengers almost fainted, and the two perps jumped up and came out with hands held high, and we found the victim's wallet under their seat.

Pat and I got along great, and I was cruising through my checkout ride. In my last week we got a tip that a guy wanted for murder out of Los Angeles was working on the groundskeeper crew at the Magness estate. Bob Magness was co-founder of a major telecommunications company and a self-made billionaire. I met him a few times and like many self-made men he never let his success go to his head. He was so down to earth and such a regular guy that you would never guess he was one of the richest men in America, if not the world. He had a very large estate and a full-time grounds crew, and it was one of these guys who was our perp. We did a quick recon from a distance using a pair of compact binoculars I kept in my "war bag" and located our guy from the description. He was down at the grounds shack a little distance from the house. Good. We didn't want to be anywhere near the house and innocent people when we took him down.

We made our approach from the north side of the grounds shack, which put us out of their view. Two other officers were with us, and we were just walking along quietly hoping to get up close without being seen. Suddenly one of the grounds crew came around the corner of the shack, and he saw us and stopped dead. Then he went back around the shack. *Damn*! We were blown. We all started running across the field, and me and Eric Nielsen started pulling a lead on the other two cops. We came running around the shack with guns drawn and to our utter amazement nobody was running. Everybody was just sitting on hay bales or on the ground talking and eating their lunches. The guy who saw us hadn't said anything to the others. But as soon as our suspect saw us he knew The Man had come for him. *Ask not for whom the bell tolls, it tolls for thee.* He jumped up to run but we were on him in a flash, taking him down in the dirt and wrestling him into the cuffs. It was fun, heady stuff for a guy still in field training. Pat gave me a nice write-up in my training log for it, icing on the cake for my graduation from the Field Training Program.

FOUR

ALTHOUGH IT HAS NOW BEEN TWENTY YEARS, I still remember the first day I went out on patrol after finishing the Field Training program. I just drove around for a couple of hours with the window down and the radio on, not doing anything but enjoying being in the car all by myself. No one sitting next to me with a clipboard and pen, evaluating my every move, every radio transmission, every decision. If I made a wrong turn now, went left when I should have went right, there would be no one to see it but me.

I began to get to know the Department and some of the other officers. It happened slowly, because when you work in a police department the only people you see regularly are the handful of other officers on your shift. Night after night, you see the same faces in the squad room and the same faces on every call. If you like each other, by the end of a one-year rotation you'll bond like family. If you even mildly dislike each other, by the end of the year you may grow to be mortal enemies. Even after I had been out of field training for a full month or more, every once in a while a cop I had never seen before would come into the squad room, look at me, and turn to the other officers and say "Who the hell is this boot?" "Boot" is a semi-derogatory term for a new guy, universal in police departments, and nobody really knows where it came from. There are fellow cops in the department that you can go weeks without seeing, because they're on different shifts with different days off than yours. Then when you see them you say "Hey, John! Where the hell have you been?" and he'll say "Right here! Where the hell have *you* been?" You've both been swirling around each other for weeks, sitting in the same squad room chairs, driving the same cars, but always just missing each other.

The Chief of Cherry Hills, Les Langford, I had already met before I got hired. The second in command was Captain Charlie "Norman" Bates, a fiftyish, tall and slightly overweight man who had the unfortunate characteristic of having more than a passing resemblance to the cartoon character Charlie Brown, and behind his back that was what everyone called him. There was a detective and a detective sergeant, a DARE Officer, an Animal Control Officer, five patrol sergeants and fourteen patrol officers. Fully twenty five percent of the department was female, but my first badge said "Patrolman" in block letters, a throwback to the old days when police work was a man's world. It was a very small and close-knit department, and I just hoped I could find my place in it.

There were other important people, like the City Manager and the Finance Director. Those two were like peas in a pod, and as befitted their positions their minds were always turned to dollars and cents. When they cancelled the annual City Christmas Party one year due to cost they earned the nicknames Grinch and Scrooge. There was also the municipal court judge, Judge James "The Terrible" Turre, who was an irascible old bear on the bench, and Suzanne Rogers, the cute and spunky prosecutor that all the male officers had the hots for. We had another judge who would occasionally fill in, an attractive woman with long auburn hair, and we would tell the new guys that when she presided over court she wore nothing under her black robe. Then you'd see these guys sneak into the back of the courtroom, craning their necks or bending down in hopes of catching a peek under that robe. I bet the judge always wondered why all these cops would come stand around in her courtroom.

The police department itself was a run-down, cramped little tan brick building with peeling paint, bad lighting, and thin tiles laid over a concrete floor. It wasn't at all what one would expect from a blue-blood, moneyed community like Cherry Hills. I suppose that tells us where we stood on the priority list, as far as the good people of the Village were concerned, when there were many homes in the city larger than the entire PD. I mentioned to Pat Weathers that it looked like we were running a police department out of someone's garage, and he guffawed with laughter. "We are!" he exclaimed, and explained this building was the old Public Works garage, where they parked their sand trucks and plows, and when they got a brand new garage the city converted this one to be the police department.

Now that I was on my own, I was assigned to a patrol team. I would be working Watch 2, the two to midnight shift. My team sergeant was a guy named Dave. Dave was a towering, gangly guy with a head topped by a mop of red hair, and he had the nickname "Big Bird", after the Sesame Street character. I immediately picked up on an interesting social dynamic at work in the Department. We would see the brass at the two o'clock roll call, and as soon as the Chief or the Captain walked into the squad room, coffee cup in hand, some of the sergeants would make a show of barking orders and calling everyone to attention. After roll call and while the officers bustled about loading their gear bags into their cars or drawing weapons from the armory, it was amusing to see some of the sergeants engage in the daily competition to deliver the most obsequious compliments to the Captain and boast about the achievements of themselves and their team. "We've really been hitting the extra patrols on the Canal, just you like you said, Sir!" would be countered by another sergeant with "We hammered the school zone today Captain, just like you wanted, got sixteen tickets this morning!" and then someone would *really* stoop down low with "Have you been losing weight, sir? You really look good!" and the other sergeants would give the offender sidelong dirty looks because they didn't think of it first. Captain Charlie Bates expected such brown nosing from his sergeants, and most of them did their best to comply and receive their pat on the head.

The Captain liked Dave, but he was not the favorite son, so Dave had reason to be concerned about his position and his career. I often thought how glad I was to be just a street cop, a slick-sleeve with no rank, and I swore I would never put in for sergeant. Dave's way of assuring his place was to be an absolute stickler for the rules and regulations. He was very smart, and we always said his oversized noggin was to accommodate his oversized brain. When I was hired I received an initial gear issue, and right on top was a giant book in a blue binder that looked as weighty and boring as the Federal Tax Code, and on the cover it read in foreboding big black letters:

POLICY AND PROCEDURES MANUAL.

Most of us took a cursory glance at it, riffled through the pages to see if there were any pictures (there weren't), then tossed it in the trunk of the car or the bottom of our lockers. Technically, we were responsible for every last one of the hundreds of pages in the Manual, but seriously now, did they expect anyone to actually read that? Well, Dave did read it, and he could spout regulations by page and section number. So could the Captain, because he wrote almost all of it. I liked Dave and he was a good sergeant, but his dogged adherence to the Policy Manual could be frustrating. One afternoon Dave and I were pulled up car to car under a shady tree, just passing the time for a few minutes. A confused looking man motored by and when he saw us he slowed down and lowered his window. He said "Officer, can you tell me how to get to I-25?" I said "Sure, just keep goin' straight up to Hampden, hang a right and go two miles and you're there." He said thanks and drove away. A minute later Dave said as he pulled away from our shady spot "Don't forget to give me a report on that." I was genuinely confused and said "A report on what?" "Per P and P a report must be generated for all Citizen Assists" came the reply, so I had to drive back to the station and first write an Incident Report, which is a quick summary report, then fill out the longer Officer's Report, make copies, put one in the mailbox on the sergeant's door and the other in the box for Records, then go back on patrol. So all told I was out of service for almost half an hour for what was literally five seconds of talking to a citizen.

One Friday night Dave stumbled across a stolen car someone had swiped in Aurora and dumped in a church parking lot in Cherry Hills. Inside the car was a Wendy's bag with a half eaten hamburger in it. The P&P Manual says any evidence available at a crime scene is to be recovered and booked in for analysis, so Dave dutifully collected the Big Bacon Classic with Cheese, took it the station, and placed it in one of the evidence lockers recessed into the back wall of the squad room. It was summertime and hot, there was no air conditioning in the squad room, the evidence lockers are small and stuffy, and the detective wouldn't be in until Monday morning. By Saturday the hamburger was starting to stink, and by Sunday night the squad room reeked of rotting onions, pickles, ketchup and mustard. When the detective came in Monday morning and opened the evidence locker, a wave of stench rolled out of it from the now green and moldy hamburger. Dave defended himself by saying we could get DNA evidence, and once again the P&P Manual says "Thou shalt collect all available evidence…"

The sergeants all lived in dread that one of the gung-ho young officers on their teams would go out and do something reckless and stupid and violate whole chapters of the P&P Manual. That was me. When I was a rookie, I hated doing paperwork and I just wanted to go out and drive fast and get in fights and bust people. Teams rotated shifts every four months, and not long after we moved to Watch 3, the graveyard shift, an officer named Joe Quaratino came to the team. He was a red-headed Italian with a hot temper, so naturally he became well-known as one of the "shit magnets" on the Department. Trouble just seemed to follow him like a cloud. One night he was driving through Denver on his way to work when some drunks in a pickup pulled up alongside him and threw a beer bottle at his car, which shattered against the driver's door. Five hundred cars on the road on a Friday night, and they pick Joe Q's.

Joe had his packset radio with him and he called it in to dispatch. I was at the station, out back loading my car when he aired it. I jumped right in the car and roared out of the lot. I was supposed to be going inside for roll call, but this sounded like so much more fun! I was going up University Boulevard toward Joe's location when he aired that both vehicles had stopped. A few seconds later Joe's voice registered an octave higher when he said that several occupants of the truck had gotten out and were advancing on him, and the driver was armed with a baseball bat. Then we could hear Joe's voice over the radio shouting *"Drop the bat or I will shoot your ass!"* I was just a rookie and I was waiting for someone else to get on the radio and take control, say something, *do* something, but there was only silence. *The hell with it!* I said to myself and grabbed the radio and told dispatch to call Denver PD to assist, as Joe was still a few miles north of Cherry Hills and in Denver's jurisdiction. Dispatch made the call and a moment later said DPD had been notified and was responding.

Dispatch started calling Joe back to check his status, but there was no reply. They tried to raise him several more times, but there was only more ominous silence. When another officer is in trouble and not responding, your imagination goes to the worst, and you feel guilty because you're not there to help. I pushed the gas down harder and saw the speedometer needle pass 100 mph. I was flying past other traffic and silently praying no drunks pulled out in front of me. I had almost reached Joe's location when he came back on the radio sounding out of breath and said the driver with the bat was in custody, DPD was on scene, and he was Code 4. I breathed a sigh of relief and backed off my speed. Seconds later I saw a veritable sea of red and blue flashing lights off to my left. There must have been twenty Denver cars there, and Joe and a horde of Denver cops were gathered around five suspects proned out on the ground.

I was walked up to the scene and saw all the police cars and thought *"My God, now that's BACKUP!!"* We only ran two cars on duty at a time, three on a good day. Our only "backup" was the other guy on the team, and these DPD guys sent twenty cars to one call. I was envious. The Denver cops were gathered around the guys on the ground and giving them an earful. One of them was leaning over the driver and said *"Hey Dumbass!* Didn't anybody ever tell you not to bring a bat to a gunfight?" and another one said "Five hundred cars on the road and you throw a beer bottle at *a cop*?! Genius!" We didn't talk to people like that in Cherry Hills. We would have said *"Sir, please rise to your feet and move to the police vehicle for transport"*. It was the first time I had ever been on a call with Denver officers, and I was at once repelled and fascinated by their way of doing the Job. Since technically all the crimes had occurred in the city of Denver, they took the occupants of the truck into custody, and Joe and I went back to the station.

We were high-fiving each other as the adrenaline dump was wearing off, but when we pulled up in the alley and walked through the back door into the squad room, Dave immediately came out of the sergeant's office and said "What the hell are you two doing stepping into shit up in Denver?! You're not even in your own jurisdiction!" We tried to explain but he wasn't having any of it. If things had gone bad and Joe had shot someone, it would have all come down on Dave as the sergeant. That was just the first of many, many times that my own sense of what needed to be done on the street butted heads with the CYA organizational culture of government agencies.

* * *

My usual partner for those first couple of years was Beth Janzer. She had been hired at the same time I was; I was badge number 95-2 and she was 95-3. The two of us had little in common and made an unlikely pair. I was a redneck farm boy and she was sophisticated and well-mannered. I was a conservative right-wing male and she was a liberal female. I tended to eat with my fingers while she knew all the social graces. Against all odds we hit it off and became fast friends. One night early on, though, that friendship was tested and cemented.

There was a man who lived in the city named Hancock. He was the son of wealthy parents and had inherited a fortune, including a beautiful mansion with manicured grounds, approached by a long gated driveway. He was also a bodybuilder, a drug addict, a steroid user, and subject to wild and violent mood swings. One night his girlfriend made a frantic 9-1-1 call saying that he was tripping on acid and was holding her hostage in the house, and she was afraid he was going to kill her. There were three of us on duty that night, and we rolled on the call.

We knew from past experiences that Hancock was really out there, that he owned guns, and we all believed he was fully capable of killing her. We also knew he was paranoid and that the house had an elaborate security system, with cameras covering the entire property and the approaches to the house. We did not roll up with lights and sirens because if Hancock was tripping that might just send him right over the edge. The house had a massive security gate across the driveway and at least two cameras pointed toward it, so we would be spotted before we got within fifty yards of the place.

We had a quick powwow and decided to try a stealthy approach from one of the back corners of the house. To get there, we had to hike a couple of hundred yards in the dark through a field that bordered the property, then hope to find a place to get in. We tromped through the tall grass of the field, with many stumbles and curses because we were using our flashlights sparingly, until we reached a dark back corner of the high metal fence that surrounded the estate. Suffice to say that we didn't exactly look like SEAL Team 6 taking down Osama Bin Laden's compound.

We searched in vain for an easy way in, and finally concluded that we would have to climb over the tall fence. Jody Sansing was tall and athletic, and he easily clambered up and over the fence and ran across the open space for the shelter of some trees. It was Beth's turn next, but she couldn't climb up over the high fence. She jumped and reached for the top, but no matter how she tried she was just too short to pull herself up and over. I cupped my hands and she put her foot into them to try to hoist herself up. Try as we might we just couldn't get the balance right on the uneven ground, and she was still trying to get herself up when suddenly a bright light blossomed and what had been black darkness was lit up as floodlights mounted on the back of the house activated. We had been made.

He had probably seen us on the security cameras or maybe he even had passive infrared heat sensitive detectors. Some of the homes here had security systems that would make the CIA envious. In any case we were caught like deer in the headlights, but luckily we were on the far edge of the reach of the lights so we still had some concealment. Jody was shouting and waving from under the trees for us to hurry the hell up. I dropped down to my hands and knees like an adult about to give a pony ride to a kid and told Beth to stand on my back. She did, and just then there was a shout from the house and the beam of a flashlight probing toward us. I was fully expecting the roar of gunshots to follow and I grabbed Beth's feet and stood up fast, heaving her up and practically tossing her over the fence. She hit the ground and I told her to run for cover to Jody. Then I started to climb up the fence myself, just as Hancock zeroed in on me with the flashlight beam. He was shouting something but I didn't bother to try to figure it out as I rolled over the top of the fence and hit the ground with a thud, then got up and ran across the open space toward the trees, illuminated by the powerful light beam the whole way. *I don't think this is how the SEALs do it* I thought as I made my stumbling run.

I knew how crazy Hancock was when he was using, and with every step I was expecting to hear the whine of bullets passing me, cursing my bad luck all the way. *If I get shot because of Beth I'm gonna kill her!* I growled to myself, but I made it to the trees. At the same moment Hancock disappeared back into his house. "What the hell took you so long!" Jody demanded when I got to the cover of the trees, and I just said "We had a little trouble at the fence."

We settled into negotiations over the phone with Hancock, when suddenly the phone line went dead. We were weighing our options, but none of us wanted to cross the yard fully exposed and try to force entry into the house, on camera and under the gun the whole way. On the other hand, he might be murdering her in there. We decided Beth would stay at the tree line and provide covering fire if needed while Jody and I sprinted across the open space. We had just psyched ourselves up for the mad dash across No Man's Land when the back door opened and the girlfriend walked out. She said he had finally got tired of waiting for us and just passed out on the couch. We went in and cuffed him without further trouble, although the DA later ended up dropping all of the charges because the girlfriend would not cooperate with the prosecution and said it was all just a misunderstanding. Jody said I should have dropped Beth and run for cover, but she was my partner and I just couldn't do that.

Like Jester said to Maverick in *Top Gun,* you never, ever leave your wingman. Or wingwoman.

* * *

It was about this time that I proposed to my girlfriend. We met in college, in *American History - The Revolution to the Civil War.* On the first day of class I sat with my buddy Wayne, and our carefully selected vantage point in the back center of the room allowed us to check out all the girls as they came in, and my eye was drawn to a very pretty green-eyed blonde who sat just a few rows in front of us. Before she sat down we made eye contact and she gave me a coy little smile, and I turned to Wayne and said "I gotta meet that one!" Just a few days later she came up to me after class, and said she had missed a day and could she get my notes? We talked for a few minutes and I told her sure, she could get my notes. In fact, why don't we just get together and study? Now every red-blooded male knows that "let's go study" is a euphemism for "let's go make out on the couch", but she said yes anyway.

We went to Pizza Hut for that first date and started going steady from that night forward. I was sort of dating two other girls at the time, and figured I had to break it off with them. One took it well (which was a blow to my ego) and the other took it very badly, as in throwing a skillet at my head (which was alarming). She and I dated all through four years of college and then moved to Denver together after graduation. We had been together for five years by this point, and I wanted to ask her to marry me, but I just wouldn't do it while I was working as a lowly security guard. Now that I had a real police job and was making some decent money, I decided the time was ripe.

She left to go to Cancun with one of her college girlfriends for a week, and while she was gone I asked my older brother

Tim to be my best man, and to help me pick out a ring. I picked out a diamond solitaire that I thought was perfect, and asked her right there at the airport when she came back. After five years I was pretty sure she'd say yes, but there's always the nagging possibility in the back of your mind that she might say no. In any case, she did say yes and we were married about a year later. On the wedding day I did not know it but Kari was already pregnant with our first child. She found out the night before our wedding but didn't tell me because she didn't know how I would react, and she didn't want to spoil the honeymoon.

After the wedding we honeymooned in the Cayman Islands, and Kari was being very careful not to do anything to cause problems with the baby. I was clueless, a typical man, and when we went out on a scuba diving trip she said she just wanted to stay on the boat. I bobbed in the water, trying to convince her to come in, and when she wouldn't I swam off, annoyed and thinking she was being a stick-in-the-mud. Then she was going to the bathroom constantly. Every fifteen minutes, it seemed, she was heading for the ladies room. We were in the airport on the way home and she passed the women's restroom and said she had to go, and I turned to her and said "Again?!" She shot me a truly evil look before stalking off to the bathroom. I was left standing there thinking *Jeez, what's her problem?!* and she was no doubt thinking she had just the made the biggest mistake of her life by marrying a moron.

The final straw was when we were on the plane headed home. Two kids about six or seven years old were sitting right behind me and they kept punching and kicking my seat and fighting over Goldfish crackers and who got to sit by the window. I have a long fuse, but I finally snapped and spun around in my seat and, ignoring their inattentive mother completely, I yelled at them that the next kid who kicked my seat would be riding home on the wing. Then I turned back to Kari and said "We are *never* having kids!" As luck would have it, it was Father's Day. Yes, if they gave a prize for Jackass of the Year I would have been the uncontested champion.

Kari didn't speak to me the rest of the flight, the whole car ride home from the airport, and the next day. She didn't tell me she was pregnant for two more weeks after we got home. After the honeymoon and the plane ride home, who can blame her? Two weeks after we got home I was sitting on the couch and she said she had rented a movie for us to watch. I was hoping for *Dirty Harry* or *Conan the Barbarian,* but instead she popped in *Nine Months*. Great. A chick flick, just what I wanted to watch. A lot of women think Hugh Grant is just dreamy, but most guys think he's an effeminate wuss. But I wanted to get myself out of the doghouse I had been in for days, so I settled in and pretended to like it.

We came to the part in the movie where the girl tells Wuss that she's pregnant, and Kari turned to me and said she was, too. I thought she was making a joke, and gave a perfunctory laugh and went back to watching the movie. See, what did I tell you? I was the typical guy who misses every single warning sign and hint she puts in front of him. She could have stuck a sign in the front yard in letters three feet tall saying I AM PREGNANT! and I would have walked right by it thumbing through the latest issue of *The Police Marksman* on my way in from the mailbox. She waited a few seconds until it became clear that I really didn't believe her and she told me again, that she really meant it, she wasn't pulling my leg, we were going to have a child, me and her. I was stunned, so what did I say to her? I said "Prove it!"

Before you women use my picture as a dart board let me defend myself by saying I'm a cop, and we demand proof! She gave me proof, in spades. She showed me the home pregnancy kit test results, and the doctor's report. Suddenly I completely identified with Hugh in the movie when he dreamed about the giant female praying mantis eating the male after they mate. After hyperventilating for a moment, I calmed down and began the process of accepting the idea that I was going to be a father.

After we were married we bought a little house in a small farm community about fifty miles north of Cherry Hills, because between me being a cop and her being a teacher we couldn't afford anything in the city. But we were happy there in our little cottage, and as the months went by and Kari got bigger, I began to grow a little worried. Our next door neighbors were a nice couple and me and the husband, Mark, talked frequently over the back yard fence. His wife was a rather large woman, easily 200 pounds and perpetually wore pink sweats every time she left the house. She looked like an enormous petunia, or the survivor of an explosion in a Pepto-Bismol factory, and Mark sighed sadly and said when he married her she weighed 120 pounds. She put on 80 pounds with their first pregnancy and promised she'd lose it all after the baby was born. The kid was practically shaving now. So like all men with pregnant wives, I was a little scared and Mark's story was not helping.

When Kari was full term and we went to the hospital, the nurses wheeled her into the delivery room and I somehow got trapped in the corner by cords and IV stands and monitoring machines and couldn't get out. I did not want to be in the delivery room. I come from a very traditional family, and I wanted very much to be out in the hallway, pacing around and waiting for the doctor to come out and tell me what I had. But like I said, I was trapped and I was afraid to try to get out because I just *knew* I was going to trip and fall and yank the IV out of her arm or pull a cord out of the socket so I just stayed put, huddling in my corner. When my daughter was born and I saw her and heard her cry for the first time, everything changed in an instant. All the fear and anxiety I had were replaced by just wanting to hold and take care of that tiny little girl. That little girl is young woman now, but that feeling is still there.

FIVE

IT WAS THE FOURTH OF JULY, and I was working as I did on seemingly every holiday. To be a cop is to miss Christmas, Thanksgiving, New Year's, Easter, birthdays and school plays, and every holiday where people get together with family and friends. Next time you're handing out presents under the tree or pulling out a chair to sit down for turkey and pumpkin pie, take just a minute to look out your living room window because somewhere out there is a police officer driving around who'd like to be with his or her family, but is instead keeping an eye on your neighborhood. Christmas at the station usually meant two cops sitting in the empty squad room toasting each other with a cup of hot chocolate. On this particular evening I was dispatched to a fireworks complaint. *Are you kidding me?* So many fireworks are going off in the city it sounds like the Tet Offensive, and some uptight citizen is actually making a complaint? The complaint came from the Cherry Hills Farm neighborhood, a gated and guarded area that was home to the very upper crust of the city, the richest of the rich.

I waved at the guard as I drove over the pavestone road and through the brick archway into the neighborhood. I was driving around with the windows down looking and listening for the source of the complaint, when a huge explosion and bright light rattled my car. *What the hell!?* I thought I was taking mortar rounds. I thought I was back in Lebanon. No wonder the neighbors were complaining! I followed the light and sound to a cul-de-sac, where I saw a group of guys with their backs to me getting ready to light another one, and they touched it off before I could get there to stop them. The thing shot up into the air and boomed and sparkled and lit up the sky. This wasn't pop bottle rockets or Black Cats. This was the good stuff, the showstopper stuff direct from China. I hollered at these guys and they all turned around. One of them immediately struck me as familiar, and then it hit me; *Hey! That's John Elway!* To tell the truth I've been a Pittsburgh Steelers fan since I was old enough to catch a ball, but if you like football you can't live in Denver and not be a John Elway fan. He brought two Super Bowl titles to Denver, not to mention masterminding one of the great moments in sports history, "The Drive" against Cleveland in the AFC Championship Game.

So there he was, in the flesh, the hero of Denver, looking like a kid caught with his hand in the cookie jar. I told him there'd been some complaints in the neighborhood about the fireworks, and he was very polite and apologetic, but he begged me to let him shoot just *one more!* I actually thought about it for a minute, and I almost let him do it, but then I thought how would it look if I get called on a fireworks complaint, then I join in and watch while he shoots some more? So I reluctantly told him *Sorry pal, no can do. Hand the stuff over.*

Elway had this big, beautiful Alaskan Malamute dog named Kimo that escaped pretty much every other week. He had the invisible fence collar on, but his fur was just so thick it didn't faze him. It got to where I knew him on sight. I'd be driving around and see this big gray and white beast running down the street or nosing around someone's yard and I'd stop and call him over to me. He was a friendly dog and would come running over and I'd get out and open the back door to let him in. Whether it was because he was so big or because he just liked being picked up I don't know, but he would put his front paws on the back seat and just look back over his shoulder at me with his tongue hanging out and panting, as if to say *"Hey cop, how 'bout a lift?"*. So I'd grab his back legs and hoist him into the car and step back with my neatly pressed blue shirt covered in so much hair that I looked like I'd been wrestling a bear. Then I'd take him back home. The Policy & Procedures Manual said we were never to transport animals in the police car. We were supposed to call the Animal Control officer if she was on duty, and if she wasn't then we were supposed to go back to the station, drop off our patrol car and climb into the lumbering old Animal Control truck and go back for the dog. Who of course by then would be in the next county. Plus, with only two officers on duty we just *knew* that we'd get a physical domestic or a burglary in progress while we were rattling around in that old truck. So it was a lot easier all the way around for us to just put the animals in the back like any other detainee and take them home.

* * *

Being a celebrity can be hazardous to your health. I'm cruising around one night in Cherry Hills Farm, and I see this car ahead of me that piques my curiosity. It's what we call a JDLR – Just Don't Look Right. First off, it's a piece of crap car, one of those rust and primer grey multi-hued little compact cars you usually see in high school parking lots. There are no POS cars in Cherry Hills. Around here people are tooling around in Bentleys and Porsches and an occasional Lamborghini. Even the goofball security guard at the front entrance drives a Lincoln Navigator. Second, the car is cruising around real slow, hit the brakes, check out the house, move on to the next one. I don't really have any probable cause, because technically this is a public road and they haven't broken any traffic laws, but I figure I got reasonable suspicion, so I light the car up and pull it over. I approach the car and shine my Streamlight in the window, and there's this petite quiet young lady sitting behind the wheel. She's very meek and soft-spoken, hardly even looks at me. I get her ID and I ask her what she's doing out here in the middle of the night. She quietly says that she's meeting someone here. "Yeah? Who are you meeting?" I ask. She says "I'm meeting John Elway."

Now I think to myself, *John's only human, so maybe...* Nah! If John wanted to fool around it wouldn't be with this mousey girl. So I ask her "Does John know you're coming?" She looks at me and calmly says "Yes. It's our wedding night." *Okaaayy...* I said "You do know that he's already married, right?"

She says "Yes, but he's going to leave her for me." I ask her "Did John actually *tell* you this?" She quietly replied "No. My friend did." I shine the light around the inside of the car again, and there's nobody in that little car but her. I'm pretty sure now I've got a whack job on my hands, so I say "Is your friend here with you? Right now?" She nods her head yes. *Yep. Whack job.* Then she adds "He's right here next to me" and she moves a backpack that's lying on the passenger seat. Right there on the seat is a big butcher knife. This thing's got a shiny silver blade a foot long and three inches wide at the base, and it looks sharp.

They say there's more than one way to skin a cat, and having actually skinned a cat in a college Biology class I can confirm the old saying is true. I also know there's more than one way to handle a dangerous situation. When you're confronted with a dangerous and unstable person you have to weigh all the variables; lighting, bystanders, your weapons and theirs, your perception of their capabilities and yours, the availability of backup, and more. Factor in that you have just a few seconds, maybe less, to figure this all out and you can start to see how things can go wrong in so many ways.

When a cop on the street makes a split second tactical decision, whether it will be viewed by the brass and by the public as a good decision or a bad one hinges completely on how it all turns out. If you talk the emotionally disturbed person down and nobody gets hurt, you're a hero. They give you a medal and put an official letter in your file saying what a great cop you are. But if the EDP flips out and stabs herself, you, or some bystander, they put an official letter in your file saying you are officially an idiot.

So, I had to decide right quick how I was going to handle this crazy chick with her big knife. I could have retreated and called for backup, in which case she might take off and we wind up in a pursuit ending with a stabbing. A lot of guys would have just cleared leather and stuck their gun in her ear, which would probably end with somebody getting stabbed and somebody getting shot. So I just kept calmly talking to her, and while I was doing it I quietly reached up and called for cover, no lights and sirens. I asked her to step out of the car and come back and talk to me. *Let's just leave the knife, okay?* She came out willingly and came back to my car, still calm, quiet, and cooperative. Now that I had successfully separated her from her weapon, I patted her down to make sure she wasn't carrying the little brother to the one in the car. You've got to be *so* careful with EDP's. They can explode on you in a flash, they're often fascinated with knives and razors, and their strength and pain resistance is phenomenal. Scary people. I'd rather deal with a street-hardened gang "soldier" over a petite little female EDP like this one any day.

My cover arrived, and we told dispatch to send the bus. The ambulance arrived and the paramedics got her to lay down on the cot, *there you go, just lay back right there, that's nice...* and strapped her in. Tight. As they were rolling her away to the back doors of the ambulance she turned to me and made me promise to tell John where she would be, so he could come get her. After all, it was their wedding night.

I figured I better go warn Elway about this girl, in case she got out anytime soon. Hospitals have this disturbing habit where if you don't have health insurance, you're not crazy enough and they let you go. You do have health insurance? You're a loon - you need serious help and we just happen to have a bed for you right here! So I drove to his house to give him the heads-up that a very amorous and equally dangerous woman wanted to make his close acquaintance. John wasn't home, but his wife Janet was. I told her all about it, but instead of being scared she said "Oh, the poor woman! I should go see her! Where is she?" Now Janet's a real sweetheart, the nicest person you would ever want to meet, but considering that she's the biggest obstacle to this girl's dreams of John and happy matrimony coming true, I convinced her that maybe she should just stay home. And lock the doors.

When John Elway retired I worked his retirement party. It was a grand party, where the food and drink flowed and everybody who was anybody in professional football was there. It was like being on the Mount Olympus of football, the NFL Hall of Fame come to life and walking around me. One of John's kids came up to me in the living room and said "Sir, would you like something to drink?" I'm looking around behind me thinking *Who's this kid talking to?* until I realize he's talking to *me*. The Elway children were always polite, well-mannered, and respectful and never gave the police the slightest trouble. John was enjoying himself immensely and I don't blame him one bit. It was a hell of a party to cap a hell of a career. I was standing outside with another cop when Elway walked up to us, said "Man, I love you guys!" then swayed out into the darkness of the park by his house. Me and Bobby looked at each other, then nodded. *We better go check on him.* It wouldn't do to have John Elway fall and break his neck at his own retirement party.

Joe Sakic of the Colorado Avalanche also lived in Cherry Hills, and I saw him out in the neighborhood one day walking his dog. He was bending down picking up dog poop. When you see a big-time celebrity doing something like that, it really brings them back down to your level. By all accounts Joe was a good neighbor and a good citizen, very involved in the community and school activities. It's nice to see guys like John and Joe to balance out the spoiled brat celebrities that are entering rehab or getting arrested every other week.

I arrested another celebrity once, for DUI. He got very huffy with me, and said *"Do you know who I am?"* I couldn't believe someone was actually using that line on me. He said I should let him go, because his stature in the community was so great that the whole community would be harmed by his arrest. I told him the community would get over it, and watch your head getting into the back seat.

* * *

Another group of very important people to police officers were the dispatchers. They were your unseen lifeline, the voice on the radio that could bring you help when you needed it, calm you down when things were getting crazy, and do a million other things for you. You need to call out a coroner? Need a translator who speaks Hmong? Locked yourself out of your patrol car? Just as we were the go-to guys for the citizens, they were the go-to guys for us. Go-to girls, actually. There was a dispatcher that we called The Dragon Lady. She had a husky, sultry, Kathleen Turner voice that would have sounded just right telling you to kick off your shoes and stay awhile rather than telling you about a burglary in progress. I never met her, but I always pictured her sitting at her desk along the row of other dispatchers, but with a red light above hers, wearing something slinky and caressing her microphone while she talked. All the cops loved to listen to her, and when she would call you your heart sped up a few beats. Somehow I always felt like I should tip her after she gave me a call.

The dispatchers wouldn't hesitate to tell an officer or even a sergeant to pull his head out of his ass if he was screwing things up, as I still remember from my very first felony arrest. I was still in Field Training and had made a traffic stop. I cleared the driver and dispatch quickly came back with "311 Six Frank." I didn't know what that meant but it sounded important, and I was thinking *Six Frank? Six Frank? What does that mean?* I knew I should know this but it just wasn't coming to me. As if reading my thoughts the dispatcher said, not too nicely "That means he has a felony warrant, 311. ARREST him!" I could hear snickers over the radio from other officers, and my face burned with embarrassment. But we grew to psychologically depend on the dispatchers so much that on long, slow nights when everything was real quiet you would reach over and just key the mike; *hello?...is anybody out there?* just to hear them and know you were still connected.

* * *

I mentioned that Cherry Hills was a very wealthy little burg, in fact someone told me it was per capita the ninth richest city in America. Rich people do not live in the same world that you and I do. Their world is easy; messes get cleaned up by the servants, problems get cleaned up with money and connections and lawyers. This way of living, of calling someone to fix anything that goes wrong, has colored their view of the world and what can be done in it. I was out on patrol when I was dispatched to respond on a citizen assist. That was very normal in Cherry Hills Village; in addition to our regular radio calls we were constantly getting called to assist the citizens with everything from fixing flat tires to getting wildlife out of their living rooms to making their kids listen to them. We were the go-to guys for the residents, no matter what the real or imagined emergency. I jotted down the address and started making my way over to it. It was in a remote corner of the city and something about the address was dinging a bell in my head but I couldn't quite put my finger on it.

I arrived at a formidable looking iron gate that was turning green with age and weather, leading down a long tree-lined lane. I got out and pressed the intercom button and identified myself, and a creaking elderly female voice told me to wait for the gate to open and drive in. The ponderous gate slowly swung open with rusty groans of protest and I drove in. At the other end I emerged from the shady lane into a wide circular drive with a bubbling fountain in the center, fronting a beautiful old stone and wood mansion. I love grand old homes, homes with a history and charm and presence of all the people that have passed through there that newer homes, no matter how spectacular or gaudy, can never have.

I was admiring the house when the old woman doddered out of the front door, balancing on a cane. Now I suddenly knew why the bell had been ringing in my head. This was one our esteemed City Council members, and a cracked old bird at that. She had a reputation for wandering off in council meetings on soliloquies of the old days and confusing herself about just which days she was actually living in. I imagined she needed help with some yard work or moving some heavy piece of furniture or the like, but instead she led me over to the edge of her yard, to a very tall pine tree. She pointed the tip of her cane to the ground and there, nestled in the pine needles, was a fluffy magpie chick. No doubt she had fallen from her nest up above while testing out her wings and learning to fly. The old lady was concerned that the little chick would be eaten by a fox or a coyote, so I explained to her that sometimes nature was harsh and that it was the way of the natural world that some animals must be eaten so that the fox can feed her hungry kits, and so that the population of one species doesn't get out of control.

As I was explaining this Wild Kingdom lesson the old woman's face hardened. She did not like the idea of adorable little magpie chicks being fed to fox kits like a TV dinner. I blame Disney. In Disney movies the foxes and bears and owls sit down on tree stumps and have tea parties with the rabbits and birds and squirrels. As a farm boy I knew the reality was very different, but when I finished talking she just smiled at me and asked me if I would be so kind as to put the little chick back in its nest. I blinked and intelligently said "What?" She smiled more broadly and said I should put the chick back in its nest. I looked up the trunk of that tall pine tree and spied the nest, about forty feet up in the crook of a branch. I looked back at the old lady and she was just standing there with an expectant grandmotherly smile, waiting for me to pick up the chick and get going.

You don't say no to city council people, because they control your pay and benefits, but I had visions of myself huffing and puffing and pulling myself up those spiky tree branches with one hand like an orangutan and holding that fluffy little chick in the other, while getting covered with bits of bark and dirt and sticky pine resin, and getting jabbed and scratched and poked in the eye by branches and needles and pine cones, only to have the mother magpie start dive-bombing me and shrieking at me, all of which would of course end with me falling out of the tree from three stories up and bouncing and cracking my way down to land flat on my back, with multiple broken bones.

I wanted to say "Are you out of your f***ing mind?!" but instead I tried to calmly explain to her the sheer impossibility of what she was asking, but the old lady did not seem very concerned by the danger to me, so I went on to explain to her that even if I could manage to get the chick up there and get back down in one piece, the chick would likely just jump out again and beat me back down. She hesitated now, but when she saw that I was not about to pick up the bird and start climbing she finally relented and turned back toward the front door of her grand old mansion, balancing on her cane while looking back and casting disapproving scowls at me over her shoulder. She'll probably cut my pay next year.

SIX

WHEN I HAD ABOUT TWO YEARS ON THE JOB, the face of the Department began to change. Some of the older officers began to retire and new hires were coming on. I was suddenly not "the new guy" anymore, and I began to have confidence in my knowledge and skills. Hiring boards were going on that summer, and I came in one day to be told that we had hired a new officer named Jody Sansing. I thought we had hired an Oriental female, so it was with no small amount of surprise when I was introduced to a six foot two, mustached guy with a deep voice and tattoos. All the girls in the office were in a flutter about him, and when he would ride in on his Harley wearing a black leather jacket and boots they would melt; just your classic tall, dark and handsome Bad Boy. I didn't have much of an opinion about Jody's attractiveness, but he did look like he had the makings of a good cop. He breezed through Field Training, and he turned out to be one of the Department's outstanding officers.

We hired another good guy named Roy Stallsworth, and still another named Joe Quaratino, whom I have already briefly mentioned. With these guys coming aboard I was happy with the way the Department was shaping up. Both of them breezed through Field Training and were farmed out to patrol teams. Joe Q came to my team while Jody and Roy went to other teams. We all wanted to get to know the new guys and see what kind of people they were and what kind of cops they might be, so we took them out for beers after work and to backyard barbeques at our houses. There is no better way to see what a person is really like deep down than to get them comfortable and put a few beers in them. If a guy was a mean drunk, that was a warning sign of some deeper issues, but if he was a happy drunk, or just mellowed out, those were good signs. Navy Commander Richard Marcinko, the founder of SEAL Team Six, supposedly tested out new applicants to his team by taking them out and getting them drunk, so maybe he subscribed to the same philosophy.

In any case, we need not have worried. All of these guys turned out to be solid guys who meshed seamlessly with their teams. Jody and Roy were both married with nice families, and Joe was engaged to be married to a rodeo queen. A few months after they were hired, I came into work one day and was told that Roy was dead. It was a tragic accident. He was fishing with his two children on his boat, and one of them fell overboard. Roy jumped into the water and pulled him back to the boat and hoisted him aboard. The investigators believed that because of the very cold water temperature Roy was suffering from hypothermia and could not pull himself back aboard, and slipped beneath the water and drowned. It was a hard blow to us all. Roy was new, but we already felt that he was one of us. His wife and children were devastated, and we all pitched in to do whatever we could to support them and help them with their expenses, and we continued to help them for years afterward. His wife said she never expected us to rally to her since Roy was so new, but we take care of our own.

Death becomes a familiar face to those in law enforcement. It's a frequent but never welcome guest, that you become accustomed to just because he's always around. You do not become immune to death, just more comfortable with it and more accepting of it. The tragedy and pathos of death is dealt with through gallows humor. It may seem to a civilian observer that police officers are cruel and uncaring when they show no emotions other than to make a joke at the scene of a car accident or a suicide or a murder. Nothing could be further from the truth.

For most people, a tragic death of a family member or a friend is a once or twice in a lifetime event, and they can cry in grief, or shout in anger, and vent all of their emotions. We can't do that. For us, tragic deaths are a regular occurrence, a part of the Job, and if we dealt with them that way we would soon be an emotional wreck, from sheer overload. We use humor to shield ourselves because we must, to keep it from eating us up inside. When you lose that shield, when you can't deal with it any longer, it's time to go.

Some deaths overpower all the defenses we throw up. When I was still new on the Job I went to a call of a man not breathing. A neighbor had called it in, checking on his elderly friend next door. When I got in the house I found him lying on the floor in a back bedroom, and I knelt down beside him and checked for a pulse and breath. He had neither so I started doing CPR on him, cycling breaths and chest compressions, and fervently trying to bring him back. The paramedics arrived soon after and took over, so I stood back and let them work but I knew already that it was no use. As they worked on him on the floor, I looked around the room. There, on the bedroom dresser right next to me, was an open birthday card where a little girl had written the words in crayon "Happy Birthday Grandpa!" and underneath she had drawn little crayon stick figures of herself with a big smile holding Grandpa's hand. That was a tough one.

Much later in my career, when my skin was a lot thicker, I was the first car on the scene of a traffic accident on Hampden Avenue. I could see that it was a bad one as soon as I pulled up, and a frantic bystander ran up to me and pointed to one of the cars and said "Please help her, Officer! She's hurt bad!" I ran up to the car and found a teenaged girl trapped behind the wheel, the driver's side of her car crushed in and pinning her. The odd thing was that her face was almost untouched, beautiful and calm, like she was only asleep. Her body was a mess, torn and mangled and bleeding. I tried to get her out of the car but I couldn't. As I was working to free her a woman came running up behind me and said she was a doctor, so I moved aside to let her work. As I moved back I started looking for the other driver. He was seated on the pavement, with his back against the front tire of his truck. He appeared to be unhurt, but when I bent down to talk to him he reeked of alcohol. He lifted his head and slurred "Don't worry, Officer. I'm okay." I stood up and fought the urge to kick his head right through the sidewall of his truck. She died right there behind the wheel of her car; somebody's daughter, a future wife and mother, maybe, with children of her own. He didn't have a scratch on him. Cops always say the Devil takes care of his own.

* * *

Being a cop changes you. Not just on the surface, like making you more watchful of people around you or making you drive more carefully, but deep down on a fundamental level. It changes your view of the world, and the people in it. It makes you cynical, jaded, skeptical. It also makes you believe in honor, duty, and heroism. What it does to you inside is a double-edged sword. Because of the shifts you work, you find that gradually your non-cop friends fade away. The buddies you used to hang out with are working nine to five jobs now, and it seems you never see them anymore. You start hanging out off duty with your teammates, frankly because there's nobody else who is off on Tuesday and Wednesday mornings, and because cops share a set of beliefs and experiences that the larger society often can't relate to or quite understand. The irony of it is that the people who are there to protect and serve society gradually become increasingly isolated from it.

One way that being a cop changes you is that you become very aware of your surroundings. It's called being a "trained observer", and is the mark of a really good cop. I started learning it back in the military. In boot camp my company commander, aside from whipping us into shape through endless physical training, continually preached to us so often that I can still hear his gravelly voice in my head saying "Recruit, pay attention to *detail!"* When I got out of boot camp I was assigned to the aircraft carrier USS *Coral Sea.* I worked on the flight deck, where a mere moment's inattention could mean death. On my Mediterranean Cruise we lost four people to accidents. One person was dog tired at the end of a twelve hour shift, and just walked right through a spinning propeller. Another did the same with the tail rotor of a helicopter, and still another walked behind a jet sitting on the catapult in full afterburner. Fatigue dulls the senses, and it can get you killed.

I was taking my annual physical, and I was sitting on the table in the examining room with my shirt off and I was hooked up to an EKG monitor. The door was open, and the nurse was checking me over. She said to me "You show a response every time a person walks by the door or you hear a noise. I've never seen anyone so in tune with their environment." I did none of these things consciously. It was all just ingrained into me by now.

My wife and I were taking a walk near our house, pushing our new baby around in the stroller when a pickup pulled up next to us. A cowboy leaned out the driver's window and asked us for directions. We walked up to the window and the first thing I did was visually scan the interior of the truck. And I saw the gun. There, between the seat cushion and the center console to the driver's right, I saw just a hint of the wooden grips of a revolver. While I was talking to him I eased my hand up under my untucked shirt and placed it on the butt of my Glock. He thanked us for the directions and drove away. When he was gone I let out a breath and said "Whew! Did you see that?" Kari had no idea what I was talking about. Her eyes had never left the man's face, because that's how we all learned to talk to people.

The world becomes so much more interesting when you really *look* at what is going on around you, and you see what you've been missing all these years. We were out shopping and pulled into a store parking lot. I immediately noticed a young couple in a car a few spaces over from us, and even though their windows were up and I couldn't hear what they were saying, after only a few seconds of watching their facial expressions and body language I said to Kari as we were getting out "He's breaking up with her." Kari said "Who's breaking up with who?" When Kari would catch me looking at pretty girls I would protest "Honey, I'm just being a trained observer! It's not my fault!" and she would say "Funny how you have extra powers of observation for girls with big hooters." It's all just a part of the Job, dear.

Another way that being a police officer changes you is the way you respond to situations in your environment. When most people see something unusual happening around them, their first response is to stop and stare, take it in, look around to see if anybody else is noticing this, and then decide what to do. Cops don't do that. We were driving through the Safeway parking lot looking for a space when suddenly we saw a man come flying out through the front door at a dead run, pursued by store security. Without even a conscious thought, or even waiting for the car to stop, I threw the passenger door open and leaped out. My wife was no doubt sitting there looking at my empty seat and wondering what madness had suddenly possessed her husband to jump out of a moving car. I cut across the angle and did a flying tackle on the guy in what I imagined was a fair imitation of Vonn Miller (no relation) and brought him down in a heap. At first he resisted and squirmed to try to get away, but I pinned his arm behind him in a shoulder lock while yelling "Police! Stop resisting!" and then he realized he was screwed and just gave up. Turns out he swiped a pack of cigarettes, two apples, and some pens. All told it came to less than ten bucks. I told the guy "You're willing to risk going to jail for eight dollars worth of junk?" He just shrugged sheepishly as the loss prevention officer led him back to the store in handcuffs.

I was standing in my back yard watering the privet bushes next to my fence when a group of school kids came walking by. There was a girl, probably in seventh grade but small for her age, who was walking down the sidewalk with her head hanging and behind her was a group of older boys and girls. They were probably eighth or ninth graders, and they were yelling some things to the small girl that were not very nice, not very nice at all. That caught my attention, and as I watched this scene unfolding the group of older kids suddenly burst into a run. The little girl didn't see her danger until it was too late. She tried to run but they caught up to her and surrounded her on the front lawn of the house across the street, and one of the bigger girls shoved the little girl and pushed her down on the ground, telling her they were going to kick her ass. Four against one? And a little one at that? *Not on my watch.*

I vaulted my fence, and just as the little girl hadn't seen her danger until it was too late, the group of older kids didn't see theirs, either. I came up behind the older boy who was talking the most shit, and he found himself suddenly being lifted into the air. I hate bullies, people who use their size or their strength of numbers to pick on the small and the weak. The boy said "This ain't got nothin' to do with you! Just walk away, man! Just walk away!" Cops don't walk away. I shook the boy like a rag doll while yelling at him nose to nose like a drill instructor, and with the other hand grabbed the girl who had done the pushing and pulled her close and gave her an earful as well. The other two bolted and ran for the hills, and the little girl took the opportunity to scamper away as well. When I was done with them, I let the two kids go, promising that if I ever saw them picking on the little girl again they'd wish they had never laid eyes on her. No one, police officer or not, should stand by or walk away when bad people are doing bad things to those smaller and weaker than them.

* * *

Since I had a wife and a baby now, my meager police salary was no longer enough. When I was a bachelor it seemed like I always had money to spare, but I soon discovered that having a family cast everything in a different light. The money that I used to spend tinkering around with cars like my classic '73 Firebird 400 or buying a new rifle with a black Kevlar stock and free-floated barrel, was now diverted to Huggies and Enfamil. And Gerber baby food. Alex's favorite was plums, and one day while spoon feeding her I decided *I like plums. What the hell, give it a try!* and had a spoonful myself. *Oy! Yeck!* Not good! How do babies eat this stuff? I also out of curiosity once decided to eat a dog biscuit while I was giving Tiki one, so I don't know what that says about my culinary tastes, although the dog biscuit was preferable to the baby food. Fatherhood was new and novel to me, and to my surprise I found myself really enjoying it. I liked playing horsey and bouncing her on my knee, or reading bedtime stories to her, or singing "Mr. Sandman" and "Goodnight Sweetheart" while she stared at me with those bright big blue eyes.

It is a culture shock of the highest magnitude for a bachelor who has only lived alone or with his college buddies to suddenly try living with a woman. I found to my surprise that it was no longer okay to leave half-empty pizza boxes laying out overnight on the kitchen table, waiting for the contents to be eaten for breakfast, and that the middle of the bedroom floor was no longer the proper place for my dirty socks and t-shirts. The first time I came in from working on the car and washed my hands with the little flower-shaped soaps in the dish next to the bathroom sink I got yelled at, and I thought to myself *"This is impossible! We have soap we can't wash with, towels we can't dry our hands on, what's next? Toilet paper we can't"*...never mind. It took some getting used to, but in the end it was of course a change for the better. I found myself sitting down at the table for nice home-cooked dinners rather than eating microwave Hot Pockets in front of the TV, and pushing the baby stroller around the neighborhood in the evening was sometimes better than bolting a new set of headers on the Firebird.

Marriage had a civilizing effect on me, and those who say that the differences between men and women are only physical are completely wrong. Women live on a higher plane than men. We occasionally come up to visit them, but we still have too much caveman in us to ever actually live there. If men and women lived on separate continents, men would still be living in caves and wearing bearskin tunics, and we would come in from the woods and lean the spear against the wall, and flop down in our state of the art reclining chairs and turn on the giant-screen hi-def TV and watch football while gnawing on a turkey leg. Women, on the other hand, would be living in modern skyscrapers and taking flying cars to work and the mall.

* * *

I needed more money for my growing family, and to get it I turned to working off-duty jobs. Most cops work off-duty jobs. Some need it to pay the bills, and some do it to buy more toys. When I later worked for the Denver Police Department all the bars downtown would hire cops to keep order in the place, the banks wanted officers to cut down on the armed robberies, and then there were the Bronco games, the Rockies, the Avalanche, and the Nuggets games, too. When I was at DPD I worked a bank job on my days off. It was in a bad area in District 4 and the banks were always getting hit, so I usually stood near the front doors to let any potential robbers casing the place from the parking lot see there was a cop working here, and maybe they would go somewhere else. Or they would plan to take the cop out first. It's a hell of a way to make a living.

But back in Cherry Hills we weren't blessed with much off-duty work; we had two big churches where we directed traffic when the services let out, and there were also weddings and private parties and bar mitzvahs, and to get a job you put your name on a list. Jobs were given out and names checked off, and when you rotated to the top of the list you got the next job. I started putting my name on the Off-Duty List, and it was not long until Eric Nielsen, the off-duty coordinator, came to me and said "Miller, you're up!" I said "What's the job?" and he replied "It's the Debutante Ball." I laughed because I thought he was pulling my leg, and said "Seriously Eric, what's the next job?" He said "I told you! They need four guys for the Debutante Ball. Do you want it or not?" *Debutante Ball? You mean people still do that?* I thought such things were just a charming relic from the past, that people like the Rockefellers or the Vanderbilts held in the parlors of their mansions in days gone by, or that it was something now found only in the pages of *Gone With The Wind* or in faded photographs. I suddenly had a vision of Scarlett O'Hara in a flowing dress being squired around by Rhett Butler. I had no idea people still did things like that.

The night came for the Ball, and the four of us drove up to the Cherry Hills Country Club to get ready. The ball was being held on the west side of the main building and everyone was taking their places. The teenaged girls, dozens of them, were resplendent in gowns of every color as they lined up along one side of the broad lawn, and their fathers were beside them in tuxedos and double-breasted suits to escort and announce them. The whole area was bedecked with lights and garlands and there was an area for the audience to sit.

When the formalities began the announcer would read off the name of the girl, like "Presenting Miss Millicent Anastasia Huffingsworth, escorted by her father, Doctor Archibald Milhouse Huffingsworth the Third!" and then the girl would step forward arm in arm with her father and walk down the line and curtsy, to the polite applause of the crowd. Then she would go stand in another line. It had a pageant air to it, and I thought the whole thing was outlandish, just more airs that rich people put on. But the more I watched the more I kept picturing my own daughter up there in a pretty dress being introduced to everyone. After the presenting of the debutantes the reception began, and since we decidedly were *not* of the social class to be taking part in either the dancing or the socializing all of us cops just went to the kitchen to see if we could score some food (which we did; blue collar workers look out for each other, and the cooks took care of us), and when we left my initial feelings of disdain for the whole affair were replaced by a strangely uncomfortable feeling that maybe these rich snots were onto something.

Rich people didn't always behave so well at their social get-togethers, though. A lot of them have a sense of entitlement, a feeling that the rules don't apply to them because they're rich. How many Wall Street bigwigs have gone to prison because they thought they were untouchable? Not long after the Debutante Ball I worked another country club job, but this was one was over at the Glenmoor Country Club. The Cherry Hills Country Club was old money, the stodgy cigar-smoking gentlemen from prominent families, who had buildings and foundations named after them, people who were sure of their solid and comfortable position atop the social ladder. Glenmoor was new money, brash and flashy and younger, openly challenging the old establishment. These were the dot.com millionaires, the hotshot young lawyers and doctors and trust fund babies. The old crowd looked down their noses at these newly-rich brats, and they in turn sneered at the old stuffshirts.

The gig was a high school reunion. Twenty years. There was a band playing the hits from the '70s; the crooning of Simon and Garfunkel mixed in with the sappy romance of Barry Manilow, set off by the disco numbers of the Bee Gees, and the rebellious spirit of a young guy named Bruce Springsteen. I knew some of these songs from listening to my older brother Fred playing them on his 8-track when I was just a kid, and it brought back memories of childhood. Fred was the picture of the Seventies to me; platform shoes, bell-bottom jeans, long hair parted in the middle, smoking some grass out behind the shed where Dad wouldn't catch him. He lit out years ago for North Carolina with his girlfriend, and these old songs made me miss him.

It didn't look like I would have a whole lot to do at this reunion. For starters everyone was dressed up. The men wore suits and ties, and the ladies wore dresses and held glasses of wine and chatted and laughed in little groups. There was quite a spread of food, much of which I didn't even recognize. When no one was looking I sneaked a few samples, and most of it was awful. Rich people's food; everything was creamy or slimy or just too fancy. I did see a pan of those little meatballs covered with some kind of glaze so I settled for pilfering a few of those. I had just had my ten year high school reunion the previous summer, and we were all wearing shorts and flip-flops and grilling burgers and hot dogs in the park, and it was much better than this spread.

As the night wore on and the wine and drinks flowed, however, the mood of the crowd began to change. People got loose and got loud, and one couple got out and did a Saturday Night Fever disco dance that got the crowd going. Suddenly a harried-looking man came rushing up to me and said his wife was missing. He hadn't seen her in probably half an hour, and he had been looking for her everywhere in the clubhouse. She had quite a bit to drink and he was afraid she would wander out onto the golf course that surrounded the club and fall into a water trap or get lost and hurt herself. I put down my little plate of meatballs and told him to just relax and I would get some help and start a search for her.

I got on the radio and called John Defelice, who was working the swing shift that night. John came up and we made a careful search of the entire club, starting in the basement. Then came the kitchen but the cooks said none of the partygoers had been here. We went back to the main floor and were about halfway through searching that when the man came back to us saying not to worry, he had found her. She was very tipsy and accompanied by another man, and she laughed and said she had just been out taking a walk on the golf course with an old high school buddy, getting some fresh air and talking about old times. Now police officers are trained observers, taught to take in multiple details about someone at a glance, and I observed right away that the wife's companion seemed a little nervous and rumpled, and also that his zipper was down. I said nothing about it until the husband and wife had moved away to rejoin the crowd, and then JD turned to me and said "Did ya see that? She was gettin' a little more than fresh air out there." I replied "Well, they say there are no lovers like old lovers" as we moved back to the meatballs.

The partiers were getting really liquored up now and the reunion was kicking into high gear. I was rousting wandering guests out of the basement and the kitchen, people were making out in the dark corners, and then the manager came up to me frantically saying that the guests were stealing the golf carts and having races with them out on the course. I went outside and there were people fully clothed in the pool, someone was out on the sidewalk grandly singing to the traffic passing by on Belleview, and there was a golf cart nose-down and half submerged in the water trap at the nearest hole. I thought to myself *Well whaddaya know!? These rich people know how to party after all!* I did my best to keep a lid on things but in the end it was no use. It was like trying to nail Jello to the wall. People were everywhere, wandering around out on the golf course, down in the basement, in the pool, and God knows where else. In any case my job ended at midnight, and when the Cinderella hour came around I bid the by now thoroughly stressed out manager goodnight and went out the door. I told him to cheer up, they only do this once every twenty years.

* * *

In addition to rich people behaving badly, Cherry Hills was a haven for wildlife, and with homes on sprawling estates with tree-covered lanes, wooded open spaces, parks, trails, ponds and golf courses it was a vast refuge in the heart of metro Denver. Every furry four-footed animal you can think of was at home here, from the cute ones like rabbits and squirrels to the not so cute ones like coyotes and snakes. We experienced a constant onslaught of predation upon the schnauzers, poodles, and kitty-cats living in the Village. Residents called weekly to report that Snookums ran off barking at something in the bushes last night and has not returned. *O where could my precious Snookums be?* I'll tell ya' where he is, lady. That thing he was barking at in the bushes ate him. He's coyote chow. Or some owl flew away with little Pookie in her talons, to take back to her nest of hungry chicks. People always say they *love* living near wildlife until the wildlife eats their prize Persian cat. Then not so much, no. Welcome to the *real* world of wildlife, the kill or be killed, eat or be eaten world.

One morning while I was sitting in the station the phone rang, and on the other end a woman was telling me that an elk was in her garden, eating all of her lovingly grown flowers, and could I please come and remove him? I immediately thought of all the times I had taken my kids to the zoo, where some bubblehead parent would point to the cheetah and say to the kids "*oooh*...look at the *lion* sweetie!" or point to the Cape Buffalo and tell their child "Can you say *rhinoceros,* honey?!" and I thought to myself "An elk in your yard? Right in the middle of a metro area of three million people? Sure, lady...it's probably the neighbor's riding horse." So I drove over to the house and to my astonishment, right there in the front yard, grazing on the daisies and sunflowers, was a full grown bull elk with an enormous set of antlers and probably half a ton on the hoof. He lifted his head at my approach and stared at me, continuing to munch contentedly, with the ends of flowers hanging out of his mouth. I'm sure he thought this was far better fare than the scrub grass and sagebrush he was used to. The woman who had called it in now came outside and pointed to the elk, saying "See? He's right there in the garden!" in case I had somehow missed him, and said "Can you make him go away?" Sure, I'll just throw a leash around him and put him in my car. *Can I keep him? I promise I'll feed him and walk him!* I told her I would have to call the Division of Wildlife, so I went back to the car and made the call. The DOW agent said "Just leave him alone and he'll wander away." They always said that. An Alaskan brown bear could be making a den in your garage for the winter and they would say "Just leave him alone and he'll go away." I told the woman there was really nothing I could do, as all wildlife was their jurisdiction. I told her to call the DOW if he moved into the kitchen and started raiding the 'fridge.

Elk in the flower garden were a nuisance, but the residents became much more concerned when a mountain lion moved in. Supposedly. Some say they saw him, while others pooh-poohed the idea. It was like sightings of Sasquatch; people would call in and swear they saw the lion crossing a bridle path, or walking along the Canal, or slinking off through the trees, or reading the paper and having a cup of tea in the back yard. Once the word got out, a flurry of unsubstantiated sightings began pouring into the police station. "Lion Fever" gripped the city and any yellow creature became the mountain lion. To calm the citizens we quickly responded to all these calls, and I found "lions" who were Golden Retrievers, yellow tabby cats, foxes, and even Shetland ponies.

We were assigned to do extra patrols along the Canal road and in the parks and trails, to reassure the citizens that they were safe. We responded to a call of the lion supposedly lurking in a field of tall grass, and my partner Matt and I were on one end of the field while a sergeant named Tom was on the other end. Tom grabbed his MP-5 and started off across the field toward us. His rifle was at port arms and as he walked through the waist high grass he looked for all the world like he was on safari. All he needed was a pith helmet and some native gunbearers. *"I say old chum, do you suppose that lion is about? Be a good chap and go into that brush there and shake him out!"* Matt and I were just watching him, and Matt said "Look at him, God bless him! That lion is going to leap out of that grass and tear him apart, and we get to watch the whole thing."

Matt may have laughed at Tom but he who laughs last, laughs loudest, because he had a lion encounter of his own shortly afterward. Supposedly. He was driving along the Canal road at night when he *swears* the mountain lion emerged from the bushes not twenty yards away, looked over at him, and then dashed across the road into the bushes on the other side. We all gave him huge amounts of ribbing over it, and he began finding stuffed animal cats and bags of catnip in his war bag, in his locker, and in his car. Every time he got on the radio you could hear *"meow"* in the background from the other officers. I never did see the lion, and the furor eventually died down, but I think it was probably there. Just like Sasquatch.

* * *

One thing that I quickly discovered about working at Cherry Hills is that sometimes, like Shakespeare said in *Henry IV,* discretion is the better part of valor. Because we were such a small department we usually only ran two officers on duty at a time, and before you stepped into something you would have to take a long look at who your partner was for the night. If I worked with Matt or JR or Jody we would charge hell with a bucket of water, because we knew we could absolutely count on each other. Mean drunk construction worker? *No problem!*

Carload of gang bangers? *We can handle that.* Convoy of Hells Angels bikers? *Well...maybe we'll let that one go.* On the other hand, there were officers who were known to run the other way, or who always seemed to on the other side of town or in the bathroom when the Code 3 hot calls came out or when an officer was calling for help.

I covered one such officer, who shall remain nameless in his shame, on a DUI arrest. The driver was from neighboring Englewood, a big skinhead with White Power tattoos all over him. When he was told he was under arrest, he started clenching his fists and pawing the ground with his foot like a bull about to charge. He said "I don't wanna hurt you, but you are *not* arresting me!" Now when a guy says he doesn't want to hurt you, then he's already *thinking* about hurting you, so don't take any comfort from that statement. In any case, that was not an acceptable answer and the next thing you know I'm rolling around on the ground punching and cussing and kicking with this guy when I suddenly realize *Hey, I'm all alone down here!* When I finally got the suspect under control and into handcuffs, I look up at my "partner" and he's just standing there on the sidewalk watching the show. He never even moved.

Sometimes even when you had a partner you could trust you still had to use your better judgment. Englewood PD had an officer-involved shooting one night, so Jody and I were shagging calls in their city. Englewood may have been our next door neighbor, but it was nothing like Cherry Hills. It was full of trailer parks, biker bars, liquor stores, tattoo parlors, run down tenements, and boarded up meth houses. We would definitely be seeing how the other half lived tonight. We got a call to check suspicious circumstances at a house, and we broke out our map books and found the right place. As we walked up we exchanged dubious glances. The house was pitch dark and set well back from the street, in the deeper shade of overhanging branches from a huge, hoary old tree. We checked around the outside and found an unlocked door. We quietly entered the house and found ourselves in the kitchen. There were old needles and cooking spoons on the floor amid a layer of dust. Meth house. We checked around the main floor, and then found there was something much more disturbing than that. On the walls were drawn Satanic symbols and pentagrams, and there was a large brown stain on a bed that looked an awful lot like old dried blood.

The hair on the back of my neck was standing on end as I slid my gun out of its holster. This place was beyond creepy. We cleared the first floor, and found a door leading to the basement. I turned the knob and pushed on the door, and it creaked and groaned as it swung open. We saw before us a flight of wooden steps leading down to a cobwebbed landing. On the wall of the landing was another pentagram, and a second flight of curving steps descended downward into a black pit. You could feel the malevolence rolling up out of the darkness. Bad things had happened in this house. It was like the *Silence of the Lambs* house. Jody and I stood there on the threshold with guns drawn, staring into the void. Jody finally said "I'm sure it's fine down there." I heartily agreed "Yeah, I'm sure it's all okay", and we backed out and went back to our cars and our own nice, safe city where the walls have Renoits and Picassos instead of spells to summon the Devil.

SEVEN

CHERRY HILLS WAS A LITTLE ISLAND OF TRANQUILITY in a sea of turmoil, a quiet bastion of stately old mansions on tree-lined boulevards, reeking of old money and well to do blue-blood family names. On three sides of our wealthy little island, however, were the ghettos and trailer parks and public housing projects common to large metropolitan areas everywhere. Along Clarkson street to our west and Hampden Avenue to our north one could readily find meth houses, crack dealers, prostitutes, homeless people, and willing players for any game you wanted to play. We called it Border Patrol, when we cruised these streets at night, keeping the riffraff on the other side of the street where it belonged.

We had good relations with the surrounding agencies; Englewood to the west, Denver PD to the north and east, Greenwood Village PD to the south, and the Arapahoe County Sheriff's deputies. We all had friends from the other cop shops, and we'd meet for coffee somewhere when it was quiet, or just pull up car to car in any handy parking lot to shoot the breeze and swap war stories. With us being from sedate Cherry Hills, however, the other guys' war stories were usually better than ours, especially the Denver cops.

Captain Charlie Bates *hated* the Denver Police Department. He thought DPD represented everything bad about law enforcement in America; they were abusive, they were corrupt, their cars were ugly, and their officers were a bunch of knuckle-dragging gorillas. None of that was true, of course, but he strictly forbade us to get involved in any way, shape, or form with *anything* that DPD was even remotely involved in. He hated car chases too, because they were fraught with civil liability, people got hurt, cars got wrecked, and he strictly forbade us, under penalty of being tarred and feathered and hung from the station house flagpole, to get involved in anything even resembling a pursuit. This is a story of how I found myself neck-deep involved with both, at the same time.

My regular car at that time was Car 6, a Ford Explorer; it wasn't fast like the Chevy Caprices or comfy like the Crown Vic sleds, but I liked it. I had recently made sergeant at that time, and sergeants had to drive the SUV's to carry all the extra stuff that supervisors carry, plus it was the only car that had a tape deck in addition to the radio, so I'd bring in my favorites of George Strait, Marty Robbins, and Alan Jackson (in case you ain't noticed, I'm kinda partial to old country) and cruise around listening to them, even though technically we weren't supposed to do that. I got the car set up just how I wanted it; seat setting, equipment, radio presets, and everything else, and settled in to my new ride.

One swing shift I was assigned a rider. He was a young kid, maybe sixteen, one of the guys from our Explorer Post. I was driving around with this kid, talking to him about the Job, when my ears perked up at some radio chatter in the background. A good cop can carry on a conversation with his buddy, clean his gun, listen to dispatch, and eat a sandwich all at the same time. On this day I caught the radio traffic that Denver PD was in a high speed pursuit with an armed robbery suspect. I turned up the radio, in time to hear dispatch say the chase was now coming down Happy Canyon Road. *Hey! We* were on Happy Canyon Road! They were coming right toward us! I wanted to get after it in a bad way, but Charlie Bates's face magically appeared in my head, shaking his finger at me and promising to hang me up by my heels from the top of the Public Works garage, so instead of turning left on an intercept course I reluctantly turned right away from the pursuit.

We were still following the chase on the radio, and dispatch coolly informed us that the suspect had just tried to ram a DPD cruiser and run it off the road. *Damn!* I wanted to get in there and get this guy! Now the chase turned down I-25 heading southbound. *Hey!* That was parallel to where *we* were right now! I looked over to my left. *There they were!* The bad guy was out of control, flying down I-25 with what looked like a sea of police cars some distance behind him. I looked up in the sky and saw at least two, maybe three news helicopters overhead following the chase. *Damn I wanted to get in there!!*

It was all I could do to just sit there on the sidelines, watching the other guys play ball. Suddenly, the bad guy lost it! His car skidded out of control and crashed in a huge cloud of dust. Dispatch excitedly aired *"Suspect has crashed! Suspect has crashed!"* No shit, I thought, looking over at the billowing cloud of brown dust not two hundred yards from me, across an open field. To my amazement, bursting from the cloud of dust at a dead run, was the suspect! The white DPD cars were all screeching to a stop and the cops were running up to the car with guns drawn. *"Oh Hell!"* I thought, *"They don't even know this guy is rabbiting!"* They don't see him through the dust cloud! This was too much; here I was being an obedient officer trying to stay away from this chase, and now the chase has come to me! What else could I do? I yelled *"Hang On!"* to the kid, cranked the wheel, and hit the gas.

We went up and over the curb and rocketed away over the field. I told the kid to hit the lights and siren, and we were bouncing over the field at breakneck speed like we were at Baja. One of the news helicopters saw it and dove on us like he was making a strafing run. The Denver guys looked up when they heard my siren and realized their suspect was halfway across the field and leaving them further behind with every step. The suspect saw me barreling across the field headed right at him and decided he had had enough. He was done. He stopped running, and wearily put up his hands while I skidded to a stop in front of him. I told the kid to sit tight and I jumped out with Heinz drawn, yelling at him *"Get your ass on the ground, NOW!"* He dropped down and assumed the position, and a moment later some DPD officers came running up. They jumped on the guy and cuffed him and searched him. The kid had not stayed in the car like I told him to, and he was standing next to me with a grin from ear to ear. This was *sooo* much cooler than Playstation! I was high-fiving the Denver guys and they were thanking me profusely, yelling to be heard over the noise of the hovering helicopter above us. *The helicopter!* Oh Crap! This was sure as hell going to be all over the five o'clock news. I told the kid "We gotta get out of Dodge, right NOW!" I grabbed him and pulled him away, threw the car in reverse, and put up some rooster tails of dirt peeling away.

That night I watched the news, dreading to see myself and hoping I wouldn't. Alas, there I was; my car bouncing across the field, me jumping out with my gun in my hand, the takedown of the suspect, all set off by the excited narrative of the newscaster. If this was my fifteen minutes of fame, I didn't want it. The next day when I came to work I snuck around back and peeked in the door. "Anybody seen Bates?" I asked. "No, not yet" came the reply. I waited in the squad room nervously for the two o'clock roll call. One look at the Captain's face and I would know. Bates walked into the room. I took one look at him and I knew; *He hadn't seen it! We were clear!* He didn't know a thing. I breathed a sigh of relief. Then I heard it. Voices in the hallway. Excited voices, voices talking about what an *Awesome!* chase we were in last night! That damn Explorer kid walked into the squad room regaling another pimply-faced Explorer with the blow-by-blow of what we did yesterday. Now Charlie Bates's ears were perking up. "What's going on?" he turned and asked, suspicion rapidly rising. I piped up quickly "Oh, we heard that Denver had a chase or something yesterday that ended in a crash and a foot pursuit. The details are a little sketchy" I said nonchalantly, while shooting the kid a warning glance. "Oh, I see" Bates said, turning away toward the hallway. Before he went around the corner, though, he took a long suspicious look over his shoulder at me.

* * *

We had an Explorer Post at Cherry Hills, which was a program operated through the Boy Scouts that allowed high school students to explore a career in law enforcement before having to make any kind of a real commitment to it. They wore uniforms that were made to look similar to a police uniform but different enough that nobody would mistake them for actual cops. The majority of them were genuinely dedicated bright young people who really wanted a career in law enforcement. We took these guys and gals under our wing and showed them the ropes. We didn't sugarcoat anything or bullshit them; we showed them the good and the bad about being a cop so when the time came they could make an informed decision about whether or not they really wanted to do this. Some of them did, and it was always nice to bump into one of your old Explorers on a call somewhere, wearing the badge and doing the Job.

One night early in my career, when I was young and foolish and would do stupid things without thinking about the consequences, I had an Explorer named Jen riding with me. Jen was a brown-haired, bubbly outgoing girl, a good kid who would eventually come to work for us an officer, but on this night we were just out cruising Hampden Avenue to see what we could scare up when I saw a bearded, tattooed biker on a Harley roll past me going the other way. He eyeballed me hard as we passed each other, but it wasn't the usual look of challenge I got from bikers but more of a look of concern, of worry, as in "I really hope that cop doesn't stop me." I've seen that look on perps a thousand times and it fairly screams *"Officer, I have a warrant out for my arrest!"* But you have to have PC, probable cause, to make a stop. When he eyeballed me I noticed he wasn't wearing eye protection, a violation of the Revised Model Traffic Code. PC achieved!

I braked and whipped the car around. The second my brake lights lit up, Harley Guy took off. He rolled on the throttle and his bike roared in response. He had a lead on me already, but I had two things working in my favor. First, he was on a Harley. I don't mean to offend any fellow motorcyclists out there who ride Hogs, but let's face it; for all their macho looks, loud pipes, and Bad Boy image, Harleys are pigs. They're heavy beasts. I've always ridden Japanese bikes, both on the Job and in my garage at home (though someday I hope to park a nice BMW bike in there), and the rice rockets will leave a Harley choking on their dust and exhaust fumes. Even a casual glance at the road test review section of *Cycle World* will tell you that a Corvette will smoke a Hog. Which brings me to my second advantage; I was driving Car 3, my favorite car, a Chevy Caprice with the LT-1 motor derived from the 'Vette's engine. It could really haul, and in no time I was right on the biker's tail. He saw me coming and braked into a hard left, nearly dumping his bike. He shot down a residential street and I came barreling down it after him like an angry black and white rhinoceros intent on pulverizing anything in front of it. The street ended in a T-intersection after a few blocks and he took another peg-scraping left turn. I was right on his tail, tires squealing in protest, making up some time in the corners before hammering the gas down the straightaways.

At each block the road dipped down slightly into a shallow drainage way, and every time his bike hit one sparks would fly up as it bottomed out. My car was bouncing into them every block, too. I glanced over at Jen; her face was white as a sheet and she was pressed back into her seat, and her hands gripped the dashboard and the chicken bar above her door with white knuckles. Another few seconds and *I had him! Gotcha!* I caught up to the biker and actually pulled alongside him, shouting at him over the PA to pull over. He was right next to the passenger door now and actually looking into the passenger side window, almost nose to nose to with Jen, who was now even whiter than before and shrinking back from the window and making whimpering noises. Harley Guy was looking at me instead of watching the road, which was a big mistake because he was heading right for the back end of a parked pickup truck. He didn't see it, but I did, and I actually thought for a split second about letting him pile up into it. But even though he was running from me I didn't want him to actually get injured, and then there was the consideration that at the Cherry Hills Police Department pursuits were strictly forbidden. It was such a strong policy that we couldn't even *say* pursuit. We called it "the P word", and the Chief was so anti-pursuit we couldn't even chase down speeders if they were going too fast. That made no sense to me and I argued loud and long to the Chief that it was unfair for us to stop and ticket the guy who was going 55 in a 40, but the guy going 85 in a 40 gets a free pass.

In any case, I had a flash vision of me standing in front of a crumpled up bike and rider, out of my jurisdiction, in an unauthorized pursuit, and calling for an ambulance and a supervisor and wondering how I was ever going to explain it all, since I had never even called it out to dispatch that I was even *in* a pursuit. With the end of my short career looming before me, I braked hard and Harley Guy, now seeing his danger with fear-widened eyes, managed at the last second to whip his bike around the truck and back in front of me. Now you would think that after that we would both be smart enough to stop this thing, wouldn't you?

We picked up the chase immediately, and as we were now out of Cherry Hills and into Denver I had no idea even where we were. The street was dark and narrow and suddenly I saw that it was rapidly coming to a dead end, with a stand of trees directly ahead. Now I knew where we were; on the other side of those trees was Colorado Boulevard, and just up ahead and to the right was a little grassy park. There was a footbridge from the street we were on that spanned a little creek and went into the park, and Harley Guy found it. He whipped his hog around to the right, went up and over the bridge, and the last I saw of him he was gunning his bike across the green grass, sending up a rooster tail of dirt and grass while looking back and giving me the finger. Oh well, it could have been worse, much worse, I told myself as I stood on the bridge and watched him go. *Lesson learned.* Jen was still sitting in the car, her face still white and her hands still gripping the dash. I think it took a while for her heart rate to come back down while we were slowly driving back to our own city, but when it did she suddenly turned to me with a huge radiant smile and said "That was *AWESOME!!*"

* * *

While the juveniles on our side of the law were a frequent source of amusement for us, the ones on the other side of the law could be, too. I was just walking out of a 7-11 with a cup of coffee in my hand when I spied a teenaged kid looking at me. He was dirty, disheveled, his clothes looked like he'd been sleeping in them, and I just *knew* he wanted to come talk to me. When you wear the badge and the uniform, it's like wearing a sign for every street person, every nutcase, everyone with a screw loose, that says "Come talk to me, please!", because they always make a beeline for us when they see us. As soon as the kid started walking toward me I inwardly groaned *At least let me finish my coffee!* but outwardly I said "What can I help you with?" and he hesitantly told me he had a warrant out for his arrest - petty theft - and he had been on the run for three days. He'd been sleeping in a field because he was afraid to go home, but he was tired, he was cold, he was hungry, and he just wanted to turn himself in.

I got his name and date of birth and cleared him over the radio, and sure enough he had an active warrant out of Westminster for theft. When you have a wanted juvenile you can't just take them to jail, because there is a whole array of laws designed to protect the tender, innocent teenagers from the hardened adult prisoners. Never mind that some of the teenagers are fairly hardened criminals themselves. When you take a juvenile into custody, you must maintain sight and sound separation at all times from any adult prisoners, as well as complying with a host of other federal, state, and local policies, regulations, and statutes. As a result, nobody wants to mess with juvies. They're just a pain in the ass, and cops avoid dealing with them like the plague. Obviously they cannot be housed in the regular city and county jails, so there are a few juvenile detention centers here and there like the Montview Youth Corrections Center or the Marvin W. Foote Center, which we all just called the Foote Locker.

With this kid, I called the Foote Locker to see if I could take him there. I told them what I had and the lady said "No, we don't want him. We're only taking felonies tonight." I hung up with her and called Montview, and they said "Nope, we're full up and we don't want him. Try somewhere else." I called Westminster PD and the duty officer said "A juvenile? *No way!* He's yours, pal!" I said "Hey, it's *your* warrant! If you won't take him when somebody catches him then why the hell did you put the warrant out in the first place?" He said that wasn't his problem, and he definitely was not taking responsibility for that kid. I hung up the phone and stared at the kid for a minute, trying to figure out what to do with him. I took him inside and bought him a sandwich and a drink, then drove him home. I told him "Go home kid. Go to sleep in a real bed tonight. Nobody wants you." He kept looking back at me as he walked up his driveway, like this was all a trick. I think he was actually a little disappointed that not even the police cared what he was doing.

The system, and society, just doesn't know what to do with teenaged criminals. Do you lock 'em up and throw the book at 'em? Some people say yes, but what if they can still be saved? Once you send a teenager to general population, he's lost. He'll be brutalized and traumatized by the other prisoners, be forced to join a gang for protection, and just learn how to become a better criminal. On the other hand, do you baby them and try to reason with them? We all know teenagers are creatures that are almost impossible to reason with, and they can spot weakness in an instant and shamelessly exploit it. I wish I had the answer. I have some ideas, but I don't have the answer.

I got an alert tone one morning and was dispatched to a call of a teenaged male running around the house with a butcher knife trying to stab his parents. John Bayman and I rolled Code 3 on the call, at one of the big mansions in the city. We jumped out of our cars and ran up to the house, and when I found the front door was locked I stepped back and did a perfect, made-for-the movies, flying leap to crash through the door. Except the door didn't even quiver. It was like solid granite, and I fell back holding my shoulder in pain. *This isn't the way it's supposed to work!* Bayman was watching me and said "Nice move, genius. Who do you think you are, Robocop?" I meekly followed him around back rubbing my shoulder, and we found some French doors that we easily pushed open and made our entry. Just as we stepped inside we saw a terrified woman run past us, followed a few seconds later by a teenaged kid with a knife over his head like Norman Bates in *Psycho*. We both leveled our guns at the kid and ordered him to drop the knife. When he saw us his eyes got as wide as dinner plates and he instantly dropped the knife. We took him down and cuffed him, none too gently, and got the situation stabilized.

With the juvenile Norman Bates now in custody, I called the Foote Center to tell them I would be bringing one down. As I was talking to the Intake person and telling them what I had, he interrupted me and asked "Did he *actually* stab anyone?" I said no, he had only tried, and the Intake person said "Well we can't take him unless he's actually committed a felony" to which I replied a little heatedly "He's running through the house trying to stab people like he's starring in *The Shining*. It's called *Attempted Murder*! Maybe you've heard of it?" but the Intake guy was unimpressed. He said "Well if it was only *attempted murder* we can't take him. Call us back if he succeeds." He added the helpful suggestion that maybe the kid could go stay with a relative or neighbor until he cools off. Our policy was that we could only hold juveniles in our own holding cells for a maximum of ninety minutes, and only then if there were no adults in our other holding cell. I called the Arapahoe County Jail hoping for a good solution, but the Intake deputy could only say that if the Foote Locker wouldn't take him, there was nothing they could do.

I went back to the family and explained the situation, and they were stunned. The mom looked at me and said "Well what good are you people?" I didn't have an answer for her. What good *were* we? As soon as we left he'd pick up the knife and resume his Freddy Krueger imitation and go chasing his family around again. In the end, I took the kid back to the station and stuck him in our holding cell while the family packed up and went to stay in a hotel for the night. Then I took the kid back home. On the way home he was being mouthy in the back seat, saying we couldn't do shit to him and everybody knew it. He gave me a smug smirk as I was dropping him off and that really pissed me off, partly because the kid was right, so I grabbed him by the shirt front and shoved him hard against the door, and told him the next time I got called up here I was just going to shoot him, and everybody would back me up on it. His smirk vanished instantly, and he scuttled inside the door. We never got called back up there.

* * *

Why do kids go bad? Is it nature or nurture? I have two kids, raised in the same household in the same way, and their personalities are as different as night and day, but thankfully neither one of them has ever been in any real trouble. Hilary Clinton says it takes a village to raise a child, but I say Mrs. Clinton has been smoking some Arkansas weed. To raise a child takes parents who are involved and paying attention; not the schools, not the government, not your neighbors in your "village" - just you, the parents. I got spanked a lot when I was a kid and it sure straightened me out, but it's in vogue nowadays to listen to the pop psychologists who say that spanking your children will turn them into the next Eric Harris or Dylan Klebold. *Bullshit.* I have a theory, born of long experience with hundreds of different sets of parents and kids, and that theory is that *all kids* that need it will get spanked; it's just a question of who does it. If the parents won't do it, the police will, or the other kids at school, or worse, the kid will smart off to somebody who is a really bad guy and may lose his life.

* * *

I did not go to the shooting at Columbine High School. I worked the graveyard shift the night before, and when I woke up I sat down on the couch and turned on the television to see that awful sight we've all seen, of the kids running out of the school guarded by police officers with rifles and shotguns. My friend Danny O'Shea was there. He was on Denver SWAT and exchanged shots with Eric Harris and Dylan Klebold while they were in the library.

There was a lot of bad press about the police response that day, but there were officers on scene whose own kids were in that school and any idea that the police were afraid to enter is pure bullshit. They responded the way they were trained to do, but what they were trained to do was all wrong for that situation. They had been trained to set up a perimeter and wait for SWAT, but ad hoc teams of officers were forming up and going in on their own. Since Columbine, the one that seemed to start the wave of school shootings that have swept the nation, all police departments now have Active Shooter protocols. Harris and Klebold planned to go back to the cafeteria and try again to blow the propane bombs which had failed to detonate, which would have been catastrophic, but instead killed themselves in the library. So maybe the police response and Danny's sustained fire did save some lives that day.

What is the answer to the seemingly random and inexplicable explosions of violence like Columbine or Parkland, and in workplaces and churches across the country? Some say it's violent video games, and others say there are too many guns out there. I think they're both getting it wrong. Prior to the Gun Control Act of 1934, you could order up from a catalog a Thompson submachine gun, just like Al Capone and John Dillinger carried, and the mailman would bring it to your door. When my dad was in high school in the 1950's, he was on the school rifle team and would bring his rifle on the school bus with him. All the kids would bring their guns to school and lean them in the corner of the classroom and go hunting after school for rabbits and squirrels for the dinner pot. The AR-15 rifle, the favorite target of every gun ban advocate, has been on gun store shelves for sale to the public since the 1960's, longer than I have been alive, and they were never used in a mass shooting until now. No, it is not the guns - something in the fabric of our society has changed.

For what my two cents is worth, it is the absence of fathers in the home that is driving the increase in mass shootings. A *majority* of male children born today grow up in a home without a father. One shooter's last social media post before he went on his killing spree was "I wish I had a Dad." I will also say that *everybody* that knew Harris and Klebold knew they were ticking time bombs, but nobody did anything. Their teachers, their fellow students, even the police. Nothing happens in a vacuum, and all the warning signs were there for more than a full year that they were going to do this. They bragged about what they were going to do to their fellow students at school, they put it out on a website, and supposedly they did a class project where they acted out exactly what they later did. The local Sheriff's Office was concerned enough that a full year before the shooting they swore out a search warrant for their homes, but it was never executed. This was right out in the open for everyone to see. We saw the same thing with the Parkland High School shooter, who posted on social media that he was going to be the next school shooter. Everybody saw it, and nobody did anything.

* * *

November 12, 1997 seemed like a typical Wednesday. I was working swing shift patrol over on the east side of town, in District 1. It had been a slow shift and I was making a leisurely cruise through one of the residential neighborhoods when the quiet calm of the afternoon was abruptly broken. Dispatch gave the high-pitched alert tone and aired that Jefferson County Sheriff's deputies were in pursuit of burglary suspects, and that Denver PD had taken up the chase to assist and the pursuit was now coming down Hampden Avenue. Hampden was the northern boundary of Cherry Hills, separating us from Denver, and the pursuit was heading directly toward us. I immediately whipped the patrol car around and started heading north while radioing in that I was moving to an intercept position, but someone from the brass came over the radio on our car to car channel, saying this was Denver's deal and we were not to get involved. Dispatch aired that the chase was coming closer and that shots were now being fired. Despite the order from the office to stand down I went up to the parking lot of the Bethany Church, which sits on a little hill overlooking Hampden Avenue. I radioed in my position but again was told not to get involved.

We were all keeping track of the chase on the radio, as it entered one of the neighborhoods just on the other side of our eastern boundary with Denver. A short time later dispatch aired that an officer was down. We all clustered around our radios, silently waiting for news. We later learned the terrible news that Officer Bruce Vanderjagt had been killed, shot to death by a skinhead named Mattheus Jaehnig. We were stunned. I felt a sense of helpless rage and guilt, both at the brass in the office for ordering us not to get involved, and at myself for not disobeying the order. I had a rifle in the roof rack of my patrol car, and sitting on the hill at the Bethany Church looking down on Hampden Avenue I would have had a perfect shot at the suspect vehicle. I could have emptied an entire magazine into the car as they approached my position, and had I known then what was going to happen no commands from anyone could have stopped me from doing it. I know that I was only following orders, and no one could have foreseen what would ultimately happen, but that was little consolation to me in the days that followed, as I learned more about the shooting and about the man. Officer Bruce Vanderjagt was a true hero, a decorated officer who had risked his own life to run into a burning building to rescue the people trapped inside, and before that was a decorated Marine in Vietnam. He left behind a wife and a young daughter. In law enforcement it is rarely the things you did that haunt you - it's the things you didn't do that keep you awake at night.

In the days that followed we learned more about the shooting and the events that led up to it. A woman named Lisl Auman broke up with her live-in boyfriend and recruited some punk friends to break into the apartment and take back some of her belongings. One of them was Mattheus Jaehning, a many-time loser and a white supremacist skinhead. Someone spotted them breaking into the apartment and called the Jefferson County Sheriff's Department, and when deputies arrived Auman and her friends raced away from them and the deputies pursued. Jaehnig was driving and reached speeds of well over 100 miles per hour, as the chase ultimately covered some thirty miles. At one point Auman held the wheel so Jaehnig could lean out the window and fire his SKS semi-automatic rifle at deputies. Denver officers picked up the chase, which came through Cherry Hills and ended in an apartment complex nearby. Jaehnig sought cover between two of the buildings, and lay in wait to ambush the officers. When Bruce Vanderjagt peered around the corner Jaehnig opened fire. Vanderjagt's body armor was of no use against the high-powered rifle, and he was killed instantly. His fellow officers were unaware that he had been killed and, believing him to be wounded, tried to organize a rescue but heavy fire from Jaehnig's assault rifle drove them back. As more and more officers arrived, Jaehnig knew he could not escape, and crawled forward to Vanderjagt's body. He retrieved the officer's gun, put it to his chin, and pulled the trigger, taking his own miserable, worthless life.

In the weeks that followed the metro area was gripped by a series of incidents that appeared to be heading toward a war between the police and the skinheads. White supremacist groups vowed revenge on the police, and a dead pig with Vanderjagt's name carved into it was thrown onto the lawn of the District 3 station. A West African immigrant named Oumar Dia was ruthlessly gunned down and murdered for no reason whatsoever while innocently standing at a bus stop by a skinhead named Nathan Thill. A Denver officer responding to a prowler call received a fusillade of bullets in an ambush. The officer survived, but the whole city was holding its collective breath, waiting for the storm to burst. The city was on the verge of a full-blown war.

The trunks of patrol cars were dragging with the extra weight of unauthorized weapons, ammunition, and extra body armor. The command staff turned a blind eye to the extra gear, because they knew the officers were badly outgunned with their department-issued weapons. At that time, almost no police departments issued rifles, and many officers had only their .38 revolvers to go up against heavily armed white supremacist gangs with assault rifles. Officers were bringing their own scoped high-powered rifles and AR-15's to work. We at Cherry Hills had MP-5 carbines which were effective out to 100 yards, but those of us who had it were bringing in more firepower. I brought in my own heavy-barreled AR-15 target rifle which would be deadly out to 600 yards; Jason McGurren brought in an FN .308 battle rifle, and John Reynolds brought in his own AR and scoped high-powered hunting rifle. One of the Cherry Hills citizens even offered us a massive Barrett .50 caliber sniper rifle.

Many of the skinheads lived in Englewood, and the Englewood police had frequent contacts and the best intelligence on their activities. They were a good bunch of officers, and they were loaded for war as well. All of the cops wanted blood after the murder of Bruce Vanderjagt, we *wanted* the fight, but to the credit of police officers in the metro area I am aware of no incident where police officers provoked a fight with the white supremacists. Tensions rose to the breaking point, and it would have taken only a single spark, a single incident, to make the city explode. A few days passed without incident, and people began to breathe easier. I believe the skinheads, like all punks and bullies who strut around and act tough, realized that for all their tough talk they didn't really want a shooting war with the police. As the days passed, tensions drained away and things gradually went back to normal, or as normal as they could ever be.

I did not go to Bruce Vanderjagt's funeral, because I couldn't bear to see his wife and daughter. Could I have prevented what happened? Maybe. Maybe not. Other officers would testify in the trial of Lisl Auman that followed that they also had an opportunity to shoot Jaehnig beforehand but did not. I wonder if they are second-guessing themselves, too. To this day, I have no answer for that question.

PART TWO

EIGHT

*"When choosing between two evils, I always
like to try the one I've never tried before."*
- Mae West

ONE OF THE TROUBLES with small police departments
is that if you get there at a time when all the guys above you are
fairly young you can suffer through years of stagnation, of going
absolutely nowhere on your career path. Cherry Hills had about
two dozen sworn officers when I arrived, but I came aboard at
a good time. There were several officers above me who had a
lot of years on the job; several senior patrolmen, and a couple
of sergeants who had 25 plus years on the force. One old-timer
sergeant, Mike Wagner, had come on the Job in the late Sixties.
When Wags retired they threw him a grand party at the Glenmoor
Country Club, and the next week the Chief put out a memo for
the sergeant opening created by his retirement.

None of the senior officers wanted it because it meant
going back to working graveyard shifts. The next sergeant due
to retire was Tim Barrett but he had the combination of several
more years left in him plus a cushy desk job, so he wasn't
going anywhere. Whoever took that next sergeant slot would be
working deep nights for a *looong* time, likely for several years.
The older guys were too set in their routines, had their family
time, or their visitation with their kids, their poker nights, all

set up around their work schedules and didn't want to upset everything just for a set of stripes.

The younger officers like me, Beth, and John Reynolds talked amongst ourselves about putting in for it, but frankly we just didn't feel ready to actually be *in charge* of our own patrol team. On the day the notice was put out at roll call all of us migrated to our usual rendezvous spot in the Public Works garage to talk about it. "Can you imagine telling Weathers or Defelice what to do?" JR said. "They would just tell you to go to hell and then go do what they wanted anyway" I agreed. Beth said she didn't want the stripes, either. Another factor of weighty consequence was that if you were a sergeant you would be spending a *whole* lot more time face to face with the Chief and the Captain, and none of us wanted that. So the upshot was that in the end no one put in for the sergeant position.

The Chief was furious, and he took our lack of response as a personal insult. He bawled us out at roll calls for being lazy, for having no ambition or drive to be the next generation of leaders in the Department. He was sort of right on all counts, but sort of wrong, too. The word started going around that he was buttonholing individual officers and grilling them about why they weren't putting in for sergeant, so we all started bolting out the door and onto the street right after roll call, to avoid getting hooked and fried by him.

In the end all his efforts and haranguing were to no avail, because the closing date for applications passed and the letter box he had placed on his office door to accept them stood forlorn and empty, save for some dust and cobwebs, and a gum wrapper someone had deposited in it. We were forced to go outside the department for a new sergeant, and we came up with a guy named Bobby Forrest. Bobby was a New Yorker, and he had grown up next to Yankee Stadium and worked for NYPD in the Bronx before moving out west. He was real skinny, he looked like his uniform was draped over one of those skeletons from high school biology class, and he still had his New York accent. He turned out to be a pretty good guy, and he could sure tell some funny stories.

Then something *really* unexpected happened. Out of the blue Tim Barrett put in his papers to retire. The rumor mill started buzzing, with some people saying "I hear Barrett got sideways with the Chief" and another guy would say "No, no, he got a sweet corporate security gig downtown." Who knew what the real story was? He was keeping his mouth shut, and all we knew was that he was retiring years before anyone expected him to. Now we suddenly had another opening for sergeant, and this time I really thought seriously about it. For one thing, if none of us put in for it this time the Chief would probably come unglued and go into orbit, and for another I was getting a little bored with my patrol duties.

Even though I only had about three years on the Job at this point, the daily routine of writing a few traffic tickets and responding to alarm calls was getting a little monotonous. Occasionally we would get a hot call, a real TV cop show kind of call, but in our sleepy little burg they didn't come often enough, and I was starting to look around for something more to do.

For the small size of the Department we actually had quite a variety of specialized units; there was the K-9 Unit (we had more police dogs than police detectives), the Motorcycle Unit, the Detective Bureau, the Firearms Training Unit, the Technical Accident Investigators, and the DARE Program. Given my background of a being a military veteran and a gun-toting redneck, I eagerly joined the Firearms Training Unit. We didn't have a SWAT team so the FTU took on the duties of training the officers in tactics as well as marksmanship, and I enjoyed that immensely.

I also thought if I didn't put in for sergeant now, it could be ten years before another opening came around. So I put in for it. To my surprise so did Beth, and Eric McCarty, so we must have all been thinking the same thing. I asked JR if he was going to put in for it, and he said "Me in charge of the city? Are you kidding? BOOM!" John was one of those all-round great guys that everybody liked, and in time he would make sergeant, and he was a damn good one.

Chief Langford was very happy with the response this time around, and he was all smiles when he briefed us on what the test was going to be like. It wasn't a test like we all took in high school where you read the questions and fill in the bubble sheets for your answers, which is kind of what I was expecting. It was actually a Selection Board, an all day series of tests and exercises, before a panel of three command officers from other departments. We had a lieutenant from Englewood, another lieutenant from Arapahoe County, a sergeant from Greenwood Village, and a woman in civilian clothes and I don't know who or what she was. The first thing we had to do was a written test, followed by an oral board where I had to stand in front of the panel and they would rapid-fire questions at me; *What would you do if...?* Then we had a role-playing exercise where we had to deal with a sexual harassment situation because apparently that's the most important skill of a police leader nowadays, and finally a report writing exercise, and the testing was over. I would rather have taken a test involving running the hundred, climbing a rope, and shooting at moving targets.

When all the testing was over and done with, we had to wait a few days while the Board officers and the mystery woman tallied up their scores, compared notes, and prepared a final report to send to Chief Langford. Langford told us that whoever had the highest score would get the job.

I was sitting at home watching TV a few nights later when I got an unexpected phone call from Chief Langford. He said "Hello? Is this Sergeant Mike Miller?" I replied "I don't know... is it?" and he said "Yes it is." He told me I got the highest score, edging out Beth by one half of one percent. Look out world! For better or worse, I was a sergeant now.

* * *

There were six of us sergeants, five on patrol and one Detective Sergeant, who was also in charge of running the evidence locker as well as scheduling all training for the officers, so he rarely got do any actual detective work. As the newest sergeant I was assigned to the graveyard shift, but as a patrolman I almost always volunteered for this shift anyway. I had enough seniority that I could have bid Watch Two, the two to midnight shift, but even though I liked the hours better it just didn't work out well with my family. I'd come tiptoeing in at one in the morning trying not to wake anyone, banging my shins on unseen objects in the dark and stepping on toys (why are kid toys all full of points and sharp edges?), cursing under my breath before sliding in under the covers. By the time I woke up at about nine the next morning my wife and kids were already gone, and since I left for work at about one in the afternoon, I was also already gone before they got home. When I worked the swing shift I would literally go three days straight every week without seeing anyone in my family. Talk about ships passing in the night. That kind of separation grows into a gulf after a while and that is not good for a marriage, so even though night shift was hard on my body it was easier on my wife and kids so I bid it every four-month rotation until I just needed it a break from it.

My first patrol team was Beth and JR. I was ecstatic because I couldn't have hand-picked a better team. They were both very good cops, hard workers, and good friends of mine. I met with them after roll call on that very first night, with my shiny blue stripes newly-sewn on my sleeves, and over coffee I told them as far as I was concerned we were the same team we had always been. Some guys changed when they got promoted, suddenly felt they were Very Important People, and forgot where they came from. I was determined that was not going to happen to me. Being a sergeant puts you in a tough spot. The people on your team are your friends, and some of them like JR had more time on the Job than I did. Now you're suddenly their boss, telling them what to do and when to do it. The worst part is when you have to discipline someone who's been your friend for years. My feelings about being a sergeant were heavily shaped by my time in the military, and the way I saw it the sergeant is the leader of the team, and leaders lead from the front. If there's a door that has to be gone through, you're the first one through it. If a big mean tattooed biker has to be taken down, you get the first crack at him. If a supermodel has to be frisked and handcuffed, well that's your duty, too.

* * *

The Denver Broncos won the big one, the Super Bowl, in 1998 with a 31-24 upset victory over Brett Favre and the Packers. It was the first championship in the team's history and things went a little crazy in downtown Denver. The celebration got out of control and some of the fans started ripping open the newspaper stands and starting fires with the papers and tipping over cars. Then some fights broke out and the next thing you know the Denver Police were out tear-gassing everyone. After that it was decided by the powers that be in Cherry Hills that our officers should go through some civil disobedience training, just in case our twenty officers ever had to go rescue the fifteen hundred officers of DPD, or our good citizens started rioting because the espresso machine broke down at the country club. Because I had been in the military and gone through riot control training there, I was tasked with setting up and running the training program. I asked for some 40mm rotary gas grenade launchers and the request was denied. Then how about some automatic Pepperball guns? Denied. Concussion grenades? Denied. Rubber bullets? Denied. Gas masks? Denied. No, wait. Can you get them cheap? Yes. Okay, get some gas masks.

I went out scrounging in the bins at military surplus stores and found enough gas masks and canisters for the twelve officers and five sergeants on patrol, all the while thinking I bet the Feds don't have to go thrift shopping for gear in Army surplus stores run by crazy-eyed veterans who spent too much time in the jungle, and who would whisper conspiratorially in your ear that you gotta be *careful*, you know, because *they* are everywhere and they're *watching you!* I figured the brass wouldn't come out of the office for a riot anyway, so I didn't bother getting masks for them. Once I had all the gear loaded into my truck I went back to the station and laid everything out on tables, fitting the masks into their cases and making sure each case had the screw-in canisters to filter the gas. I've been both tear-gassed and pepper-sprayed and neither one of them is any fun at all so I knew those canisters were pretty important.

I planned to do training at each roll call until I had everyone covered, and pass out the masks once the officers had demonstrated they knew how to use them. At swing shift roll call the following day I set out all the gear on a table in the front of the squad room, and after the shift briefing by the sergeant I started in with the lesson. I passed out all the masks and canisters, and while the officers played with them like new toys I told them what the mask would protect them against and what it wouldn't, how to screw in the filter canisters, how you arranged the straps to carry the mask in its case for quick deployment, and then told everyone to pick up their masks and practice the proper method of donning them. In the military you don't say "put the mask on" or "take the mask off"; it's called "donning the mask" and "doffing the mask". I don't know why they call it that, I just work here. Getting a good seal with the mask was critical, because it becomes very hard to focus on the Bad Guys when your face is full of tears and snot and you're doubling over and coughing up a lung. I demonstrated the proper method and told everyone to do the same.

There was one guy in the back, a brand new officer that I had never seen before, who wasn't putting his mask on, just sort of holding it up to his face. This guy was a little on the short side, maybe five six or five seven, with a head of perfect, slicked back brown hair that reminded me of Arthur Fonzarelli, the Fonz, from the old TV show *Happy Days*. He didn't want to put the mask on because it would mess up his hair. I turned to Eric Nielsen who was sitting next to me and said "Who's the prima donna back there?" Eric said "He's a new guy, his name is Matt. Oh, and by the way, he's yours." *"What!?"* I protested. Eric laughed and said he was coming to my team. *Great* - just what I need, some short primping metrosexual.

When Matt did come to my team, however, I soon discovered he was turning out to be a very good cop. For one thing, he had a silver tongue, a gift for talking to people. He could get people to tell him anything. We would go to a domestic or a family disturbance where nobody wanted to see us and nobody would talk to us, and Matt would pull one of them aside into the kitchen or sit down with them on the living room sofa and within five minutes they would be telling him their life story. I never had the knack for that. My approach was always more the bull in the china shop, so having him there brought a new set of skills to the team. I found out he had been a dispatcher before he put on a badge, so none of this was new to him and maybe that helped him with talking to people, getting them to calm down and focus, because when you're a dispatcher your voice is the only tool you've got. I came to believe that he could talk a nun into giving him her panties. I also found out however, that he had a mischievous streak and wasn't above playing practical jokes on his teammates, or his sergeant.

He arrested a girl one night for DUI, and she was hammered, wasted, stumbling around the booking room barely able to stand. The whole time he was trying to process her she kept slurring "Please Officer, I'll do *anything* you want, just don't arrest me!" Matt calmly reminded her that she had already been under arrest for the last half hour, but she was undeterred in her efforts and she unbuttoned her blouse and took it off, revealing rather impressive breasts under a black lacy bra. When that wasn't enough, she took off the bra too and was following him around the booking room half naked with swaying bare breasts and promising Matt all kinds of special favors if only he would not arrest her. Matt called in another officer to be a witness, and they convinced the girl to put her clothes back on. *Look sweetheart, it's not that we don't like your equipment, but we just can't take it for a test drive, you know what I mean? So put your shirt back on...there you go. Good girl.*

After the Detox van hauled her away Matt checked the holding cell per the Policy Manual, and found she had left the lacy black bra behind. *A ha!* He took the bra and tied it to the roof rack of my truck, and I was too dog tired to notice it there when I went home, so here I was driving down I-25 with a sexy 36C black bra flying behind me like a pirate flag on a ship. *Heave to, scallawag! Or walk the plank and wear the bra!* I got home and crawled into bed, but it seemed my head had just the hit the pillow when I was rudely shaken awake. I regained consciousness to find a very angry Kari holding a black lacy bra in her hand and demanding to know where it came from. In my befuddled state I said *"Hey, you gonna wear that?"* She replied icily "It's not my size." I literally had no idea where it came from, and I had a devil of a time convincing her of that. The more I puzzled about it, the more I began to suspect one of my fellow officers was somehow behind this, and I finally tracked it back to Matt. He just laughed uproariously, and when I told him how much trouble I had gotten into that only made him laugh more.

On the other hand, I began to increasingly find myself standing at attention before the Captain's desk answering for things Matt had done. The first time was when he was driving too fast around a curve on a rain-slick road surface, and he lost it and put the front end of the car into a dirt embankment, bending the push bar. Then he backed into a fire hydrant in the police lot, crunching in the bumper of a different car. Then one morning I came in to work an off-duty job, and when the Captain came into the squad room I said "Good morning Captain! How are you?" I was in a good mood but one look at his face changed that. He glared at me with storm clouds brewing in his eyes, and said "How am I? How *am* I!? I have one officer on this department who is single-handedly destroying the fleet!" I winced and said hesitantly "Matt..?" Captain Bates exploded "Yes Matt!! Who the hell else would it be!? I want to see you in my office right now, Sergeant!" *Thanks, buddy* I thought to myself as I glumly walked down the hall to the Captain's office. A line from a movie with Chris Tucker came into my head; *You got to be a stupid motherfucker to get fired on your day off!* his voice said to me as I walked down the hall. I closed the door and stood at attention while the Captain chewed me out. Apparently, Matt was driving down University Boulevard last night and the steering on the car felt all mushy, so he got out and looked and discovered he had a flat tire. He looked to the south where the lights of the police station beckoned, only half a mile away. The Policy & Procedures Manual said when you got a flat tire you were supposed to stop and call Hinson's, our towing contractor, to send out a truck to change the flat. That could take an hour, so Matt had a quick debate with himself and thought *"What the hell? I can see the station from here!"* so he got back in the car and drove it in. Well, as it turned out that half a mile was just enough to chew through the rubber and bend the rim of the wheel, to the tune of six hundred bucks to replace it.

You have to understand Charlie Bates. He thought of the cars like they were his own, and he always wanted them clean and sparkling and preferably undamaged. You put even a scratch in it and you had to answer for it. Now along comes Matt putting three different cars in the garage in short order for various dings, dents, and bends. The Captain told me he was suspending Matt without pay for a couple of days, and I argued with him that this was police work, we weren't running a flower shop here, and that police equipment was used hard and a few dings and dents were inevitable, a part of the business. He didn't buy it, and Matt got his suspension. Alas, it would not be his last. They say you only get one chance to make a first impression, and he wasn't doing so hot with the Captain. The Captain got the impression that Matt was reckless and had a cavalier attitude toward police work, and it shaped their stormy relationship from then on. Between me, Matt, and Beth he thought of our team as a band of misfits. But we got the job done, put a lot of bad guys in jail, and had fun doing it.

* * *

There was a teenaged girl who lived up in the northeast part of the city who was physically and developmentally disabled, and she got around strapped into a motorized wheelchair, the poor kid. We were on swing shift now, and one afternoon we got a call that this girl had somehow fallen and injured herself. The ambulance was responding, but I was the first car on scene. I rushed into the house and found her tipped over sideways, still strapped into the chair. She had blood on her face, and her live-in nurse was an older woman who was unable to lift the heavy chair. I was trying to help this girl but they had this little black dog, Molly, one of those hairy little blow-dried-rat dogs, that kept barking at me and biting my leg or my backside every time I turned around. I finally had enough of this little pest and

I whirled around and grabbed it by the back of the neck. I lifted it up and was carrying it to a back bedroom when the little rat somehow twisted around and sank her teeth into my hand. It actually drew blood, and the dog was grunting and twisting as it bit into me, trying to get a better hold. She got me pretty good, and as I opened the bedroom door I'm afraid I wasn't too nice as I flung my arm out sending that little dog flying across the room onto the bed, with a little chunk of my skin still in its jaws. When the ambulance arrived we got the girl back upright and found that her injuries were minor, only a bloody nose when she hit the floor. The ambulance crew checked my bleeding hands and gave me an antibiotic and a dressing. The official "Report of Injury" read:

> Dog Bites: One inch tear on right thumb. Half inch tear on left index finger. Half inch tear on right wrist. Numerous scratches on right forearm.

The next day I found a fake Purple Heart in my mailbox with teeth marks cut into the corner. In all my years of law enforcement the worst I ever got beat up in a fight came from an eight pound dog.

A few months later, we got a terrified 9-1-1 call from the same address. The girl had motored into the back yard and somehow fallen into the swimming pool while still strapped into the chair, and the frantic nurse couldn't get her out and she was drowning. The first officer on scene ran to the back yard and saw the girl lying motionless at the bottom of the pool, still in the chair. He started stripping off his gun belt to shed the weight, when Matt came running up behind him and plunged headfirst into the pool, gun belt, body armor vest, boots and all. He dove to the bottom, freed the girl from the chair, and brought her sputtering back up to the surface. Turns out he had been a lifeguard and could swim like a fish. He said he only did it as a summer job at a water park to meet girls. Now that I could believe. He got a Lifesaving medal for it, and I know it really pained Bates to have to read the glowing citation and pin that medal on him.

Matt and I were the only officers on duty when we got a call around midnight of a woman who had overdosed on cocaine and was unconscious. We rolled on the call, and I recognized the address as Hancock's, the psychotic and paranoid bodybuilder where the year before I had tossed Beth over his fence when he was holding his girlfriend hostage. We were extra cautious approaching the house, because you just never knew what was going to happen with this guy, or what planet he was on today. He could be fairly rational and normal on one call and on the next he would be running through the yard stark naked screaming that the aliens were after him.

When we got to the house the door opened and Hancock met us on the porch. He was only a little drunk, thank God. He led us back through the house, telling us on the way that he and his girlfriend had been drinking for a while, then she started doing lines of coke. We found his girlfriend lying on the living room floor. This was a different girlfriend than the hostage of the year before. She was not an unattractive girl, brunette, and barely conscious. I called for an ambulance while Matt checked her vitals. He lifted her shoulders off the floor and her head rolled back lifelessly. I turned and started to say something to Hancock when I was interrupted by a loud sharp crack as Matt slapped the girl across the face. I jumped involuntarily, and so did Hancock. He had tagged her pretty hard, and he started shaking her and yelling *"Come On! Stay with me!"* and let her have it again. She stirred and started to come around, her eyes blinking but then she started to fall back and Matt slapped her hard again.

Hancock was starting to get one of those perplexed *"What the hell is he doing?"* looks on his face, so I decided maybe it was time to get him out of there. I led him into the kitchen, taking care to be out of sight of where my partner was smacking his girlfriend around. I was gathering information from him but I could still hear in the background the occasional pistol-shot slaps and Matt yelling at her. I was just trying to keep Hancock in the kitchen, because he was already as jumpy as a nervous cat on his good days, and I didn't want him to get mad and have us end up in a fight with him. Luckily the ambulance soon came rolling up and they loaded her on the bus and whisked her off Code 3 to Swedish Hospital, where she would make a full recovery.

As we were walking out I said to Matt "If she has bruises on her face we'll just say Hancock did it." I was kidding, of course, but Matt told me he was also an EMT and he knew that she was checking out right there on the living room floor, so he had to do something fast to bring her back. He tried a sternum rub and she wasn't responding, so giving her a good smack was all that he could think of at the time. I said "Yeah, but couldn't you be a little quieter about it?"

* * *

When my team rotated to the day shift I discovered the down side of what it meant to be a sergeant. My shift started at six thirty in the morning with roll call, to hear the pass-on of what had happened over the night shift. Then I would sit down at the one desk shared by all five sergeants and review all the paperwork and reports from the off-going shift. I felt like a teacher, checking for grammar, spelling and what not, with my red pen in hand. I hated doing the paperwork and would much rather have been out on the road, but the administrative tasks were a big part of the duties of a sergeant, so I settled in each morning and got it done. One morning I caught a glimpse of myself in the locker room mirror, with a cup of coffee in one hand and a stack of papers in the other and thought *Oh God, what am I turning into?*

One of the most important and difficult jobs of a sergeant is to make the tough decisions. Unlike soldiers in a military unit, the individual police officer out on patrol operates independently, evaluating a situation, making decisions, and taking action all on their own. They only come to the sergeant when the situation gets sticky, tricky, or looks like it could go *really bad* and they want the sergeant to make the call and take the fall. One night soon after I made sergeant, I found myself in just such a situation. An officer named Nate was dispatched to an alarm down on Clarkson Street, on our western border with Englewood. The alarm company placed a call inside, following standard procedure, and to the alarm tech's surprise a male answered the phone. He did not give the password and hung up, and then there was no answer to the call placed into the residence by our dispatcher. John Reynolds and I moved in to cover Nate.

I recognized this house as belonging to a resident who was one of those anti-police / anti-government types and with whom we had trouble before. As we met for a quick huddle in the darkness around the house we could see the shadow of a lone figure moving in the semi-lighted house. We didn't know if it was a burglar or the homeowner. We held a quick team debate about how to handle it. JR said "Look Mike, what if that guy in there really is a burglar? We know he's in there, he's not giving the password, and what if he's holding the family hostage? I say we go in." Nate said "No, the guy just hates cops and that's why he's not answering. I say we don't go in." While we were debating, some Englewood cops showed up, and when we explained the situation to them they got excited and called two more guys who were on the EPD SWAT Team. They agreed with JR and wanted to go in, too. But it was my call. I had the Englewood guys take up perimeter positions while me and JR went stealthy, sneaking and peeking around the house with guns at the ready, checking as much as we could.

We found no signs of forced entry, heard nothing, and saw nothing that set any of our cop senses tingling. We went back to the ad hoc command post under a big oak tree, and found that *two more* Englewood SWAT guys had showed up, plus Kelly Martin, the Team sergeant. Kelly was forming up his team to go in, until I reminded him that we were in *my* city, not theirs, and it was my call. If we went in and there was no burglar, and we got into a shooting with the homeowner and ventilated him, that would be a little difficult to explain. On the other hand, if we drove away and left the family hog-tied in the living room with a kidnapper, that might also be a little difficult to explain. Damned if you do, damned if you don't. All of the officers were looking at me; *Whaddaya wanna do, Sarge?* I pondered for a moment, then made my call. My report that I typed up later that night ended with this; *"The Englewood SWAT officers offered to fire tear gas grenades into the house and force entry. I declined their offer. Upon consideration of the totality of the circumstances I declined to force entry and we broke down the perimeter and departed the scene."* Sometimes you just gotta let it go.

* * *

When I started at Cherry Hills we had just twenty four sworn officers, and we would go for years with no turnover at all, the same old faces in the squad room year after year, and then we would have a sudden rush of old cops retiring and young cops getting bored with sedate Cherry Hills and moving on to bigger and more exciting departments. When those events coincided we might turn over twenty to twenty five percent of the Department in a single year. One of my jobs as a sergeant was to sit on hiring boards to select new police officers. I was happy to do it, because in any organization good people are everything. A dependable, happy coworker is worth their weight in gold, and a bad one can cause no end of headaches and problems and spread conflict and discontent throughout the ranks.

Despite the fact that they hired me, I felt like the current administration had done a hit and miss job with picking people to become Cherry Hills cops. We had some great ones and we had some losers, so I figured that sitting on the hiring boards would at least give me some influence in picking the people I had to work with and supervise, and in shaping the future of the Department. When I sit across from an applicant listening to him or her telling us about themselves and how much they want to be a police officer and help people, the thing I'm thinking about the most is "Would this person be good to work with?" That's what matters the most to all of us in coworkers, when you get right down to it. We've all worked with people who were good at their jobs but whom we also really wanted to strangle and bury the body, and we've also all worked with people who were average workers but were very likable and easy to get along with. Which one would you rather spend eight hours a day with?

We often had as many as fifty applicants for each officer slot we had open, so we had a lot of preliminary work to do before we even got to the interview stage. We would start by gathering four of five of us at tables set up in the municipal courtroom and each of us would get a stack of applications to pore through, separating them into three piles; Looks Good, Maybe, and Hell No. We had no set criteria to evaluate them other than our own judgment and experience. Sure we looked at education, law enforcement experience, the other jobs they've had, and stuff like that but on that first go-around through the files what we were really looking for was red flags, if there was something about an applicant that jumped off the page at us, things that just didn't feel right. Like one guy whose work experience consisted of several jobs as a male nanny, each one not lasting more than a few months. To me, that was creepy. First of all, that any guy would want to be a "nanny" at all and second, why did he keep moving on? What kept happening? I showed some of the other guys and their first thought echoed mine; *Pedophile*. Maybe he was, maybe he wasn't, but with fifty other people to look at why take needless risks? He went into the Reject pile.

And so it would go, as we went into the second round, talking back and forth to each other about this or that applicant, trying to get a feel through the papers in my hands for who this person was. The problem is that people lie. The person you're picturing in your head is often not what walks through the door when you call them in for an interview. For instance, one girl looked really great on paper so we set her up for an interview. Right off the bat we started getting some weird vibes from her. She was very intense, and would lean across the table and stare deeply at each one of us in turn while she answered our questions. It was kind of freaking us out, and after she claimed she was a "dog whisperer" and could hear animals' thoughts we said *"Okay!* Thank you very much! Don't call us we'll call you. Right through that door there, that's it. *Goodbye!"* As she was being herded out the door she turned back and said "You'll call, right?" Yeah, sure, we'll see, no, probably not. Law enforcement is a field that attracts every nut job, wacko, sexual deviant, Rambo wannabe, and closet psychopath society has to offer. It's the intoxicating combination of guns, handcuffs, authority, and power. That's why screening is *so* important in police departments, to catch the crazy people before they slip through the process and end up wearing a gun and a badge.

When we would interview a likely looking candidate we would run them through the standard set of questions like "Why do you want to be a police officer?" or "Tell us your strengths and weaknesses", or "How will you contribute to fostering trust and interaction between police and the community?" and fluff like that. I didn't think questions like that, coming straight out of hiring manuals prepared by the International Association of Chiefs of Police or other police management organizations staffed by people with law degrees and who hadn't actually seen the inside of a patrol car in decades, were any good at finding out who these people were, deep down. The standard questions got the standard answers, which could be prepared and rehearsed ahead of time. We wanted to catch people off guard, to see the gears turn in their heads, so we decided to just junk all the standard questions and started coming up with our own. We asked them things like "What have you done that you are the most proud of?" If someone says "Being a good provider for my family" or "serving my country in Iraq", then heads would nod around the table. If someone says "*I chugged twelve beers at a frat party, dude*" or "*I got first place in a wet t-shirt contest!*" then that might raise some appreciative eyebrows but it wasn't exactly what we were looking for.

After the array of questions, we would run through some hypothetical scenarios and ask them what they would do. They weren't cops and we didn't expect them to know police procedures, but it did give us some insight as to how they were thinking. After all the questions were asked and all the scenarios run through, we had *one last thing* we liked to do. A guy named Paul was our detective who did the background checks on the applicants, and he had to have been the biggest detective in the state of Colorado. He was six foot seven and tipped the scales at 280 pounds. He was built like a grizzly bear, but he was actually quite soft-spoken and professional, a true gentle giant. We called him Father Paul, because whether it was his size or his mannerisms I don't know, but people would just confess everything to him. So the last thing we would do with a new applicant was that Paul would come and sit next to him or her and lean forward looming over them and say that the background check and the polygraph were bound to turn up anything they were being untruthful about, and if so they were they were finished in the process and would never get a job in law enforcement. *So, is there anything that you want to tell us right now?* It was a wonderful tactic, because we would hear some amazing things. One guy looked great on paper, gave a fantastic interview. He was sincere when he was supposed to be, funny and congenial at other times, and gave all the right answers. We were looking around the table at each other and thinking *"Sign him up!"* Then Father Paul came in and sat next to him and gave his speech, and the guy said "No! Nothing at all. I've told you everything!" We nodded our heads and started to rise from our chairs when he said "Well…there is this *one thing*, but it's no big deal." He gave a self-deprecating grin and said "When I let my dog outside in the morning I like to masturbate while I watch her take a shit."

The weirdness didn't stop there, though. That was just the tip of the iceberg with the parade of applicants we got. We were running another seemingly good candidate through the scenario questions when in the very first one he made an offhand remark about stealing panties. We wrinkled our foreheads and exchanged quizzical looks. When he managed to work in stealing panties into all of the next three scenarios, about burglary, drunk driving, and domestic violence, we said *"Okay!* I think we're done here! Thank you for coming, and just go out through that door behind you." He turned as he was leaving and said "You'll call me, right?" Yeah, sure we will pal. Just wait right there by the phone. I'll bet he was wearing stolen panties *while* we were interviewing him.

Sometimes we got to the end of the pile and pulled out a winner, but even that could be a problem. We hired one great officer, a cute little Italian girl who spoke three languages fluently, was a hard worker, had a great sense of humor, was liked by everyone and as far as we could tell had no sexual deviancies. So she quit and went to another department. We hired another guy who was such a promising young man that the Chief said "I don't want to hire him, I want to adopt him!" So he quit and went to another department. I told the Chief we needed a new strategy. We stopped hiring the young superstars, the hotshots. We started hiring the first runner-up instead of Miss America, David Schwimmer instead of Patrick Dempsey, Ellen DeGeneres instead of Jennifer Aniston. And it worked for us.

The scariest candidate we ever had, for me at least, was a young female who was already a cop in another department and wanted to make the jump to Cherry Hills. She set up a ride-along and I got the slip in my mailbox that morning to take her out and show her around. Every cop groans when they get a rider, because you've got your car set up just the way you want it, with your gear bag here, your clipboard there, your nightstick and flashlight over there, and a rider just screws it all up. And then they ask all the usual questions; "Did you ever kill anyone? How many dead bodies have you seen? I have this friend who got a DUI…" and so on. But I figured this girl was already a cop so it was okay with me, and it might even be fun. We never rode with a car partner because we didn't have the manpower, but in all the cop shows everybody had a partner. Starsky had Hutch, Riggs had Murtaugh, Crockett had Tubbs, and so on, so I was actually looking forward to what I saw not so much as having a rider but having a car partner for the night.

When she showed up, she was hot. She had long blonde hair put up in a ponytail, a pretty face and a nice trim figure, and she was in uniform. We exchanged introductions then got in the car and headed out of the station. We talked about the usual stuff cops talk about and as the shift wore on we both got more relaxed and even started joking around with each other. She was talking about how she liked to work out and she suddenly put up her arm and said "Feel that! It's really toned!" *Okay, I can go along with that, I guess.* I reached up and felt her arm, and it was indeed toned. After a while and a couple of calls later we were standing in back of the station and she was talking about working out again and she said "Feel my thigh! It's really toned!" *Okaaay…*I'm not so comfortable with that, being a married man and all. She said "Come on, just feel my leg!" So I did. I just touched her thigh for a second and pulled my hand away, and she was indeed toned, and I was thinking my wife would kill me if she saw that. Later in the shift we had dinner, or breakfast, or whatever you call it at 3 a.m. Twenty years as a cop and I never did figure out what to call it.

After dinner we were talking outside the station, and she did a little half turn from me and went up on her toes on one foot and said "Feel my glutes! They're really toned!" I looked down at her ass, perfectly poised for me to just reach out and feel it, and it did indeed look very toned, but I was not about to put my hands on it. She said "Go on, feel it! It's okay!" I mumbled that it looked really toned and walked hurriedly back to the car before she asked me to feel any other parts of her. When we got back in the car she asked me if I was going to be on her oral board, and I said "Yeah, probably." She leaned in closer to me and I noticed her red lipstick and that she smelled good, and she purred in my ear "Well, what can I do to score some brownie points?" *Oh my God, how is this happening to me?* I thought as I looked up at the roof. I needed to go to the station and get this vixen out of my car before this all ended up on the news or on *Jerry Springer*. Afterward I told the Chief she seemed like a nice person, but for the male officers' sake please don't hire her.

NINE

CHERRY HILLS WAS THE LAND OF BEAUTIFUL WOMEN. I think they had a rule against unattractive women living in the Village. You could pass through or visit, but sorry, you can't stay. You take a professional athlete or a successful corporate exec or a doctor, they are not going to marry Plain Jane. They're going to go for something tall, curvy, and leggy, something that looks really good on their arm at the Country Club and cocktail parties. There must be a store that you have to be a millionaire to go into, or even to know its secret location, where you go to find women like that, because you never see them pushing a shopping cart around at Walmart. Blonde, brunette or redhead, shop for the one that really catches your eye!

Even if the rich husband was not a very handsome guy, the good looks genes of the wife usually were enough to overpower his homeliness genes and still produce good looking children. I went to a doctor's house on a call, and the doc looked for all the world like Pee Wee Herman. He was skinny, frail, nerdy, and he was also wearing two different colored socks. When he saw me looking down at his mismatched footwear, he got very embarrassed and tried to hide one foot behind the other, standing on one leg like a stork. Then I hear a Swedish-accented voice calling "Honey, are the police here yet?" and his wife comes into the room. She's a knockout, a six foot blue-eyed Scandinavian blonde. How did he land a girl like that? I'll tell you how; because he knows where that store is, and the rest of us guys don't. Despite the doctor's appearance, their kids were beautiful.

I wondered as I left if he was a mechanic or a roofer instead of being a doctor, would she still be with him?

The trophy wives (and especially the trophy girlfriends) were under pressure; they knew that if they didn't keep up their looks and their charm they might be replaced by a younger, cuter model. Many of them took up jogging, or biking, or just taking their dogs for brisk walks. They didn't have regular dogs like Labradors and Golden Retrievers and don't even *say* "mixed breed" around them. They would recoil like you just suggested they eat lunch at the soup kitchen. They had fancy dogs with fancy breed names like Beaucerons and Borzois, dogs with *pedigrees* and fancy titles like they were nobility, and that sometimes cost as much as a working man's car. So while the cops were making our rounds, patrolling the city and cruising the neighborhoods, we would often see these women out and about on the sidewalks, the bridle paths, or the Highline Canal, biking, jogging, and dog-walking. We would slow down a bit, give a wave and a smile, before going on with our business. They liked the police and were always friendly to us, I think partly because they liked the attention and partly because they knew we were there to protect them. Maybe it was the uniforms.

Out of professional courtesy we would always tell each other when a particularly hot mama was out and about. Since all radio transmissions were monitored we couldn't just come right out and say "Check out the babe jogging down Quincy Avenue!" We'd be trucked off to Sensitivity Training faster than you can say French bikini. So we had to have code words, and every team had their own. Me and Matt and JR would call each other on the car to car channel and say "Out with a traffic hazard in the 2600 block of Quincy" or we would say "I just clocked a 46 on Meade Lane", with 46 meaning 4+6 = a 10. Yeah, men are pigs, and cops are the worst. We admit it and make no excuses for it. But before you sit in judgment, you should know that the girls almost universally liked it and were willing participants. They would lean down in the car window to talk to you, giving you an eyeful of their equipment while they were doing it. Or when I would ride the police motorcycle along the bike paths or the Canal they would flag me down to stop and tell me how much they appreciated us being out here *and so...do you have a girlfriend?* A few of the guys did have girlfriends in the city, and they would pull the squad car into the garage and pull the door down and take their Code 7's, their meal breaks. With dessert.

* * *

Some of the families in our city were suspected of being involved in some shady deals and underworld criminal activity. One family was reportedly part of the Russian Mafia, and they lived in a big, secluded house set well back from the road and completely surrounded by a high metal fence and heavy growth of trees and bushes. They had a large iron gate across the driveway, guarded by some very tough-looking guys in suits and dark sunglasses. Either they didn't want anybody to see what was going in there, or they *really* wanted to keep the Jehovah's Witnesses and vacuum cleaner salesmen out. I took one look at these impressive security arrangements and drove up to the gate, got out and introduced myself. On the one hand, I really wanted to scope out these guys and this house, and on the other hand I wanted them to be very clear that however things may have operated back home in Mother Russia, here in America there would be no free pass from the cops. We weren't afraid of them, and we would be keeping an eye on them.

They had a team of security people, headed by a hulking shaved-head giant named Leonid, who was reported to be an ex-Spetsnaz commando. I talked to Leo and told him I had been in the U.S. Navy, and he brightened up immediately and started talking to me like we were old war buddies. Leo spoke with a thick, James Bond movie villain Russian accent, and I began to suspect that because of the language barrier he somehow thought I had been a Navy SEAL, a Special Forces guy like him. I thought about correcting his mistake, but we were getting along so well now that I didn't want to spoil it. When I left we shook hands, and my hand was engulfed by his enormous paw. Since we only ran with two or three officers on duty at a time, I thought if the shit ever really hit the fan one night, if we had a North Hollywood Shootout right here in Cherry Hills, I might need Leo's help. Those guys were probably a lot more heavily armed than we were.

* * *

The DEA called the squad room one day and I answered. They said they were about to go raid a house in Cherry Hills and would I like to come? *Would I!?! Oh Boy!* It seems one of our residents had been regularly taking two trips a year to Colombia on his private plane, and the fed boys for some reason thought that was a little suspicious. After all, Colombia is not exactly a vacation paradise, and there is no *Fodor's Guide to Best Colombian Beaches and Night Life*. Some Internal Revenue Service agents were coming along as well. They all suited up in their black armor and raid jackets and exotic weaponry, and when we got to the house, instead of forming up in a stack and ramming the door, the DEA agents politely asked me if I would please go up and ring the doorbell. *Oh sure, let the local cop get shot first.* They hid around the corner while I walked up the front walk like I was delivering flowers and rang the bell. A very pretty, pleasant blonde haired woman answered the door and said "Hello, Officer. What can I do for you?" I told her there were some people here to see her.

The federal agents all came out then, from the back yard, from behind trees, and seemingly out of the ground, but they didn't rush the house screaming and yelling and pointing guns. Instead they very nicely asked if her husband was home, because they *really* wanted to see him. She was clearly alarmed at what was going on, but said her husband was at work. The lead agent informed me they had already sent a team to his work, and to the airport to seize his plane. The DEA agents were very professional and very courteous to the woman. It was the IRS agents who were the assholes. Penny pinching, tightwad accountants with guns. They unceremoniously told the lady that effective immediately they were seizing the house and everything in it. The house belongs to us now, you don't live here anymore, goodbye. They told her to leave, right now, just as you are. The woman was in utter shock when she found out what was going on, and said that she and her husband had been married less than a year. She knew he was a pharmacist but other than that she didn't know anything about his business. I pulled one of the IRS guys aside and said *"Come on man. At least let her get some of her clothes, whaddaya say?"* He thought for a minute, and then told her she could pack one suitcase, then get out.

She packed her suitcase and was ushered out the door, and as she walked down the front walk with tears in her eyes she turned to me and said "Where am I supposed to go? What am I supposed to do?" For a second the famous line from *Gone With The Wind* popped into my head; *Frankly my dear, I don't give a damn!* but I suppressed it. I really did feel sorry for her, because I don't think she had a clue that her new husband was an international drug dealer and money launderer. So I let her use my phone to call her mother, and then I gave her a ride to the bus station downtown. She looked so forlorn and lost standing there crying on the sidewalk as I drove away. But then I told myself that beautiful women never seem to run out of men willing to take care of them. She'll be alright.

* * *

People think the rich have it easy, and in most respects they do have it easier than you and me. They have a gardener to take care of the lawn, a chauffer to take care of the car, a nanny to raise the kids, and a lawyer to make their troubles go away. Our parents were right though, when they told us adversity builds character, and when everything is easy, when every problem is handled by calling someone else to take care of it, there is no opportunity to build character or a core of inner strength. That's why so many rich people, particularly rich young people, engage in destructive behavior like binge drinking, drug use, and crime. So many young girls want to be the next Lindsay Lohan or Britney Spears; fame and fortune, followed by drug rehab.

What I have learned from two decades of working daily around very wealthy people, of seeing them at their very best and absolute worst, is that I feel sorry for many of them. I know that sounds completely wrong, but it's true. I pity them because most of them desperately look for money to buy them happiness, and that is never going to happen. I have responded to more calls than I count of people who had every material pleasure at their fingertips and were on the brink of suicide. I've talked down people who were at the end of their rope and didn't know where to turn, to put the pills away, put the gun down, let's talk about it. Most of them told me they just didn't see the point of living, of going on anymore. For most of us, the point of living is to *make* a living, to go to work, to take care of our families, buy a nice house and find the American Dream. I used to feel a sort of contempt for these people, thinking *What have you got to complain about, pal?* but I came to see how having all those things just handed to you, things that the rest of us have to work for, left these people like a ship without an anchor, adrift with no purpose, no rudder, no direction, nothing to work toward. When you feel your life has no meaning, then it's easy to feel your life has no value.

Curiously, I don't recall ever going to a single suicide when I worked in the housing projects in Denver. The people who have nothing today and no hope of anything better tomorrow are the very people you would think would want to just end it all, but just the opposite is true. The struggle gives them purpose. Just waking up and getting through the day, not getting mugged or shot, finding enough food to put on the table for the kids, gives them meaning. They don't have the time to think about the deep meanings of life. Their focus is on the next twelve hours. There is a great purity in simplicity.

I sat with a woman on her porch, in front of a grand mansion house. She was wearing a mink jacket and diamonds and had a bottle of prescription sleeping pills in her hand that she was going to end her life with, but at the last desperate second she decided to call someone instead. I sat with her and listened while she told me that the happiest days of her life were when she and her husband were just starting out, with no money and heads full of dreams. They lived in a run-down apartment eating cheap Chinese take-out, talking about how their lives together would be. They did things together back then, they *had fun* together. Since he became a successful corporate executive he was so busy with work and always stressed out, and even when he was home his mind was back in the office. He just didn't have time for her anymore. It had been so many years since they had fun together she couldn't remember it. She looked behind her at the great house and the fancy cars and said she'd gladly trade it all to go back to that run-down apartment again.

* * *

A maintenance man found a body on the playground of St. Mary's School. It's a private school, with students coming from prominent families of Cherry Hills and Greenwood Village. When I later worked in Denver we would get dead body calls all the time, where street people would die of exposure, or someone would overdose, or a hit and run driver or a homicide.

We'd take some pictures, wait for the night shift detective to come out and take a look, then call the wagon to haul him off. That didn't happen in Cherry Hills. If there was a dead body out in a public place something had gone very wrong.

It was my call, and I rolled up into the parking lot. It was a school day and all the kids were in their classrooms, and we were met outside by a very distraught principal. Angel Strickland was with me and we went over to take a look at the body. One look said it all. White male, business suit, briefcase, lying on his back looking up at the sky. At least he was with his right eye, because the left side of his face was just gone, blown away by the blast of the exit wound. Lying in the grass near his right hand was a silver large-caliber revolver. I glanced at the heater and turned to Angel and said "Charter Arms Bulldog .44" I bent down and checked his pulse, not that I had any doubts, but you have to cross the t's and dot the i's. If I didn't do it, someone would ask me why I hadn't.

We didn't touch the body or the weapon, and I called out the detectives, the paramedics, and the coroner, in that order. The only reason I called the paramedics is so they could give an official pronouncement of death, because there was no doubt about this one. I then walked back over to the principal. "Who found him"? I asked, and she said "The groundskeeper, Jose" and pointed to where two Hispanic men were standing on the grass a short distance away. I walked over to them and saw they were both wearing work shirts with their names sewn on patches on the chest. I looked at the first guy and his name patch read "Jose", then I looked at the second guy and his name patch also read "Jose." Maybe they were having a sale on Jose's at the shirt shop. Neither man spoke a lick of English and I spoke Spanish *poquito*, so I didn't have any luck questioning either Jose 1 or Jose 2. I found a teacher who could translate, and together we found the right Jose.

He said he found the body when he was mowing the grass, and he said he didn't touch anything. When the detectives arrived we just stood back while they took photos and processed the scene and took fingerprints from the body. When they were done with the preliminary work they checked his pockets. They found his wallet and his driver's license. They next checked the gun and one of the detectives called back to the other "The weapon is a Charter Arms Bulldog, forty four caliber." I looked over at Angel, and she just rolled her eyes at me and said I had "issues."

One of the detectives pulled an envelope out of the dead guy's jacket pocket and looked inside. The envelope contained a note, a suicide note. It went on for a few pages, and revealed he was a lawyer, a rising star in his firm, and while I don't think it's my place to reveal the tortured inner thoughts of a man who has reached such desperation that he takes his own life, the letter said that he had been living far beyond his means, trying to keep up the appearances of being a big success, and had bankrupted his family and couldn't bear to tell them. So he killed himself instead.

Listen to me on this, folks. Most of us middle-class people spend our lives dreaming about someday being rich, getting promotions at work, "getting ahead," and then we'll find success and happiness. Ahead of what, we are never sure, but we must strive to get ahead. But are we chasing a shadow, a phantom dream? Money doesn't buy happiness. Never has, never will. It can make you comfortable, bring you a measure of financial security, and those are very good things. But beyond that it has little ability to bring us happiness. Don't expect it to do something for you that it has no power to do. Happiness comes from inside, and nowhere else.

What is really sad is when even kids reach a point where the only option they see left to them is to kill themselves. JR and I were working the night shift as usual when a frightened teenaged girl called dispatch. She said she had been talking to her friend on the phone, and the friend had been very depressed and despondent lately, and she had just told our witness on the phone that she had a knife and she was going to just end it all, and abruptly hung up. Dispatch gave us the address and we jumped in our cars and rushed Code 3 to the house. We ran up to the door and rang the doorbell, and a woman opened it. "Where is your daughter!?" we asked, and the woman said "in her bedroom upstairs. Why, what's going on?" We sprinted for the stairs yelling down to the mother that her daughter might be trying to commit suicide. And do you know what the mother's response was? She yelled back to us *She better not get blood on my white carpet!"*

* * *

Sometimes people tried to kill themselves in creative ways. There was a very prominent and well-to-do attorney living in Cherry Hills who had been disbarred, for among other things being an unrepentant alcoholic. He had been arrested a number of times by us for DUI, and his family finally had him committed to a treatment program. One day I got a phone call from his doctor asking me to go check on him because he had been drinking aftershave. I went to his house and was let in by his daughter and the young live-in nurse, who showed me where he had downed three bottles of Aqua Velva and two little bottles of Scope mouthwash. Mint flavor. I found him passed out upstairs naked in the bathtub. I called for the paramedics, and the family was saying they had scoured the house and removed anything that had alcohol in it, and he didn't drive anymore, so they had no idea where he was getting this stuff from, but while we were waiting for them and I was investigating the situation further my cop instincts led me to another conclusion. It was the live-in nurse. She was probably sleeping with him, and she was setting herself up to marry him, bribe him, or blackmail him, and plying him with more alcohol so that when he finally downed one bottle too many she would suddenly be a rich woman. And the family was utterly clueless. I pulled the daughter aside and had a heart to heart talk with her.

We had another case where an extremely wealthy man died when his private jet crashed in the mountains, en route to a business meeting in California. The FAA and the authorities in California were handling the investigation, but we did some follow-up on our end. Turns out the millionaire's regular pilot had called in sick that day, and within just a few months after the mysterious crash the grieving widow and the pilot were married. Like the old song says, *Things that make you go "Hmmm..."*

* * *

When you are out there on the night shift and all the city is quiet and peaceful, and you and your partner are just hanging out having a Coke because you need the caffeine, you tend to get a little poetic and philosophical at times. Police work is a job that really makes you think about life and death and human nature, in those rare quiet moments when you have time to reflect on just what it is that you are doing for a living. Matt and I had done a death notification one night. This poor couple's son had OD'd in his college dorm, and the family had taken it very hard. When we rang the doorbell and the mother and father saw us standing there, they somehow just knew. The investigation hadn't made a finding yet whether it was suicide or an accidental overdose, but the mother broke down crying and collapsed on the floor, and we did our best to console her. People think cops are always tough and in control, but the constant flow of misery and crap you see right up close and personal gets to you no matter how hard and thick your shell is.

So now, a few hours later, we were out back of the station sitting on the little benches overlooking the pond, and we were both feeling a little melancholy after what we had just had to do, and we were talking about death and why people commit suicide. We talked about all the death notifications, suicides, and accidental and intentional overdoses we'd worked, and we concluded that people commit suicide because they just don't know what else to do. They didn't have a backup plan for when their life fell apart. So right then and there we came up with The Backup Plan. We decided if we ever came into work and the Chief fired us, and then we went home and found our wife in bed with another man, our dog bites us, and our kids run away and join a Goth cult, then we would just drop everything and go straight to the airport, purchase a one-way ticket to Maui, and when we got there enroll in one of those one-week bartending schools and just serve drinks to the tourists in one of those little beachfront bars under the straw palapas. The more you think about it, the better it sounds.

* * *

The most unpleasant job I had to do as a sergeant was Internal Affairs investigations. In every cop movie the IA cops are always the bad guys. Remember that line from the movie *Internal Affairs*, with Richard Gere and Andy Garcia, when Garcia joins IAD and his boss tells him *"Remember all those friends you had on the force? You don't have them anymore."* In some cities like New York, IAD will try to pull stings on the street cops, have a "citizen" walk up to an officer and hand him a wallet and say "Officer I found this wallet on the subway" and of course the money inside is carefully counted and marked. It the cop doesn't turn the wallet in, or turns it in with half the money, they bust him. NYPD did that and *every* cop turned the wallet in. With all the money.

One of my officers was making a Code 3 run on a hot call down Belleview Avenue and came upon a woman driving in the left lane, who wasn't moving over to get out of his way. So he yelled at her "GET THE FUCK OUT OF THE WAY YOU STUPID BITCH!" Now of course he was inside his car with the windows up, so he didn't think there was any possible way she could have heard him, but as luck would have it she was a sign language teacher and an expert lip reader, so even from looking into her rear-view mirror at him she knew exactly what he was saying. She came right down to the station and gave the Captain an earful, and an Internal Affairs Investigations was launched for Unprofessional Conduct, which naturally came down to me. I pulled the cop in and asked him about it, and all he had to say was "Wow! She could actually tell what I was saying!" He was so impressed with her abilities that he immediately confessed in full.

A police sergeant often finds himself in the difficult position of protecting his officers from themselves. One night dispatch routed a call to me from an irate citizen, and when we got connected the first thing the woman said to me was "Why is there a Cherry Hills police officer buying a hooker over in Denver!?" *Come again? What was that?* She repeated her demand for an explanation, so I asked her to tell me exactly what she saw. She said she saw a large Hispanic male officer in full uniform and a marked police car stop in front of a sleazy motel in Denver. He stepped out of his car and went around to the passenger side and opened the door for a woman who was clearly a hooker from the very skimpy and revealing outfit, frizzy hair, and too much makeup she was wearing. When the hooker got out of the police car, the officer pulled out his wallet and peeled off some bills, put them into her outstretched hand, whereupon she turned and went into the motel.

Now I didn't know *what* the hell was going on, but I assured the good citizen that this was not what it looked like. Thinking fast, I told her the hooker was actually an undercover female police officer and they were getting ready to set up a sting operation. I couldn't really give her any details because this was a very sensitive operation, you know. The woman got a very conspiratorial tone in her voice and assured me she wouldn't give anything away, and she was glad we were out there getting that kind of scum off the streets. I thanked her for her concern and made her promise to keep this operation quiet since she was now "in the know", and she promised she would.

As soon as she hung up the phone I immediately rang up Tony, one of my precocious new officers, and as soon as his cheerful voice answered I said "Tony are you buying a hooker in Denver?" "NO - no, no, no!" he replied. Then he paused and said "Well...not exactly." It seems he was driving down Colorado Blvd. when he came across a car on the side of the road with its flashers on. He pulled over and contacted the driver, who had curly brunette hair, big blue eyes, and soft pouty lips. She had plenty more equipment to go with that, so naturally Tony (who was young and single) and the damsel in distress struck up a conversation. As it turned out, she was a stripper just getting off work when her car conked out. Tony said in his best manly voice "Pop the hood and I'll have a look!" She pulled the hood latch and he raised the hood and told her "Start her up!" The girl cranked the engine and Tony looked and listened as the engine tried in vain to kick to life. Tony admitted to me that he didn't have a clue what he was looking for, but it seemed like the right thing to do at the time. Having failed to bring the car to life by lifting the hood and staring at the engine compartment, Tony had reached the end of his auto repair capabilities, so he told the girl he could give her a lift home.

She gladly accepted, telling him she lived about fifteen minutes away in Denver. She climbed out of her car and slid into the patrol car seat next to Tony. As he drove her home they were soon deep in conversation. Somewhere along the drive they decided they really liked each other. In fact they were starting to like each other so much that they decided to go on a date, just as soon as Tony got off shift. She said her roommates were home so they decided she would just go to a motel and wait for him to get off work in a couple of hours. Tony changed direction and took her to a nearby motel in Denver. Once there, they got out of the car and she told him she didn't have money for the motel. So out there in plain view of the irate citizen who had called, they stood on the sidewalk while Tony pulled out his wallet and peeled off some bills so she could go in and get the room for their date, where she would wait and get warmed up for him. Thus the call came to me that a Cherry Hills officer was buying a hooker in Denver. Is there no room in this cold world anymore for love at first sight? Or at least a good substitute for it?

* * *

One night an officer named Rob contacted two hookers at a motel. Rob was a big strapping South Dakota farm boy that we nicknamed "Handsome Rob." He took one look at these girls and knew what they were about, and he asked them if they were working girls. The girls got *very* incensed and insisted they were not that kind of girls. One of them called Rob's sergeant, Tracy, to file an angry complaint on Rob, and while Tracy was talking to them on the phone he Googled the phone number she was calling from, and it immediately popped up the girl's sex ad on Backpage.com. Her profile showed her in various states of undress and in various seductive poses, offering her services to discerning gentlemen. Tracy asked her "Do they still call you Daisy?" The girl was taken aback and a little flustered, and Tracy repeated the question "Do your friends still call you Daisy?" The girl said that yes, some of her good friends did call her Daisy, and Tracy then asked "Daisy, do you still have that butterfly tattoo on your left ass cheek?" The girl hung up on him, complaint over.

Tracy stuck up for his team to the brass, and I have to give him major kudos for that, because we in the military and in law enforcement have all worked for sergeants who wouldn't. And I imagine in the civilian world people encounter the same situation, of an immediate supervisor who tries to climb the corporate ladder over the backs of other people. A Commander would come downstairs and complain to Tracy that his guys were doing this or not doing that, and Tracy would go rounds with the Commander for his guys, even at the expense of his own good evaluations. He was told he was not progressive, that he was old-fashioned, that he was stuck in the old ways of doing police work. That sounded just perfect to us.

* * *

Morale was not so great in the Department, and I knew it was often the little things that boosted spirits and made people like coming in to work. We were paid twice a month, and with every paycheck came a little newsletter telling what was going on in the city and part of the newsletter was the "Movie Quote" quiz where there would be a line from a movie and if you guessed the movie title you got a prize. The prizes were usually pretty good; gift certificates to restaurants, Starbucks gift cards, and the like. The problem was that the newsletter and the movie quotes were prepared by the girls upstairs so the movies were always chick flicks like *Pretty Woman, The Notebook,* or anything with Julia Roberts or Sandra Bullock so none of the cops ever had a prayer of winning. So I started up "The Manly Movie Quote" as a counter to the sappy love stories. Every payday I would think of lines from guy movies like *Lethal Weapon, Dirty Harry,* and *American Pie* or anything with Clint Eastwood or Adam

Sandler. I had to pay for the prizes out of my own pocket, but it was a hit with the troops.

Our shifts were bid strictly by seniority, and as I was the newest sergeant I always found myself working the graveyard shift. Night shift is hard on the body, because the human animal is just not meant to work nights and sleep days. Some animals are nocturnal, like raccoons or lions, but the only human beings that are habitually out all night are the twenty-something party animals, the criminals, and the cops. Our bodies have what is called a Circadian Rhythm, a cycle of hormone production that is geared toward keeping us alert during the day and sleeping like babies at night, and you can only disobey your body for so long before it bites you back.

When I was younger I could ignore or overpower my body's desire for sleep, but as my twenties slipped into my thirties the sweet siren song of sleep became harder to ignore. We called it "hitting the wall", when around 3 a.m. there would come a time when you were fighting just to keep your eyelids open and your head was doing touch-and-go's off the steering wheel, yet your shift was barely half over. To make matters worse, Cherry Hills had no street lights on the interior streets, none whatsoever, so it was really black dark, what we called "deep nights", and it was worst in the dead of winter when it was bone-shaking cold and you were driving around with your coat on and the heater blasting and lulling you to sleep and you were just waiting for the sun to rise so you could get warm and go home to bed. The interior streets of Cherry Hills were a maze; we had twisty little roads that led only to dead ends, and circles inside of circles that travelers and even the new officers could never find their way out of.

I was in one of these spider webs one night, and I was tired and decided I had better go to the station to put a cup of coffee inside me, and I could have sworn I was heading for the way out, but I must have dozed off at some point because when I looked up I was sitting in front of a big house. *Who put this house in the road?* I had driven right down to the end of somebody's long tree-lined driveway, and as I blinked away the fog shrouding my brain I began to wonder where I was and how I would get out and please God don't dispatch me to a call right now. I looked over to my left and saw the face of a giant St. Bernard dog drooling at me through my window. At first I thought I was hallucinating, but my next thought was *okay, now I knew where I am.* I lowered the window and reached out and ruffled the dog's ears. "Hey Digby, what are you doing out at this hour boy?" I asked him, but in response he only drooled some more and wagged his tail. He belonged to the family that owned the Digby Trucking Company; you've probably seen their trucks with the name in big orange letters rolling down the highways.

The mind plays tricks on you at times like that. I was driving down Hampden Avenue in the wee hours of a morning when suddenly the entire sky lit up as bright as daylight and a huge fiery object hurtled across the sky at incredible speed. Just as quickly it was gone and the world descended into darkness once more. I stopped the car right there on Hampden and pondered for a minute. *Nah! Couldn't have been!* I said to myself and moved on. *I gotta get off these damn deep nights.* Just then the radio crackled and John Reynolds called me. "Hey Mike. Say, did you, ahh, *see* anything just now?" he hesitantly asked. "You saw it too?" I replied, and he said "Yeah, just making sure I'm not going crazy."

Another night I had just finished checking on a little park and was driving slowly down one of the dark inner streets of the city when suddenly I saw a shapeless white form just ahead, bobbing in my headlights. I thought *Spirits? Now I really am losing it!* as I pictured some episode like *A Christmas Carol*, where the Ghost of Police Past would come show me what my life would be like if I had never become a cop. The shape suddenly morphed into a person, a running man with no shirt on and he flew right past my patrol car, close enough for me to have reached out and touched him but he never looked at me, never said anything, or even gave the slightest indication he knew I was there. I was thinking *Well that was odd* when another running, shirtless person flew by, once again close enough to touch and once again paying not the slightest attention to me. Since my only backup was an officer who usually ran the other way on dangerous calls, I decided I must have just seen an apparition, shrugged my shoulders and drove on. *Ghosts. Yeah, that was it.*

One officer, who shall remain nameless, fell asleep at the wheel while driving down Colorado Boulevard and drove right off the road where it comes to a T-intersection with Quincy Avenue, and ended up launching his car into the air and coming to rest out in a field. Another officer at least pulled off the road before he fell asleep, but when he woke up some kids had done a first class job of TP'ing his car while he slept like a baby inside. He must have been out for a long time. Things like that scared me, so when I got really tired I would get out of the car and do checks on foot around the churches. I always liked to walk the St. Gabriel's church, because in the courtyard around back they had a life sized statue of Jesus. I always reached out a hand and touched it when I walked by - just for luck.

The flip side of working nights is sleeping days. As bone tired as I was when I would get home, it was almost impossible to get any sleep once I got there. I would dream of crawling into my bed, but as often as not once I did I couldn't get to sleep. It was always something; a crack of light through the window shade that was landing right on my face, the neighbor starting up his lawnmower, some asshole on a Harley with loud pipes blowing down my street. Light and noise became my obsession. I tried several different window coverings; aluminum foil, room darkening shades, drop-down cellular blinds, everything, but what I eventually settled on was two big rectangular cardboard shooting silhouette targets duct- taped to the window. You've seen them, the cardboard police targets that have an outline of a human form on them. Those covered with a bed sheet sealed out every crack and glimmer of light. Living in constant darkness both day and night I began to feel like Dracula, standing at my window looking out over the city like the Count standing at the window of his castle listening to the wolves howl. *Ahhh, listen to them...the children of the Night!* The other Enemy was noise, and I bought every sleep sound machine I came across, looking for just the right rhythm to lull me to sleep. I tried waterfalls, chirping crickets, loons, jungle sounds, seashores, and finally settled on a plain old fan. Despite all my efforts, in all those years I never once got a full eight hours of sleep in the daytime.

* * *

My days off were mostly spent alone. I tried to do something productive with them, like learning to speak Spanish, going to the shooting range or to the gym, but I mostly ended up taking my dog Faith to different parks for walks. I got enough of police work during the week and I didn't have much stomach for it on my days off, too. Sometimes I would meet up with Matt to hang out, but usually I was by myself. It kind of makes for a lonely life, because you never see any friends on your days off, the kids are at school, and the wife is at work. Even while you were at work, despite having your fellow officers out there, most of the time police work is a solo job. You only call for a cover car if it's an alarm or a good call like a fight or a burglary.

However, there was one *really great thing* about my days off, and that was when my kids were in kindergarten. Kindergarten was only half a day, so when Alex was five I would get her ready in the morning, picking out her clothes for her, brushing her hair and making her breakfast before I took her to school. She was such a strong-headed and independent little child that whatever I picked out for her to wear she wouldn't like, because she wanted to pick it herself. So I soon learned to just bring out two little outfits, and she would stand there with her hands on her hips looking at them and would pick one of them and then everyone was happy. Then I would drop her off with a kiss and a hug and watch her run inside with her little backpack bouncing on her back. Then just four hours later I would pick her up again and we would have a "Daddy and Daughter Day" where we would go down to the Platte River valley for a picnic lunch, or we would catch a movie. She was really into dinosaurs at that time, so we would go to the Natural History Museum and look at the skeletons and fossils, or go back to the river and find rocks worn smooth by the water and she was just convinced they were dinosaur eggs and she would bring them home and put them under a light bulb and try to hatch them. I knew every single kid in her kindergarten class by name, and I knew I was involved in her life in a way that very few fathers ever got to do.

When Alex moved on to first grade, I was sad that our dad and daughter days were over. Going to lunch or to the river by myself was just depressing now, but it was only a year later that my son Nick went off to kindergarten too, and now I had Dad and Son Days and I was happy again. When Nick was being born my wife swears I was actually watching *The Simpsons* on the overhead TV in her delivery room, but I dispute that account. That's my story and I'm sticking to it. I wanted to name him Nick because that's a laid back, mellow, cool guy name. No one named Nick could ever grow up to be an uptight, stuffed-shirt pompous ass. Nick is a name for a surfer, a chef, a ball player. Nick wasn't into dinosaurs, he was into Power Rangers and Transformers. I don't know how a grown man with a college degree can't figure out how to change those stupid things from robots into cars, but a five year old can just say "Here, just give it to me Dad" and whip through it in seconds. I got to know all of Nick's friends and classmates too, and when he graduated kindergarten and moved to first grade, I knew those great dad and child days would never be quite the same. But you know what? *They* remember it, to this day.

TEN

ONE MORNING our Technical Accident Investigator came to me for help. We had just had a terrible accident at Belleview and Holly where a woman was killed. It was a major intersection and during a storm the traffic lights went out. We came out and put up some temporary stop signs to control traffic, and when the storm cleared the traffic lights came back on. Glenn Bailey went out to the intersection to start picking up the temporary signs, when a car coming from the south and a Jeep coming from the east each thought they had the right of way and collided in the intersection. The driver of the car slammed on his brakes, and the effect of that car's hood dipping down when he braked was to create a ramp that the Jeep's left front tire went up and over and flipped the Jeep onto its roof. The Jeep slid across the intersection on its top and hit Glenn, sending him flying. The poor woman who was driving the Jeep was killed and Glenn was injured. This was too much for Chris to handle alone, so the next day he asked me to help him with the follow-up investigation.

As we did the investigation, using a drag sled to calculate coefficient of friction of the road surface, and took measurements and calculated speeds and yaw and departure angles, Chris carefully explained to me what he was doing. I found it fascinating in its complexity and detail, and I wanted to learn more. Chris approached the Chief about making me his assistant, and the Chief agreed. I spent much of the next few months going to accident investigation schools, and when I was finished I became the Department's official backup Technical Accident Investigator. Chris was ecstatic, because he was tired of being on-call twenty-four seven and was only too happy to share the duty with me. It wasn't long before I had my first call-out, and it was a doozy.

We had a juvenile delinquent in the city named Gavin. Some kids are just born to be trouble, and his first brush with the law was when at the tender age of nine or so he started shooting out his neighbor's windows with his BB gun. As he got older he graduated to more serious crimes like assault and buying and selling drugs, until he got busted by the South Metro Drug Task Force. Gavin was out late one night, up to no good I am quite sure, and was walking home because his driver's license was suspended. He was tired, it was late, and his course home took him by a local fire station. And there was a big shiny red fire truck parked right outside. With the keys in it. Gavin walked over, climbed in the cab, and fired it up. The sleeping firemen inside heard the truck start up and rushed outside just in time to see their half-million dollar truck heading up University Boulevard with Gavin behind the wheel.

Gavin didn't actually intend to steal the truck, he just wanted to drive it home and in fact he did just that. The only problem was that the entrance to his neighborhood was a sharp turn on a narrow street, bounded by a steep drop off into a wooded ravine. Gavin later admitted that he had never driven a fire truck before, nor did he stop to ask the firemen *"How does she handle?"* because he miscalculated the turning radius and sent the big fire truck plunging down the ravine, where it came to rest with its front end buried in the ground and its back end sticking up in the air with its tires still freely spinning. Gavin just climbed out of the cab and walked home and went to bed.

Maybe I'm just jaded after all these years of police work, but I believe that there are people out there who quite simply have no concept of right and wrong. To tell them that something was *wrong* was as alien a concept as the dark side of the moon. Why can't I take all the money in the bank? Why can't I force this girl to have sex with me? For Gavin, he was tired, the truck was there, he drove it home, *so what's the problem?*

I was home in my bed, sound asleep and blissfully dreaming that Elizabeth Hurley was feeding me strawberries while whispering sweet nothings to me in that delightful British accent. When the phone rang it was Matt. *"Hey buddy! Gotta good one for you! Get your ass out of bed! You weren't sleeping were you?"* I don't know what irked me more; that I was trading Elizabeth for Matt or that he sounded so damn cheerful and happy to be waking me up. I groaned and rolled out of bed, got dressed in the dark, and with many bumps and muttered curses made my way downstairs, grabbed a granola bar and a water bottle, and headed out.

When I got on scene I was frankly feeling a little overwhelmed. Matt didn't tell me what we had; the mischievous imp in him wanted to see the look on my face. I wasn't really expecting a forty foot, half-million dollar fire truck on my first call-out. But I took a deep breath, told myself *Start from the point of rest* and scrambled down the hill. The investigation took some time, needless to say, while the other cops tried to figure out how the hell they were going to get this fire truck out of there. Our normal towing contractor didn't have anything even remotely capable of dragging this giant beast out of the dirt. We ended up hooking up two of those really big tow trucks that haul tractor-trailers around, and their combined power dragged the fire truck out. Meanwhile a small army of South Metro firemen showed up and kept getting in the way. They were climbing around in the cab, getting up on the back, and I kept telling them "Guys, come on! I'm tryin' to work here! You don't see me draggin' a hose around at your fire scenes, do ya?" The upshot of all this was that a friend of mine, Eric Schmitt with Greenwood Village PD, had just the week before stuck a note on that very fire truck telling the firemen they probably shouldn't park that truck outside with the keys in it. The firemen took the note inside and drew pictures on it and used it for a dartboard. *Oops! Who's laughing now, hose draggers?!*

I can poke a little good-natured fun at firefighters because I used to be one, after a fashion. I went through two firefighting schools when I was in the military. I went through Shipboard Firefighting School and later through Aircraft Firefighting School, and I was on an Aircraft Crash Rescue Team. For that job, most of the time we just barreled around on ATV's in the desert, scaring the crap out of the coyotes and finding jumps to go over. The major problem with aircraft firefighting is that military aircraft tend to have big bombs hanging under the wings, and bombs don't react well to fire. I'll never forget going through "The Smokehouse" during shipboard firefighting school.

It was an exercise designed to show how difficult it can be just to navigate through the corridors and hallways and ladders aboard a ship during a fire. The room was dark and full of smoke and I could see flames shooting into the air around me. It was a controlled exercise, but the smoke and flames were very real, and you soon completely forgot that it was a training exercise. You have to fight the claustrophobia and the rising panic as every instinct in your body is telling you to get the hell out of there. My mask didn't have a good seal on one side, and it was filling with smoke and my eyes were stinging and I was doubling over and coughing. I was trying to get out by feel because I couldn't see squat, and when I eventually got out I pulled off my mask and breathed in deep draughts of the fresh air. The other guys all started pointing at me and laughing, and when I looked in the mirror my face was as dark as one of those old minstrel show actors. After that experience, I'll face down a man with a gun any day before I'll run into a burning building.

* * *

I was at the station, sitting in our little report writing room with its two computers side by side on a little table, clacking away on the keys when the phone rang. I picked up the receiver and said "Police Department how can I help you?", and the man on the other end started off by saying "Okay, I'm not crazy". Now here's a lesson in psychology; when someone starts off by telling you something they are *not*, that frequently means that is precisely what they are; they're not crazy, they're not guilty, etc. etc. What they usually mean is that yes they really *are,* but they just want to tell you their side of the story before you cart them off to jail or the nuthouse. I'm sure there's a technical term for the phenomenon that shrinks use that I can't pronounce - I just know it from experience. It's like when someone says "Well I don't want to be a pain..." and then in the next breath go right ahead and do what they said they didn't want to do.

So this guy tells me that he's on the seventeenth hole of the Cherry Hills Country Club golf course, and he's on the green getting ready to putt when he's distracted by a dog barking. Only the funny thing is that he swears the sound of barking is coming from *underneath* him, right under his feet. The man puts down his putter, staring at the grass and listening, and sure enough he hears it again, a dog barking from underground. The man is alone that day and looks around to make sure he's not on hidden camera. He doesn't know what to do, and he's understandably reluctant to call someone for fear of being taken by the men with white coats. As I'm listening to him talk about barking dogs underground I'm thinking about calling those very guys, but my curiosity was aroused so I told the guy to stay there and I'd be right up. Matt was in the squad room pretending to do some work but actually reading a comic book so I told him to come on, I need a witness for this if I'm going to do an MHH, a mental health hold, on this guy.

We drove up to the golf course, and although we tried to stay on the little cart path I'm afraid our black-and-whites were a bit wider than the standard golf carts and we left some tire tracks on their beautiful manicured fairways on our way out to the seventeenth green. When we got there the golfer was waiting for us and when we walked up to him he pointed excitedly at the ground and said "He's right under there! Listen!" We listened... and heard nothing. Stone silence, nothing but the breeze blowing. The guy started to become insistent. "I'm not crazy! I really heard it! I'm telling you there's a dog under the ground right here!" Matt and I exchanged dubious glances. I started to open my mouth to tell the guy not to waste our time when suddenly, faint but clear, right under our feet came a *Woof!* I was dumbfounded. This was like The Twilight Zone. The golfer was practically jumping up and down feeling vindicated. I'll bet that for a minute there he was wondering if he really was going crazy. Matt and I had a powwow because we weren't sure what exactly to do now. We figured there must be underground water or sewer pipes running through the golf course and somehow this dog had gotten inside one.

We decided to call our friends at the Fire Department and see if they had any ideas. Now here's a little known fact about the fire department. They don't get to "run Code" as often as the cops do so they run Code to *everything*. They'll be coming in hot, with lights and sirens going like they had mass casualties. Cops often don't run Code even when they're allowed to. When I get an emergency call late at night I don't even turn my siren on when I'm driving through the neighborhoods because as a guy who works shift work I know the value of a good night's sleep. So before too long we hear the wail of sirens and look to the south toward the entrance to this prestigious country club and there, charging across the course like a column of Patton's Sherman tanks crossing the Rhine is a big pumper truck, a ladder truck, and the Fire Captain's Suburban. At least we had *tried* to minimize the damage to the golf course when we were driving over it, but the fire trucks were so much wider than the little cart path and weighing in at several tons each their tires were kicking up rooster tails of beautifully manicured Kentucky bluegrass. This brought the manager of the country club flying out of the clubhouse in great distress. I bet those fire guys were having a blast.

The fire guys walked up to the green and asked what was up. I told them there was a dog underground, and to just listen. They paused, with ears cocked...Nothing. *Silence.* I could see the firefighters exchanging dubious glances among themselves. Now I was starting to be afraid that the fire guys would think *I* was crazy. Now I knew how the golfer felt. Matt was backing me up on it, but the fire guys were probably thinking *These cops have been sniffing too much gunpowder* but to my relief just then Subterranean Dog started barking again. The fire guys brightened up and looked at each other like "Okay, these guys aren't crazy. Now let's get to work!" A crowd was starting to gather now, attracted by all the lights and cop cars and fire trucks. There were other golfers, grounds keepers, club officials, and finally even a news truck showed up. The media guys didn't know what was going on but figured it might be something good for the evening news. When we told them it was a dog stuck in a water pipe they groaned audibly, like "We came all the way over here for *this*!?" It must have been a slow news day because they decided to stick around anyway, and broke out their cameras. I don't really care for the news media so I declined an interview.

Everyone spread out and searched around for the entrance to the underground pipe and with the help of some groundskeepers we found it. Maybe. Turns out there were a number of underground pipes and we had no idea where the entrance to Subterranean Dog's particular pipe was. The entrance to the pipe we found was actually pretty big, and talk was starting to go around about putting somebody in there to crawl in with a flashlight and see if they could find the dog. Matt pulled me aside. He was getting a little nervous because he was the smallest guy there and if somebody was going to get nominated to get into that pipe it was going to be him, and he didn't like the idea of crawling around in water, dirt, and worms like a Vietnam tunnel rat looking for the Viet Cong. "What if I get stuck?" he protested. "I could die in there! What if I can't get any air? What if I get claustrophobic and can't turn around? What if.." I cut him off and said I'd take care of it. I went and talked to the fire captain and told him all the reasons why we *shouldn't* put somebody down there, or why if we did it should be one of his firemen and not one of my cops. "We don't really have any equipment for this kind of thing" I said. "How about you guys?" The fire guys huddled up and conferred among themselves, then the Captain came over and said "Yeah, I think we got something."

They got on the radio and a few minutes later I heard the cough of a diesel engine and turned to see a big yellow backhoe tractor trundling *directly across the fairway,* not even bothering to stay on the golf cart path. The giant knobby tires were tearing huge chunks out of the beautiful grass. The Club Manager's hands flew to his face in horror when he saw this and came running up to *me,* because I was wearing the stripes on my sleeve, pleading and protesting, but I told him it wasn't my show anymore. And truly this had now become a spectacle, an event that was bigger than any of us. We had a crowd of spectators, we had news cameras, we had heavy equipment. It had taken on a life of its own.

The big backhoe drove up and settled onto the green. The firefighters were really enjoying themselves now - they're just big kids who like to take things apart and smash things and get paid for it. They were debating about where to start digging, and after a bit of haggling they marked their spot. The backhoe engine throttled up and the big shovel came down. As soon as the shovel bit down into the green the club manager groaned. The backhoe kept digging, lifting out big scoops of grass and dirt and dumping them in a pile. Soon we had a hole several feet deep, and every couple of minutes a fireman would jump in and dig around to see if we had reached the pipe. Then he would climb back out and signal the backhoe operator, and down the shovel would go again. Finally a fireman suddenly began shouting and waving excitedly, and the shovel stopped. We had found the pipe.

Now more firemen jumped down into the hole and cleaned it off, exposing the dull gray surface. One of them started tapping on the pipe and the dog started barking excitedly. That got the firemen excited and they started breaking out saws and torches and fearsome looking cutting tools. Of course they couldn't start excavating right on top of the dog, so by tapping and listening for the responding barks they figured out exactly where the dog was. They decided to cut open the pipe a short distance away from the dog, and that meant they would have to make the hole *much* bigger. At this news I thought the Club Manager was going to faint. The backhoe went to work and eventually turned most of the seventeenth hole into a deep, gaping pit. Then the firemen climbed down and went to work, hammering and sawing and cutting a hole into the pipe. Several minutes later one of the firemen called for a halt, and then reached deep inside the pipe and pulled out a haggard, wet Golden Retriever. The crowd cheered. Seconds later the crowd reeled back as a big angry raccoon shot out of the pipe and up the bank and into the crowd. Then everybody laughed. The news cameras zoomed in on the happy dog and the hero firemen, and it was one of those great warm human interest moments. After that the crowd eventually began to break up and drift off. The news cameras packed up and left. The firemen got in their trucks and drove away. We couldn't get our cars out until everyone else was gone so we were stuck there. The Club Manager was horrified, looking from the gaping pit that used to be the seventeenth green to the mass of mud that used to be the fairway, and demanded to know who was going to pay for all this? I shrugged my shoulders and told him to do what I did; call the Fire Department.

* * *

Charlie Bates was one of those well-meaning but misguided police administrators who really believe that any problem can be solved by just sitting down and talking about it. This new "soft" approach is catching on and spreading across the country, and it is a very dangerous development. It is going to get people killed, both police officers and the citizens who look to them for protection. When we ordered leather jackets for the motorcycle guys he ordered blue ones instead of black. That's right - blue leather jackets. He said that black just sent the wrong message, looked too mean and tough, and blue was softer and friendlier. He liked that word, "soft." Soft and cop do not go together, and us motor guys revolted and said we would all drop out of the unit before we would wear those ridiculous blue jackets, and we meant it. Who ever heard of a motorcycle cop in a blue leather jacket? Did Ponch and John wear blue jackets on CHIPS? Do SWAT guys break down the door wearing blue BDU's? Does Darth Vader wear a blue helmet? Bates relented at last when he saw the level of resistance and we got some very un-soft looking black leather jackets. And we were happy.

As part of his friendlier, gentler approach to police work the Chief sent us all to classes called "Verbal Judo", which we immediately renamed "Gerbil Voodoo." This is supposed to be a sort of modern Zen way of mixing Chinese philosophy with anger management to teach police officers to try to get people to comply without resorting to force, to create monkish "Peace Warriors" (I'm not making that up - it's in the Manual). The idea has some merit, but it's been taken to ridiculous extremes. First let it be said that the guy who invented this thing was an English professor, which apparently qualifies him to tell cops how to do their jobs. In the class we all sat in our rows and dutifully repeated "strip phrases" and "combination phrases" and "metaphrases" to "deflect" and develop "reverse-empathy", so that when a suspect or a good citizen tells us something like "You can kiss my ass, pig!" instead of cracking him over the head we are supposed to say *"Sir, I appreciate that but I still need to see your driver's license"*, or if they say "Go fuck yourself, asshole!" we're supposed to say *"Sir, I understand where you're coming from..."* As a veteran cop and possessing at least half a brain I will tell you that if you allow suspects to talk to you this way, to walk all over you and get away with it, they will lose all respect for you, for the badge, and for all cops they meet in the future, and that is a very dangerous thing to do. People will not do violence to people they have respect for. Maybe in an English class that doesn't mean anything because the students are not going to shank the teacher, but out on the street it can get people hurt and killed. Here is a life lesson that is applicable to everyone, in all walks of life; people will treat you exactly the way you allow them to.

They also sent us to learn Spanish For Law Enforcement, a rather amusing class that taught us how to say things like *COO-chee-yo* for "knife" and *MAH-tah-low* for "kill him", as well as more useful phrases like *ALL-toe / oh / dees-PA-row* for "Stop or I'll Shoot" and *LOW / VOY/ ah-rees-TAHD* for "I'm going to arrest you." Those were all well and good, but the best part of the class was that we learned to curse like a native of Old Mexico. The instructor didn't want to teach us the bad language, but we badgered and begged her until she finally relented. We took turns happily calling each other every Spanish curse word we learned in our new-found language, and we all ventured back out to the street now brimming with cultural awareness and sensitivity.

We soon got the opportunity to test our skills when we got a BOLO (Be On The Lookout) for a stolen car occupied by three Hispanic males. One of the officers spotted the car and we initiated a felony stop on the vehicle. I was crouched down using the trunk of my car for cover, and looking down the sights of my 12 gauge shotgun toward the suspects. One of the other officers got on the PA and began shouting instructions in Spanish: *Get out the vehicle! - put your hands up! - lie down on the ground! - do not move!* The three suspects complied, and we quickly had them hooked up and safely in custody in a jiffy. However, when we got a closer look at them we saw they were not Hispanic at all. Turns out they were all Cambodian and spoke Spanish about as well as I speak Swahili. Which is to say not a single word of it. I guess police officers pointing guns at you and yelling at you is a language all its own, one that is universally understood.

* * *

I responded to a cold burglary over on the west side of town. A young couple had gone away for the weekend, and when they returned they found that a window had been jimmied open and their house had been burglarized. I went to the house and the homeowners were waiting outside, and we stood on the porch for a minute while she filled me in on what happened. I started to go inside and look the place over, and the wife (who did all the talking; the husband meekly stood in the background and uselessly nodded his head once in a while) hesitated. She said "You know, we're pacifists, and we don't believe in guns or using violence, so would it be asking too much for you to leave your gun in the car before you go in?" My first reaction was that I thought she was just kidding, making a joke, but when I quickly realized that she was serious I got a little angry at such a stupid request, but I have always prided myself on being professional, so I said "Ma'am, your house has been burglarized, and until I check it out I'm not 100% sure that the burglar is not still in there. Now what if I searched your house and found the burglar and he was the only one holding a gun?" She failed to see the logic of that, and repeated her request. Now I let a little anger show and I said "Ma'am, either I come in *with* my gun or I don't come in at all!" She hesitated, but eventually moved aside and let me enter. I told them to stay on the porch while I searched the house. The burglar was no longer there, but he had cleaned them out pretty good, and I took photos and dusted for prints and made my report. When I left the woman was not at all friendly to me, and banged the door shut behind me.

When I drove away from the house I got to thinking about that couple, and I have come to the conclusion that pacifists are cowards. They think they are being courageous, taking the high moral ground, sticking to their non-violence creed, yet when push comes to shove the first thing they do is to start looking around for help from people who are decidedly *not* pacifists. They will not own guns or do violence themselves, but they are certainly willing to call people who do and who will. If I had told that woman "I can't go in there because the burglar might still be in there, and wouldn't you know it I'm a pacifist too and I don't want anyone to get hurt" she would have looked at me like I was crazy. I don't recall who coined the phrase, but there's a saying that Americans rest easy in their beds at night only because armed men are willing to do violence on their behalf. It is rather in vogue nowadays to call yourself a pacifist, to be anti-war and put a peace sign or a Coexist bumper sticker on the back of your car, but it takes no conviction, no courage, to drape the mantle of pacifism over yourself, and thereby excuse your cowardice and failure to act. The brave ones are those who love peace and justice and will fight for it. The soldiers, the police officers, the everyday citizens who refuse to stand by when bad men do bad things to innocent people, those are the ones who deserve our respect and honor.

ELEVEN

I HAD ABOUT FIVE YEARS ON THE JOB NOW, and I was feeling pretty good about myself and the progression of my career. Being a recently promotoed sergeant meant taking on a lot of new responsibilities, but most of them were administrative paper-pushing duties that if anything made me even more restless to really do something meaningful and exciting, some real police work. John Bayman was the sergeant in charge of the Motor Unit and was our resident DUI expert who handled all the training and certification for the officers. John was about ten years older than me and one of the very few sergeants besides myself that refused on grounds of principle to play the brown-nosing game with the brass, and I respected him for that. He also had an excellent Fu Manchu mustache that made him almost a dead ringer for one of The Village People, the one who always wore the black leather outfit. Picture him in your mind, and you got John. More than any other sergeant, John really helped me out when I first got promoted, guiding me through his own example and much advice over cups of coffee on how to be a good team leader while not getting on the wrong side of the powers that be in the city.

On one of those coffee meetings he said to me "Why don't you come out for the Motor Unit? You've got riding experience and we need good people." I told him I was already pretty busy with being a sergeant and with the Firearms Training Unit but when he told me I could combine the motorcycle riding with shooting that sold me. I like motorcycles. There's just something visceral and primal about bikes; the noise, the speed, the freedom, the attitude. One of my childhood memories of my father was seeing him riding a Harley around the trailer court where I grew up, a cigarette dangling from the corner of his mouth like James Dean in *Rebel Without A Cause*. That's where it began, and I guess that also tells you a lot about my childhood. I once saw a bearded biker wearing a t-shirt that said "You'll never see a motorcycle parked outside a psychiatrist's office". Bugs in your teeth, wind in your face, and a hundred horses under the throttle in your right hand is a kind of therapy all its own.

My dad was always tinkering around with motorcycles and go-karts and mini-bikes for us kids. We had a powder-blue 5 horsepower mini-bike with the fat knobby tires that could get up to maybe 35 or 40 miles per hour. The problem was that the throttle was stuck wide open, so you had to use a special technique to ride it. You'd hop on it, get your feet set, get your brain focused, make very sure the road was clear in front of you, and push the electric starter button. As soon as the engine kicked to life the little bike would rocket away like an F-14 Tomcat catapulting from an aircraft carrier deck, reaching top speed in about three seconds. It was a blast to ride, but like a Tomcat coming back to the boat the landing was more hazardous and exciting than the takeoff. You had to guide the bike in toward your pre-selected landing spot and when you got about fifty yards out you cut the engine and coasted in, jumping off and hauling the bike down to a stop when you got close. My mom would come in the house and yell at my dad "You need to fix that damn throttle! One of those boys is going to get killed riding that thing!" and my dad wouldn't even look up from reclining back in his easy chair and football game, but would say "Yeah, probably, but what are you gonna do?" and take another sip of beer.

As I got older I graduated to bigger machines, the little mini-bike giving way to a Kawasaki KM100 and then to a Suzuki RM 125. We had carved out a dirt track in the open field south of our house, and me and my brother Tim and our friend Sean LaCroix, who had a green Kawasaki KX 125, would burn up the track and see who could catch the most air on the jumps. See, being a country boy opens up a whole new world of possibilities for fun! Also for hurting yourself, as I discovered.

As a teenager I was a fan of Roger DeCoster, the Belgian motocross champion, and one day at the track I did a huge jump. *Huge.* I caught so much air migrating ducks were flying past me. I thought I must have looked incredibly cool had anyone been there to see it, and at the apex of the jump I turned my front wheel in an imitation of the pros. Problem was, the pros remember to straighten their wheels back out before they land. I landed with my wheel still turned and immediately flipped head over handlebars and went sailing through the air. When I hit the ground it knocked the wind out of me and my ribs hurt. A moment ago I wanted an audience. Now I wanted an ambulance. I just lay there for several long minutes catching my breath and assessing the damage. I finally got up and pushed my bike home.

Now that I was all grown up I had a blue and white Yamaha YZF600 in my garage, and I still liked to ride. When Bayman suggested I try out for the Motor Unit I jumped at the chance. The class was scheduled and I went out for the training. Jody Sansing decided to go out for it, too, as he already had his Harley and thought riding the police bike would be fun. With us were four guys from Englewood PD; Eric Lutz, Brian Mueller, an older deputy chief, and another guy who I only remember from his radio call sign "Romeo 69." Of the several agencies that surrounded us we had the closest relationship with the Englewood cops. We cross-trained with Englewood now and then so I already knew Lutz, and one of our officers, Sue Baril, had gone over to Englewood a couple of years earlier so they were sort of family. In addition, either department could monitor the other's radio transmissions with the flip of a switch and we occasionally covered each other on calls.

I had ridden motorcycles all my life and thought the training class would be a piece of cake. I was painfully, completely, totally wrong. The Kawasaki KZ1000 Police Motorcycle has almost a hundred horsepower and weighs 595 pounds dry. The first few times I dropped the bike I quickly heaved it back upright, out of embarrassment and trying to save face. After a while the pickups got slower and harder, and by the end of the first day I would just stand there and stare morosely at the downed bike, lying there on its side as if to say *C'mon...pick me up just one more time!* I would get my tired legs underneath me and heave it upright again and take a breather before remounting it. I thought motor training would be fun, but it was turning out to be the most physically exhausting law enforcement training course I had ever taken. The Firearms Training Unit sometimes trained with Englewood and Arapahoe County SWAT, and although that was intense as well as more fun, it was still not as demanding. After all, SWAT gear is heavy but it doesn't weigh 595 pounds.

That first week of motor training consisted mostly of riding in formations with names like The Snowman, The Intersection, and The Serpentine where the courses, marked out with orange cones, got increasingly smaller and tighter until it seemed physically impossible for a motorcycle to even fit inside them. As the week went on we got better with each day, and as our skill and confidence improved we found ourselves easily performing things we thought impossible on the first day. We could ride in a circle with the handlebars cranked into a full lock right up against the tank, so it seemed the front end was moving in a circle while the back tire was almost stationary. We could climb and descend stairs, and ride in formation with four bikes abreast moving and turning seamlessly as one, or we could put three bikes in The Snowman, running in a tight high-speed circle with the front tire of one bike almost rubbing the back tire of the bike in front of it. It was a thing of beauty.

When the first week of cone courses and formation riding was over, it was time to get out on the road. We went out on the highways and city streets to get used to maneuvering through traffic, splitting the lanes, threading through traffic jams, and even riding on the sidewalk. That sure surprised some pedestrians! Some stuffed-shirt businessman would be walking along with a briefcase and yakking on the cell phone when seven police motorcycles would suddenly appear roaring down on him. The Englewood guys were a wild and crazy bunch. Whenever we rode by a pretty girl they would start hooting and hollering and blipping their sirens and air horns, and as often as not it was the deputy chief that started it. If Chief Langford ever caught one of us doing that he'd yank us off the Unit and send us away for a solid month of Sensitivity Training conducted by man-hating lesbians with whips. We were riding along the Platte river and we saw a kayaker roll over and go into the water, and the Englewood guys were yelling and laughing and sounding their air horns. Me and Jody were looking at each other uneasily and thinking maybe we should go down there and see if he was okay. The next day I read in the paper that a kayaker had drowned in the Platte. What were the odds, you know? I was just praying that it wasn't that guy.

We did a day at the shooting range, practicing jumping off the bike and laying it down, using it for cover while we engaged targets with live ammo. Bayman told us "If any of you mother#*&*%s shoots the bike you're off the Unit!" The trick was you had to make sure you killed the engine *before* you laid the bike down, otherwise you would be lying there proned out in the dirt with your gun out, watching your bike go trundling riderless across the range until it crashed into something. Nobody made that mistake more than once.

What could be more fun than a day riding motorcycles and shooting? How about doing it at the same time? The testosterone was flowing in overdrive now, and we were screwing around and riding down the firing line controlling the throttle in one hand and shooting at the targets with the other, like some modern version of Cowboys and Indians. That wasn't really an official part of the course, but it was sure a lot of fun. Our last day of the course was a mountain ride. It was a gorgeous day, with perfect May weather and the snow-capped Rockies towering majestically above us. It was a perfect end to a challenging but immensely enjoyable training course.

Once training was over we put the motors to work. Motorcycle cops do *not* call their police bikes "motorcycles", they are "Motors" and the unit is the "Motor Unit", and we were just deadly on traffic. We could hide in places a car never could, anything that would even break up the outline of the bike or partially hide it would work; a bush, a sign, even the shade of a tree right out in the open. An officer in a patrol car was expected to write a minimum of two tickets per day in addition to his other duties. On the motors we could write ten tickets an hour, just as fast as we could zap a speeder with the laser or the radar, pull them over and write the ticket, and go back for the next one. Every police department denies they have a ticket quota, and every citizen knows that's bullshit. Officially, Cherry Hills did not have a ticket quota; instead, the two tickets per day was called a "Performance Expectation." Shakespeare said a rose by any other name would smell just as sweet, and I say a ticket quota by any other name stinks just as bad.

John Bayman was passionate about the Motor Unit, which I think is great. You *want* the head of a unit to be passionate about it, just as I was with the Firearms Training Unit, to have a drive to make it succeed by sheer force of will. Still, there were times when I couldn't always share Bayman's enthusiasm. He had a "no warnings" policy when on the bikes - everybody you stopped got a ticket, period. Me on the other hand, I gave a lot of warnings. Sometimes people were just having a bad day, like one lady I stopped for going 43 in a 30 on Happy Canyon

Road. When I walked up to the car this woman was just crying uncontrollably. I said "Take it easy lady! It's just a speeding ticket. I've even had a couple myself!" But she sobbed "It's not the ticket! I just came from court and I lost custody of my kids." I told her to get out of here, just slow down and be careful. She rolled away and I caught Bayman giving me a disapproving look. He knew I hadn't given her a ticket, because I'd let her go too fast. Instead of trying to explain it to him, I just mounted up on my motor and went off to find another one.

Captain Bates was always riding my ass about giving people warnings. I consistently had one of the highest numbers for making traffic stops, but one of the lowest for tickets. I only wrote about one out of three people I stopped. Bates would complain to me about my ticket numbers and I would protest "But Captain, we don't *have* a ticket quota, right?" Every cop has their own threshold where they'll stop people at. Some go with 10, or 15, and some as low as 7. I would stop people at 13 over, because I figured 13 was an unlucky number anyway so it had a kind of symmetry and logic to it. I would clear everyone, looking for wants and warrants, but after a few years on the Job I would only write people "attitude tickets." I know people will say that's wrong, it's unfair, blah blah blah, but in the real world most cops do it. If you were nice, if you had your license, registration, and proof of insurance, you would get a *I'm going to give you a warning this time, just be more careful* and you would be sent on your way. That's all most people need to get their attention. But the jokers who wanted to play street lawyer and argue with me about the properties of laser or radar, or make snide comments like "Don't you have any real criminals to catch?" or my favorite "Is Cherry Hills running out of money?", that was an automatic ticket plus whatever else I could find; cracked windshield, bald tires, light out, or registration not signed. The residents of Cherry Hills had enough money to fill Fort Knox, but they wouldn't turn down a little more. A friendly word of advice: if a cop stops you, just be nice. Don't argue, don't pop off with an attitude, have all your stuff, and your chances of getting a warning go up exponentially. We are human too, and we don't like dealing with jerks any more than you do at your job.

One evening I was pulled up on the bike in the shade of an elm tree, working traffic on Belleview. I looked to the east and saw a black Lincoln Navigator heading westbound right towards me. I could tell the driver was getting on it, and I made a quick visual estimate that he was going 58 or 59 in a 40. I raised my laser and put the red dot in the scope right on the license plate and pulled the trigger. Bam! 59 mph. *Gotcha.* I pulled the Lincoln over and walked up to the driver's window. When you wear the helmet and the aviator sunglasses and the black leather jacket and boots, you just sort of develop a natural swagger in your walk. You just can't help it because motor cops are *sooo* much cooler than regular cops! I contacted the driver, a young black guy in his twenties. I told him why I stopped him and he said "Aw man! I was almost home, too!" Home? In Cherry Hills? *Not likely.* I asked him where he lived and he pointed into Cherry Hills Farm and said "Right in there, man!" *Sure you do, pal.*

I made up my mind to write him a ticket for lying to me, and I asked him for his paperwork. I looked at his driver's license and sure enough, right there it listed his address as Cherry Hills Farm. I looked at the name and looked at him. It was Champ Bailey, the star cornerback for the Denver Broncos. *Well shut my mouth!* He was pretty cool and we talked for a few minutes about the Broncos chances this fall, and I sent him on his way. I probably could have written him the ticket and sold it on e-bay for a grand. It was also a bit of a wake-up call to myself, a realization that I was starting to pigeon-hole people, to let the Job make me a little too cynical and skeptical. It's something that happens to every cop after a few years, a trap that's all too easy to fall into if you don't watch for it.

On another summer day I was parked on the Highline Canal's entrance to Hampden Avenue shooting laser at the eastbound traffic when a jogger came by. He was mid-thirties, fit, with dark hair, and looking at me curiously. He said "Hey, are you a Cherry Hills cop?" Now it said Cherry Hills Police in block letters right across the fairing of my motor, so I figured this guy wasn't the sharpest knife in the drawer. I just said yes, and he next asked "What are you doing?" Now here I am, sitting on my bike with a laser gun in my hand, so it doesn't take a genius to figure out what I'm doing. I was starting to lose my patience with the stupid question routine, so I just grunted that I was working traffic. He said "You guys do that a lot, huh?" I ignored him, hoping he would take the hint and keep jogging. But he didn't take the hint, and instead commented "Yeah, I hear that's about all you guys do." This guy was starting to get under my skin, but in the interest of public relations I replied "No, we do a lot more than that, but I'm on traffic detail today." But the guy kept it up, saying "Yeah, I heard you guys like, get cats out of trees and help old ladies cross the street." *That's it. I've had enough of this asshole.* I set the laser down and started to get off the bike, saying "Listen jack-off" but the guy suddenly put his hands up and started laughing and said "I'm just kidding! I'm Charlie 30 with the County! I'm just giving you shit!" Charlie 30 was a deputy sheriff who worked this side of Arapahoe County, and I heard his voice on the radio all the time. "You asshole!" I said to him, but I was laughing too. He knew very well what kinds of calls we got, but we still had our professional pride. Maybe we did get cats out of trees and help little old ladies cross the street, but we did it with style.

I got bored with writing traffic tickets all the time, so I came up with a new strategy. Right after roll call I would head out to a couple of different hotspots and write half a dozen tickets, then I was on my own for the next few hours. I would ride the Highline Canal and the many bridle paths and walking trails in the city.

People were always startled to see me, but when they recovered they often flagged me down to say they were glad because they never saw the police out here. Score one for public relations! I liked being on the bike because you weren't tied to the radio and could jump any call that sounded good. Still, we could only ride the motor when there were three of us on duty, which wasn't often enough, so the motor days were only a welcome but infrequent break from my normal patrol duties.

* * *

I was cruising Hampden Avenue in the patrol car late one Saturday night, hoping to pick up a DUI when a light blue minivan caught my eye. The driver was keeping up with the traffic flow just ahead of me, but he was doing the slow drift from one side of his lane to another. Technically, weaving within a lane is a violation of the Model Traffic Code but I was not one of those cops for whom any excuse will do to pull someone over. For my own satisfaction, I want to see a clear violation. The van crossed the white line into the next lane about half the width of his vehicle, then drifted back into his own lane. Okay, that was enough. I pulled in behind him and lit him up with my red and blue lights, and he slowed down but kept going. I blipped the siren and he slowed down some more, and then finally made a right turn onto Sedgwick Drive. Just around the corner he eased to a stop, and I pulled in behind him.

I aimed my spotlight onto his side mirror so he couldn't watch me walk up, because I already thought he was acting squirrelly. When I was just about to the back of his van he poked his head out the window to look for me, squinting his eyes against the bright light, then he gunned the engine and took off down Sedgwick at a high rate of speed. I just stood there and watched him go, laughing to myself. Sedgwick Drive was a big circle, and the only way out was to come right back here to where I was standing. If you're going to run from the police it helps to have at least some idea of where you are.

I called dispatch and told them where I was and what I had, and I requested a cover car to respond to block the entrance. Nate and Matt were the other officers on duty with me, and both of them piped up that they were responding. I walked back to my car and popped the trunk and pulled out the Stop Sticks, the portable tire spikes. They are a really nifty little device that comes folded up in three sections, covered in cardboard so you don't accidently stab yourself and open up an artery. The steel spikes are cone shaped and hollow, and when you see the runaway car approaching, you toss the sticks out into the road (while remaining behind solid cover), the car runs over the spike strip, and the spikes deflate the tires without causing a blowout that could send the car careening out of control. I got the Sticks ready to deploy in case I saw his headlights coming at me from my left, where the other end of the drive came back out. Matt and Nate arrived and I briefed them on the situation, and I had Matt take up a position at the entrance. Since it had been several minutes and the guy hadn't come out yet, I figured he had probably gone to ground somewhere in the neighborhood. I told Nate to go left and I would go right, and we would go in and hunt him down.

I was ghosting through the neighborhood, spotlighting the cul-de-sacs and driveways looking for that blue van. I passed by the big house of Joel Brownstein, one of the pillars of the Denver legal community, and stopped. I backed up, and way back there in Brownstein's driveway, half shaded by the overhanging trees, was the back corner of a blue vehicle. I radioed it in to dispatch, and got out on foot. I am a big officer safety proponent, and that means never driving up into an unknown situation. I didn't know if this guy ran because he was drunk, because he had a warrant, or because he had an axe and a dismembered body in the back of the van. So, I slipped out of my car and using the shadows for concealment I eased up to where the vehicle was. That was it. It was the van I was looking for. *Now, where was that sneaky driver?*

I peered into the semi-darkness scanning for movement. Here's a tactical lesson; what gives people away are shape, shine, color, and movement. Whether you are in a jungle in Vietnam, a desert in Afghanistan, or somewhere above the Arctic Circle, the giveaways are the same. In dim light colors and shapes disappear but the human eye, like that of all predatory species, is highly attuned to detecting even slight movements and soon I saw a little shift in a patch of deeper darkness off to my left front. It was very subtle, just a turn of a head, but I had him. He was crouching next to another car in the driveway, looking back for me. But he was looking in the wrong direction, because I had now moved up to his left. I eased my flashlight and gun up into a two-handed Harries hold and turned on the switch. The bright light lit him up and he jumped to his feet. I yelled *"Police! Freeze!"* and he froze. He stood there, blinking in the bright light. He was a black male, maybe twenty-five, thin but wiry. I ordered him to get down on the ground. He didn't respond but kept peering around and trying to shade the light with his upraised hand so he could see me. I repeated the order, more forcefully this time, and he slowly got down onto his hands and knees. I moved in a little closer, and he suddenly started getting up again. I could tell he'd been around the block a time or two in the legal system because he wasn't afraid of me at all, in fact he was acting quite nonchalant about the whole business. He got to his feet and with a last look he turned his back on me and started walking away, almost casually.

There's a time for talking and there's a time for going hands-on, and I could see that we were now past the talking stage. I moved up behind him and he suddenly broke into a run. He went up and over Brownstein's back yard fence as easily as if he was stepping over a child's toy on the floor, and I went over it after him, with a little less grace and a little more struggle. *The pursuit was on!* While I was running I got on the radio and called out my location and that I was in a foot chase and gave a description of the suspect. It's not easy to talk on the radio while you're bouncing up and down running and jumping fences, but I was hoping they got all of that. Dispatch called a Code Red for me, which means that all other units were to maintain radio silence for the duration of the emergency, unless they were involved.

Matt called out that he was on his way, and cars started to converge from neighboring jurisdictions. Foot chases are always dangerous; you never know when the guy you're chasing is suddenly going to turn and lay in wait for you, and many good officers have been lost during foot chases. In the dark it was doubly dangerous. The chase went on, through back yards and over fences. On his side he had youth and athletic ability. On my side I had stubborn persistence and the paranoia of the people of Cherry Hills. Like most well-to-do upper class people, they lived in fear of the lower classes, the criminal element, like the nobility of France in dread of the peasant uprisings of the French Revolution. Nearly every back yard had motion sensor lights, so although my quarry was faster than me I could follow his movements by watching for the motion sensor lights to pop on ahead of me.

I heard a dog barking furiously in a yard just ahead and a startled yelp from my suspect. The people of Cherry Hills also have a fondness for large guard dogs, and I wondered if the dog had taken a bite. I was smiling at the prospect until I realized I had to go through the same back yard, and I hoped the dog was too focused on my runner to notice me. He wasn't. He was standing at the other end of the fence barking furiously where my suspect had gone over, but when I was only about halfway across the yard he turned his head and saw me coming. He was a big black dog of some breed I didn't recognize, and as soon as he saw me I could read his furry face like a book; *Hey, here comes another one!* and he took off across the yard toward me, barking and growling. I was swatting at him with my flashlight to keep him at bay and yelling to him that I was the police and that he was a bad dog for biting me, but he didn't recognize the good guys from the bad guys. As far as his canine brain was concerned, anyone in his yard was an intruder and therefore a Bad Guy. Luckily he was just a family pet and not a genuine guard dog, and he didn't really try too hard to bite me. His job was just to bark and harass me and get the attention of his masters, and he had done that, so his duty was done. I went over the fence with just a final nip on the leg from him, and the chase resumed.

I was getting tired. I cleared yet another fence, with much huffing and puffing and a lot slower this time, but I damn sure wasn't going to give up and I wasn't going to let him get away if I had to chase him clear to Timbuktu, wherever that is. But first I needed a short break, so I stood in the back yard for a minute to catch my breath. I looked around the neighborhood and I didn't see any more motion lights turning on or dogs barking. In fact it was very, very quiet. I was thinking about which way to go when I suddenly got the uncomfortable feeling I was being watched. I looked around the yard I was in and spied a deep patch of shade, darker than the rest of the yard. It was cast by a big pine tree a few yards away from where I was standing, so I brought my flashlight up to it and pressed the button. The bright light flooded the shady area and right in the middle of it, peering between two branches, I saw two large eyes staring back at me. *Gotcha!* He bolted out from behind the tree toward the far fence, and it was apparent that he was growing tired too, because rather than simply vaulting it like he had been doing he had to climb up each rail now, and as he swung a leg up and over it he turned to look back at me. That look was his undoing. I gave him a blast of pepper spray that caught him full in the face. He was straddling the fence like he was riding a horse, and when the spray caught him he tumbled over onto the far side and I could hear a stream of startled curses and profanity coming from him. I climbed up over the fence and I saw that he was getting to his feet and starting to run again. I shook my head and doggedly set out after him, just telling myself to keep putting one leaden foot in front of the other. We had come clean through the neighborhood and he was running across a front yard toward the street ahead of him. I was thinking *I'll buy you a beer if you just stop already!* I didn't know how much longer I could keep this up.

Just then I saw a wonderful sight. I saw brilliant red and blue lights flashing like a Christmas tree and rapidly approaching from the opposite end of the street. I heard Matt's excited voice come over the radio *"I've got 'em! Coming on scene now!"* My runner must have seen it too, because he just collapsed in the front yard. On the other hand he may not have seen anything because the pepper spray was finally kicking in, and he was rubbing his face and yelling "My eyes! My eyes are burning! Give me water!" Matt came screeching up and jumped out of his car. I had caught my runner at last. I cuffed him and searched him, and called an ambulance to treat him for the pepper spray. When the firemen arrived they ran water over his eyes continually for about ten minutes, while he kept saying "Man, you didn't have to spray me with that shit!" When his eyes stopped burning and weren't so red and puffy I put him in the back of Matt's car to take him to jail, but not before I congratulated him on a hell of a good chase. I thought he earned it. I was always a fast runner and played football and ran track in school, and it remains a point of pride with me that in all my years of law enforcement I never had anybody get away from me in a foot chase.

TWELVE

I WAS CRUISING AROUND on the west side of Cherry Hills one afternoon when I spotted two kids walking down one of the little dirt roads that ran all through this part of the city. They were about nine or ten years old, a boy and a girl, obviously brother and sister, and with matching little freckles and turned-up noses they were two peas in a pod. They looked like they were either lost or had lost something, so I pulled up next to them and rolled the window down. "Hi!" I said "Are you two lost?" The little girl piped up "No, we're not lost but Elvis is!" Now I know that Elvis was even before my time, and I have childhood memories of my Dad sitting in his easy chair listening to the crooning of The King. There were still a lot of people who claimed to see Elvis at gas stations or grocery stores, but they were a lot older and weirder than these kids. "Do you mean Elvis the singer?" I asked. The little girl replied "He doesn't sing, but he does make a lot of noise. He's a donkey." *Oh, okay, that makes sense now.* They explained that Elvis had broken loose from his pen because a section of the fence had been hit by their neighbor's pickup truck and Elvis, apparently being a resourceful little donkey, had taken advantage of the breach in security to escape. Now the kids were trying frantically to find him and bring him home before their parents got back. Well, donkey-wrangling wasn't exactly a part of my normal duties, but I couldn't just leave these cute little kids in their desperate state, and after all I had done stranger things than that on this job. I told the kids to hop in and we'd go look for Elvis together.

We had been driving up and down the little roads for about ten minutes when the girl, who was apparently the spokesperson for the two, shouted out "There he is!" and pointed excitedly. I looked to my left and saw standing in a field a little brownish donkey, contentedly chewing a mouthful of grass and staring at us with sleepy eyes. I stopped the car and got out, with the kids piling out behind me. I asked the girl if she had a rope, but she didn't. I rummaged around in my war bag and found a six foot blue nylon dog leash that was handy not only for catching stray dogs but also for wrapping up the feet of prisoners who tried to kick me. Leash in hand, I started off across the field with the kids in tow. Some people are scared of horses and other large animals, but I was a farm kid and I had a black Appaloosa named Lady when I was growing up (she was not a lady at all, and had a disagreeable streak that was wide and deep) so I wasn't too worried. That was my first mistake. The little donkey continued to chew his grass and stare at me with an unconcerned look on his face. I reached the little four-footed escapee, and he was actually kind of cute and looked a lot like that little donkey in *Shrek,* and I gave him a pat and rubbed him behind the ears, talking to him to make friends and show him I wasn't dangerous. Mistake number two.

I slipped the leash over his head and fastened it, and clucked to him to go. He didn't move. I pulled harder on the leash and said encouragingly "Come on Elvis, let's go home now." Elvis liked it just fine where he was because he dug in his little hooves and wouldn't move. The harder I pulled on the leash the more he squatted on his heels and dug in, until his backside was practically touching the ground and his little front legs were stiff and straight out in front of him. No matter what combination of cajoling, encouraging, threatening, pulling, and tempting him with select bunches of grass I tried to use, Elvis stood firm. I moved around behind him and put my shoulder up against his haunches and pushed. I knew horses would kick, and my own horse nearly connected with me a couple of times with a flying leg, but this little guy's legs were shorter than my own and I wasn't too worried about it. I pushed and shoved to no avail, while Elvis continued stolidly munching his grass. I turned around and put my back against him and dug in my feet and pushed hard using the strength of my legs and back. I felt him give and my expectations soared, but all that happened is that his back feet came up off the ground, so there we were with his back feet dangling a foot off the ground and his rear end up in the air, while his front legs stood rooted and he just stared across the field munching his grass, unconcerned as to the goings-on at his other end. I gave up and stood up, and Elvis's back feet dropped back to the ground. I stood back for a minute puzzling over what to do. I was fiddling with the leash in my hand and that suddenly gave me an idea. With a *swish* and a *smack!* I brought the end of the nylon leash down across his back side. That worked! With a start the donkey jumped forward, then started walking rapidly across the field. *Hurray!* I had him moving.

He was moving alright, but his fast pace was hard to keep up with, and when he broke into a trot it became too much. I was half running, half stumbling across the uneven ground and I was afraid I was going to get dragged down. I had to slow this runaway donkey down. I hauled back on the leash and said "WHOA!" That worked with my horse, but this donkey had apparently never heard this term before because he paid no heed to it. He kept trotting along with his little short donkey legs pumping and his neck straining forward. I pulled back harder, and harder, to no avail. By now I was giving some choice words to Elvis, until I remembered there were children present. I glanced back fearfully and the kids were staring at me with wide eyes. *Oops!* I went with what worked before, and smacked the leash against his flanks while yelling "WHOA Donkey!" It worked. Elvis slowed down, and obediently walked with me across the field toward my car. I smiled to myself, satisfied that

I had shown this little beast of burden who was boss. Mistake number three.

Near the edge of the field a little tree was growing, and Elvis started steering toward it. I tried to head him off and get him back on track, but he kept veering toward that tree. He was very strong for his size, and a strong bullheaded donkey is hard to steer. As we passed close by the tree the donkey suddenly gave me a tremendous shove. I was lifted off my feet and thrown bodily into the tree. Branches jabbed at me and leaves covered my face, but by some miracle I managed to hold onto the leash. I emerged from the tree covered with bits of bark, leaves and dirt, and ready to kill. I started to tell Elvis what I thought of him and his ancestry but caught sight of the kids staring wide-eyed at me again and held my tongue. I yanked on the leash and Elvis, now quite satisfied, walked obediently with me the rest of the way to the car while I muttered curses under my breath and wondered what a Taser would do to a donkey. I got him back to the road and turned him over to the kids. The donkey followed the kids home like a puppy at their heels while I drove slowly behind them still filled with dark thoughts and wounded pride as I stared at the back end of that donkey ahead of me. Suddenly I had to laugh out loud, and Elvis turned his head at the sound, rolling his eyes at me. We got the donkey back home, and the neighbor who had knocked the fence down was already out there repairing it. So we got Elvis safely back in his pen and I said goodbye to the kids, and as I was walking back to my squad car Elvis turned to me and let out a bray like a giant rusty wheel turning. I'm pretty sure he was laughing at me.

* * *

There are some people who treat their dogs like they were children. They dress them up in little sweaters, talk baby talk to them (which is very annoying to everyone around them) and even let them eat off their dinner plates. If police dogs were relatives, they would be Cousin Eddie in *Christmas Vacation,* the slightly deranged one you try to hide from your friends and neighbors, but you still have to accept them because they're family. At Cherry Hills PD we always seemed to end up having police dogs with personality disorders. We had a coal-black German Shepherd named Poker, who bit Pat Weathers right in the butt on a building search, because Pat strayed a little too close to him and he just wanted to bite *somebody.* Despite his injuries, Pat refused to drop his drawers for the female paramedic who showed up, saying he'd just put up with the pain rather than having a bunch of strangers looking at his bare ass. Poker also took the time out while searching for a burglar in a house to pee on a beautiful Italian leather sofa. That cost the department almost the price of a patrol car, and the Chief was loudly calling for Poker's hide to be pegged out on the wall of his office.

Some people are just born psychotic, like Charles Manson, and so are some dogs. Magnum was an oversized black and tan German Shepherd with one notched floppy ear and a crazed look in his eye. John Reynolds was Magnum's handler, and there was just something a little off with that dog, like he had been born with some crossed wires in that brain of his. Magnum had this bizarre trait that he didn't like anybody looking at him. In the squad room he would come and sit near you while you were working on reports, and he would just stare fixedly at you until it would start to bother you and you looked over at him. Then if you looked him in the eye he would take it as a challenge, and he would get this low rumble in his throat and he would stand up and start advancing on you. So everybody swirled around him at roll call, careful not to get too close to him or look directly at him. I felt sorry for Mags, because I figured his mental problems were not his fault.

Magnum got an ear infection once, and when his ears would bother him he would whine and shake his head, which made his big ears flap and hurt more, and if you were anywhere near him he would think *you* did it and would lunge and snap at you. While in a rage from the pain he grabbed a fire extinguisher in his mouth and ripped it right out of its mounting bracket on the wall and started attacking it, biting and snarling. We all jumped up and ran out of the squad room, expecting any second to hear a *BOOM!* when the highly pressurized extinguisher exploded, and to see bits of fur floating back down. John bravely rushed in and fought with Magnum for the extinguisher and he eventually got it away from him, though not without suffering a few bites in the process. Magnum was a little scary to us - and we were his friends. To Bad Guys he was a holy terror.

John and I stopped a drunk driver one night. Some people are happy drunks; you've seen them, getting lit and dancing on the table, or kissing everyone and saying *I love you man!* Others just sit out on the couch and mellow out and talk philosophy over their fourth glass of wine. Then there are the mean drunks. This guy was one of those. He was a big angry construction worker, with a big mouth and the big muscles to back it up. It was just John and I on duty that night, and although neither one of was would ever back down from a scrap, we knew that on this one someone was going to get hurt, probably all three of us.

We were trying to reason with this guy and calm him down, the term now in vogue is "de-escalation", but think back to the times when you have tried to reason with an angry drunk; how successful was that? Since we were getting nowhere and the situation was escalating, John decided to see if perhaps Magnum had anything to contribute to the negotiations. He did.

As soon as that big hundred-pound German Shepherd bounded out of the car the dynamics of the situation perceptibly changed. I told you that Magnum had some wires crossed to begin with, and when he gets amped up they start sparking. Mags took one look at the guy and went ballistic. He wasn't so much barking as he was roaring, snapping his flashing white teeth and straining at the leash with his front feet off the ground to go get this man in front of him. This big guy who was ready to fight us knuckle and skull thirty seconds ago was now a lying face down on the ground whimpering and begging us to put him in the patrol car where he would be safe from this beast.

Magnum served for several years, but he was getting a little long in the tooth and eventually had to take a well-earned retirement. He still wanted to get up and go to work every day, and every day he had to stand at the door and watch while John drove away. Like all cops, retirement didn't sit well with Magnum, and he passed away a few years later. We all took the news with sadness, and Magnum was buried in a place of honor in John's back yard, and when we go to John's house we all still drink one for Mags.

* * *

I have always had a personal and professional interest in mob psychology, in the way that ordinary, law-abiding citizens can suddenly and unexpectedly transform into rock-throwing, window-smashing, looting thugs, then just as suddenly revert to being the kid next door or the girl in the coffee shop on the corner. When I was an MP in the military I took a training course on it, but my interest in the phenomenon actually began through absolutely no efforts of my own. This is how it began...

When I was a young man and a sailor in the United States Navy, I got transferred from San Diego to Virginia Beach. Tough duty, I know, to be transferred from one sun-soaked beachfront paradise to another. All you Army guys shivering in the cold mountains of the DMZ in Korea, I feel for you, brothers. I will lift a margarita for you, from my poolside lounge chair. I wasn't quite *in* Virginia Beach, but it was a short drive. My roommate in the barracks was my bosom buddy Tom McCoy, who I still stay in close touch with today. Tom was a 20 year old farm kid from Kansas, a perfect match for a 22 year old farm kid from Wyoming. We were both young and single, and every weekend after we got off work at the squadron we would head for the coast and the night life. Sometimes we were too drunk or too tired to drive home, and we would either sleep right on the beach or on someone's beach chairs on their back porch. More than once we woke up to being unceremoniously shooed off some indignant person's patio furniture. Then we would drag our butts back to the base for work on Monday.

On one occasion Tom finished up his work early, but I still had a few things to do on my airplane so we agreed that he would just go down to the beach first and I would meet him later on the wide wooden boardwalk that ran along the shoreline, just a few yards from the water. My duties at the squadron took longer than I expected, so I was already late when I rushed back to the barracks. I opened the door and to my surprise there was Tom, sitting on his bed. I asked him what the heck he was doing back here when he was supposed to be down there waiting for me, and he said "Don't go down to the beach, it's crazy down there." "Crazy how?" I asked. It was *always* crazy down there on the weekends. Tom answered "Trust me, you don't want to go down there!" I thought to myself *Whatever* and shrugged it off figuring Tom just didn't really feel like going out tonight. I showered and cleaned the grease off myself, then put on a pastel outfit that resembled something the guys on *Miami Vice* or the band *Wham!* would wear. Hey, it was the height of style back then! Then I went to find my friend Rich Goedel.

Rich was one of those genuine good guys, straight out of one of those black and white 1950's TV shows like *Leave it to Beaver,* or Richie Cunningham from *Happy Days*. He was a real Boy Scout, which made me like him a lot because you just don't see too many people like that, but when girls are your prey for the evening, guys like Rich are not really what you're looking for in a sidekick. Tom was a boyishly handsome rascal with a shock of blonde hair and possessing no morals to speak of, which made him perfect for cruising for chicks. He also had a silver tongue, the gift for gab that I never had. We would be cruising Atlantic and Pacific avenues in a '66 Mustang convertible we occasionally borrowed from a friend of ours, and at a stoplight we'd pull up next to a carload of girls and Tom would lean over and start talking to them, and the next thing you know half of them would be in our car. But Rich was available and Tom was not, so we climbed into his staid grey Chevy Celebrity sedan and headed for the beach.

When we got near the beach I was floored. Tom was right; there were people everywhere, by the thousands, most of them young males in their late teens and early twenties. They were filling the street corners, standing around in groups and knots, crowding the sidewalks, and the streets were jammed with cars pumping out a thumping bass. We didn't know it at the time, but every summer all the fraternities from colleges up and down the East Coast would gather for one huge weekend celebration in Virginia Beach, called Greekfest. The locals knew all about it and stayed away, because trouble erupted all too frequently but Rich and I, displaying a stupefying lack of awareness of the tactical situation, found a place to park and started walking around to see what was happening.

We walked around like tourists, with our eyes bugging out and gawking and pointing things out to each other. The police presence was heavy, because they had been in this rodeo before and knew what was coming. We stood on the sidewalk and watched while a police officer ordered a carload of young men to get back in their vehicle and get moving. They had seen a group of their friends going the other way, so both groups just stopped their cars right there in the middle of the street and got out to talk. That of course had the effect of jamming up traffic even worse than it already was, and the group just ignored the officer who was telling them to get back in their cars so he could get traffic moving again. A K-9 officer with a big Doberman on a leash arrived, and the two groups quickly thought better of it and climbed back into their cars and the traffic resumed its crawl.

That should have been a warning to us that things were starting to go downhill but we paid no heed. As Colonel Jeff Cooper (God rest his warrior soul) would say, we were fully in Condition White. If you don't know what that means, Google it. We had walked further down the street by now, and after a while it was beginning to seep into even our oblivious heads that the mood of the crowd was starting to get ugly, as booze and a restless energy did their work. A few minutes later we saw a guy in the street getting the crap kicked out of him by a circle of about a dozen males surrounding him. The crowd was by now getting openly hostile and looking for their next victim. Rich and I quickly ducked into a storefront alcove to get out of sight. Then someone threw one of those portable newspaper stands through a store window, and that was it, the little spark that fueled a firestorm. The riot was on. The crowd surged in and began smashing storefront windows and looting the shelves, while others smashed car windows, passersby, and each other. I turned to Rich and shouted that we had to get out of here, and we turned and made our way quickly through the crowd, ducking into doorways, dodging flying bottles, running into people, and just staying low. I got shoved a lot and somebody hit me with a punch, but I just kept moving. Then somebody started a fire, and the other rioters must have thought that was a great idea because within minutes there were several fires burning, and the wail of sirens filled the air as police and fire units moved in en masse.

Rich and I eventually made our way out of the madness and down to the quiet calm of the water. Along with us were a fair number of other people, and we all stood in silence on the sand and watched the city tear itself apart. Eventually we walked up the beach back to the parking lot, where to our amazement Rich's car was undamaged. We decided to leave before things

Michael Miller

got worse, and turned our car west for the safety of the Navy base, guarded by burly Marines with rifles.

That was Labor Day weekend, 1989, and the worst rioting in the history of the state of Virginia. Entire blocks of stores were looted and burned out, and dozens of people were injured and several were shot. It took police two days to restore law and order in the city, and the governor of Virginia declared a state of emergency and sent in the National Guard, vowing that Greekfest would never again be held in his state. To this day, I don't like being in crowds of people. Wherever I go, I sit facing the door and always look to see where the exits are. I like the Broncos, but I don't like going to the stadium to watch them play, and when I go out with my family I always have the comforting heft of a pistol and a spare mag or two with me. The way the anonymity of the crowd releases the ugly beast in people is both fascinating and frightening. I saw it magnified then, and I have seen it many times on a smaller scale since.

There are those who believe that people are basically good and those who believe that people are basically bad. I couldn't tell you who's right, but I can tell you that there is a significant portion of our fellow human beings who obey the law only because they have to, only because they fear the consequences. I'm not just talking about the known criminals here; I'm talking about the guy wearing a suit and sitting in the next cubicle over from yours, or sitting next to you at the stoplight on the morning commute. For those people, the beast is just below the surface, waiting for the enforcers of the law to take the day off. You've no doubt heard the expression "the thin blue line" but you never realize just what that means until it's gone. It doesn't mean the line between the police and the public, us and them. It means that the men and women who stand in front of the mirror each day and pin on the badge, and hoist up the heavy gunbelt, are the all-too-thin line literally standing between law and order and anarchy and chaos.

* * *

I got a call one day that every officer hates to get. A woman called dispatch and reported that she had been walking on a path near her home when a Hispanic male walking the other way suddenly grabbed her, forced her down to the ground and raped her. There is no other crime except for child abuse that makes a police officer's blood boil, and makes us want to find the perpetrator and just pray that he resists arrest and allows the officers to mete out some street justice. But they never do, because they're cowards at heart preying on the weak and the helpless. The victims of rape can be very uncomfortable and difficult for a male officer to deal with. Maybe it's because male police officers tend to have old-fashioned values where women are to be protected, and we have a sense that somehow we failed them because we weren't there. Or maybe it's because men are fixers by nature, and when you have a rape victim there is nothing you can do to fix it. So in either case you feel helpless and sort of useless. I went to the area and located the victim, who had remained at the scene after calling 9-1-1 on her cell phone. I saw her ahead on the walking path waiting for me, and I was going over in my head how to best handle the situation and the scene. I walked up to her, expecting her to be crying and distraught, but found her completely calm. This took me aback, but then I reminded myself that crime victims, even of terrible crimes, react in many ways. Some scream, some cry, some go into a rage, some take it out on us, and some seem calm and collected.

We made introductions and I told her an ambulance was on the way. She was a slender and plain woman, mid-thirties I guessed, with straight brown hair to the shoulder. Since she was acting calm and rational, as if we were discussing the weather, I did the same. I told her to describe the attack. We were standing in a field, on a dirt path that was often used by people out riding their horses, and in this neighborhood all the homes were on acreage so it had a very rural, out in the country feel. The victim said she had been out for a walk on this path when she saw a Hispanic male walking toward her from the other way. She pointed off to the east, and as I looked over to where she was pointing I saw a few houses under construction a couple hundred yards away. There were probably thirty or forty guys on the work crews, and many of them would no doubt be Hispanic. I could see that he might have easily snuck away from the job site and come down here in just a minute or two, and been back before anyone even noticed he was gone. The description of the suspect had already been aired and other cars were checking the area for him, so I radioed Angel and Joe to check out the construction site. They affirmed, and I turned back to the victim. She said he was a young guy, maybe twenty or so, wearing a white t-shirt and blue jeans. Well, that described pretty much half of all the Hispanic male construction and landscape workers in the city, but maybe I could elicit more details out of her as the interview went on.

She said as they approached each other she could see him looking her up and down and it made her very uncomfortable. As they passed each other he suddenly grabbed her and pushed her down onto the ground. She struggled and screamed for help, but he was too strong for her. He pulled her dress up above her waist and pulled down his pants and raped her. As she was talking about him pulling up her dress, I looked at what she was wearing, and something struck me as odd. She had on a peach colored sun dress that came to just above the knee, and a matching wide-brimmed floppy sun hat. What was odd was that there wasn't a wrinkle or a smudge of dirt on it. I asked her to show me exactly where the attack happened, and she turned around and walked to the right of where we were standing. That movement also showed me what I wanted to see, namely the back of her dress. Not a wrinkle, not a smudge. Same with the floppy hat. I told myself the hat could have flown off or gotten knocked off and that could explain why it was clean, but the area she showed me where he pulled her down was soft dirt and weeds and grass. I was having a hard time seeing how her dress didn't have a single streak, spot, or smudge of dirt or grass on it. But stranger things have happened, so I continued the interview.

I asked her if she had screamed for help and she said "Oh yes, as loud as I could. But nobody ever came." I looked over to the construction site, probably two hundred yards away. With the noise of hammering and sawing…it was entirely possible that they didn't hear her. I told her I had to take some photos of the scene, but she asked if I could do that later, because she had already called her husband and he was on his way home and he would be very upset. I looked at the scene, and there was nothing immediately apparent of evidentiary value, in fact you could not even tell there had been any sort of a struggle there at all.

I took her home and we waited in the kitchen for her husband to arrive. I asked her several more questions, and gave dispatch our new location. She insisted she did not want an ambulance or to go to the hospital, and I tried to explain to her the need for what we call a SANE Kit, to collect evidence, but she was adamant. The ambulance crews were more experienced at this, so I decided to let the argument die until they got here. While we waited I digested what I knew so far. The more I thought about, the more I didn't like it. Call it cop instinct, but it just didn't feel right. I heard the gravel crunch in the driveway and the hum of the garage door opener. The victim turned to me and said "Do you want to tell him or should I?" I was confused for a moment, and said "But I thought you had already called him, didn't you?" She said she called him and told him it was an emergency and that he needed to come home right away, but she didn't tell him why. I sure as hell didn't want to break it to a guy that his wife had just been raped, but if she didn't want to do it I would.

I didn't get to answer her question before the door suddenly opened and her husband walked in. He was a good bit older than her, maybe by twenty years, and he had graying hair and a hurried disheveled appearance about him, as if he was always too busy to straighten his tie or comb his hair. He came striding into the room and paused when he saw me sitting at the table. I stood up and he said "What's going on here?" as he looked from me to her. I looked at her to see what she wanted to do, and she looked at her husband and said simply "I was raped." I expected her husband to go into hysterics, with shock and disbelief, scream with rage, or rush to her side to comfort her. That's what I had seen other husbands do and God forbid if it ever happened to my wife I imagined that's what I would do. Instead, he simply stood there and said "Oh really?" She nodded her head and repeated "Yes, I was raped." He turned and walked over to the sink and turned on the water, while asking "And where did this happen?" She said "Out on the bridle path". He pushed the lever on the soap dispenser and started washing his hands, and said "With all those people around?" as matter-of-factly as if they were talking about a stray dog she had seen.

I was watching the exchange up to this point and thinking *What the hell is going on here?* This was not going at all like I had expected it to. Something struck me then about the *way* she had told him she was raped. Without any shame, embarrassment, or anger. She had said it almost triumphantly, with her chin up and forward, almost an in-your-face way. I was now starting to believe this woman was fabricating the whole thing, making it up to somehow and for some mysterious reason get to her husband. All the pieces I had seen so far; the clean and pressed dress and hat, the calm demeanor, the refusal of medical attention, the lack of ground disturbance at the site of the attack, this bizarre exchange with her husband, it all fit better with the theory that she was fabricating it for some personal reason, than with a real rape.

I knew I was in dangerous waters. The last thing you want to do is accuse a woman of making a false report of rape. For one thing, despite all the evidence I was seeing, she might actually have been raped, and for the police to then accuse her of lying would be a double injustice to her. Second, if you made the accusation and you were wrong, or even if you were right, you would be crucified by victim's rights groups, the media, and your own Department. It could actually mean the end of your career. You better be 100% right and be able to prove it before you even drop the mere suggestion that a victim was lying. So after a quick mental assessment of the dangers I planned to just ride this out, make the reports, and let it go down in the books and she and her husband could work out whatever bizarre personal problems they were having. But Fate was not going to let that happen.

Joe Q suddenly came up on the air and said he was out with a possible suspect. *Damn!* This just got a lot more complicated. He radioed in that he was detaining a Hispanic male matching the description, at a bus stop on University Blvd. about two miles north of where we were. I told her to come with me, and the husband started to get up but I told him to stay put, he couldn't go on this. I was forming a plan in my head and I didn't want him there screwing it up. If he was in the car with us, there was no telling what she would do or say to get to him.

I drove her up in my patrol car to where Joe was waiting, and on the way I ventured some some casual, open-ended questions about her husband. She immediately jumped on the subject, and bitterly complained about how much her husband worked and was never at home, and how things used to be so much better between them. I next switched to questioning her about what the suspect looked like and what he was wearing. She stuck to her vague, generalized description, even as I zeroed in on my questioning. Did he speak English? Yes. Did he have an accent? Um, I think so. What did his teeth look like? White, yellow, dirty, caps, what? Um…I don't remember. Did he have any tattoos or scars that you could see? Um…I don't remember. Did he have any facial hair? Clean shaven, goatee, beard? Um… maybe but I'm not sure. The more questions I asked, always in a nice, casual way, the more she squirmed in her seat and looked away from me out the window and retreated into "I don't remember", to the point she was actually turning away in the seat so her back was turned to me. This had happened just thirty minutes ago. By the time we got to where Joe was detaining the suspect, I knew beyond any doubt she was full of it. She had not been raped. Not today, at least. For whatever reason, whatever weird relationship thing she had going on with her husband, she had made this up to get to him, to get a rise out of him, to get him to pay attention to her. How far would she go with this game, this desperate bid to get her husband to notice her? Would she send an innocent man to prison for rape to make her point?

We arrived at the bus stop and Joe marched him out, a scared-looking young Hispanic guy in handcuffs, not knowing what was going on and terrified of what might happen to him. I knew that if she said it was him, he was done for. His life was over. I knew that for many prosecutors the actual guilt or innocence of the accused was often merely an academic question that didn't really affect their day to day work. My own experiences with some of them were that as far as they were concerned there was no such thing as a wrongly accused man. They would bury this guy, and the white jury from this area would see a young Mexican male, probably an illegal immigrant to boot, accused of raping a white woman, and she would tearfully testify to what he had done to her, and they would pound the nails in his coffin. All because he pulled a white t-shirt and blue jeans out of the hamper this morning.

I pulled the car up in front of him, and I turned to her and said "Look, if you are not *one hundred percent* certain that this is him, do not say it was, you understand?" She looked at him for a long moment, standing there just five feet from the hood of my car, and I could see his scared round eyes and his legs were shaking. I turned to look at her and I could see the mental struggle going on in her head, as she considered whether her conscience would let her sacrifice this kid. She said "Um…I'm not" and she didn't get another word out before I got on the radio and said "Negative. It's not him" and threw the car into reverse. Neither of us said a single word all the way back to her house. We both knew the score here. When we were waiting there for that long moment while she looked at him, I had told myself if she said it was him, that I would testify for the defense. It would cost me my job, but I had to do it. I could not let an innocent man go to prison to solve some rich bitch's problems with her marriage. While I was en route the detective sergeant called me and said she wanted a meet. I dropped the girl off at her house, and she got out and shut the door and walked away without a word. I knew it was pointless to try to charge her with false reporting. Not only would it never fly, it would rebound on me like a ton of crap.

I left her house and went to meet with the detective sergeant and Angel back at the construction site. The three of us had a powwow in the street, and the detective told me to start rounding up the construction workers and bringing them to the station for questioning. I breathed out a sigh, then started to tell her about what I had seen, that I thought she might be lying, and why I thought that. As soon as the word "lying" came out of my mouth you would have thought I just accused their mothers of being Colfax hookers, because they both lit into me with a vengeance. I was catching it from both sides, with the detective and Angel both poking me in the chest and shaking their fingers at me and saying that it was just like a man to say a woman would lie about something like that. "Next you're going to say she was asking for it because of the way she was dressed!" they railed. You see what I mean when I say this is treading dangerous waters? People get so emotionally charged up about it that reason, logic, and good basic police work can just fly right out the window.

I weathered the storm for about five minutes, until they ran out of steam and stood there glaring at me in feminine indignation and catching their breath. I started to speak again but the detective immediately shut me down, and told me I was off the case because I would only make it worse, and *how dare I* question a rape victim?! and then they were off on another rant against me and all men. Thankfully, this one was shorter, and ended with the detective sergeant telling me to go disappear somewhere out of her sight, and she sent Angel up to the house to finish interviewing the victim. Angel shot me a look filled with daggers, and I slunk away back to my patrol car. I knew going into it that if I said a rape victim was lying that the whole world would stack up against me, but on the other hand I could not let her later just accuse a different innocent man. Sometimes you're damned if you do and damned if you don't, and you just have to accept it and roll with it.

A few hours later Angel called me on the radio and wanted a meet. *Oh, Great!* I figured she had just finished talking to the victim and was all fired up again and ready to deliver another tirade against me. I pulled up car to car with her in a church parking lot and prepared for the verbal assault. To my surprise, Angel said the victim was full of it. She said that while she was interviewing her the victim didn't want to talk about the attack at all, just about how mad she was at her husband for ignoring her for years. Angel kept trying to steer her back to the details of the attack, but she didn't want to go there. She only wanted to talk about her husband. At one point she leaned in toward Angel and said conspiratorially "Maybe *now* he'll pay attention to me!" Angel apologized to me, which was gracious of her, and I suggested we go talk to the detective together. Angel thought about that for a minute and said "Maybe you better stay out of it. I'll go talk to her." Thank God. Staying out of it was exactly where I wanted to be.

We both knew it was futile to try to bring false reporting charges. How do you prove that a crime *didn't* happen? It was almost impossible, and considering the political and emotional firestorm that could result if this hit the media, we decided to just file it and forget it, and let this lady and her husband find their own way to work out their issues. I drove away thinking about what depths of desperation people will sink to just to get their wife or husband to look at them the way they used to, with the old fire and desire in their hearts and in their loins. I had seen it so many times it was almost a cliché. When couples are young they live on dreams and sex and cheap Chinese takeout, and they think someday when they've got careers and a family then things will be perfect. Then when you get those things they consume you, until you forget what you are doing them for. Sometimes the perfect days *are* those early days. If there is one thing that I learned from spending many years around the rich and famous it is that money can't buy you either love or happiness. Those things can only come for free.

PART THREE

THIRTEEN

"Here's a rule I recommend. Never practice two vices at once."
- Tallulah Bankhead

One morning we got some shocking news. Tony Trujillo was leaving. *Not Tony!* Tony was one of the most well-liked guys in the whole Department, and we all button-holed him about why he was leaving. He had secretly put in his application to go to the Denver Police Department, and he didn't tell anyone because he didn't want the Chief and the Captain to find out. Denver had given him the call, and so he put in his resignation notice at Cherry Hills. For some unknown reason, the Chief and the Captain had it in for Tony right from the start. If you were on their bad side, everything you did was wrong. If you were on their good side, you could do no wrong. Tony was never on their good side. They rode him mercilessly about his paperwork, his decision making on calls, his public relations, the way he parked the car, everything. I didn't get it. Tony was just one of those all-around great guys that *everybody* got along with. He was very much like Joey Tribiani from *Friends*. He was always happy, always had a great attitude, the citizens liked him, and I never heard a complaining word come out of his mouth. But for whatever reason, as far as the brass was concerned, he was a bad seed and needed to be pruned.

The last straw for Tony came on a burglary in progress call. He and Matt got dispatched to a frantic call from a homeowner that someone was breaking in through her back door. Tony and Matt hit the lights and sirens and raced up to the house. They pulled their cars onto a bike path that bordered the main road, pulled their guns, and raced in to save the day. It turned out the "burglar" was only one of the kids trying to get in the back door, and everyone breathed a collective sigh of relief. Tony and Matt laughed it off and went back to their cars. They were soon called into the station, however, behind the closed door of the Chief's office.

I wasn't there so I only heard about it the next day, but the officers who were in the squad room said they could hear the Chief and the Captain yelling at them for a solid half hour. Why? Because they used poor tactics? Because they drew down on a kid and scared the crap out of him? Because they were rude and insensitive to the homeowner? No. No to all of them. They were getting yelled at because they parked on the bike path. The Chief told them "You were denying the residents of this city the use of the bike path. That shows very poor judgment and very poor community relations. I expect much better performance out of my officers than that." Matt and Tony reminded the Chief and the Captain that they were on a burglary, *in progress*, with the homeowner stating someone was breaking in through her back door, at that *very moment*. "Irrelevant" came the response. You were blocking the bike path and you will be punished. They each got written reprimands placed in their files, and Tony knew then that no matter what he did he could never take that target off his back, so he started looking for someplace else to go.

So, we all said a sad goodbye to Tony and wished him well at DPD. There were only seventeen of us on patrol and we were a tight-knit group, and we missed him. I had been with the Department over eight years now, and a lot of the people that I started with were gone or going. I was considered one of "the old guys" now, and at thirty five I was starting to feel like an old guy some nights. Matt and I started talking a lot at this time about leaving Cherry Hills. We had many long debates about it over coffee at work, and over backyard hot dogs and hamburgers at our houses, as we weighed the pros and cons. When we became cops all those years ago we had an idea in our heads of what it would be like, and writing traffic tickets and shagging alarms every day was not what we had in mind for our careers. Being a cop at Cherry Hills was easy, not usually dangerous (for which reason our wives loved it), we got paid well, and we had good friends here. For all those reasons, I wasn't ready to go. Matt was a little more restless about it than I was, but he wasn't really ready either. It was just an idea, hanging out there on the horizon. Matt bid my team regularly now, and he had joined the Motor Unit in the class after mine, so we were like Mutt and Jeff these days, although we preferred to think of ourselves like Riggs and Murtaugh, or Starsky and Hutch. Our wives and kids had also become close friends over the years as well. We played off each other's strengths and weaknesses, because I was more serious and technical minded while Matt was more of a people person. He was always one for playing practical jokes, and it was during this time that Matt acquired his nickname "Boom Boom." I can't tell you why, because the statute of limitations might not have run out yet.

On slow nights we tended to wax philosophical. Maybe you've heard of philosopher-kings, or warrior-monks in the old days? Well how about philosopher-cops? About three in the morning when your brain is only half awake you tend to think you're wise and deep, when in reality you're just punchy and sleep-deprived. In any case, one night we found ourselves once again sitting on the bench out back of the station by the pond, this time discussing the nature of God, and we came to the conclusion that Heaven simply *must* be different for everyone. I think it was Dante who wrote that the mind can make a hell of heaven or a heaven of hell. So we looked at the people we worked with and decided what Heaven would be like for each of them. Joe Q loved boating and his dearly departed dog Reno, so we figured his heaven would be zooming around on a pristine lake in his boat, reunited with his dog in the seat next to him, tongues happily flapping in the breeze and water spray. Tom L. was a pack-rat, and on trash day he would actually dig through the trash cans the rich people put out, placing televisions, dishes, and furniture in the trunk of his patrol car. He found a diamond ring once, and actually rang the lady's doorbell to give it to back to her, figuring it must have been thrown out by mistake, but the lady told him it was no mistake because that no-good cheating lying double-crossing skunk had screwed his secretary for the last time! So we figured Tom's heaven would be an endless line of trash cans, each one containing something marvelous. Jody's would be to own his own Harley shop where all the sales girls and mechanics were biker babes in black leather. On cold winter days when our breath was coming out in clouds Matt would always tell us "It's 85 in Maui" and he was always talking about Hawaii, so his Heaven would be a beautiful beach house with island girls rubbing suntan lotion on him and feeding him grapes all day. And me? Well that biblical description of streets of gold didn't do much for me, so being a country boy I figured Heaven would be a big ranch house in a beautiful green wooded valley, with a creek out front and where all the ranch hands would be cowgirls in chaps and Stetsons.

* * *

Matt and I had an alarm call in the wee hours of a morning, a burglar alarm originating from a back door. The address was a castle-like structure, on an estate of several acres with the mansion house reached by a long curving driveway, and the entire place was surrounded by a tall metal fence. The security was impressive, but what was *really* important to us and to potential burglars were the three massive black and tan Rottweilers that constantly patrolled the grounds, and the signs placed every few yards saying WARNING! Trained Guard Dogs Will Attack! As we turned the corner into the neighborhood we cut our lights and cruised slowly up near the house. We got out and walked quietly up to the gate, and we stood watching and listening for several minutes, for some sign of the dogs. I called softly *"Here Killer! Fresh meat at the gate!"*

I expected to hear a rush of feet and ferocious growls, but there was only an empty, ominous silence. I turned to Matt and whispered "Maybe they're on vacation" to which he whispered back "Yeah, and maybe Cujo and his brothers are ten feet away lying in the grass waiting for two stupid cops to hop this gate so they can eat us!" *Good point.* In the end we decided not to risk the unknown dangers lurking in the dark, and we walked around the perimeter of the fence spotlighting as much of the house and grounds as we could see. We didn't see anything out of order, nor any sign of the guard dogs either. I suggested again that maybe we should hop the fence and take a closer look. I grew up around dogs, and my dad was always sending me out to shoo away the dogs that were constantly trying to catch our chickens. I knew from experience that even dogs that stand their ground and growl and look fierce are almost always just putting on a show and will quickly fold and run when they see the show isn't working, so I was willing to take more chances with dogs than the other officers were. "But Mikey" Matt reasoned "these aren't your average dogs. These are trained killers, Rambo with teeth, and there's *three* of them. They're going to pull you apart like a big blue gummy bear and I'm just going to stand here at the gate and watch because I'm not stupid enough to go in there!" *All good points.* In the end we decided to call it good and pack it in, and if any burglar had gone in there we'd recover his body in the morning.

The next night I went to work, changed out in the locker room, and went to my mailbox for the nightly memo from the Captain. Instead of a memo there was a sticky note saying the Chief wanted to see me in the morning, so stick around after shift. When your boss leaves you a note like that it's never because you did something good, so I thought back to what we had done over the last few days and I couldn't think of anything that was bad or even questionable. Later on, I asked Matt over coffee and he thought for a minute and said no, he couldn't think of anything we'd done lately either, so I just put it out of my head and finished my shift. At seven the next morning, when my shift was supposed to end, I sat around in the squad room waiting until the Chief arrived. Everyone was razzing me about being in trouble, and I knew I was, I just didn't know what for yet but I figured it had to be something minor.

Les Langford had recently retired, and Charlie Bates had been promoted. When Chief Bates arrived at eight he called me into his office. "Close the door" he said. When I sat down he asked me to tell him about the burglar alarm call up on Lynn Road. I told him about it and he said that he got a call from the owner this morning, and the owner was very upset because there had been an actual break-in and some stuff had been stolen. "Why didn't you go in?" he said. Now I knew what this was all about. Monday morning quarterback session. Wonderful. I told him about the dogs, and he said that lots of people have dogs and that was no reason not to go in. I asked him if he had seen these dogs, or driven by the property and seen the warning signs on the fence. He said he had not, and then we began a long exchange of "you should have done this", followed by my explanation of why I did not, followed by his rejection of my explanation.

If there is one thing I cannot stand, it is the armchair generals, the Monday morning quarterbacks. People who work in nice offices in the safe light of day, tapping on their keyboards and shuffling reports and going to lunch with the secretaries, and whose biggest danger is getting a paper cut or spilling hot coffee on themselves, yet who have the nerve to sit in judgment on the people who are actually out there doing the job, making decisions on the scene, and who have the added danger of being ground into puppy chow by three very large, very aggressive trained killers. The desk-drivers and paper-pushers have the luxury of reading and re-reading the reports, taking the Policy and Procedures Manual down off the shelf and flipping through it, and holding meetings to discuss it all for hours before deciding the officer made the wrong decision in the moments or sometimes seconds he had on the scene. Oversight is necessary of course, but if the officer's decision on the scene is a reasonable one under the circumstances, they should be given the benefit of the doubt. What makes it more irksome is that it is all outcome-based. If the house had not been burglarized, we wouldn't be having this conversation. On the other hand, as I pointed out to the Chief, if I had gone over the fence and been attacked by the dogs and I had been forced to shoot them to save my own life then the owner would be complaining about *that* and suing us as well. Damned if I do, damned if I don't. Just another day on The Job. Oh, and the burglary? Turns out it was someone who knew them and knew they would be on vacation and the dogs would be boarded while they were gone.

Not all the animals that caused me problems were of the fanged Cujo variety, however. One of my favorite guys I worked with was Jason McGurren. I always liked working with people who were dedicated to the getting the job done but at the same time could laugh at themselves and others. Jason was that kind of guy. He was a "gun guy" and a history buff like me, so we could down a pizza while talking about Rommel versus Montgomery in North Africa, or the relative merits of the Remington Model 700 versus the Winchester Model 70. We had more than ample opportunities to laugh at ourselves on an unusual call we got on the day shift. A distressed resident called and said that, responding to a call of nature, she had entered her bathroom and lowered her skivvies and started to sit down, when she felt something *touch* her bare backside. She screamed and leaped away, and turned around just in time to see an equally terrified squirrel go ballistic trying to find a way out and escape from the Giant Screaming Woman. Its running and chattering scared the woman half to death and she ran out of the bathroom while pulling up her pants and slammed the door, trapping the fresh rodent inside. Then like every else who wasn't sure what to do, she called us.

Jason and I knocked on the front door and a harried looking middle-aged woman answered. "Oh Thank God you're here!" she said breathlessly, motioning us inside. She led us quickly to the bathroom door and whispered "He's in *there!*" Normally, we just open the door and whisk the rodent out with a broom, but as the bathroom was too far from the front door I didn't think that would work. He might run up the stairs or get into the pantry and make the extraction more complicated. So I simply asked her to get me a big Tupperware bowl. She looked dubiously at me, but I told her *"Trust me, we're trained professionals, ma'am"* so she brought me a big one. I took it and told the lady to stand back, as Jason and I cautiously, silently approached and opened the door. We entered the bathroom and noticed right away that it was about the size of a middle-class home's bedroom, and secondly that there was no sign of the squirrel. We split up and did a grid search. Nothing. We opened cabinets and drawers and looked under the sink. Nothing. We stood there, perplexed, and I was looking at the toilet where it all started and Jason caught my gaze and said "You don't think he went down *there*, do you? Like those alligators everyone says lives in the sewers in New York?" I wasn't thinking that, but it gave me an idea. I went over to it and got down on my hands and knees and peered up behind the bowl. There, with big frightened round eyes, was the squirrel.

He was huddled up under there, with twitching bushy tail, and how he was hanging on to the porcelain I don't know. We debated ways to get him out of there, and tried various methods. First I tried to fit the Tupperware bowl underneath him and sweep him into it with a broom I obtained from the lady of the house, but that didn't work. Next I tried the more direct approach of just pushing him off his perch. This tactic only produced an outburst of indignant chattering and biting at the broom. Then Jason, who was not an animal lover and was losing his patience, said "Just jab him with your baton! He'll move!" I thought that sounded reasonable, so I pulled out my black hickory baton (I never liked the newfangled polycarbonate or metal nightsticks - call me old fashioned) and began gently pushing the squirrel out. "Come on, *give him the stick!*" Jason shouted. I pulled the baton back, drew a breath and apologized in advance to the squirrel, and gave him a good jab.

The squirrel exploded out from behind the toilet and immediately went into a full-blown rodent meltdown, flying around the bathroom at maximum warp and scattering everything in its path in its desperate flight, while Jason and I tried in vain to catch him. He leaped through the air and landed on the counter and sent the dish of little soaps scattering with a crash along with some pictures and candles. Next he tried to run up the towel rack and scattered the towels and all the while me and Jason were laughing our asses off, so much that we couldn't concentrate on catching the little bandit. I don't know what the lady standing outside must have been thinking. Finally the squirrel saw the mirror and, thinking it was another room, leaped for it. He was probably thinking "I've done it! Escape! Hey look there's another squirrel coming right towards me!" right before he crashed headfirst into the mirror and knocked himself senseless. Then I clapped the Tupperware bowl over him. He was caught! I closed the lid and we opened the bathroom door, to see the woman standing there with a look of deep puzzlement and concern on her face. I told her not to worry, we would take him to a nearby park and release him. She liked this idea, but no sooner had we stepped out onto the front porch, with many thanks from the lady of the house, when the alert tone blared over our portable radios. "310 and 311 copy a physical domestic." That was us. I told the lady *"Sorry, we gotta go!"* The best I could do was to take the squirrel to the end of the driveway and open the lid. He bounded out like he was shot from a cannon and disappeared up the nearest tall tree. I told the lady not to worry, he wouldn't be back. But just to be on the safe side, look before you squat.

FOURTEEN

IN MARCH 2003, THE DENVER AREA GOT SOCKED with the Storm of the Century. The mother of all blizzards roared in overnight and buried the city under a deep blanket of snow. It was the heaviest snowfall in a hundred years, and the second snowiest in the history of the city. The entire metro area shut down for nearly a week; airports, highways, bus stations, gas stations, grocery stores, everything in a bustling city of three million came to a slow, wet, grinding halt. Of course the weatherman said it was going to be a light snow, not to worry, so the command staff at the police department decided to go with "standard patrol staffing", which in real terms meant "Mike and Matt." We arrived for work on the graveyard shift, and a light pretty snow was falling. Soon the trees and the streets were covered with a soft white blanket. It was beautiful, like a Christmas postcard. The snow kept on falling however, faster and heavier all the time. Soon there were several inches on the ground, then quickly rising to more than a foot.

I was driving Car 6, my Ford Explorer, and I was getting around okay in four wheel drive, but Matt was driving a Crown Vic and even though the sheer mass and weight of the car kept it moving, if he stopped he got stuck and would give me a call on the radio "Hey Sarge, a little help here?" and "Mikey, I need a push! I'm spinnin' my wheels over here on Mansfield!" Finally, I told him to just park the sled and get into the Animal Control truck. He was grumbling about it, because no self-respecting cop wants to be driving around doing police work in the dog-catcher truck. It would be like having to drive your daughter's pink Barbie Corvette electric toy car to the office. We started getting worried when the snow in the parking lot passed our knees and rose to mid-thigh. Matt had a Mitsubishi Galant and by morning all we could see of it was a piece of the side view mirror sticking out of a hill of snow. Sometime during the night the roof of our covered patio out behind the station, where we had our midnight Coke and Philosophy sessions, collapsed under the weight of the heavy wet snow. When the grey light of dawn broke, the familiar city we had been patrolling for years was gone, replaced by a white moonscape, like the ice planet Hoth in *Star Wars V: The Empire Strikes Back*. In the early dawn, before all the cars and the people woke up, it was eerie and beautiful. I saw a fox running lightly over the crusted snow, looking for mice that would show up brown against the white background.

During the long cold night we didn't get many calls, but we got a few. We pushed several cars that were stuck, and helped a few people get out of or into their driveways. The real trouble began in the morning when people were trying to get to work. I had called the Public Works guys out about three in the morning, and they had been hard at work clearing the main roads. We had three major highways running through the city; Belleview Avenue, running east and west on the south side, University Blvd running north and south right through the middle, and Hampden Avenue running east and west spanning the north side. All three highways were gridlocked, with long lines of cars spinning their wheels and sliding and honking and flipping each other the bird, and no one could tell where any of the lane lines were so cars were all over the place. Jody Sansing had a big Dodge Ram pickup so he made it in to work, but nobody else did. Jody was one of those guys that would make it in to work if he had to go through hell or high water. I've seen him come into work when he was so sick he laid on the bathroom floor for half the shift puking his guts out. It was partly because he was just that kind of a guy, and partly because he knew that if he didn't make it in, somebody else would have to stay over and cover his shift, and he simply would not let his fellow officers down. So the three of us went out to do what we could to get everything moving.

I pushed so many cars up hills and out of traffic that I lost count. The hills were icy and most of the cars just couldn't get any traction so they would sit unmoving with their wheels spinning. I would start at the front of the line and push one up, then go back for the next one, and the next one until I had the whole line moving in a disjointed automotive symphony. Sometimes with light little cars that couldn't even muster the traction to get going on level ground we just had to say "Sorry pal, but you're blocking traffic and your car's gotta go" and then we would just push their car off to the side of the road so other traffic could get by. *Keep it movin'.* One pompous ass in a nice pearl white Lexus was having trouble making it up the hill on University. His car was rear-drive and his back tires were just spinning. I pulled up behind him in my SUV and got out to talk to him, and I told him I could ease up behind him and push him up the hill. He glanced at my Ford with such a look of haughty disdain, as if I had suggested he sit down for dinner with homeless people, and said "You're not touching my Lexus with *that!*" *Oh, a wise guy, eh?*

My patience had worn pretty thin by this point, so I said to him "I'm not *asking* you pal, I'm *telling* you! Either I push you up the hill or I push you over into the gutter, but either way I *am* pushing you out of here! So what's it gonna be!?" He relented and I pushed him up the hill, but it didn't matter. Most of the cars behind him weren't going anywhere either. Despite having every sand truck and snowplow the city owned being out on the road we were just overwhelmed. Most of the people eventually just gave up and walked back home, so now there were stuck and abandoned cars littering the roadways, like an icy automotive graveyard. If there's four feet of snow in your driveway (which we got) why do you even bother to take your Honda Civic out of the garage? Stay home, pop some popcorn, and put in some movies. Relax, because your boss isn't going to make it in to work either.

Emergencies don't care about the weather, and we got a call of a lady possibly having a heart attack. Matt and I drove up as close as we could get to the address, and then we had to hike in the rest of the way, plowing through snow up to our waists. We got to the house and the woman was still conscious and breathing, but she was clutching her chest and she didn't look too good. We decided we needed to get her out, but the fire trucks and the ambulance couldn't get in either. So me and Matt just looked at each other and shrugged; *ya gotta do what ya gotta do*. I grabbed the old lady and slung her over my back with her arms around my neck, and out the door we went. It was still a long walk back to our cars, and Matt and I took turns with one piggybacking the old woman and the other going in front and breaking trail. In that fashion we got her down her long driveway and out to the street where the ambulance was waiting. She was still conscious and breathing, so Matt turned to me and said "If she ain't dead yet, she'll be alright."

When our shift was supposed to end we just kept on working. We couldn't get home, and no other cops could get in, so what else could we do? Climb back into the car and get back out there. Later that day I was driving west on Belleview and made the right hand turn onto northbound University. Sometimes, Fate puts a guy in the right spot at the right time. Just north of that intersection is a long, steep hill before the road levels out, and about halfway up that hill was an RTD city bus, and he was in trouble. He was trying to climb the big hill but he had lost traction and all his momentum, and now he was slowly starting to slide backward. As he was sliding backward the front end of the bus was starting to swing around to the left. I knew that as he slid down the hill he was going to pick up speed and as he did so his front end was going to come around wider and faster, until he came down that hill sideways like a roaring avalanche right into the crowded intersection, where it would send cars and the people in them flying like bowling pins.

I was the Department's accident investigator, and I knew that all it would take was a "trip factor", a rock or a piece of debris or a pothole, that would catch the side of one of those big tires and that bus would roll right over onto its side, like a whale going belly up. With forty people inside. Not good. I could only think of one thing to do, so I quickly crossed myself and gunned the engine of my truck. I sped up the hill and with a solid thump put the nose of my truck's push bars right up against the side of the bus, up near the front and just behind the driver's window, to stop the nose from swinging around any further. I put on the brakes but that had no effect and the twelve ton bus was just pushing me backwards. My biggest fear was that the big bus would just roll right over me and crush me underneath it, but if it did there was nothing I could do so I just tried not to think about that. I peered up through my windshield and saw the pale white face of the driver of the bus gripping the wheel and looking out his window, and he looked scared shitless. I shifted to 4 Low and pressed the gas, and my tires spun, caught, and spun again, but I could see and feel that the bus had stopped its ponderous slide. *It was working!* The bus was now half sideways and blocking two lanes of northbound traffic, and the really amazing thing was that people in cars behind me were actually *honking* and yelling for me to get out of their way. *Are you kidding me?* With the situation I was in, I had the proverbial tiger by the tail. As long as I sat here with my foot in the gas, the bus wasn't moving, but I couldn't push it up the hill either.

So there we sat, with my tires spinning and my little engine wailing just to hold it in position. I needed help, and from somebody big. Jody was driving the Tahoe, but I needed something bigger. I needed a T-Rex, or King Kong. I switched over to the Public

Works channel and got one of the snowplow drivers and told him I could use a little help with a bus. He asked what kind of help, and I started to try to explain it but then said he just better come see for himself. I switched back to our channel and got Jody and told him to come down and give me a hand. Traffic was still snarled up everywhere so it took a few minutes for the cavalry to arrive, and during that time I just kept my foot in it, and then I could smell the acrid odor of the transmission starting to burn itself up. I eased off the gas a bit, but no sooner had I done it than I felt us start sliding back, so I put my foot in it again. I could see people looking at me through the windows of the bus. A kid waved at me, and I waved back to him. *Hi there, kid.* Just your friendly neighborhood policeman out pushing a bus. The great thing about kids is that they don't think anything is weird. A pink dragon could fly in and sit down next to a kid and start talking to him and the kid would just offer it a bite of his sandwich.

Finally, I saw a beautiful sight! A big red snowplow came rumbling up behind me. We held a window to window conference, yelling over the noise to be heard, and we came up with a plan. He drove up ahead of the bus and laid down a bed of gravel, then he was going to come back and push the bus. While he drove ahead to lay the gravel, I saw some flashing red and blue lights in the mirror, and I looked up to see Jody coming up behind me. He got up there with me, and with the added mechanical muscle of both trucks pushing we got the nose of the bus straightened out. Then Jody backed up and got behind the bus and eased his push bars up against it and started pushing. Behind that big bus he looked like a Dachshund pushing an elephant, but he slowly but surely got it going, and in a few minutes the bus was over the hill, back on level ground, and off to make its rounds. Jody and I met up to breathe a sigh of relief and wait for the next call to come in. I ended up staying and working all through the first night, all the next day, the next night, and finally went home the next morning. We slept in shifts on a couch in the break room, snatching a couple of hours before going back out. We didn't have any food except what was in the vending machines in the Public Works garage. I was so bone-tired going home that I could barely see the road. The streets in my neighborhood weren't plowed, so I had to park my truck and hike in. I had never been so tired, and I was already asleep before my body hit the bed.

I was on my days off now, and both me and the city got ourselves back to normal during that time. I rested up and the streets got plowed and businesses started to reopen. When I went back into work the Chief was waiting for me, and he was not happy. Needless to say, he had not come in during the three days of the snowstorm. He had a piece of paper in his hand and he shook it at me and said through his red face "Do you know what this is?!" *No sir, I don't.* "This is a bill for $1200 for transmission repair to Car 6! This is abuse of equipment! I ought to take this out of your paycheck!" he thundered. Now I didn't expect any medals or accolades for the work we had done, but the fact was we had gone with little sleep and little food for almost three days, busting our asses to answer calls, get traffic moving, and probably saved a couple of lives in the process while the Chief was sitting at home by the fireplace sipping hot cocoa and looking at all the pretty snowflakes through the kitchen window. I said "I'm sorry sir, next time I'll just let the bus tip over. Some people might get hurt, but at least it won't come out of our budget." He told me not to get smart, and he didn't take the twelve hundred out of my paycheck, but he did write me up for abusing the police equipment. I just shook my head and signed the paper. Just another day on the Job.

* * *

If you are a burglar there is no better place to ply your trade than Cherry Hills. While it is true that many of the residents of The Village had security akin to Fort Knox, complete with sophisticated alarms, video cameras, massive safes like bank vaults, and armed ex-Special Forces types for bodyguards, a surprising number of them took no heed whatsoever for security. I've never seen people with so much to lose who were so careless about it. They leave doors and windows unlocked, keys in the ignition of their cars, garage doors open at night, all the things that warm the hearts of professional criminals. There is one guy there who has had three Lexus cars stolen out of his driveway because he leaves the keys in the car at night. He says he refuses to let criminals force him to change his ways. I'll bet his insurance company disagrees. Some people just have more money than sense.

Maybe a couple of decades in police work has made me paranoid, or maybe it's just made me aware, but I don't go to bed at night without doing my perimeter check inside and out to make sure all the windows and doors are secure, and my wife jokingly calls our house "Fortress Miller." My kids don't go to the park without me, and if someone gives me a bad feeling I know that on some subconscious level there's a reason for it. It takes only mere seconds for a life-altering tragedy to happen. Kids have literally been taken right off their front porches while their mothers and fathers were watching television on the couch. I don't mean to create paranoia, but you should realize there are some truly evil people out there, like the serial rapist Brent Brents who was operating in my district in Denver while I was there. We wanted to catch him in a bad way, but people made it so easy for him, leaving doors wide open in the daytime, and unlocked at night. We did get the son of a b****, but not before he'd committed a whole string of unspeakable crimes.

Most criminals are more like petty thugs than hardened professionals, but every once in a while we would get a professional burglar operating in Cherry Hills. They come here because, like Willie Horton famously said when asked why he robbed banks, *"'Cause that's where the money is!"* Unlike the opportunistic thief looking for the open garage door or the purse foolishly left on the seat, the professionals take a certain amount of pride in their work, and some of them are quite good at it. They case their marks, they bring tools, they make plans. We captured some pros who had actually phoned in false calls to the police department and clocked our response time. Others have kept notebooks, and actually observed officers in secret and made notes about the habits of individual officers. There was a jewel and art thief who made so much money from his trade he actually bought a mansion in Cherry Hills, living right among his prey. When he was finally arrested and his house searched, at first we couldn't find anything, not a scrap of evidence in the house. It was baffling, because we knew he moved a decent volume. We started in again and searched carefully and thoroughly, into every crevice and crack. We finally discovered he had secret compartments built into the walls of his house where he kept the stolen paintings. One day his elderly neighbor had a heart attack and was rushed off by ambulance to the hospital, so he sauntered over and burglarized the house, and that moment of indiscretion is what got him caught.

We had another set of thieves working our city, but they weren't the suave *Mission Impossible* types who took pride in their work, they were just smash and grab thugs, and the leader was known to carry a gun. They were hitting us hard, so we set up a sting for them. There was a big society soiree going on at the Cherry Hills Country Club one Saturday and we knew they would probably show up, to break into the cars or sneak into the club to pick pockets or steal purses. We positioned a couple of officers in plain clothes inside, and a couple more in unmarked cars in the parking lot. Eric Nielsen and I were in uniform and in black and whites, waiting out of sight but nearby to swoop in if one of the undercover officers spotted them. We were circling and waiting when one of the undercovers called out a tally-ho. Our prey had arrived.

They were cruising the parking lot, three people in the car, slowly driving along the rows of cars, and a woman would get out of the passenger seat and look into a couple of car windows, then get back in and they would move a little further on. I heard the call and moved into position just a block away, and other units were moving in. *Just one more minute and we would finally have these bastards!* Bates moved too soon. He got so excited that he couldn't contain himself, and he shifted his car into drive and started moving in behind them. They spotted him instantly and gunned their engine, screeching through the lot and out onto University Boulevard. They flew right past me, and I spun around and hit my lights and siren *and the pursuit was on!*

They fled north, then made a squealing right turn onto Hampden Avenue, in a mid-size sedan. I was in a slower vehicle, a Ford Explorer SUV, but I was a better trained driver and was staying right with them. They realized after a moment that they were not going to outrun me, so the driver made a hard right into the circular drive in front of the Nazarene Church and skidded to a sudden stop. Nielsen reported he was coming in to cover me, and for some odd reason which is utterly inexplicable to this day, Bates radioed everyone to hold their positions and not cover me. *What the...?* I didn't have time to wonder about it because the driver, the one known to be always armed, threw open the driver's door and jumped out, just as I was throwing my own door open and jumping out. He turned towards me, while reaching his right hand underneath the waistband of his hoodie. I drew faster. His hand was still under his jacket but his arm was coming up when my gun barrel came level with his chest. I ordered him to freeze, and we stood there for a moment with eyes locked, each waiting on a knife edge to see what the other was going to do. I told myself if his hand continued to come out and I saw a gun butt I was going to fire, put two hollowpoints in his chest.

I yelled again for him not to move, but instead of freezing his face split into an evil grin, then he turned and climbed back into his car. He sure looked like he was reaching for a gun, but I wouldn't shoot him unless I actually saw him pulling one out. I didn't want it on my conscience if I killed someone pulling out his driver's license, and besides I figured for all the little things I got in so much trouble for around here Heaven knows what they would do to me if I actually shot someone.

He got back behind the wheel of his car and accelerated with squealing tires out of the church parking lot and back onto Hampden Avenue, headed westbound back the way we had come, with me close behind him with my lights and siren wailing. The Wellshire golf course is a nice course, if a little pricey, that runs along the north side of Hampden Avenue, and he suddenly made a dive to the right, cutting across all three lanes of traffic, leaving the roadway completely, and bouncing up onto the golf course. I was mentally in full-blown pursuit, catch 'em and skin 'em, mindset and I followed him right onto the golf course. I soon saw however that the course was crowded with people and that the driver of the other car was careening across the fairways with reckless abandon, so I shut down my lights and siren and came to a stop, hoping he would back off too, and not endanger all the golfers on the course. He didn't back off, because he's a no-good criminal and didn't really care if he hurt anybody or not. The last I saw of him he was rooster-tailing grass across a fairway before he disappeared.

I had his license plate number, and with that we got a name, an address, and a hit on a warrant. We pulled up his booking photograph and I confirmed that yep, he was our guy, our pistol-packing burglar and golf course hot-rodder. The address was in Englewood, and the Englewood SWAT team hit the house. The guy had prepared a clever hiding place in a crawl space in his attic for just such an occasion, and he was secreted up there as the SWAT guys searched the house in vain for him. Fate intervened however, as the bad guy hadn't calculated how much weight the piece of roofing he was lying on could hold, and the drywall suddenly gave way and our man came tumbling down in a heap right amongst the SWAT cops. *Busted! By good police work and the force of gravity.* In the end, he went to prison for a long time, and got exactly what he deserved.

* * *

Every civilian ride-along I have had asks me if I have ever killed anyone. Like most police officers, I have never been in a position where I had to take someone's life. I am thankful for that, because I don't know how that would weigh on my mind. Decent human beings have an inborn, innate reluctance to kill another human being, and it takes an extraordinary set of circumstances to overcome that. I have watched patrol car camera video of police officers who were ultimately killed because they simply could not bring themselves to shoot another person, even when that person was shooting at them.

That natural born reluctance to kill another person can be overcome in various ways. One way is by training, as we did in the military and in law enforcement. It might surprise you to learn that even on a battlefield, a significant percentage of soldiers historically will not fire their weapons at the enemy. They will fire them into the air, or in the general direction of the enemy, but they simply will not zero another person in their sights and squeeze the trigger. I spent twelve years in the military, active and reserve, and twenty years in law enforcement, and I can tell you definitively that in every military unit and police department, there are those few "hunters" who will do the majority of killing for that unit. To them, they will not hesitate to kill. You might be forgiven for thinking they do this so easily because they must be psychotic or filled with bloodlust. You would be very wrong.

I have spent all of my adult life in the profession of arms and I can count on the fingers of one hand the number of people I met who would fall into those categories. Believe me, we don't want those people in our ranks, and we go through extensive screening and background checks to weed them out. So how do they do it? How do those "hunters" in every unit switch off that reluctance to kill and calmly take out dozens or even hundreds of enemy soldiers?

One of my personal heroes is the legendary Marine sniper Carlos Hathcock. He served two tours in Vietnam and had 93 confirmed kills and hundreds of probables, and he said in interviews that he never lost a wink of sleep over anyone he killed. He put it this way; every enemy soldier that he killed saved the life of a fellow Marine. Navy SEAL sniper Chris Kyle, with more than 160 confirmed kills, said the same thing. We kill to save the lives of our brothers.

It is worth pointing out that both Hathcock and Kyle had grown up as country boys, the former in Arkansas and the latter in Texas, and they had been tracking and hunting deer and other animals since childhood. Same with the famous Russian sniper Vasily Zaitsev. They had, in a sense, been training for this all their lives. For "normal" people, this reluctance to kill must be overcome by realistic and repeated training. When the military switched after World War II from the traditional round circle targets to human silhouette targets on firing ranges and qualification courses, the percentage of soldiers who will kill went up dramatically during the Korean and Vietnam wars.

Now this is just my two cents worth, but I firmly believe that violent video games train our youth to kill. As a firearms instructor in both the military and the police, I used video simulators using real actors to train troops to instantly recognize threats and engage them with lethal force. Violent video games do *exactly* the same thing. The players are rewarded for killing, the graphics and blood splatter are incredibly life-like, and this continued exposure to it gradually overcomes that natural reluctance to kill another human being. Repetition and Reward are the single most effective tools for changing a person's behavior, for good or evil. When I was growing up in the 1980's, school shootings were unheard of, in fact they were unthinkable. Columbine was so shocking it stunned the nation, and extensive Congressional hearings were held, task forces created to study it, and voluminous reports generated. Now, school shootings have become so common they don't even stay on the news for more than 48 hours. After nearly every school shooting the investigators find out that the shooters spent hours each day playing violent video games. Repetition and Reward. Getting off my soapbox now.

You can fairly call this type of killing that soldiers do to be killing as an Act of Duty. Duty to your country and your fellow soldiers. There are two other ways that human beings will kill others. One is self-defense, kill or be killed, or defense of others such as your spouse or your children. Even timid and peaceful people will attack with the savagery of a wild animal if anyone tries to hurt their children.

The other, and the most interesting to me as a police officer, is what in law is called a "depraved heart." These are your classic serial killers, psychopaths, such as Ted Bundy, John Wayne Gacy, the ones who are seemingly incapable of feeling any empathy or remorse for their victims. This brings me to the point that a depraved heart is not something that any person is born with. People are not "born evil", generally speaking. A depraved heart is something that is *learned*, through emulation and through the environment a person grows up in.

Even among serial killers, they have almost universally been physically, sexually and emotionally abused as children. Whatever goodness was in them was choked out and replaced by a simmering anger and hatred. Why has there been an explosion of murders in the cities of Chicago, Baltimore,

Detroit, and others? Chicago had more than 2,000 people shot in the first nine months of 2019. Murders exploded in cities across the nation after the rioting of 2020. What is fueling the senseless violence? Simple; the shooters learned it from their mentors. Most of these young men grow up in homes with no fathers, no one to teach them how young men should behave, so their role models become the gang they run with, and they adopt the values of the gang. The idea that it is the guns, or bullying, or a lack of after-school programs is simply nonsense. They do it because they have been taught to do it. Repetition and Reward.

I have personally been in several situations that could have turned deadly in the blink of an eye. These were situations wherein if the suspects had done *one thing* differently, I would have shot them. I was ready, willing, and I know that I would not have hesitated. In law enforcement, an officer who has been in a lethal shooting achieves a certain status among the other officers, a strange mix of admiration and not wanting to get too close to them. Admiration, because they won the gunfight, they showed their courage and skill in the ultimate test. At the same time, you feel an unconscious urge to not get too close to them, *because* they have killed another human being.

I am glad that I never had to kill anyone. My partner and I were involved in a foot chase with an armed robbery suspect, and my partner shot him. I watched him bleed out and die from just a few feet away, with our eyes locked on each other. Even though the shooting was fully justified, his face kept coming back to me in my dreams for years afterward, looking at me again. His is not the only one. I have seen many deaths, both deserved and undeserved, people I have tried to save and failed. In police work, the deepest scars we carry are all on the inside.

* * *

One of the most bizarre cases I ever worked in all my years of law enforcement started with a morning jog. I will not reveal the victim's name, because of the truly horrible things that happened to her, but I will say that she was the bravest, most remarkable victim I have ever encountered. The Highline Canal is a wide and slow-flowing irrigation canal that enters Cherry Hills from the south, running underneath Belleview Avenue, and from there winds its sedate way north with many gentle turns through the city for several miles before flowing out again on the north side, passing underneath a little bridge on Hampden Avenue. All along the entire length of the canal the banks are completely overgrown with brush and bushes and Russian Olive trees flanked by stately old massive cottonwoods with shady branches overhanging the water, so that it looks for all the world like a gentle forest river running like a green ribbon through the city. The canal is flanked in many places by wide, grassy fields dotted with trees and populated by furtive wildlife going about on business of their own. A gravel service road runs alongside the canal, not quite wide enough for two vehicles to pass. Normal traffic is not allowed on the canal, only the trucks that service the intermittent pumps and valves and flow gates, and the police vehicles that frequently patrol the canal as well. The Canal road is heavily used by joggers, walkers, bicyclists, equestrians, and others out for a quiet stroll.

The victim didn't live in Cherry Hills, but she liked to come here and jog on the Canal road, soaking in the beauty and the morning solitude of the place. She would park her car in one of the little turnouts on the main roads intersected by the canal, do some stretches and set off on her morning run. But one morning she was not alone. She was being watched. As she jogged down the canal on her usual course, she noticed a strange man walking slowly the other way. He was not wearing workout clothes, which by itself was not unusual. Lots of people came here just to walk and think or to enjoy the outdoors, yet something about this man just didn't feel right to her, but like most people in this modern and supposedly civilized world she rationalized and minimized her fears. This was the Highline Canal, there were lots of people around here, she had jogged here before without even a hint of trouble. She didn't listen to that inner warning voice and turn around and jog the other way. No one can blame her; we are a peaceful and civilized society now, the theory goes, not some third world country where revolution and ethnic cleansing threaten our lives. We are not living like our ancestors in the Pleistocene, dwelling in caves and depending on our fires and sharp spears to keep us safe from wild animals and marauding tribes. The truth of the matter is that although we now live in houses instead of caves things haven't changed all that much in substance, but only in form. The predators are still out there, as the more than 17,000 homicide victims a year can mutely attest, and now we depend on calling 9-1-1 instead of brightly burning fires, and many of us no longer carry our own spears but pay police to do it. Try to reconcile the notion that ours is a civilized world with the fact that every four months more Americans are murdered in their own streets, homes, and workplaces than were killed in more than seven years of the Iraq war.

But on that day as she jogged past the man she may have breathed a little sigh of relief as she passed him, but suddenly she felt a crushing weight on her back as she was grabbed and dragged down to the ground. The man held her down, with her face in the dirt and pressed a gun into her side. He was dirty, and his breath smelled as he leaned his face very close to hers and he said if she screamed he would kill her. He told her to get on her feet, and when they were up he told her to start walking, back down the canal the way she had come. He walked slightly behind her, with the gun in his hand and held to her back. As they walked her mind was racing. She knew she was being abducted, that she should do something, but what? She knew she could outrun him, but she could not outrun his bullets. They saw other people ahead, coming towards them. Maybe she could scream and run to them for help, but even as she thought it he pressed the gun into her back and said he would kill her and them if she cried out for help. So the people passed, and maybe they thought this was a strange couple but once they were gone they dismissed the thought and returned to their own affairs.

They passed still more people, and the victim was again silent. They arrived at his car and he ordered her to get in. He tied and blindfolded her and ordered her to lay down in the back seat. As they drove she was terrified, wondering what was going to happen to her and if she would be killed when it was over. At last she felt the car stop, and heard the sound of his car door opening. Then her own door opened and she was roughly dragged from the car and led inside a house, and down a hallway to a bedroom, where she was forced to lie down on the bed. He tied her hands and feet to the bed and removed her blindfold. Then for the next three days and nights she endured a living hell. He stripped her clothes from her, then set up a video camera at the foot of the bed and videotaped himself repeatedly raping and beating her.

During the day he would leave, maybe to go to work, maybe to plan his next attack, who knew? During those hours she was alone, tied to the bed, she screamed for help until her lungs were hoarse, but no help came. She didn't know where she was, but she could see now that she was in a trailer house. Whether it was in the midst of a trailer court or away by itself in some remote area she had no way of knowing. Then in the evening she would hear his key in the lock, and he would come in and make his way back to her, and the rapes would begin again. This went on for three long and horrible days and nights. The search for her had already begun, when she didn't show up for work and her friends began to worry about her. When another day had passed and her car had been found, it was suspected she had been abducted and an organized search began for her. Teams of police, firefighters, and civilian volunteers searched the length of the canal and the brush looking for her or her body. We got down in the canal itself and formed a line, sloshing through the water and hoping against hope we wouldn't stumble across her body. We used search dogs, and Denver PD joined in using their police helicopter equipped with thermal imaging.

On the second day the Arapahoe County Sheriff's Office set up a Mobile Command Post in a church parking lot near the Canal, and from there we fanned out each day in the search. We wanted desperately to find her, and officers worked night and day with no thought of going home. Meanwhile, she was far away in a torture chamber. During the day as she lay in bed, she began to understand the horrible truth that no one was ever going to find her. No police would rescue her, her family would never see her again. She would be killed, and her body buried somewhere in a cold grave in the mountains or at the bottom of a lake. She grimly realized that if she were going to get out, she would have find a way to save herself.

As she took stock of her surroundings, she saw a magazine on a nightstand, and by straining her head she saw the mailing label, and a name and an address. Okay, now she knew something. She knew what was probably the name of her abductor, and she knew where she probably was. She also saw something horrible. In the room with her was a large crate, like a wooden trunk. It was big enough to hold a person if they were compressed down into it. And it had holes drilled in the sides and bottom. As she looked at it, she knew in her heart this crate was for her, and she knew then that when he was done with her he was going to kill her.

She knew that she needed to make a connection with him. She needed to become more to him than a helpless victim, a piece of meat for his sadistic torture fantasies. So when he would rape her, she began to talk to him. She called him by his name. She told him she knew how the world had treated him wrong. When he raped her, she pretended to him that they were making love.

And she was getting through to him. He had indeed planned to kill her when he was done with her. His plan was to kill her, fold her body into the trunk, then drive to a reservoir and take a boat out to the middle and dump the crate. The holes drilled in the sides and bottom were there so water would flow in and weigh the crate down so it would sink. But now, he found that he was not sure that he could bring himself to kill her. She was the only woman he had ever had any kind of relationship with, and in his twisted world she was the closest thing to a friend he had.

After three days, he couldn't keep her anymore. There was too much news coverage, people were looking for her everywhere. He came to her and told her that he had to let her go now, but that he was afraid she would go to the police, so he *had* to kill her, didn't she see? He didn't want to, but he had to. She knew her life was hanging on the gamble that she now tried. She told him she was a paralegal, and she would draw up a contract swearing she would not reveal his name or his identity or where he lived. They would both sign it, and if she ever did tell, it would not be admissible in court against him. She could hardly breathe while she waited for his answer, knowing if he said no, he would then kill her and place her body in the trunk, and from there take her to the depths of a cold, dark lake where no one, not her family, not her friends, would ever know what had happened to her. He thought for a moment, then untied her and brought her a pen and paper.

He drove her, still naked, to a hotel in Aurora. He pulled up in front of the hotel and told her to get out of the car. She was afraid he might still kill her, but she opened the door, stepped out completely naked, closed the door, and walked away praying with every step that she wouldn't feel a bullet fired into her back. Instead, he simply drove away.

With the information she gave us about his name and address, he was quickly tracked down and arrested, as officers kicked down his door and swarmed into the trailer. Because she had been abducted in Cherry Hills and the rapes occurred in Aurora, the two departments jointly handled the investigation and prosecution. With the videotapes, the semen-stained sheets, and her testimony, it was an airtight case. Rather than face life in prison without parole, he agreed to a plea bargain that gave him almost seventy years in prison. The victim did not want the publicity of a trial, and the term he got would effectively put him away for life anyway, so she agreed to the plea arrangement. Thanks only to her cool head and strength of character, she is alive today and a true monster will spend the rest of his days in a steel cage.

* * *

With that case behind us, we went back to our normal routines. One of my small pleasures was still riding the motor whenever I could. Between my normal sergeant duties supervising my team, preparing the monthly reports in my job as Technical Accident Investigator, and planning training and keeping track of inventory and records for the Firearms Training Unit, I had little time for the motors. Sometimes I would just say *the hell with it* and drop the paperwork, throw a leg over the big machine, and roar off for a few hours of fun. I had been on the Motor Unit for a few years now and I was a good rider, but Jody had a phenomenal natural ability. He and John Bayman entered the Top Gun motorcycle competition, which is the Holy Grail for motor cops. It's a multi-day event drawing riders from law enforcement agencies all over the state. Bayman took third place and Jody took fifth, and the following year Jody won it all, the best rider in the state.

We were scheduled for a training day, so we all rode up to the big parking lot of the Colorado Community Church. It was an early weekday morning and the air was cool and crisp, so the lot was almost empty. We put out the cones to set up the courses, did our maintenance checks, then did some warm-ups to heat up the tires so they would stick better. I was the first rider up, and the first maneuver was one called the Brake-and-Escape. The rider approached at 40 mph, then on a signal from John we were to brake and turn hard to right or left, wherever he pointed. The purpose of the exercise was to simulate evading a car suddenly pulling out in front of you, and what made it nerve-wracking was that John wouldn't give you the signal until you were practically running him over. Considering that at 40 mph the bike is covering 66 feet per second, by the time he signaled we had only a fraction of a second to complete the maneuver while staying within the course, marked out with orange traffic cones, and he had a radar gun aimed at you to make sure you didn't dog it on the speed in order to make it easier to do the drill. I always hoped those radar beams he was dousing me with weren't giving me brain cancer or making me impotent.

I had done the exercise many times before but it was far from easy, and on this particularly fateful day I rode back to the starting line and on John's signal I rolled on the throttle and the big bike leaped forward. I was at almost 40 mph and John was gesturing with his thumb for me to kick the speed up, so I goosed the throttle a little more. A little too much, as it turned out. I was getting awful close to John and just when I thought I was surely going to run right over the top of him he suddenly shot his right arm out, signaling for me to go left. I pulled the front brake lever simultaneously with pressing the pedal for the back brake and in an instant, in the blink of an eye, the bike went down under me and I found myself sailing through the air at 45 miles per hour. I don't know what happened; if there was a fine layer of sand or dirt on the pavement, if the brakes were still cold and sticky that morning, too much speed, I pulled the lever too hard, whatever, but all I knew is that one second I was on the bike executing the move and then too fast for me to even comprehend it the bike was no longer under me.

The parking lot of the church had tall metal light poles with big round concrete bases about four feet across and two feet high and I remember as I was airborne sending out a swift silent prayer *"Please God don't let me hit one of those!"* I came down on my hands first, and if I had not been wearing Kevlar-and-leather gloves my hands would have been ground hamburger. My head hit next, then my body crumpled into the asphalt and I rolled over and slid on my back for what seemed an eternity. When I finally stopped I just lay there, stunned. The other guys came rushing up to me but Bayman wisely told them to back away and don't touch me. We had seen a case where a well-meaning person moved an accident victim and ended up paralyzing him.

I was conscious and in surprisingly little pain. I told myself to just lie still, don't move, until I figured out how bad it was. I began down at my feet, flexing my toes, then my calves. *Okay.* I moved up, flexing my leg muscles and bending my knees. *Okay.* I tightened my stomach muscles. *Good.* Then I gingerly raised my left arm and that was okay, too. Now the right arm. A wave of excruciating pain shot through my arm as soon as I started to lift my shoulder. *Not Okay!* It felt like someone very large and very strong was grinding broken glass into my shoulder joint. I was afraid to even move my head and my neck, but I gingerly did and they seemed okay. I told John that as far as I could tell only my right shoulder and arm were injured. He called for an ambulance and before long I could hear sirens coming, and soon the paramedics and firefighters from South Metro Fire were bending over me. They probed and prodded me, all the while giving me a ribbing for my bad riding. These were guys we knew, from Station 38 across the parking lot from the PD. For all the natural rivalry between cops and firefighters when the chips were down we would be right there for each other. They gently pulled my helmet off of me, then gingerly loaded me onto the gurney. On the ride over to Swedish Medical Center they told me I had probably broken my right shoulder. It was starting to throb with pain now.

When I got to the ER they wheeled me in and the doctors shot me full of painkillers, then they cut my shirt off and took me down for some x-rays. *Yep, busted.* My right shoulder was obliterated. When I came down on the pavement at 40+ miles per hour the scapula and the clavicle just came apart. They wheeled me back to my room, and as I was laying in my hospital bed Chief Bates poked his head into the room. He didn't ask me how I was doing, or if I wanted someone to call my wife, or what happened, or anything. He just looked me up and down for several seconds with a detached, emotionless expression on his face while his eyes examined me like a side of beef he was thinking about buying - or throwing out. I just looked back at him, expecting him to say *something*, but he turned away without a word. John Bayman was right outside the door to my room, and I distinctly heard the Chief ask "How's the bike?" *That son of a bitch.* Sergeant Bayman just said "What?" and the Chief said "The bike. Is it damaged?" Bayman said the bike was banged up but it would be okay, which was more than I could say for me at the moment. Then the Chief asked "Which bike was he riding?" and Bayman answered "17." Bates then asked "Why wasn't he riding Unit 15, the training bike?" to which Bayman replied "Because 17 is his assigned motor." I was doing a slow burn listening to this, and I yelled out "I'm a little banged up in here too, in case you were wondering!" Bates stuck his head back in the door, then out again without saying anything. At some point he left, but I didn't see him go and he never did say a single word to me.

A parade of officers began to come through my room over the course of the day, and it was touching to see them all coming in to see me and wish me a speedy recovery. The guys had to act macho of course, and just punched me in my good shoulder and told me to hang in there, while the girls gave me hugs. I was a little embarrassed about the whole thing frankly, being laid up in bed and only half-dressed with my arm in a sling. Even some of the Englewood cops I had gone through motor training with stopped by. Then my wife arrived. *Hi honey! I had a little accident today*...She took one look at me laid up in the hospital bed and once again told me I was a fool for wanting to be a cop. The doctors eventually decided they would not operate, since I was fairly young and in good shape and they thought it would be better to fit the scapula and clavicle back into position and see if the bones would heal on their own. They gave me my cut-up shirt back and Matt and my wife led me hobbling on a crutch out to the car. Matt said "Hey buddy, you might want this for a souvenir" and handed me my helmet. It had a long black gash in the left front where my head hit the asphalt, and up until then I had not at any point felt scared, but when I saw that long ugly smear on the helmet I felt a chill go through me. That helmet had surely saved my life. I was supposed to give it back to the Department but I snuck it home, and to this very day it sits on a shelf in my study, as a reminder to be thankful for each day that we have, because it can all be taken from you in an instant.

I was out for two months. I stayed at home nursing my painful shoulder, laying around the house watching a lot of Schwarzenegger and Eastwood movies over nachos and popcorn and pain-killers. I watched all the *Dirty Harry* movies in sequence, until I was hearing Inspector Callahan's gravelly voice in my sleep. I had a bizarre dream where I was back on the motor in the church parking lot, doing the Brake-and-Escape maneuver, only where Bayman was supposed to be standing there was Harry, growling *Do you feel lucky, punk?* then he pulled out his Smith & Wesson .44 Magnum and shot me in the shoulder. Sleeping was the worst; I couldn't lay down in the bed because every toss and turn I made in my sleep sent stabs of pain shooting through me. I had to learn to sleep downstairs in a recliner chair, so I wouldn't keep my wife awake at night. I think I slept about six hours total in the first week.

I hated the meds they gave me because they made me feel all loopy, like my head was detached and floating above my body. So I flushed them down the toilet and gritted my teeth and lived with the pain. I remembered a line from *The Terminator;* "Pain can be controlled – you just disconnect it." I also remembered the words of a Marine Recon buddy of mine, Staff Sergeant "Ranger Rick" Ricketts, one of the toughest men alive, as we were on a field exercise in the burning Nevada desert heat he grinned and said to me "You make a friend of pain, you've got a friend for life." So I tried to disconnect my pain and make friends with it, and you know what? That went a long way to making me feel better.

I had to go see the doctor for physical therapy a couple of times a week, and usually Matt would drive me. One time he took me there and helped me fill out the usual paperwork on the little clipboard they give you when you walk in, and we waited for the nurse to come get me. The waiting room was busier than usual and there were a fair number of people in there, including two cute girls across the room. Matt and the girls were making flirty eyes at each other, but I was in no mood for it. I looked terrible and didn't feel much better. At last the nurse called me and I got up and dutifully followed her into the back. When we got back to the therapy room she asked me for my paperwork, and I realized I had forgotten to take it from Matt and he was too busy smiling and winking at the girls to notice either. I said "Oh, my partner's got it out in the waiting room. Sorry, I'll go get it." She waved me back down and said she'd go get it.

The nurse went out into the crowded waiting room and said out loud to Matt "Are you his partner? He says you're his partner and you have his paperwork." All eyes now turned to Matt, and there were a few raised eyebrows. Without thinking, Matt said "Yeah, I'm his partner!" and got up to give her the clipboard. He suddenly realized that all these people in the room were not cops, he and I were both in street clothes, and every person in that room now thought we were little lovebirds. Matt stammered out "Well, I'm not really his *partner...* " but the nurse had already grabbed the clipboard and walked away, leaving him standing in the middle of the room with everyone watching him. Matt turned red as a beet and suddenly exclaimed to the group "I'M NOT GAY!!" Everyone just looked uncomfortably down at the floor or back at their magazines, and to his horror Matt suddenly thought of the cute girls. He quickly looked over at them and saw that they were now looking at him with a mix of curiosity and disdain. "Really, I'm not gay!" he protested, but they only rolled their eyes at him and looked away, pretending not to notice him anymore as if to say *"Sure pal, you're only lying to yourself..."* Matt sat down dejectedly, muttering curses at me under his breath.

When I came back out of my physical therapy session he was still sitting in his chair with a downcast expression on his face. When I walked into the waiting room every person in there turned toward me, looking me up and down with curiosity, like some big novelty item. The cute girls especially were sizing me up, like girls do with other girls, and I noticed it immediately and thought *Okaaay...why is everybody looking at me like I'm a side of beef?* I walked up to Matt and he stood up and hissed "As soon as you recover, I'm gonna break your other arm!" He couldn't resist one last plea and turned to the girls and said "I'm not gay, I swear!" One of them said *"What-ever!"* and turned away. I had no idea what was going on but as soon as he said the word "gay" I put my arm around him and said "Let's go honey."

* * *

The two months passed, and eventually I felt strong enough to go back to work. On my first day back I suited up and put the uniform on, and slid my familiar pistol back into the holster. When that was done I looked at myself in the locker room mirror. The guy looking back at me seemed older, a few more wrinkles and lines in the face, but wiser. I flexed the shoulder and thought I'd better take it easy for awhile, stay in the office more and catch up on things. The shoulder was still a little sore but it was mostly healed. The bones of the scapula and the clavicle never grew back together the way the doctors had hoped, there was just too much damage, and I now have a noticeable bump sticking out above my right shoulder. It didn't hurt, and as it turned out it was kind of handy for keeping the strap of my gear bag from sliding off my shoulder.

I started getting bills in the mail from the hospital and from the physical therapist. It was an on-duty injury, so the city was supposed to be taking care of the bills, but every week I'd get another one in the mail. I would bring each bill to the Finance Director and he would say "Yeah, yeah, we'll take care of it", but they didn't take care of it and the bills kept coming and they got more threatening with each one. At first it was *"Just a friendly reminder that your account is overdue. Please send in payment as soon as possible. Thank You!"* This was soon followed by *"This is your third notice. Your account is overdue. Please remit payment as soon as possible."* After that all the friendliness went away. *"Your account is delinquent. You must remit payment immediately!"* A week later it was *"Your account is seriously delinquent. You must remit payment immediately or the matter will be turned over to collections."* The next one said *"We're sending Sammy the Bull and Vito over. Unless you want your other arm broken, you'll have our money."* I went to the Finance Director with all the hate mail from the hospital, and he impatiently tried to wave me away, don't bother him with this trivial stuff. I told him if a collections agency came after me, then I was going to have to get a lawyer and sue the city. Now that I was talking a language he understood, the bills got paid. It was just ridiculous that it had to go this far.

I wasn't ready to get back on the bike, either physically or mentally, so I stuck with my patrol car for awhile. I had been getting my regular paychecks while I was out, but on my next pay stub I noticed that all my leave balances were zeroed out. Vacation, holiday, personal time, comp time, all were down to 0.00 hours. I went to the Chief and asked him about it and he immediately got defensive and said "I didn't have anything to do with that! You'll have to go upstairs and see the Finance people!" I went upstairs, and as I walked up the steps I was already starting to do a slow burn, getting the sinking feeling that I was about to get screwed again. It never ended with them, it was always something, some new way to stick it to the workers. I went to the Finance clerk and she said "We didn't do that. That was by order of the Chief." I went past the clerk and into the Finance Director's office and showed him, and he hemmed and hawed and cleared his throat and looked uncomfortable, and finally said "Well, that was for the time you were out."

I started to speak, then reined myself in and took a breath and as calmly as I could manage I explained to him that I was not on vacation, I was not away on holiday, I wasn't taking a little *me* time, I was home nursing a broken shoulder from an on-duty, work-related accident. The Finance Director tried to snowball me with a bunch of official-sounding talk of workmen's comp regulations and labor law statutes, but I know when I'm being bullshitted, and I in turn tried to not reach over and throttle him. In the end things got a little heated and the City Manager came out of her office on her broom and said they were cleaning out my time banks and if I didn't like it I was welcome to go work somewhere else. Then she said "Why should the City have to pay because you can't ride a motorcycle?" Angry words rose to my lips, but before I could say them the Wicked Witch turned on her heel and went back in her lair to stir her bubbling cauldron. The Finance Director gave me a smug little smirk that made me want to punch him, but I turned around and walked away before I got myself fired. *Just shut up, bend over, and take it.* The administration never passed up an opportunity to remind us they were an at-will employer and if you couldn't take a screwing with a smile on your face, then you were history.

You know, the Good Book says that *Vengeance is mine, sayeth the Lord* and the Big Guy must have been watching, because we all got some payback on the City Manager, or The Grinch as we called her. Also the Wicked Witch, Scrooge, and some other choice and fitting names. She booked one of those exotic, "Adventure Vacations" for an Amazon River cruise down in Brazil. Well, she caught some horrible tropical disease down there that the doctors couldn't even identify. You know it's bad when the doctors don't even know what it is, when the doctor examining you says to the other doctors *"Hey guys, look at this! What do you think that is?"* She was deathly ill for months, and needless to say, when she was in the hospital she didn't get any *Get Well Soon!* cards from the cops.

They never did give me any of my leave time back, and we had to cancel our vacation plans that year. I decided the hell with the motor squad, and I told Bayman I wasn't coming back. Matt quit too, in a show of support, and because he knew that could just as easily could be him if he ever got hurt on the bikes. Not long after I quit the Motor Unit we got the news that Brian Mueller, one of the Englewood motor guys I had gone through training with, had been in a horrific accident. He had been going to a call with lights and sirens on when a pickup truck suddenly pulled right in front of him. Brian couldn't avoid it and hit the truck with full force. His body was crushed against the truck and they transported him to the emergency room, unconscious. The ER doctors worked feverishly on him, not sure if he was going to live or die, but they finally got him stabilized. The accident left him partially paralyzed. He has a wife and a child. At around the same time another motor officer, Denver officer Dennis Licata, was killed in another horrible accident, leaving a wife and daughter behind. When I heard it I breathed a silent prayer for his family and one of relief that I had quit the motor unit when I did.

FIFTEEN

AN IRATE MOTORIST WALKED INTO THE STATION ONE DAY and wanted to sign a complaint against another driver. All the cops hated these walk-in traffic complaints because they were a pain in the ass; somebody cut somebody else off on the highway and their pride or ego was wounded or their righteous indignation was inflamed, which meant *you* had to track down the other driver who usually lived in another city, go find him even though you've never seen him before and don't know what he looks like, and serve him with a summons even though you never saw him do anything, and come in on your day off to go to court and testify that you don't know anything about it but you gave him the ticket. Nine times out of ten by that time the complaining driver has already forgotten about it and doesn't even show up for court, so the case is dismissed anyway and you wasted hours of time. So it was with no enthusiasm that I took this guy's complaint.

The indignant citizen told me he was driving down University Blvd. in our fair city when a guy in a pickup suddenly jumped into his lane, cutting him off and forcing him to hit the brakes to avoid an accident. The citizen was very irate and as he was telling the story he got very animated and angry all over again as he was reliving it and ended, as these complaints inevitably do, in a tirade against the police as he demanded to know *where were the police when you needed them anyway, sitting in a doughnut shop?!*

Nevertheless, I calmly explained to him how the process worked. I told him that I would have him sign the complaint,

254

then I would track the guy down and serve him, then he, Mr. Outraged Citizen, would have to go to court and testify against the guy. Outraged Citizen wanted to know, like they always do, why *he* should have to take time off work to go to court and testify. After all, isn't that *our* job? I resisted the urge to reach across the counter and smack him and instead calmly explained that *I* did not see the other guy cut Citizen off, did not write down his license plate, or get a description of his car, or see what he looked like, therefore *I* could not testify to *anything*. Mr. Outraged Citizen harrumphed and grabbed the ticket and signed it, and then with a disapproving glare he stalked out of the station. I already knew in my bones that this guy was not going to show up for court and everything I did from this moment forward was a complete waste of my time, but the Policy and Procedures Manual is an unforgiving master, and I had to do it.

I ran the plate and got the address, but dispatch couldn't get a matching phone number from the COLS directory, which meant I had to go there in person to serve the ticket. As it turned out the guy only lived a couple of miles outside of our city so I figured this would be quick and easy, just run out there, give him the coupon, and be back in service within the hour. Now I like to read Richard Marcinko's books about his days as a Navy SEAL operator, and he's always talking about how Murphy of Murphy's Law fame always shows up when he's least expected and throws a wrench into all your best laid plans, and I may be only a cop and not a Navy commando but I believe Richard so I took Matt with me to serve the ticket, just in case Murphy showed up. Murphy showed up.

I cleared out my gear to make some room in the front seat for Matt, called dispatch to tell them where we were going and why, and headed out. We arrived at the target house in just a few minutes, and when we pulled up to the house we could see it was a run-down dump of a place, with a one car attached garage. I parked a block down like always and we walked up. Luckily the garage door was the type that had those little windows at the top that I could peek in. *Bingo!* There was the truck.

We walked up to the front door. Now before we knocked on the door we could tell there was a bathroom just to the right of the door. How could we tell that, you ask? Because there was a large frosted glass window that apparently was losing its frosting because we could pretty clearly see the form of a shapely naked woman standing in there. It was nighttime and the bathroom light was on, which made her stand out all the more. We stood in the shadows for a minute assessing the tactical situation, if you will, and debating her measurements. When the light clicked off we knocked on the door. A moment later the young lady from the bathroom opened the door wearing a bathrobe. We asked her if the guy, let's call him Joe, lived there. She said yes, that he was her roommate. Where was he, we asked, and she replied he was right down the hall in his bedroom. I told her to ask him to come out but *not* to tell him the police were here. People tend not to come out when they know they've done something wrong and the cops are at their door. Tell him the toilet's flooded, or that you made cookies, or something, I said to her. We were standing in the living room, and the door to his bedroom was down a short hallway of several feet. She stepped into the hallway and called to him, asking if he could come out. He mumbled an incoherent reply but didn't come out. She tried again to no avail, and then looked at us and shrugged her shoulders.

Time for Plan B. Plan B was the "Direct Approach." I moved down the hall and banged on the door and said "Joe! It's the police. I need you to come out and talk to us." There was no answer, and I said "Joe I know you're in there. Come out and talk to us." Joe's voice came back "Whaddaya want?" I told him that someone had made a complaint about his driving and I needed to talk to him about that. He asked through the door if he was going to be arrested. I told him no, I was going to give him a ticket and leave. This discussion of stupid question followed by our answer went back and forth for another minute, and Matt was starting to get a little pissed off at Joe. Matt's got a bit of a temper, you see. I was starting to get pissed off at Joe, too. A part of me wanted to stop screwing around and just boot the door and drag Joe out by his hair and stuff the ticket in his ear. But the smart part of me, the weapons and tactics instructor part of me, said only a fool needlessly boots down a door when he doesn't know what's on the other side. I finally said "Joe, you can deal with us now or deal with us later, but we're not going to leave you alone until we get this taken care of."

Isn't it funny how the smallest little sound can echo like a drum? I was listening for Joe's reply when I heard the faint but very distinctive sound of a weapon slide being carefully racked. The narrow hallway I was in was a deathtrap, a fatal funnel, and I backpedaled down it expecting any second for a hail of bullets to splinter the door. As I went back I drew Heinz, my Sig P229 .40, and yelled back to Matt "He's got a gun!" Matt dove for cover drawing his Glock, and I yelled to the girl to get the fuck out. She saw the guns and bolted like a rabbit. Matt and I both settled into position covering the hallway, and I got on the horn and told dispatch to give us the air, we had a barricaded subject with a gun.

Dispatch immediately called a Code Red and sent all non-essential radio traffic to Channel 2 and started calling in units for cover. The dispatchers were real pros in situations like this. Cars started calling in from everywhere that they were en route to cover. In that couple of minutes between calling it in and the arrival of backup, Matt and I engaged in a quick whispered discussion about our next move. As the sergeant it was my call, but I always listened to the input of my officers. I considered whether we should pull out and let SWAT deal with it, but right now we knew exactly where he was and he was contained. He could not come through that door without getting mowed down like Custer at Little Big Horn. If we pulled out he could move freely through the house and the SWAT guys would have to go in and hunt for him, and he had the advantage of being on his own turf, creating a much more dangerous tactical situation for the SWAT operators. I decided we would remain in place unless he just started randomly shooting through the door. We couldn't return fire because we didn't know if there was anyone else in there. Now I was thinking maybe I shouldn't have sent the roommate hustling out of there so fast. *Damn!*

That's the way it goes with dynamic tactical situations, but I could already hear the Chief's voice in my head giving me the armchair quarterback speech; *Sergeant Miller you should have done this, or you should have done that.* Still, I have always been a believer in making a decision and running with it, and I made my decision and we stayed put. It was only a matter of minutes before we had a sea of police cars surrounding the house. I could see the flashing red and blue lights in every window, and I'm sure Joe could too and he had to realize that he was now thoroughly f***ed. An Arapahoe County SWAT sergeant came into the house and I gave him a quick sitrep. I expected him to pull us out and put his own guys in but he left us in place, partly because he could see that we knew what we were doing and partly because some of the SWAT team was still assembling, and he deployed some other patrol officers in the house with us. I was glad to see some guys with shotguns. Nothing is more decisive in a close quarters fight than The Big Boomer.

Now that the perimeter was secure negotiations began. Dispatch called Joe on the phone and a negotiator began to talk to him. While they talked we stayed in our position and waited, but I was now feeling better about the outcome. When a situation first blows up is the time of greatest danger. Tempers are hot, emotions are high, and the perp doesn't know whether to fight, run, or surrender. Sometimes the cops inflame the situation, too, because cops by nature and by training are take-charge people and their natural reaction to resistance is to overpower it. But if those first tense moments pass and nobody gets hurt and things kind of settle down, then the chances are very good that the situation will be resolved without bloodshed.

We waited from our positions in the living room, and believe me a two pound pistol can feel like a two hundred when you're holding it up for twenty minutes. After about half an hour dispatch called me; "330 he's coming out". The hall door opened and all guns came up to cover it, in case he had decided to commit suicide by cop. But he came out unarmed, with his hands in the air. I ordered him to lie face down on the floor, and he got down and assumed the position. Other officers moved in and cuffed him, and the situation was over. In the bedroom we found a small arsenal of loaded weapons laid out and ready for use on his bed. He had a Beretta 92F 9mm pistol, which I believe is the weapon I heard being racked, and a shotgun and a couple of rifles. When they pulled him off the floor I walked up to him and stuffed the ticket in his shirt pocket.

When a dangerous and stressful situation suddenly comes to an end, you feel a sense of relief and something like euphoria come over you, and Matt and I were laughing and high-fiving each other on the way back to the car. "Wait'll they hear about this at roll call!" But that thought suddenly sobered us up. We had a Chief of Police who had openly stated that in thirty years of law enforcement he had never drawn his gun and never been in a fight. The unspoken part of that was that we better not, either. The more we thought about it, the more we knew that in the eyes of the brass this was going to be viewed as Matt and Mike out stirring up shit again, calling out SWAT Teams, screwing off and violating policy, and not even in our own jurisdiction. By the time we got back to the station Matt said "You know they're going to fry us for this! They're going to suspend us, we're going to get fired, they're going to shove that Policy & Procedures Manual so deep up our asses" I stopped Matt before he got to us being hanged from the flagpole - *Not Helping!* I knew he was right, but I told him to write it up just like it happened, then I went into my office to write up my own report. I was the sergeant, I was in charge, and it was my responsibility.

I knew the Chief would sit down and pore through that Manual with a fine-toothed comb to find every single section we violated and use it as a hammer. They were going to tell me that as soon as I heard the pistol slide rack I should have just turned around and left. I could hear the Chief's voice in my head already *What were you thinking, Sergeant Miller? I'm very disappointed in you.* But I couldn't do that. I could not allow someone to threaten police officers with a gun and just back down and leave. What kind of society would we live in if the police were afraid of the criminals? If rather than risk a confrontation we just surrendered the field to the bad guys? How could regular citizens expect to feel safe if the police would not protect even themselves? So I sat down and wrote up my report, exactly as it happened, and before I left for home at the end of my shift I made a copy for the Chief and placed our reports squarely on his desk in front of his big leather chair. When Matt and I came in for our shifts the next day we met outside in the parking lot. "Well, here goes" we said, and went in to face the music.

We saw the Chief in the squad room. We saw the Lieutenant. Nobody said a word to us. Nothing was said about it in the pass-on of events at roll call. We didn't get called in to the office to explain it. It was like it never happened. After roll call we picked up our gear bags and went out to our cars and headed out on patrol. *Unbelievable.* I was relieved at first that we didn't get in trouble, but the more I thought about it the more pissed off I got, because it dawned on me that the reason they didn't ask about it is because they didn't think it was important. We didn't write any tickets, we didn't generate any revenue, we didn't do any of the things *they* thought were important. In their minds we were out on a lark, screwing off for fun instead of doing our jobs like the officers who stayed in the city and dutifully made traffic stops.

Matt and I talked about it, and with bitterness we concluded that despite what we did there, when the end-of-month performance evaluations came out those officers who stayed behind and wrote tickets would get better evals for the day than we would, because what we did generated no countable stats. In the city's Pay-for-Performance plan there was no category for "Successfully resolve barricaded gunman situation." I wrote Matt up for a commendation, for acting with bravery, coolness, and professionalism in a dangerous situation. The next day the writeup was back in my mailbox, denied. No explanation was given. The incident was never mentioned in our performance evaluations and never discussed or even mentioned by anyone. I wrote a memorandum to the Chief saying I wanted to discuss it with the officers at shift briefings as a training tool, since we very rarely encountered barricaded armed subjects. The memo was back in my box the next day, denied. It was like they wanted to pretend it never happened. And the traffic complaint from Mr. Outraged Citizen, that started this ball rolling in the lobby of the Police Station? He didn't show up for court.

* * *

We had a detective slot open up when John Defelice decided to come out of Investigations. He was a brilliant detective, the best we ever had, but he just wanted to go back to the street. Being a detective is sort of the Holy Grail for cops, and all the cop movies are about detectives. No one makes a movie about a street cop writing traffic tickets or going to alarm calls or settling a domestic disturbance. JD had been doing it for awhile and had enough of it, so he put in a request to go back to Patrol Division. The memo was posted on the board in the squad room for the opening, and everyone was talking about it. Matt was putting in for it, because all he ever wanted to be was a detective. It was his dream. There were several officers that put in letters, and the Chief and JD sat down in the Chief's office to go over the applicants and decide who would be the best candidate to take JD's place. They each had copies of the letters and were looking them over when Chief Bates saw Matt's letter. He exclaimed "Him! What's he doing in here? Throw him out!" JD looked up in surprise and told the Chief he was thinking Matt was the best officer in the bunch to replace him. Bates replied "He'll make detective over my dead body! Matt will never go anywhere in this Department as long as I'm the Chief!"

The detective slot went to another officer, who was brand new and had practically no street experience. Matt was thoroughly dejected, which quickly gave way to being pissed off. We talked about it over the next few days, with me trying to console him but at the same time we both knew that for whatever reason the Chief had it in for him and Matt had no future here. He told me one day that he had been talking to Tony Trujillo, and Tony was telling him how much he loved working at Denver PD. He was over in District One, and he was telling Matt he just *had* to come over. Matt and I had a lot of talks about it, and Matt said "When I'm old and retired and looking back over my career, I don't want to say that I was a traffic cop for twenty five years. I want to do *more* than what we can do here." I had to agree that he had a good point there, so Matt went down to the Civil Service Commission and picked up an application for Denver PD.

I was sad to see my best friend go, after all we had been through together, all the things we had seen and done as partners, but I knew it was best for him. All that had happened got me thinking about leaving myself, but I wasn't quite ready for that. Despite all the bad things, I had a lot going for me at Cherry Hills. I was a sergeant, I was the head of my beloved Firearms Training Unit, I was the Technical Accident Investigator. Over the next few months Matt went through the hiring process with

Denver, taking tests, filling out paperwork, and moving forward. Matt told the people at DPD that he wasn't on good terms with his bosses at Cherry Hills, and naturally they wanted to know why. When Matt sat down with the background investigator and told him about all the many times he had gotten in trouble at Cherry Hills, all his suspensions, the detective just nodded his head now and then and listened while Matt talked. When Matt was done the detective said "You're Chief sounds like an asshole, and I think you'll fit in just fine at Denver PD."

Matt also told the detective that, for obvious reasons, he didn't want them to contact Cherry Hills until the last possible minute, because he had the very well-founded fear that Chief Bates would fire him on the spot. As it was, the regular DPD detective doing Matt's background check was off one day and another one was filling in. He apparently had not gotten the word about not contacting Cherry Hills because he showed up at the station asking to see Matt's personnel file. Of course, this was the first the Chief knew about Matt applying at Denver PD, and he hit the roof. He refused to show the personnel records to the DPD investigator and rudely showed him the door, and when Matt came in to work Bates met him in the squad room and they had a shouting match right there in front of everybody. Bates accused Matt of being disloyal and blindsiding him, and Matt brought up Bates's comment that "Matt will never go anywhere in this Department as long as I'm the Chief" and asked him what else did Bates expect him to do when he clearly had no future here? Bates didn't know JD had told Matt what he said and that caught him up short. He blustered and yelled some more and ended by telling Matt "You better hope you get hired at Denver, because you're finished here!" and stalked out of the squad room.

Matt was now feeling more dejected than ever, because if Denver didn't hire him his police career was probably over. Bates would never give him a good recommendation to any potential police employer, and now he wouldn't release any of his personnel records to the Denver investigators either, so they couldn't complete his background check. Luckily the Denver detectives handling his background investigation knew what was going on. It would have been so easy for them to be like every petty bureaucrat and say "We're sorry, but the proper boxes on the paperwork are not checked, so we are unable to process your application", but they liked Matt and wanted him on board, and so they moved past the petty squabbling at Cherry Hills and pushed him forward. The year was almost over when Matt got a letter in the mail, saying *Congratulations and Welcome to the Denver Police Department*! and instructing him to report to the Denver Police Academy in January to become part of Academy Class 04-1.

* * *

With Matt gone, I turned back to my duties but it just wasn't the same place anymore. So many of the guys I had come on the Job with were gone now, either retired or moved on to other departments and other places. I had almost ten years on now, and as I approached that significant (or as I felt, ominous) mark I felt I had a decision to make. I needed to either fully commit myself to the rest of my career at Cherry Hills, or to follow Matt to Denver. DPD was really the only other department I considered going to. Over the years some of my buddies had gone to our neighboring agencies at Englewood or Greenwood Village, but they were not much bigger than Cherry Hills. I had my fill of small departments with their inbreeding and petty squabbling and favoritism, and if I left here it would be to find something as far away from that as possible. Denver was huge by comparison, with nearly fifteen hundred officers, six district stations, the gang unit substation, and headquarters, too. A guy could get lost in there, and that might be just what I wanted right now. But my decision would have to wait awhile, because Duty is a jealous mistress, and she can be a bitch sometimes.

* * *

We were a few months into the new year, and Matt had graduated from the DPD Academy. He was assigned to District Five, out on the east side of Denver which included Denver International Airport. He worked in a neighborhood called Montebello, or simply "The Bell" to the cops that worked there. It was a crack and crime ridden area, gang infested and one of the worst in the entire metro area. But he loved it. I asked him if he thought it was a good move to go to Denver, and he said "Mikey, it's everything I hoped it would be and more." He told me to come out and do a ride-along with him, and out of curiosity as much as anything I did. We went to a shooting, and to a robbery, and got into a foot chase. It was adrenalin pumping and exciting, and as I was watching my old friend it struck me that he was having *fun* again on the Job. It had been years since either of us actually had much fun at work. I was happy for him. Jealous, but happy. He was telling me that I needed to get over here, but I wasn't ready for that. My wife did not want me even thinking of going to Denver, and I was making a good living as a sergeant and would take a steep pay cut to go to DPD. So even though it was fun, I wouldn't be going anywhere any time soon. Or so I thought.

A drunk driver was out for an evening on the town and passing through the lovely city of Cherry Hills, down in the quiet southwest corner of the Village and ran his pickup truck straight into a brick wall. Judging by the way his truck was halfway through the wall with a fan of ejected bricks and debris spreading out in front of him, I estimated he must have been going about forty miles per hour at impact. The driver managed to extract himself from his vehicle and stagger up to the house the wall belonged to and ring the doorbell. The people inside the house heard the sounds of the collision of truck versus brick, and when they looked out their window and saw the bloody apparition standing on their porch they called the police. They had a push-button intercom at the front porch of the house so they could tell the vacuum cleaner salesmen and Jehovah's Witnesses to go away without actually having to open their door and see them face to face. They used the intercom to tell the injured, intoxicated driver that they had called for an ambulance and for him to go back out to the street and wait for it. The dazed driver dutifully turned around and swayed and staggered back across the yard and crawled out through the hole in the wall to wait for the ambulance.

John DeFelice and I were on duty that night and got the call of an injury accident. We flipped on the lights and sirens and headed that way. Amazingly, the ambulance and the Fire Department had actually beaten us there, which almost never happens. In fact when we got there the paramedics already had the drunk driver sitting on a gurney and were talking to him and treating his injuries. This guy didn't look so good. He obviously wasn't wearing his seatbelt, because when his truck hit the wall his face immediately followed by hitting the windshield. His forehead had a big open gash with bits of embedded glass , and there were little rivulets of blood running down his face. The paramedics working on him were trying to sponge it up and stop the bleeding and get him stabilized before they transported him. I walked over to the house to get some information from the homeowners, and when I returned the ambulance and my demolition derby driver were gone. JD went to the hospital with them while I stayed on scene for the accident investigation. When I was finished I called for a tow truck, and when the truck arrived the driver hooked up his cables and winched the truck back out of the big dark hole it had made in the wall. Some paperwork was signed and the tow jockey was on his way, and I went back to the station and made my report. Another night on the Job done and put to bed.

The next day I was walking through the hallway to the squad room when the detective passed me. We exchanged hellos and then he turned and said "By the way, we'll need that Use of Force report from you and JD before you get off shift today." I was a little puzzled and said so, and the detective said "You know, for when you beat up that guy last night." Now I was really perplexed. I enjoy a good brawl as much as the next cop, but I think I would remember it if I had been in one, so I said "What guy?" He replied "You know what I'm talking about! That guy in the truck on Belleview." I said "Wait a minute! What *are* you talking about? That was a traffic accident. We didn't fight with that guy!" The answer came back "Well, he had blood all over him, didn't he?" and as he said this a subtle change crept into his voice. A note of accusation had crept into it that I couldn't help but notice. I pointed out that he *did* just run into a brick wall at forty miles per hour with no seatbelt on, which has been known to cause injuries and bleeding. The detective threw his cards on the table and said "You and JD beat the crap out of that guy! *Before* the ambulance arrived! We know you did so don't deny it!" Now I was getting hot under the collar and said "The ambulance arrived before we did. Call them and ask! And how do you know we did?" He said coldly "We have witnesses. The Chief expects that report on his desk before you go home today" and with that he turned and walked down the hall to his office.

I stood in the hall a moment wondering just what the hell was going on. I decided I had better nip this in the bud early, because these things have a way of taking on a life of their own and growing and mutating like some B-movie monster until it didn't even matter if you did it or not. I walked down the hall and straight into the Chief's office. He looked up from his desk and when he saw it was me a sour look crossed his face as I said "Chief, what's all this use of force business about? We never laid a hand on that guy." The Chief set his pen down and leaned back in his chair, and said in his best official-sounding voice "Sergeant Miller, an Internal Affairs investigation has been launched. I would advise you not to say anything right now. You will have a full opportunity to make a recorded statement at a later time. You may want to consider contacting an attorney." So, it had already begun. The laboratory lights were on, the mad scientist was at work, and the monster was coming to life.

Here is Police Work 101: when you are conducting an investigation into *anything*, from a barking dog complaint to a homicide, you talk to all sides. You interview the victim, the witnesses, the accused and anybody who has information about the case. You examine the physical evidence, you investigate the scene of the crime. You gather records and documents if there are any. Only then do you evaluate what you have and make a decision. That's what *good cops* do. These Command Officers wouldn't know good police work if it ran them over in the street. They were impulsive, they made snap decisions based on whatever the first person they talked to told them. The Chief didn't like cops. I know that sounds like a strange thing to say, but it was true. I should say he didn't like real cops that went out and busted real bad guys. He liked the social worker kind of cops, the touchy-feely, group-hug kind of cops. The son of wealthy parents himself, he had grown up in a quiet upper-class neighborhood and he had lived and worked in sheltered little communities all his life. Now, having spent the last fifteen years driving a desk and pushing paper had driven him so far from the realities of the street he didn't even recognize them any more. To him, any use of force was suspect, and in any dispute between an officer and a citizen or suspect, the officer was guilty until proven innocent.

Right behind the secretary's desk at the front door of the police station, hung on the wall were large color photos of every officer in the Department, so if someone came in to make a complaint the Chief would just turn to the wall and say "Which officer was it?" For me and JD, they had heard that we had beaten a suspect senseless, and from that moment on we were guilty. We were the Rodney King cops, the Amadou Diallo cops, the bad apples that had to be rooted out. They were so sure of themselves that they never, at any time, even asked us what had happened. We were never given any kind of hearing or opportunity to present our side. All investigation was done in secret. We were simply notified that an Internal Affairs Investigation was ongoing, that criminal charges could result from it, and that a disciplinary hearing would be held at a date to be determined. I tried to talk to the Chief again but he wouldn't talk to me. They just looked at me and JD like we were lepers. We didn't even know who our accuser was.

I realized that this hearing was going to be like the Salem witch trials, where a mere accusation was all that was required for the exalted guardians of purity and truth in the community to bring their righteous wrath down upon the heretics. I told JD that if we were going to save our careers and stay out of jail it was all up to us. You can bet that if their "investigation" uncovered any exculpatory evidence it would be squashed and somehow get "misplaced." I started preparing our defense by trying to pull up the case file, but it was missing. It had been removed and I was not allowed access to it. I went across the street to South Metro Fire Station 38, and with their help I tracked down the ambulance crew that had been the first responders and I got signed statements from them and from the firefighters on scene, confirming that the guy was already being treated before the police ever arrived on scene. I talked to the homeowners whose wall had been hit and got written statements from them. The amazing thing to me was that of all these people I talked to, *none* of them had been contacted by the Department in the course of their "investigation" into these charges of police brutality.

I dug into the bottom of my locker and blew the dust off my Policy and Procedures Manual and began studying the Internal Affairs section. The next day the Chief called me into his office and closed the door. He was red in the face and angry, and said he got a concerned phone call from the people who lived at the house where the truck crashed, and he wanted to know just what the hell I thought I was doing talking to those people. I told him I was preparing my defense, and he ordered me not to call those people and bother them anymore, and not to talk to *anyone* about the case. I pulled their statements from my briefcase, and the statements of the paramedics and firefighters that had been on scene and shoved them at the Chief. He took them and glanced over them and said "What the hell is this?!" I told him what they were and told him to read them. I also told him that the Policy and Procedures Manual mandated that officers who were the subject of internal affairs investigations were to be informed of the charges against them, be notified who their accusers were and who was heading up the investigation. Furthermore, officers were to be given the opportunity to make written statements presenting their side. He brusquely dismissed me, but kept the statements.

We didn't hear anything the next day, but the day after that the Chief called me and JD into his office. He was all smiles, telling us to please sit down, make yourselves comfortable. He said this had all been just a little misunderstanding. Water under the bridge, right? No hard feelings, go back on patrol, investigation over. When we walked out of the office I said to JD "Water under the bridge? I'd like to show him water under the bridge by holding his head under it for a few minutes." JD heartily agreed, and the next day we found out from Angel who their "witness" was that launched this whole fiasco.

He was a 15 year old high school freshman who happened to be driving by with his mother when the pickup driver was sitting on the gurney with his face bleeding and we were all standing around him. The kid went to school the next day and told his friends he saw the cops beating the hell out of somebody last night on Belleview. Those friends told other friends, and the story grew in the telling until it reached the ears of a child of a police officer. That kid came home and told his parents, who went and told the Chief, and the witch-hunt was on.

This whole incident just sickened me when I heard the full details. To think that JD and I were facing the loss of our jobs and threats of criminal prosecution based solely on the fertile imagination of a teenager driving by a scene. I was sick of the politics of small town departments and the small minds that often run them. You couldn't draw a breath around here without someone noticing it and evaluating it. It occurred to me that with the events of the past few years I had sort of established myself as the Problem Sergeant, because I just couldn't shut my mouth and go along with it when I thought something was really wrong. I felt like I was walking around with a big target on my back and it was just a matter of time before someone hit the bullseye.

SIXTEEN

THE CIVIL SERVICE COMMISSION building in Denver is located at 1570 Grove Street. It sits on a hill near Invesco Field, home of the Broncos since they bulldozed Mile High Stadium, and it has a breathtaking overlook of the city to the east. After I picked up my application packet for the Denver Police Department I walked over the to the edge of the parking lot and just stood there for several minutes, looking out over the city and imagining all the stories of all the lives going on down there, and hoping I would soon be a part of it. Suddenly the opening line of *Dragnet* came to my mind; *This is the city...*

The decision to make the move to Denver PD had been a long time coming, like a pressure cooker building until it bursts out in a whistle of steam and noise. The small town politics and the small town minds were becoming too much. I felt like I needed a place where I could just blend in and disappear. But that wasn't the whole reason, as I thought back to a conversation I had with Matt before he left, where we agreed that we didn't want to look back on our careers and say "I was a traffic cop for twenty-five years." At Cherry Hills, what you were doing on Day One was probably exactly what you would be doing on Day Ten Thousand. You came in driving a sled on patrol, and you would go out driving a sled on patrol. When I thought back to those early days, now seemingly so long ago, when I first decided I wanted more than anything to be a cop, I had visions and dreams in my head of what that exciting life would be like, and after ten years at Cherry Hills PD an awful lot of those dreams were still out there, and a lot of those visions were still unfulfilled, and I knew they never would be if I stayed where I was. Denver was big, bold, exciting, and action-packed. It was the kind of police work they made television shows and movies about, and I wanted to be a part of it.

I turned in my application, but kept my plans secret from everyone at Cherry Hills, even my closest friends Jody and JR. I didn't want anything blowing up in my face like it had with Matt. I went about my patrol duties during the nights and plodded through the DPD hiring process during my days off. I was sitting in the squad room with Angel and Jason one night when the alert tone sounded. We stopped talking and turned up the volume on our portable radios. Dispatch called me "330 investigate a possible drowning" and she gave out the address. We flew out the squad room door and into our cars and raced the short distance to the scene with lights and sirens going. The house we were looking for was set well back from the road by a long and curving tree-lined driveway, and as we pulled up in front of the house we saw no one out there to meet us or guide us.

We entered through the front door and began searching through the house, knowing almost nothing about the call. The house had an indoor swimming pool, and there we found the tragic scene. Several people were huddled in a group on one end of the pool, and beside them was a man bending over a motionless child. I rushed up to him and he turned to me with anguished tears in his eyes and said "Please...save my son!" I bent down to the child, a slight slim blonde haired boy of maybe five or six years old. His eyes were closed, and he was cold to the touch. I knew in an instant we would be fighting the odds to save this boy. I picked him up and carried him away from the edge of the pool, shouting for Angel to grab an AED from the car. As I carried him to a dry place I looked down at him. He was so small, and so light in my arms, and I suddenly had a vision of my own little five year old son, lying helpless and cold and still.

I shook it off and set the boy down, and I grabbed a towel and dried him off. Angel came in with the AED and stuck the pads to his little chest and connected the leads. The machine spooled up, but it would not send the shock. There was no heartbeat. The Automated External Defribillator does not revive people who have no heartbeat, it shocks the heart to stop it from going into ventricular fibrillation. I bent down to the boy and felt for a carotid pulse. His skin was so cold. I thought I detected a slight pulse, but it could have been my own heartbeat that I was feeling through my fingertips. I bent down to him and began giving him mouth to mouth resuscitation, giving him slow breaths so as not to overfill his tiny lungs. I gave him two breaths, then moved my hands down to his chest and pressed off fifteen compressions, then went back to giving him breaths. I kept this up for several minutes, the rhythm of breaths and compressions, but the little boy never responded, and I knew we were losing him. Suddenly I felt a hand on my shoulder, and I turned to see a paramedic standing over me. "We'll take it now."

They took the boy, his name was Matthew, out to the ambulance. They worked on him inside for several minutes, then drove to Swedish Hospital with lights and sirens. I knew it was over. Matthew died there on that cold, wet pool deck. I tried my best, but I couldn't save him. That night on my way home at the end of shift, alone in the dark on the empty road, I suddenly pulled my car over onto the shoulder and just lost it as the tears flowed unstoppable, for that small little boy and all the things he would never be, the life he would never get the chance to live. In all my years of police work that was the only time I ever cried for a victim.

* * *

I got my letter from the Denver Police Department, with the news that I had been hired. I waited just a couple more days to tender my resignation. It was pleasant to drive around the city those last two weeks, with winter snow coating the branches of the trees and icing the lakes. I didn't arrest anybody, and I didn't write anybody a ticket.

I'll never forget my last call. My very last radio call as a Cherry Hills cop went like this;

Dispatch: "320?"
Me: "320"
Dispatch: "Can you respond to 822 Sanford Circle? Resident reports a large, hairy spider on her back porch"
Silence...
Me: "Can you repeat that call dispatch?"
Dispatch: "Affirm. Resident at 822 Sanford Circle reports she was sitting on her back porch when she was approached by a large, hairy spider."
(Laughter in the background at the dispatch center)
Me: "Copy, en route"
Dispatch: "Use caution 320"
Charlie 30 (smartass deputy piping up): "Does 320 need cover?"
Dispatch: "320, do you need a cover car?" (more laughter)
Me (blushing red with anger and embarrassment): "Negative, dispatch. I think I can handle it."

That last call was a microcosm of life as a Cherry Hills cop. I should say of one aspect of being a Cherry Hills cop. I went to the house, the spider was gone, I told the homeowner to call back if the spider returned, and left her feeling reassured that her brave blue knights were there to save her whenever she needed us. I went back to the station, gassed up my old companion Car 6 and put her to bed. I went to the locker room and changed out of my uniform for the last time. It was a symptom of how times had changed over ten years that the two guys I was working with that night were both new guys, guys that I barely knew. Most of my old friends from the Department were gone, moved on to other departments or to civilian life. It was just as well, I figured, as I walked through the squad room. The new guys said goodbye but without feeling. To them I was just Sergeant Miller, a stern guy they hardly knew. I walked out the back door and stood in the darkness of the alley for a moment, all the memories of the last decade rushing up in my mind. I walked across the lot and out to my car, and with one last look around I got in and drove away. There were no tears in my eyes; I took satisfaction in knowing I had done a good job here, and I had met some great people that I am still good friends with today. I was looking forward to my new career at Denver PD, and I believe one should appreciate where you've been but don't dwell on it. All the good times and bad times, the good people and bad, were all in the past now.

PART FOUR

SEVENTEEN

*"Oh dear, I never realized what a terrible lot of
explaining one has to do in a murder!"*
-Agatha Christie, *Spider's Web*

I WAS EXCITED TO BE MAKING THE MOVE TO
DENVER, but the process of actually getting hired was far
from smooth. I didn't think that would be a problem, given
my experience, but I was wrong. Getting hired at blue-collar
DPD turned out to be far more complicated than getting hired
at highbrow Cherry Hills. I found out that Denver PD does not
directly hire its officers; it's all done through the Civil Service
Commission, and I had to go down to their main office to pick up
an application packet. I filled it out and turned it in, and after my
packet went through I had to take a written test which I passed
with no problem, and that was followed a week later by a physical
agility test. Before I took the agility test I had to have a physical
exam, to make sure I wouldn't collapse and have a heart attack
halfway around the course. I made an appointment and went
to the clinic, and the nurses put me through the usual regimen;
height, weight, blood pressure, sticking that cold stethoscope
against my back and telling me to take deep breaths. I swear
they refrigerate those things just for laughs. Then I laid down
on a table while a doctor moved my legs around and poked and
prodded me, checking for what I don't know, then I was told to

go into the next room and get undressed down to my underwear. And that's where it all got a little weird.

I got undressed down to my skivvies, and I was standing there reading the charts on the wall, looking at the little plastic model of the knee or whatever it was, flipping through old magazines and waiting for someone to come in. I believe they have a rule in hospitals - I call it the Time/Nudity Rule, which says the more undressed you are, the longer you will have to stand around waiting for someone to come in. When someone finally did come in I was surprised to see it was a woman. I don't know about you, but I find it very uncomfortable to be minutely examined in the nude by a person of the opposite sex. In the half-light of a bedroom, or even the back seat of a car at the drive-in, I have no problem getting naked. I'm all for it in fact, and do it as often as I can, but under the bright revealing lights of a hospital clinic, with someone poking and prodding you and minutely examining you with furrowed brows, like you were a strange new specimen pinned to the science tray, then no, not so much.

This woman was a dark-haired nurse in her thirties I would guess, and she was very friendly and chatty, trying to set me at ease, no doubt, as she moved around me, doing more examining and prodding. Then the moment came that every guy dreads. She told me to drop my shorts. I slid them down thinking *let's just hurry up and get this over with, okay?* but I found that she was in no hurry at all to get this over with. In fact she pulled up a chair and sat down, right in front of me at crotch level. She continued talking to me about nothing in particular while she moved and lifted and examined my equipment. Then she cradled my package in her hand and just sat there, looking up at me and talking, as if we were having lunch at a cafe. I can tell you that it is very difficult to carry on a casual conversation with a woman who is seated with her face twelve inches from your unit, and holding it in her hand no less. *Okay lady, you either gotta do something with that or let go of it!* Finally after a couple more minutes of talking she released it, and let me pull up my shorts. The whole episode was so bizarre that I mentioned it to Matt, and he immediately said "Yes! The Fondler! She did it to me, too!"

* * *

The agility test was administered at the Denver Police Academy. I had never been there before so I had to call and get directions, and when I found it I saw it was on the grounds of a long defunct airport and the Academy building itself was an old paint-faded airplane hangar completely surrounded by a tall chain link fence topped with strands of barbed wire and locked gates. It looked more like Area 51 than a police academy. I drove in through the gate, parked, and went inside. Once inside, the building looked even older and drearier than it had on the outside. It reminded me of my old barracks at boot camp, long ago back in San Diego. It had a large bare central room with a painted concrete floor and around the periphery was set up an obstacle course, with fences to jump, tunnels to crawl through, and a heavy-looking dummy with handles on it.

I joined a group of other guys and we were just standing around making small talk when a short, slightly chubby Hispanic guy with a mustache and wearing vintage 1970's grey sweats emerged from an office and began barking at us like a drill sergeant. We all reflexively jumped to attention, and he bawled out that he was Corporal Chagolla, and we would do exactly what he said, when he said it, and how he said it, is that CLEAR!? "YES SIR!" we all shouted in unison. This was already looking a whole lot different than Cherry Hills, where even when you were neck deep in trouble and they were about to shove something very deep into your backside, they never raised their voices. Chagolla demonstrated the agility course, and I gotta give the guy credit, because even though he was older and a little paunchy, he fairly flew through the agility course. The rest of us went in turn, and I easily passed the agility test with time to spare. I had always felt that while a police officer doesn't have to look like Arnold Schwarzenegger he should at least be in decent physical condition. I've seen bad guys size me up on many occasions, deciding if they want to take me on, plus your uniform just looks and fits better, and you feel better and more confident in yourself.

I took a polygraph test a couple of weeks later, and then got a letter from the Civil Service Commission saying I had passed all the tests so far and things were looking good.

The next step with Denver was a psychological screening. I think this was the MMPI, the Minnesota Multi-Phasic Personality Inventory, a test that, judging by the questions, was designed by eggheads in white lab coats who don't have a clue how regular people think and behave. I remember some of the questions; *Do you like fire?* If I'm camping in the woods and there are marshmallows roasting over it then yeah, I like fire. If it's burning down my house, then no, I don't like it. *Do you like tall women?* I didn't know how to answer that one. Yes, I like tall women if they look like Tyra Banks or Katherine Heigl, but not if they look like Janet Reno. So then you start wondering just what are they looking for and you find yourself trying to get into the heads of the people who wrote the test. Only you can't do that because you're a regular Joe and they're all Ivy League nerds who were in the Chess Club at Harvard. I just don't trust psychologists. I have a sneaking suspicion that most of them went into the field to try and sort out their own confused minds.

I got a phone call from a woman at the Civil Service Commission who told me I needed to come in because they had some…um…*irregularities*, on my psychological exam. *Uh oh.* The nerds were after me. I had to make an appointment with Dr. Nicoletti, a police psychiatrist. I went to his office on the appointed day, seeing my chances of becoming a Denver cop receding away from me. Nicolleti was flipping through some papers and charts he had in his hand, and he was frowning as he was reading. He said the people who scored my tests had some concerns, because my answers to the MMPI were significantly different than the average DPD recruit. No offense to DPD, but they hire a lot of guys who aren't exactly rocket scientists. When you have around 1,500 cops, you can't be too choosy about who comes through the door. The doc talked to me for a while, chatting about my childhood, my previous experiences as a cop, and why I wanted to go to Denver. I just answered each question straight up, and after about half an hour Nicolleti said that as far as he was concerned I had both paddles in the water and I was okay by him. *Whew!* I had escaped from the clutches of the nerds.

That psych eval was the very last hurdle and the final thing I had to do was go in for an interview. I showed up in my suit and tie and waited patiently in the hallway with half a dozen other guys, and when one of the officers stepped out into the hall and called my name I got up and went in for what I hoped was the last test. As soon as I walked in right away I saw that I knew one of the guys on the interview team. Neither of us said anything about it, and we continued the interview with them firing questions at me and me doing my best to give what I hoped were good answers. When it was over, they said thanks for coming and they would be in touch. It was about two weeks later that I got a letter in the mail saying *Congratulations and Welcome to the Denver Police Department!* I was to report for duty to the Police Academy on January 10. That was the week of my birthday.

* * *

I drove up to the gate for my first day at the Denver Police Academy with a mix of anticipation and anxiety, and as I walked through the entrance I looked up at the words painted above the door: Through These Doors Pass The Finest Police Officers In The World. *Let's see if I'm one of them*...I met my classmates in Class 05-1, just thirteen of us. The usual Academy classes numbered fifty or more, but we were a lateral class, officers with experience and all coming from other departments, rather than rookies. We milled around, making introductions and wondering what was going to happen. The Academy building itself was a huge old airplane hangar that looked like it dated back from World War II, still retaining its giant hangar doors on the south wall, and as I stood in the vast bay I could almost hear the guttural thrum of supercharged Merlin V-12s and spinning props. There was an addition built onto the north end for classrooms, and in the open center bay there were lockers, a gym with free weights and machines, the two-story tactical training house, and piles of equipment and odds and ends. It all had a very functional, industrial feel to it.

We met our class commander, Sergeant Jim Mair, himself a lateral to DPD. Mair was a very sharp yet laid back guy, and he told us that since we were all experienced officers we wouldn't be subjected to the same boot camp treatment that the green recruits would get. On the other hand, because we were veteran cops, he would cut us no slack and expected us to be a model class for the boots. If we failed, we would pay dearly for it. We were all wondering just what that meant, but before we got an answer we shuffled into a classroom for badge number assignments. We were the first class of the year, so our badge numbers started with double-0, for example 05-001. We all wanted 007, but I got 006. *What the hell*, I figured, *maybe I'll be one better than James Bond.* We soon settled into a daily routine of running and PT in the morning, followed by classes ranging from drug recognition to gang intelligence to sexual assault investigations. This would be followed by lifting weights or more running in the afternoon. Denver PD was heavy into the "ridin', ropin', and shootin'" aspects of law enforcement, and considering the neighborhoods they worked and the violent criminal gangs they encountered, maybe that wasn't such a bad thing. It seemed we were always at the shooting range, out at the driving track, or in the gym practicing arrest control techniques. When we weren't doing those, we were practicing building searches in the two-story "kill house" in the center of the hangar. The whole atmosphere was very militaristic, with PT, uniform inspections, saluting and shouting "YES SIR!" every other time you opened your mouth. It reminded me of my military days and Senior Chief Salazar molding recruits into warriors. It was right up my alley, and I loved it.

As the weeks passed and we began to get to know our instructors, we took it upon ourselves to assign them names from *Star Wars*. Corporal Dave Sconce was a towering, intimidating figure who was always yelling at us so he became Chewbacca. The handsome Lamar Sims from the DA's office who taught us search and seizure became Lando Calrissian. Our own Sergeant Mair became Han Solo. Corporal Chagolla was our most frequent instructor, our mentor in most subjects, and as he was quite short he became the most famous Jedi master of them all, Yoda. One morning we were at the driving track, and we were all standing outside in a group while he was explaining the physics behind high-speed driving when Mike Anich standing somewhere in the back quipped *"Teach You To Drive I Will!"* in an excellent imitation of Master Yoda. We all laughed and Corporal Chagolla immediately demanded "Who said that!?" No one said anything and Chagolla's face got red with anger and he shouted "I want to know who said that, RIGHT NOW!" Still, no one would give our classmate up and the Corporal thundered "Either you tell me who it was or you'll *all* being doing pushups until sundown!"

We didn't give Mike up, and for the next two hours Yoda was as good as his word as we ran sprints, cranked out pushups, and did lunges all the way across the driving track until our legs burned.

But we didn't give him up. Disgusted, Chagolla sent us back to the hangar, then went to talk to Sergeant Mair. Mair came back and called us all to form up in ranks and stand at attention. We all were already beat and thinking *Oh crap! What's he going to do to us now?* Mair stood there grim faced for a moment staring at his disobedient troops, then he began "Corporal Chagolla has informed me of what you did. He informed me that he punished you for two hours and you still wouldn't tell him who made that insubordinate remark." He paused for a moment and then said "I'm *damn proud* of you! Hit the locker room!" Sergeant Mair drilled it into us so often that I can still clearly picture him standing in front of us and saying "Remember, at Denver PD we take care of our own!"

We fell into formation one morning as usual, and received some exciting news. It seems the NBA All-Star Game was coming to Denver, and the patrol guys needed more bodies for crowd and traffic control. Our class and the class ahead of us, 04-4, with whom we shared the Academy would be working traffic control during the event. Each of us would be paired up with a patrol officer and be assigned to a particular intersection. They loaded us all on a bus and drove us down to the Pepsi Center where the action would be taking place, and there we were paired up with our assigned officers. They told us to wear our jackets so no one would see we didn't have guns. I was assigned to a crusty, grumpy old codger at an intersection near the Pepsi Center, and as he stood out there directing cars to go this way and that way he kept up a steady drone of curses, and at one point a passing motorist paused and politely asked "Do you know where I can find a parking space?" I opened my mouth to give him a couple of suggestions, but before I could say anything my partner for the day shouted "What do I look like, a friggin' parking attendant!? Keep it movin' buddy!" The rest of that day passed in a similar vein, and as we rode the bus back to the Academy we all talked about how they did things just a little differently here in Denver.

We had a "Community Tours" day about halfway through the Academy, in which they loaded all of us on a bus and drove us around to meet the people in the community. We went to an Islamic Center, where an imam got up and railed at us about how evil the police all were. Then we got back on the bus and went to a Hispanic Center, where a guy got up and railed at us about how evil the police all were. Then we got back on the bus and went to a battered women's shelter, where a woman got up and railed at us about how evil men all were. It was actually refreshing to be called evil for some reason other than being a police officer. *Welcome to the community and fuck you!* Then we went back to the Academy for dinner.

As the weeks passed I began to take closer notice of my surroundings. In the main hallway that ran through the Academy there were glass display cases that lined each wall, containing memorabilia from the past; old ticket books from the 1800's, uniform items, billy clubs, Denver City Marshal's badges from the days of the Old West, yellowing newspaper articles about Indian depredations, and rumrunners from the time of Prohibition. There were faded black and white photographs of grim-faced men in Denver Police uniforms, and I thought that even though they and I were separated by a hundred years if we could somehow sit down over a beer we would understand each other completely. I began to feel a great sense of history in this place, and in this Department, and could almost feel the ghosts of generations of men and women who had walked these halls, mustered in the hangar bay, and been yelled at by other, time-forgotten Corporals. At formation once a week they made us call out one a time the names of each of the sixty Denver police officers who had given their lives in the line of duty, followed by a moment of silence to honor their sacrifice. I started to feel a swell of pride in being here, in being a Denver Police Officer, that I had never experienced in the other law enforcement agencies I had worked for over the past decade.

Graduation week came at last, and on our final day in the Academy we gathered in the classroom for our District assignments. Everyone was eager to find out where they would be going, and some said "Two is the place to go!" or "No, no, Four is where the action is!" or "Six rocks! That's where you wanna be!" I didn't know anything about the Districts, not being from around here, but the consensus was that Four and Six were the hot districts for action, and Three and Five were the slow, country club districts. District Three, which bordered Cherry Hills, was known as "Hollywood" because there were a lot of rich people and big mansions out there. Six was called "Disneyland" because anything you can imagine would happen there. Five had the airport, DIA, and a whole lot of prairie east of that. Four had a large Hispanic population and Little Saigon. Sergeant Mair called us to order and the speculation died down, and all of the other instructors were there in the room as well and it was almost a festive, Christmas-like atmosphere. *What did Santa bring me? I've been good!* Mair began to call off names and assignments, while each of us waited breathlessly for our turn. At last he called out "MILLER! You're goin' to Six!" *Yippee! Thank you Santa!*

On Graduation Day we lined up in formation with white gloves and dress uniforms, sans badges, and listened while Chief Gerry Whitman stood on stage framed by a large American flag behind him and made a stirring speech about duty, honor, and sacrifice. My mind drifted back to my swearing in at Cherry Hills, where I stood in t-shirt and jeans before the secretary, who didn't even get out of her chair to administer the oath. I glanced out in the audience to my wife and children, and the hundreds of people at rapt attention seated out there. *Now this is more like it!* When the speech was over we were called to attention, and one by one as our names were called out we marched across the stage and stood at attention while Chief Whitman shook our hands and pinned our badges on our chests. It was a proud moment for me, and I knew I had done the right thing to come here.

EIGHTEEN

I REPORTED FOR DUTY AT DISTRICT SIX, pulling into the station at Colfax and Washington. I drove up to the gate at the tall chain link fence surrounding the parking lot and had to push the intercom button and ask permission to enter. While I waited I glanced around to see what my new home looked like. The station house itself was a reddish-tan brick building with few windows that looked to be about four or five stories, with a vast parking lot and another low building (which I later found out housed the bikes of the Downtown Motor Unit) all surrounded by the fence. The whole effect was that it looked like an outpost on a hostile planet. The station was surrounded by rundown apartment buildings, a liquor store, a porn shop, and a theater where concerts by off-beat bands were held.

The gate creaked and at last began to move, and slowly rolled aside so I could enter. When I came inside the station I found out that no one was expecting me. I kept telling the desk officer that I was a new officer just graduated from the Academy, that I was assigned to District Six, and I had been ordered to report for duty this morning. He kept looking at his clipboard and shaking his head and saying "Nobody said nothin' about boots from the Academy coming here." He finally went and got a sergeant, who also shook his head and said no one told them I would be coming. He went in the back and conferred with some unseen authority, then came back out and told me to come back tomorrow.

I came back the next day and again had to push the intercom and ask to be buzzed in. I certainly wasn't being made to feel very welcome. I came into the station again and approached the desk officer and this time I was expected and was passed through. The desk officer walked me to the back where a large, dark-skinned guy was sitting at a desk and tersely said "Ranjan Ford, Mike Miller. Miller, Ford" and with the formal introductions done, he turned on his heel and walked back to his desk.

As it turns out I was supposed to be assigned to a Field Training Officer named Mike Wyatt, but he was on his days off so Ford was babysitting me for a couple of days until he got back. I called him "Ford" because I wasn't sure how to pronounce "Ranjan'. Was it ran-jan? Or run-yun? Or Ran-jun? *The hell with it, I'll just call him Ford.* I learned later that Ford had been a detective in Texas, and had cracked the sensational case of a black man who had been kidnapped by white supremacists, then tied and dragged behind a pickup truck until there was nothing left of him but rags. Ford was a good guy and we got along well, and as luck would have it my wife, who was a kindergarten teacher, had Ford's daughter in her class. Ford would later become Matt's partner in the Detective Bureau, and we all became friends. Small world, isn't it?

Corporal Mike Wyatt was a quiet, reserved guy who started our training by giving me a tour of the station. Downstairs in the basement were the locker rooms and a nicely equipped weight room. On the first floor was the desk officer who dealt with the public from behind thick bulletproof glass, and the holding cells, report writing rooms, sergeant's offices, filing rooms, and all the accoutrements of a modern, if a bit run-down, police station. It looked to me like the police station in the old TV show *Barney Miller.* Upstairs was the patrol briefing room, and above that was the Detective Bureau. Atop it all were the lofty offices of The Brass, the District Commander and her entourage of Lieutenants.

Technically, Wyatt (and therefore me) was assigned to Precinct 612, City Park West, but since I was in training he took me all over, showing me the boundaries and the different neighborhoods that made up District Six. In the center of it all was Capitol Hill, with the gold-domed State Capitol building where the governor and the state legislature worked, and the nearby Governor's Mansion where the gov lived when he wasn't at work. Directly across from the Capitol, across the broad green lawns, walkways, and stone statues of Civic Center Park was the imposing Denver County Courthouse with its wide grey steps and broad columns topped with intricate carvings and script in Roman letters. I always liked that courthouse, because in an era when all the new courthouses are built to look like impersonal office buildings this one still retains the grandeur and majesty befitting its position.

There was also the Central Business District with its tall skyscrapers of cold glass and steel, and several blocks of shops, bars and trendy cafes known by one and all simply as LoDo, or Lower Downtown. Out on the east side of the District was Cheesman Park with its large gay community and flamboyant collection of artists, musicians, and tye-dyed tree huggers. There was also the Auraria Campus and Metro State University, as well as the crime and gang infested neighborhoods of Five Points and Lincoln Park. All that sin required ample opportunity to do confession and penance, so there was the spectacular Cathedral of the Immaculate Conception, right on Colfax Avenue where it was most needed. Nearby was the almost as grand Cathedral of Saint John. The district that was to be my home was truly the beating heart of the entire metro Denver area of three million people, the political, business, and cultural center of it all, an eclectic blend of politicians, lawyers, executives, artists, students, junkies, gang bangers, and prostitutes. It was not so much a melting pot as a colorful tossed salad with every topping.

There were maybe a hundred or so officers working out of Six, and most of them took no notice of me, being too busy with their own cases to spare a word for a boot. As they passed me in the hall or in the locker room they might grunt out a half-greeting or else look right through me like I wasn't even there. I started to walk through a little hallway once when I was abruptly stopped by a hulking blonde-haired sergeant who looked like a lineman for the Nebraska Cornhuskers. He said "This is the *Sergeants'* breezeway, boot!" I looked at his nametag - Addison - and beat a hasty retreat. I knew the drill here - I was a boot, an FNG, and I needed to prove myself to these guys before they would accept me. They weren't going to waste time befriending someone who might not even be here in a week or two, so I took no offense. Yet I was delighted to find that I had friends here after all. I was on a call and ran across Todd Ondrak, the new husband of my old Cherry Hills partner Beth. Todd was assigned to Precinct 616, the Golden Triangle, and he was an easy-going, laid back guy who loved backyard cookouts and beer. He also bore, for better or worse, an uncanny resemblance to Homer Simpson. I soon found out that Danny O'Shea, my old buddy from my Navy Reserve days that now seemed like ages ago, was also here in Six, assigned to the Downtown Motor Unit and the SWAT team. When the other officers discovered that these two would vouch for me they suddenly became much friendlier to me. The world of police work is a close-knit family, albeit with a few embarrassing relatives, but what family doesn't have those?

As I traveled with Wyatt over the next couple of weeks of Field Training, learning the lay of the land and the creatures who populated it, I also began the dizzying task of learning the arcane lore of paperwork and procedures at DPD. Every call seemingly had a different collection of forms and reports that went with it. For example, if you rolled on a domestic and you decided to charge the perp under the Denver Revised Municipal Code you had to write up a Domestic Violence Case Summary, a GSS&C or General Sessions Summons & Complaint, get a video-taped interview with the victim, get written statements from all involved officers and any witnesses, and do a Neighborhood Survey. On the other hand if you decided to charge it under the

Colorado Revised Statutes you had to do all the same stuff but you had to charge the perp under a CS&C or Criminal Summon & Complaint but you still had to do your Probable Cause Statement on the GSS&C. See?

One night we were parked outside of a bar on Colfax called Charlie's. It was closing time and we were just watching the outflow of patrons into the parking lot and keeping an eye out for fights, muggings, petty thefts, drug deals, and drunk drivers climbing behind the wheel. As I watched the ebb and flow of the people making their way to their cars or standing around in groups and knots talking I suddenly felt that something seemed different here. At first I couldn't put my finger on it, but then it suddenly hit me. *Hey, where's the chicks? This is a bar - there oughtta be chicks!* There were indeed no chicks. No honeys, hotties, or babes either. It was all dudes. Dudes in leather, in satiny polyester, and in way-too-tight pants. I had never seen a gay bar before, so it was both interesting and a little uncomfortable at the same time. I was to find that there were a few gay bars in the District, including one that was rumored to have Buttless Chaps Night on Thursdays.

I was in my third week of Field Training now, and I was getting comfortable with finding my way around the District and learning to deal with the people who lived here, and who required a whole different approach than the residents of Cherry Hills. If you approached a report of a man with a gun call here and politely said "Sir do you have a firearm in your possession?" you would probably be immediately shot. The biggest change for me was retraining my brain to deal with the entirely different class of people who inhabited the mean streets of District Six. Six had been carved out of the worst parts of three other Districts, and if you wanted action you came to Six. I found out one night just how mean those streets could be.

It was around midnight and we were cruising down Colfax Avenue in the Capitol Hill area, and I was behind the wheel.

Colfax Avenue, or "The Fax" as everybody called it, was sort of like the spiritual heart of downtown Denver. It was the epicenter of all that was good and bad in the Mile High City. For forty miles Colfax Avenue cut like a ribbon through the center of the entire metro area, from Golden in the West to Aurora in the East. It was and is the longest continuous main street in the United States and for all that length it was the central artery that pumped the city's lifeblood. By day it was crisscrossed by lawyers and executives going to their cool metal and glass high-rises to work million dollar deals, and politicians and their staffs and reporters going to and fro at the Capitol, and the homeless people on the street corners begging those people in suits for their spare change. Sometimes they got it, sometimes they didn't. By night the Fax was transformed into the hangout of drug dealers doing swift furtive deals in the bus shelters, hookers trolling the passing cars for johns, the mentally disturbed stumbling down the sidewalks having conversations with people that weren't there, the suburban yuppies coming downtown to go bar-hopping and carousing, and watching over this nightly parade was us; the cops, the heat, Five-O.

On this night we were cruising the Capitol Hill area. There were a few bars in the neighborhood that had been the site of more trouble than usual recently, so we were keeping an alert eye out. It seems a big guy had been robbing people leaving the bars, and even when they gave him all of their money, he would still pistol-whip them. I was near Logan Street, heading westbound and at the same time watching the people on the sidewalk, when out of nowhere a man suddenly appeared right in front of my patrol car. His head and his shirt were bloody, and his eyes were wild. He thrust his hands out toward my car like he was going to use The Force to stop it, and was yelling "STOP! STOP!" I slammed on my brakes and nosed down to a stop just inches from the psycho's legs. He then started to run around to the driver's side window, which was down on this warm summer night. The thought immediately flashed into my mind that this might be some crazy suicide-by-cop attempt, so when he started coming around toward my window I skinned my Sig 9mm and brought it up in a close two-hand hold and leaned back away from the window.

His bloodied head appeared in the window and he started jabbering at me loud and fast. I couldn't understand what the hell he was saying because he appeared to be Middle Eastern and had a thick accent. I yelled at him to move back away from the car, and when he saw the muzzle of my gun pointed at his chest he got the message. He took a couple of steps back but kept shouting. "He robbed me! He beat me! He took my money!" I got him to calm down a fraction, but he was still very excited and kept repeating "He robbed me! I gave him my money and he beat me anyway! He had a gun!" I said "Who robbed you? Where is he?" He said "He had a gun! He robbed me! *And he's right there!*" and with that he pointed back to the sidewalk. Standing on the southwest corner of Colfax and Logan was a big black dude with dreadlocks and a white sweatshirt. His right hand was at his waistband, up under the shirt, ten short yards away and he was looking right at me. I yelled at Bloody Man to *Move!* and I thrust my gun up and out the window to aim it at Dreds, and I yelled for him to freeze. He was one cool customer, I'll give him that, and he just looked at me and my gun nonchalantly, and slowly turned around and started walking down the sidewalk, heading south on Logan.

Usually when a suspect commits an armed robbery he can't get out of the area fast enough. This guy stuck around, and even when the police showed up and were talking to his victim, he just stood right there, thirty feet away, watching us. *Something was very wrong here*, I thought to myself as I watched him turn his back and start walking away. Wyatt was out of the car and running down the street as I was starting to open my car door. He had his gun out and up, and was yelling for the suspect to stop. Without even turning around the suspect started to run. I slammed the door and gunned the engine, forcing our witness to leap out of the way.

I bore down on them fast, but I didn't want to get right on top of the suspect because he had a gun and might start shooting. When I got right behind them I skidded to a stop and jumped out and started running after them. I could see past Mike and saw the suspect's right elbow going up and down. *What the hell is he doing?* It suddenly dawned on me that he was trying to get his gun out but it was snagging on his pants. We were both yelling at him to stop, but he kept going. We were running next to an apartment complex now, and just ahead at the corner of the building there was a big tree growing right up next to the wall. Just a few steps away from that tree the suspect's gun came free. He slowed and turned, and I could see him swing the long black barrel of his revolver around toward us. My gun was up but I was a step behind Mike, and I was afraid if I fired I might hit Mike if he suddenly made an evasive move. So I held my breath and held my fire, and I heard the report of a single shot just as the suspect disappeared around that tree.

In emergency situations, for some people the mind works at the speed of light. You could recite the entire Declaration of Independence in two seconds. For others time slows down so that every movement feels as though you are swimming through molasses. For me it did neither, as my long years of training automatically kicked in. As the suspect went out of sight around the tree I thought to myself that the shot did not sound like the boom of a .357 Magnum, which I believed the revolver was. It sounded more like a pop from the nine millimeter Mike carried, which was just like mine, a Sig P228. So I figured it was Mike that fired. We both skidded to a stop by the tree and fell right into our combat training mode. We sliced the pie, just as we had been trained, slow and careful as we edged around the big tree. I was in front now, and as my angle around the tree increased I saw a leg, and then a torso, and then the whole body.

The suspect was lying on his stomach, with his head slightly raised, and he was looking up at me. His hands were underneath his body, and I started yelling for him to put his hands out. He didn't speak, didn't move, just kept looking at me. Then I saw his gun, lying on the ground several feet in front of him. It must have flown from his grasp as he fell. I looked back at him, at his face. His face did not show any anger or hate, just an odd calm, with a wince of pain around the eyes. It suddenly struck me that he was dying. Dying right there in front of me, in that hot dirty parking lot. All of my anger, adrenaline, and righteous indignation left me. I didn't know what to do, or say. We just stared at each other for a moment, six feet apart. In that instant, I did not see him as a robber, a criminal. I just saw him as another human being, one whose life was draining away. I wanted to reach out to him, to help him hold on to it before it slipped away forever. But the spreading blood stain on his white shirt, and that look of death in his eyes told me it was far too late for that. Our eyes locked for a few seconds more, then his head slowly fell forward to the street. He was dead.

There were many more things that happened that night, but right then I just felt numb. Maybe he was a bad guy, maybe the life he was living had led him inexorably to this end, but that didn't make it any easier to be there, at the end. I still think about him sometimes, though it has been years now. Some nights I lie down in my bed, and in the darkness his face comes back to me, and there I am again in that dirty parking lot, with our eyes locked on each other. It was a sad and surreal moment, like we were sharing something of great significance. As strange as it may seem, I felt kind of dirty, and unworthy, to watch another human being drawing their last breath of life. He should have had family, a friend, someone else he cared about to be there with him when night fell forever. All he had was us.

* * *

After he was dead, pandemonium broke out. Somewhere along the way Wyatt had managed to grab his radio and call out that we were in a foot pursuit and gave our location, and after he fired his pistol he radioed out *"Shots fired!"* The radio came alive as cars all over the District started calling in that they were en route to cover and asking for more information, and you could hear their engines racing in the background as they came running to back us up. I could hear dispatch and the sergeant repeatedly trying to raise us on the radio to check on our status but they couldn't get through. I was in turn trying to answer them but could not, for the same reason. I caught a lull in the frantic radio traffic of just a few seconds and keyed the mike and said "This is 612, Miller. Slow everybody down! Both officers are uninjured. The suspect is down with a gunshot wound to the back. We need an ambulance and cars to seal off the scene." As soon as the words "to the back" came out of my mouth I wanted to reach through the radio and grab them. Matt was on duty over in District Five and they were all gathered around in the squad room listening to the foot chase play out, and he later told me that as soon as I said those words every cop in the room winced and said *"Oooh!! Why did he say THAT?!"* I figured those words would came back to haunt me later, but right then I had other things to think about. As it turned out, Mike's shot was perfect, on the run and in the dark, and had entered underneath the suspect's armpit when he swung his gun barrel back toward us and the exit wound was in the back.

Out of nowhere, an angry crowd had formed like they sprang right out of the ground. One minute it was just the three of us out there in that dirty parking lot, and the next minute it was ground zero for an angry mob. *Where the hell did all these people come from?* One black guy in particular was playing the instigator, whipping up and inflaming the crowd. He was walking back and forth in front of them waving his arms and shouting "They did it again! The white cops killed another brother!" For a minute there it was just me and Wyatt, and the crowd sensed their power of numbers and surged in on us. I thought to myself that if we were going to have shoot our way out of this I was determined to start with The Instigator. I got back on the radio and told backup units to step it up, the crowd was getting hostile. Just then I heard the sweet sound of sirens. Sirens are beautiful music to a cop who is in trouble, who needs backup in a hurry. Seconds later the cars came screeching in and blue uniforms started jumping out.

We soon had enough officers on scene to drive the crowd back, and while they were busily getting things under control something suddenly dawned on me like getting hit over the head with a bat; we had a dead body - shot by us - an angry crowd, a sure big news story, and when they asked us why we chased him and shot him, we would say because some guy on Colfax told us the dead man robbed him. *And where is that guy now?* the lawyers would ask. And we would look at each other and shrug our shoulders. We needed that victim! Without him, I could see us being sued, fired, and even prosecuted. I didn't even bother to tell anyone where I was going, I just sprinted back up Logan Street to Colfax. When I got back to Colfax I looked left and right, searching through the moving crowds for our witness. I tried to remember what he was wearing but couldn't. *No luck. Damn! Where was he!?* I picked a direction, heading east figuring he probably was not going back to the bar where he was just robbed. I pushed my way through the crowds, with many a polite "Excuse me!" which garnered many a "Screw you!" in return. I saw up ahead a t-shirt and matted black hair that looked familiar and I ran to catch up to him. It was Bloody Man. *Thank the Lord!* I brought him back with me to the scene and turned him over to another officer and said "Do NOT lose this guy! He's our key witness!" The other officer put him in the back seat of his car and when the door clunked shut I breathed a sigh of relief.

The crowd was under control but now the news media started showing up, jumping out of their trucks with cameras on their shoulders and the talking heads speaking rapidly into their microphones for the breaking news. A sergeant grabbed me and told me not to talk to the reporters. *In fact, just have a seat in my car and don't come out until I tell you.* I climbed into the passenger seat and he climbed in the driver's seat. He said Internal Affairs was on the way and when they arrived just go with them. Then he got out and shut the door, and I was all alone. My head was spinning, and as the adrenalin dump was wearing off my hands were shaking. After all the hectic events that had just happened the quiet of the car was eerie, watching but not hearing the activity of the other officers, the crowd, and the reporters through the window, like a silent movie. *Internal Affairs was coming.* That scared me. When was being taken to Internal Affairs ever a good thing? I took a deep breath and let it out, trying to calm myself and collect my thoughts.

Like most cops, I had played the "what if" game while driving around on patrol, running possible scenarios through my head and deciding what I would do if they happened. Every police officer tries to mentally prepare himself for a shooting, and I'll tell you that a cop's biggest fear is not being shot – it's the fear of not being brave. You always picture yourself being the hero, being Gary Cooper in *High Noon*, but you never know how you'll perform until you've actually "seen the elephant" as the late Colonel Jeff Cooper was fond of saying. *Will you rise to the challenge, or will your courage melt away like running water?* I've seen it happen. While I was running down the sidewalk, and coming around the tree, I did not feel scared, and did not experience some of the things that police magazine articles said can happen like auditory exclusion or everything slowing down. My training kicked in and I found myself focusing on distance, cover, watching my front sight, slicing the pie. So I was satisfied that I had sort of passed a personal test.

Suddenly I noticed through the front windshield a guy in a suit walking around in the crime scene. He was obviously a cop, a middle aged guy with an ill-fitting jacket and I saw him ask a uniform a question, and the uniform turned and pointed right at me. He walked over and climbed into the car. He sat down heavily and looked over at me. *Internal Affairs. Here we go.*

He stuck out his hand and introduced himself. He was a detective in Internal Affairs, and he needed me to go down to Headquarters with him. We got out of the sergeant's car and moved over to his unmarked sedan and set off for HQ. I thought he would start grilling me about the shooting, asking me for the play by play of how it went down. But he didn't. Instead he talked about good restaurants in the area, how the Rockies would do this season, anything but the shooting. It was hard to focus on what he was saying, because although I'm a Rockies fan at the moment I didn't really give a shit about how they would stack up against the Dodgers. It was a short ride to 1331 Cherokee Street, and we soon pulled onto the ramp that led down to the police garage underneath the imposing grey building of Denver Police Headquarters.

Once inside we took the elevator up to God knows where, and the detective escorted me to a little windowless room with a couch and couple of chairs and a table with some magazines and nothing more. He told me to wait there and someone would come for me in awhile, then he turned and left. I sat down and reflected on the situation. This was not at all what I expected. I thought they would whisk me off to a meeting with detectives and lawyers and a whirring video camera who would want to hear every detail of the story, several times over. Instead the minutes ticked by, and turned into half an hour and still no one came by talk to me in my isolated little room. Was this some kind of stress test? Were they watching me even now from some hidden camera to see what I would do or say to myself in my isolation chamber? I glanced around the room and up at the ceiling tiles with suspicion. I figured if they were watching me I had better act natural, so I picked up a copy of a magazine and started thumbing through it, trying to look unconcerned. I could not concentrate on the words in front of me, because my kept running in a loop back over every step of what had happened, wondering *could we have done anything different?* Suddenly the door to my little room opened and Sergeant Steve Addison walked in. Addison was a big, blonde haired handsome fellow, and he was on the swing shift while I was on nights, so I didn't really work with him directly, but I liked him.

Addison sat down with me for awhile, asking me how I was doing, making small talk, trying to set me at ease. I asked him why no one was talking to me, and he patiently explained to me how the process worked. Whenever there was an officer-involved shooting, the cop is the very *last* person the investigators talk to. First they talk to the perp (assuming he lives), then they talk to witnesses, then they talk to officers present but not involved, and only then do they interview the officers directly involved. Of course I was ignorant of all this and thought the longer it was taking for them to talk to me must mean they thought something was wrong with what we did and they were deciding what to do about it, so I felt much better after talking to Addison. He told me that all the guys at the station house were behind us all the way, and even though I instinctively knew they would be, it made me feel better to hear it said out loud. He asked me if I wanted something to eat, and it dawned on me that I hadn't eaten since yesterday and I was famished. I ordered a beef burrito, smothered with green chile, and topped with lettuce and tomato. Hey, if he was offering I was going to take him up on it! Addison slapped me on the shoulder and told me not to worry and he was off.

I started to settle back into the couch but a second later someone else walked in. I glanced up as an older man in a perfectly creased uniform walked in. He looked vaguely familiar, then I saw the row of gold stars on his collar, the gold shield on his chest, and then the gold nameplate that said "Whitman". As in Gerald Whitman, Chief of Police. Now in a small department the Chief is a guy you see all the time; hanging out in the squad room holding a cup of coffee, droning on at staff meetings, flirting with the secretaries, and occasionally even out on a call. He's human, a regular guy. In a big department with a thousand plus officers, the Chief is a guy you see in press conferences on TV. Denver PD has six district stations, the gang unit substation, the traffic bureau, and headquarters downtown. The beat cops live and work in their district stations and you don't go downtown unless you have some reason to. If you have to go see the Chief you are either getting a medal or you're getting fired. The Chief lives at the top of headquarters, he is *not* a regular guy, and you will *never* see him out on a call. To see the Chief out on a call would be like a soldier diving into a trench in Afghanistan and looking over and seeing a four-star General in the dirt there beside him. So when Chief Whitman walked in I jumped up and saluted, both because of my military background and because I wasn't sure exactly what I was supposed to do. He grinned and told me to relax and sit down. I did, and he sat in the chair across from me. I thought *Well I'm not getting a medal so I must be getting fired.*

The Chief started by asking me how I was doing, to which I said I was fine. Then he said he wanted me to know that he backed us all the way and if there was anything he could do for me just let him know, and I could tell he meant it. He asked if I wanted him to call my wife, or the FOP attorney, or anyone else I wanted. I said no, thank you, and then he shook my hand and got up and left. I wanted to see Wyatt and check on how he was doing, but then a steady stream of people started coming through; captains, deputy chiefs, lieutenants, patrol officers, people that I didn't even know, and all saying they backed us one hundred percent.

Even one of my old Academy instructors dropped by to give me his support. I was flabbergasted. In the police academy Jim Mair always hammered into us that at Denver PD we take care of our own. I always thought it was just words, an encouraging slogan to build teamwork and spirit, but now I saw it in action. In my old department, if some citizen made a complaint against you or you got involved in some hairy, scary confrontation you were considered guilty until proven innocent. The brass just assumed you had violated some policy or other, and they just had to find the right one to shove up your backside. Of course, I was too young and hard-headed and full of piss and vinegar back then to ever let that stop me from jumping with both feet into every mess I could find. I always figured if it went bad it was easier to take my licks and ask for forgiveness than to ask permission. The two departments were as different as night and day when it came to the command supporting the troops, and after ten years operating in that oppressive Us-versus-Them environment I just naturally assumed that now I would have to defend myself for what we had done.

Addison finally came back with my burrito, and maybe it was just the combination of being glad to be alive, stressed out, and famished but it was the best-tasting burrito I ever ate. Steve was a big boy with arms like hams, so he figured as long as he was getting me one he might as well get two for himself. So we ate and talked and got to know each other. He told me a funny story. One day he was having lunch with his wife down in the Cherry Creek shopping district, which is a very posh, ritzy area full of quaint shops and European style little outdoor cafes. He and his wife were sitting out on the patio under an umbrella enjoying lunch when a couple of gang members hanging out across the street recognized him. They started taunting him, calling out *"Aaaddison! Aaaaddison!"* He wasn't too happy about it because like every cop he doesn't want his family exposed to the crap we have to deal with every day. You try to insulate them, protect them from the world you become a part of every time you put on the badge and gun. He ignored them and finished his meal and left, taking care they weren't following him. A couple of days later while on patrol he saw one of the guys sitting on a porch drinking 40's with his homies. He cruised by and slowed down, and rolling down his window he called out to the guy and said "Hey, thanks for the info! It was a good tip!" and drove away. He could see with great satisfaction in his rear view mirror that the homies were now all surrounding the guy and demanding to know what the fuck was up.

My little isolation room did not have a clock in it so I don't know how long I was in there, but it felt like four or five hours, when at last a detective poked his head in the door and told me to follow him. It was at last my turn. As we walked down the hall he stuck out his hand and said "Lieutenant Priest, Homicide." Jon Priest needed no introduction. He was a legend in the Denver Police Department, indeed in the whole metro law enforcement community. He practically wrote the book on investigating human-caused deaths. When Jon Benet Ramsey was murdered, scuttlebutt was that Denver PD offered to lend Priest to Boulder PD to help with the investigation, but they turned down the offer. I know there are a lot of Denver detectives who are quite certain that if Boulder's chief had accepted the offer that sad case would have been solved.

Priest led me back to a small interview room and held the door open for me. Inside, to my surprise I saw Lamar Sims seated on a chair at the table. Sims was the Chief Deputy District Attorney for the Denver DA's Office. He had been a frequent instructor at the Police Academy, and seeing as how I had just graduated three short weeks ago he remembered me. He stood up and warmly shook my hand and said "Welcome to the streets, Officer Miller." He was a tall, muscular, handsome black man. He was the one we nicknamed Lando Calrissian back in the Academy. He also has a mind that's as sharp as a knife and a great sense of humor, and I would not be surprised to see him in the Governor's office or Congress someday.

After the pleasantries we all sat down at the table and Priest began. He told me he was going to ask me a lot of questions about what happened, and just to relax and tell it exactly the way I remembered it, omitting no details and being as complete as I could be. He said the interview was going to be recorded but don't let that distract me. He pointed to a TV screen hung on the wall and said "Now, we're just going to start with some photos, to set the scene. When I place a photo up on the screen I want you to identify what is in the picture for us, okay?" I said sure, no problem, and waited while he loaded the first picture.

The first picture popped up on the screen. It was a picture of a parking lot, taken at night, with a scattering of cars in it, and a distant apartment building in the corner of the picture, and no people were visible. I looked closely at it, but try as I might nothing in the scene looked familiar. They were waiting for me to speak, and I racked my brain to come up with something, some landmark that I would recognize but there was just nothing there that was ringing any bells. Finally Priest said "Well, do you recognize this picture, Officer Miller?" I sat back in my chair and said "I'm sorry but I don't." Priest's jaw dropped and he said "What do you mean you don't recognize this scene? You were just there a few hours ago! You were just involved in a shooting there! How can you not recognize it?!" He turned to look at Sims and they exchanged a look that said plainer than any words *"What kind of brain-dead idiot are we dealing with here?"* Priest turned back to me, and speaking slowly asked me to explain what exactly was my major malfunction. I told him that yes, it looked vaguely like that parking lot but the angle was all wrong. We looked at it some more and finally figured out that yes it was indeed a picture of the parking lot where the shooting happened, but the snapshot was taken from *the far side* of the lot, on the opposite side from where all the action had taken place and from that angle you couldn't see the big tree and everything looked different.

When we got that straightened out Priest was at last satisfied that I really did have an IQ above room temperature, and the interview continued. We were there for about an hour, I think, with Priest asking questions while Sims sat off to one side, and me reflecting back and trying to replay for them the events exactly as they unfolded, from the first contact, to sighting the suspect, the foot chase, seeing the gun, the firing of the fatal shot, everything play by play. Finally the time came when Priest had no more questions. He went back over a couple of points just to clarify things, and we were done. I got up, shook their hands, and Priest escorted me out. I was surprised to see it was bright daylight out. At the door, Priest told me to take a few days off and unwind. He said it looked like a good shoot and not to worry about it. Then he closed the door and went back inside. I was done at last.

* * *

On the way home I tried not to think about anything. I was dead tired and just wanted to crawl into bed and sleep for three days. I thought about calling my wife, Kari, but she was at school and I thought she'd freak out if I told her what had happened, then she'd rush home to see me and she'd want to hear the whole story. I didn't want to upset her, and I figured there would be plenty of time to talk about it *after* I got some shuteye. I got home and crawled into bed, but it seemed like my head had barely hit the pillow when Kari was standing above me and frantically shaking me awake. As soon as I regained semi-consciousness she grabbed me and hugged me. She was crying and asking if I was okay and telling me what an ass I was for ever becoming a cop. *Now how the hell did she find out about this already?*

Whenever there is an officer-involved shooting the Department does not immediately release the names of the officers involved, not until the brass and the media relations people have had a chance to sort things out and figure out exactly what happened. Only then do they release a statement. In our case that didn't happen - somebody let something slip, because my name and Mike Wyatt's name went out on the radio and TV almost before the smoke cleared. All the morning commuters sitting in traffic sipping their Starbucks heard all about it. Some of those morning commuters were Kari's friends, and they started calling her. The first one called Kari just after she got to school and asked her if she was okay. Now as it turns out Kari's uncle Bob whom she was close to had just passed away the day before, and Kari thought they were talking about *that*. She doesn't listen to the radio on the way to school and so had no idea what had happened. She just told her friend that yes, she was okay, she was dealing with it but she'd be fine. Minutes later another friend called and in the same soothing, concerned voice said she had just heard and was Kari okay? Kari thought how nice it was that her friends were all calling to see how she was doing, and said yes, she would be fine. Then the friend asked *is Mike doing okay?* Kari thought to herself that yeah, Mike liked the old guy but they weren't close so why wouldn't he be okay? She just said that Mike was fine, he wasn't really too upset about it. Now it was the friend's turn to think that was a little strange.

When the phone rang again Kari thought this was getting a little weird. Why were these people all calling at the same time, and how did they even *know* her uncle had died anyway? The next call was her best friend Suzie, and Suzie was asking her if she was okay. Kari said she was alright, and then Suzie asked if Mike was okay, and had he got home to talk to her about it yet? Kari said Mike was fine, then got the feeling she was missing something here, and said "Wait a minute; got home to talk to me about what?" So Suzie told Kari that she'd just heard it on the radio that I had been involved in a shooting early this morning. Kari freaked out and told another teacher to take over her class and ran home. When she saw me sleeping in bed she first wanted to hug me, then brain me with a skillet for not telling her about it right away. I told her I figured she wouldn't have heard about it yet anyway, so I would just get some sleep and talk to her about it when she got home this afternoon. That sounds perfectly logical to me, but I have since learned not to trust my own figuring when it comes to women. In many situations since then I have calculated what I thought would be the appropriate thing to do and then I do the opposite. That plan has actually worked out pretty well for me, at least as far as my wife is concerned.

So I got things straightened out with my wife, got some sleep, and after I woke up I was curious about how the story would play out in the media. I sat back on the couch and turned on the tube. It wasn't long before there was a commercial break and the suntanned anchor man from a local station came on with his perfect hair and perfect teeth, and he leaned into the camera and said with a serious look on his face "Coming up at five, Denver police gun down a father of three!" then the TV cut to another commercial.

I sat back on the couch, stunned. This guy was out there with a gun prowling for victims, robbing and pistol-whipping people, aiming his gun at police officers, and in an instant, with the power of the media he had been transformed into The Good Guy. Where there's a good guy there has to be a Bad Guy, and we were it. Over the next few days all the local news channels repeatedly featured his wailing mother, crying out that *my baby wouldn't hurt nobody!* and those white cops just shot her baby down. The local television stations showed over and over his Glamour Shots photo that showed a young man with a red sweater and a big sweet smile and his hand resting on his chin. The picture looked like it had been taken several years before, and I didn't see that guy out there on the street that night. By that same power of the media me and Wyatt instantly became the Evil White Racist Cops, we had become the Rodney King cops, and the so-called "community leaders" were out giving interviews to anyone with a microphone, decrying the injustice, and Joe and Jane Citizen out there dutifully believed whatever the talking heads told them to believe.

As it turns out there *was* a citizen witness to the shooting; a woman coming home late saw the entire event, saw the foot chase, saw him pull his gun and point it back toward us, and heard us yelling for him to drop it. I didn't find out about her until the next day. It was partly on account of her that we were cleared by the DA, cleared by the Department, and no lawsuit was ever even filed. Of all the news stations in the metro area only *one* interviewed her. You see she threw a monkey wrench into the whole packaged story that the media was selling; Bad White Cops, Innocent Black Man, Police Brutality. That's the stuff that makes headlines, gets people excited, sells newspapers and creates a frenzy. It amazes me to think that there are still people out there who really believe the media just wants to find the truth, get the real story out, still has journalistic integrity. You know what the news media wants? Scandal. They want dirt, sex, violence and corruption. They want to get their viewers' blood pumping, and if they have to spin the truth and twist the facts to get it, trash a few good people along the way, hey it's a small price to pay for ratings.

* * *

My first phase of Field Training was over, and the night before my second phase was set to begin I got a phone call at home. It was a sergeant from the station telling me to report to District One tomorrow. I would be going there for my next phase instead of doing it in Six. I didn't even know where the District One station was, and had to ask the sergeant for directions. He said my next FTO would be a Corporal named...well I'll just call him Vic. One of my friends from the Academy named Matt had been assigned to One, so I called him and asked about the District and about this guy Vic. As soon as I asked there was a pause on the other end, then Matt said "I'm sorry Mike. Vic's an asshole. He takes pride in washing recruits out, and he's washed out more guys than any other FTO." *Wonderful.* At least I was forewarned.

I reported for duty the next morning, and met Vic. He was an older guy, a little pudgy, and when we met he looked me up and down with a sneer on his face. This was going to be a long four weeks. For starters, he was lazy. Vic began every shift after roll call by going to the home of a friend of his who lived in the District. They would sit at the kitchen table and talk and have coffee for about an hour, while I sat on the couch and listened to the other guys handling all the radio calls. Then he would ding me on my daily evaluation for missing radio calls. I had never been in District One before, and he would tell me to go find some obscure address then ding me on knowledge of district geography when I didn't drive right to it. He ripped me constantly on my daily evals and told me I wasn't cutting it and I should just quit. I ignored him and went about my business, and by the third week we weren't even speaking to each other anymore. I would handle the calls, he would write on my eval that I did everything wrong, I would sign the eval and hand it back to him. And we'd do it all again tomorrow. If I didn't know beforehand what he was doing, if I was really a raw recruit just trying to make it, I would have been a nervous, stressed out wreck thinking I was doing everything wrong. He was just an asshole trying to pump up his own ego by washing out recruits. I figured I could put up with anything for four weeks and would just ride it out.

One morning I had to run a report upstairs to the detectives, and to my delight the detective was Tony Trujillo, my old pal from Cherry Hills. I knew he had gone to Denver a few years before but I had no idea where he was working. Tony and I sat and talked for a long time, and he told me Vic was a prick and to just ignore him and ride it out. I remembered hearing that Tony had been involved in a shooting the year before, and he told me about it. He had responded to a fight with weapons at a seedy bar, and the suspect had met him out front in the parking lot, with a pistol tucked in his waistband. The guy was drunk and belligerent and threatening to shoot Tony. Tony drew down on him and told him not to move, but the guy went for his gun anyway and Tony was forced to shoot him. Tony is a truly decent human being and the killing deeply affected him. It was good to see an old friend again, considering what I was going through now.

One morning I came to roll call and there was a guy there I hadn't seen before. He was in a suit, and I smelled Internal Affairs on him. Vic walked past me (we never sat together) and said "IA's here for you." I said "sure they are", thinking he was just messing with me, but to my surprise right after roll call the IA detective came walking right up to me and said he needed to talk to me. I followed him to an interview room, wondering what I could possibly have done. Was I going to get an IA in every phase of FTO? The detective closed the door and told me that an investigation had been launched because a black male had come down to Headquarters and filed a complaint against me. He said that I had arrested him and while transporting him to the jail I had repeatedly called him a n****r, had hit my brakes so he would lurch forward and hit his head on the cage, and in the jail parking lot I had dragged him out of the car, knocked him down on the ground, and beat him.

I reminded the detective that I was in Field Training, and so could never have transported anyone by myself. We did some more investigation over the next couple of weeks and discovered that the guy said it was me because my name was on the Criminal Summons & Complaint, but another officer had actually transported him. Furthermore, the guy making the complaint apparently didn't realize that there are cameras everywhere in the jail parking garage, and a review of the footage showed him being led out of the car by Corporal John "The Sled" Schledwitz, and he took the guy out of the car and calmly walked him up to the door. No dragging, no beating, no name calling, just a leisurely walk up to the door. The next time he makes a false claim about police brutality, he should check for cameras first.

I finished my second phase of FTO, and Vic submitted a recommendation that I be terminated from the program. They called back to Six and talked to Mike Wyatt, who said I was one of the best recruits he ever had, and the recommendation was summarily denied. I was happy at the thought of going back home to Six, but I got another phone call telling me I would be staying in One for the rest of my FTO. My next training officer was a funny guy named Mike "Dolly" Parton, and we got along great although nothing of note happened during the four weeks I was with him. In fact, he stopped even doing my daily evaluations after the first week, saying if he had any concerns he would let me know. My next and final Field Training Officer was a guy named John Calvetti. John told me on the first day that he had reviewed my record and as far as he was concerned we were partners, not trainer and trainee. I liked him, and we got along just great. We would go to this fleabag motel at 6th and Federal and clear cars in the parking lot because the place was a dumping ground for stolen cars, and we got a lot of them out of there. Calvetti was a very street-smart cop and I learned a lot from him about how police work should be done in Denver.

We mostly worked Precinct 125, Sun Valley, a ghetto near Invesco Field which at that time was the highest crime neighborhood in the entire state of Colorado for six years running. We made drug busts, we had foot chases through the projects, we picked up felony warrants, and we had a lot of fun. One hot day we stopped at a 7-11 for a Coke, and Calvetti told me that shortly before I came to him he had stopped at this very 7-11 to use the bathroom. He tried the door but it was locked, so he waited, and waited, and finally went and got the clerk and told him to unlock the door because he couldn't wait anymore and whoever was in there would have to zip it up and go. The clerk got the key and put it in the lock, and when he swung the door open they came face to face with a guy standing over the toilet who looked up at them in surprise. He had a smudge of white powder under his nose and a baggie of cocaine in his hand. As soon as he saw a cop he threw the baggie into the toilet but before he could flush it John jumped on him and tackled him. The panicked clerk slammed the door shut behind them, locking them both in the tiny bathroom.

People who are jacked up on cocaine and adrenalin have superhuman strength, and this guy was just throwing John around and bouncing him off the walls. He was still fixated on getting rid of the evidence, and he tossed Cal to the floor then turned back and tried to flush the toilet, but Cal kicked his hand away from the flush handle. Then the guy reached down and wrapped his arms around the bowl of the toilet and *ripped* the toilet right off the floor. When John saw that, he got scared. This guy was like The Hulk, or Superman. Water was spewing everywhere, the guy was frantically trying to stuff the baggie of cocaine down the drain pipe, and Cal was hitting the guy with everything he had but it wasn't even phasing him. They fell back down on the slippery floor, both of them now wet and tired. The guy was like an octopus, wrapping him up and squeezing him on the floor. They had been fighting in that small, cramped wet bathroom for several minutes now, and John was so tired he could barely lift his arms. He had lost his radio mike somewhere, and he decided he just had to shoot this guy, but his gun was underneath him pinned to the floor and he couldn't get to it. Suddenly the door opened and other Denver officers were there, pulling the guy off of John and wrestling him to the floor. John was so worn out he just laid on the wet tile for a few more minutes. That's police work; one minute you're just waiting to take a leak and the next minute you're fighting for your life.

NINETEEN

NOW THAT I WAS FINISHED with Field Training I was assigned to Watch 1, the graveyard shift. District Six was divided into Sector 1, roughly the south and east areas, and Sector 2, the north and west areas and LoDo. Each Sector was subdivided into several Precincts, each comprising a few neighborhoods or a number of city blocks. It was considered to be a feather in your cap to be permanently assigned to a Precinct, and once you "earned your Precinct" you were held responsible for it and were expected to get to know it and the creatures who moved through it like the back of your hand. Officers who were assigned to a Precinct became inextricably identified with it and were referred to interchangeably by either their name or their Precinct number. For those of us like me who didn't have our own Precinct, we got assigned to work a particular area on a nightly basis, wherever the shift sergeant decided he needed bodies.

Denver PD had a regular brass parade of command officers; Deputy Chiefs, Division Chiefs, Captains, District Commanders and more, but they were creatures of the light, of daytime and Headquarters downtown, while we were creatures of the night. Down here working deep nights the highest ranking officer we ever saw was our Lieutenant. The District Commander's office was on the top floor of the station but it may as well have been on another planet as far as we were concerned. We never took the elevator any higher than the third floor roll call room. Our LT was a good cop and a good boss. He was a working Lieutenant, out there in a car driving around and showing up on calls rather than pushing paper in an office.

Working at Denver PD was a culture shock for me, not only because I had moved from the raised pinky, wine and cheese country club set to the crack pipe and needles ghetto set, but because of the culture of the Department and of the city. On one occasion I responded to a report of a loud juvenile party in an apartment building. I know you'll be shocked to hear this, but the report said that alcohol was present and there were no adults around. When I got there, along with three or four other officers, we saw that there was one of those floor to ceiling sidelight windows next to the door, and when we looked through it we could see a large and raucous party going on inside. The music was thumping, everybody was drinking, and there wasn't an adult in sight. We banged on the door, not that anybody heard, but then one of the kids inside saw us in the sidelight window. From my previous experience in Cherry Hills I now expected the kids to kill the music and run and hide. But this was Denver, and even the kids do things differently here. The kid who saw us quickly got the attention of the other kids, and they came up to the window and started giving us the finger and laughing and taunting us by taking long pulls from their beer bottles right next to the window, proof that alcohol really does make you stupid.

Now as luck would have it, the phone company had just delivered the new phone books like they do every year, and the residents of this apartment had not yet taken theirs inside. One of the officers on scene decided to follow the advice of Gunnery Sergeant Tom Highway in one of my favorite Clint Eastwood movies, *Heartbreak Ridge*, and Adapt, Improvise, and Overcome. He reached down and picked up the phone book. Now the metro Denver Yellow Pages is a hefty, substantial piece of literature, and he weighed it in his hand for a moment, doing the mental calculations, then yelled out "PHONE BOOK DELIVERY!" and heaved the phone book into the sidelight window. The sidelight window exploded in a shower of glass, and he reached around the window frame and unlocked the door. He pushed it open and the cops walked in and started grabbing the shocked and now subdued kids. As the cops were walking in I was standing in the hallway thinking *Did that really just happen?*

However, in our defense you have to look at the kind of people we were dealing with on a day to day basis. In Cherry Hills I would deal with doctors, lawyers, and businessmen on a typical call, people who were educated, polite, and had a lot to lose. For them, throwing a punch at a police officer was unthinkable. In Denver we dealt with gang members, hookers, and drug addicts on a day to day basis, people who were decidedly impolite to say the least, and with nothing to lose. For those people, well *why not* throw a punch at a police officer?

* * *

I was dispatched one night to the big downtown bus station on a report of a man acting strangely. If you have ever spent any time in a bus station, you know that people acting strangely sort of goes with the territory. In any city or town across America, bus stations are the gathering points for the drifters, the runaways, the transients, and all those who just don't quite fit in with the rest of society. They stream in on the buses, huddle together in the dim tiled stations for a while, then board different buses to take them away to new promised lands, where they hope to find new starts. The people who work in the bus stations have seen it all, so I knew if they were calling me it must be something extra strange. I eased my patrol car up to the front entrance on Arapahoe Street and went up to the door. All eyes were watching me, ready to run if I suddenly turned toward them. At least half the people in bus stations have warrants, but I wasn't interested in them at the moment. I went inside and was met by a security guard. We exchanged pleasantries, then he led me across the station and pointed out the object of this call.

I beheld a thin Asian man, maybe twenty-five, dressed in an oversized rumpled dirty blue jacket and raggedy jeans. He was wearing glasses and had a wispy goatee sprouting from his chin. He looked like an engineering student who had gotten quite lost. Except for the fact that he was crazy, that is. He was pacing around the bus terminal staring up at the ceiling, talking to himself, and every few seconds he would give an emphatic double middle finger gesture up toward the roof. "See what I mean?" said the security guard. "Yeah, I see" I replied. The other patrons of the bus station took no notice of him, as most of them were too busy talking to themselves and dealing with their own inner demons to pay attention to anyone else's. We approached him slowly, and when I got his attention I asked him, just out of curiosity, why he was giving the double bird to the roof of the bus station. Was there someone up there he didn't like? "Yeah! Yeah!" he hissed, very intense and leaning closer to me. "It's God! I'm flipping off God!" *Okay...*I pointed out that God had done a lot of good things, you know, like making the heavens and the earth, giving us food and water, creating man and woman, etc. He replied "That's just it! He cast me out of Heaven, the bastard!" *Okay. Let's start with some basics.* I asked him what his name was. The answer was not what I was expecting. "My name is Lucifer, the Prince of Darkness" he said with a straight face. I asked Lucifer if he had some identification, you know to verify that he was not merely *pretending* to be the Prince of Darkness.

He produced an ID card with his name and picture on it. I mentioned that if he was indeed Satan then the downtown bus station was a little out of his usual neighborhood, and I asked him what he was doing here. He said he was looking for his ex-girlfriend, Allison. I asked him why he wanted to find her, and he said "She is the whore of Babylon! She is the Bride of Lucifer, and I am Lucifer!" I was starting to become a little concerned for Allison, whoever and wherever she was, and I asked him what he intended to do when he found her. "I'll fuck her and lick her body from head to toe!" he said. I proposed the idea that maybe Allison would not want to do that, and he replied "SHE MUST!! She is the Bride of Lucifer. Lick lick lick lick lick lick!!" When he did this his tongue flicked in and out like a hungry snake. I noticed a notebook sticking out of his rumpled jacket pocket, and I asked him what he liked to write. He eagerly pulled it out and showed it to me.

With his permission, I flipped open the notebook. He had spidery, scrawling handwriting and on one page he had written "When I see a thing of beauty, I want to seize it in my hands and choke the life out of it, then drink it in." On another page he wrote about "Little Zikki." He wrote "Little Zikki is shooting nice, tight groups now. I am very satisfied now." I had read quite enough now. I asked him if he knew where Allison lived, and he immediately spouted off an address in the city and said he was on his way there now to meet his bride. This guy was clearly unstable and he needed to go to a nice padded room somewhere, complete with a fashionable straight jacket. I decided to place him on an M-1, a Mental Health Hold, until he could be evaluated by a psychiatrist. Without saying a word I subtly nodded to the security guard. You have to be very careful in dealing with emotionally disturbed people. They can turn on you in a flash, and they can have freakish superhuman strength. They also are frequently armed, usually with an edged weapon of some sort. I don't know why, but blades are unusually fascinating to EDP's. The security guard began to talk to him, and he turned around to face the guard, while I slipped out my handcuffs and quickly, neatly snicked them on his wrists.

Ho did not even appear to notice that I was putting the cuffs on him, but I was ready to sweep his legs and drop him at the first sign of a fight. You do not mess around with EDP's. After I cuffed him, I searched him. The first thing I found was a big, long shiny Bowie knife inside his jacket. It looked like Crocodile Dundee's knife. The blade was over a foot long and sharp. I asked him what he intended to do with this knife, and he immediately said "To take my bride, the whore of Babylon!" I kept searching him and found ten bottles of Robitussin in the pockets of his jacket. He had already drank three. I called dispatch and told them to send me the bus for a mental health hold. The ambulance crew arrived and I briefed them on their patient. They strapped him down to a gurney and took him away to see the nice men in the white coats. The security guard went back to his post and I went back out into the waiting city, ready for the next one. Allison, wherever and whoever you are, you owe me a beer.

* * *

I was working the day shift on a quiet morning, which was unusual for DPD so I was enjoying the silence. We suddenly got an Amber Alert over the radio that a 9 year old girl had just been abducted. Suspect information was very thin, just that a white Mercedes was involved. That wasn't just thin, it was anorexic. Time is usually of the essence in child abductions because all too often it ends badly if we don't find the child quickly. I was driving around keeping my eyes peeled when I spotted a white Mercedes sedan in a bank parking lot. I aired it and pulled in behind the Benz. The driver saw me pull in and got out of the car. He was a black guy in a suit, and I could see the apprehension on his face. I told him why I was contacting him, while scanning the inside of his car for any sign a child had been in it, as well as scanning him for any nervous "tells" that cops always look for. I asked him if I could look in his trunk. He said "You want to look for a kid, *in my trunk?*" I nodded, and he said "*Man, your job is fucked up!*" Yeah, but what the hell, it's a living. We did find the girl, safe and sound, by the way.

* * *

If you venture into downtown after 2 a.m., in any large city in America, you will find among the dark alleys, the trash, and the flickering neon signs, a colorful collection of individuals known only as "street people." You will see the drug dealers doing quick, furtive deals with their hungry clients, desperately needing their next fix; the homeless guy who tugs at your sleeve as you walk by and asks for your spare change; the crazy lady pushing a shopping cart full of aluminum cans and bags and what-not, talking and laughing to herself; and no night street scene would be complete without the hookers. You see them slowly walking along the sidewalk in stiletto heels and very short, tight dresses, looking at every car for a glimmer of interest from a passerby. The way it works is a john drives slowly down the street, and when he sees a girl he pulls up next to her and rolls down his window and asks "Are you working?" and then she gets in.

Contrary to movies like *Pretty Woman*, most hookers are decidedly unattractive. Some of them are downright ugly. Sure, most of them may have been decent looking in their past, better days, but after a while of working the streets they all begin to acquire that hard and used look. Most of them are drug addicts. Many have kids to support. Cops don't usually harass the prostitutes, unless some citizens' group complains to the mayor about the deplorable state of the city, then the mayor's staff gets on the horn to the Chief, who sends the word downhill to crack down on the hookers and junkies and clean up the city. That usually lasts about a week and fades away. It's like sticking your finger in a bucket of water; as soon as you pull your finger out, the water fills back in.

Prostitution has been called the oldest profession, and decent society has been railing against it even as far back as the Old Testament. But it's still around, because it's a service that will never suffer from a lack of demand. Heidi Fleiss, the "Hollywood Madam" made a very good living using her stable of girls to serve the needs of rich and famous guys like Charlie Sheen and former New York Governor Elliot Spitzer. That kind of makes regular guys feel better knowing that even these guys have to pay for it now and then. Sometimes the girls are not above picking up a little more money than they contracted for, too.

I was with Todd Ondrak one night when a man in a black Mercedes flagged us down. He was a middle-aged white guy who obviously had money, and he reported to us that his wallet got stolen. By who? we asked. He said he was driving down Colfax and a girl flagged him down for a ride. He pulled over and gave her a lift, because he's such a nice guy and a good citizen, so he gave her a ride and somewhere along the way she stole his wallet. Where was your wallet? was our next question, but this story already wasn't passing the smell test, and we knew there was more to it than what he was telling us. At first he automatically replied that it was in his back pocket, until he realized the difficulty that presented with his story, then he changed his mind and said it was in the glove box. We asked him where he lived, and he gave us an address in a nicer part of town. Do you always like to drive around Colfax at midnight? was our next question. Yeah, he just liked to go out and see the city at night. *Sure pal, because Colfax at night is so scenic and beautiful.*

We'd had enough of his bullshit by now and told him so, and that either he could tell us the real story or we'll run him in for false reporting. He finally admitted to us he picked up a hooker at Colfax and Broadway, looking for a blowjob. They pulled into a dark parking lot and he pulled down his pants, and she slid across the seat and went down on him. While she was doing her thing she sneaked a hand around and lifted his wallet out of the back pocket of his slacks, which were down around his ankles. He wanted to press charges, and he wanted his wallet back. We said "Look dumbass, you just admitted to us that you committed a crime. If we bust her, we gotta bust you too." I noticed he was wearing a wedding ring, and I asked him how his wife would feel about coming down to the jail to bail his ass out. He decided that maybe he just lost his wallet somewhere else, after all.

I don't know what it is about people from the wrong side of the tracks, but those from the "right side" of the tracks find them irresistible. The girl in the tight black leather and the come-hither look in her eyes is far more interesting to men than the nice girl in the flowered dress and bobby socks. They know the girl in the black leather is bad for them, like smoking and drinking, and that no good will come of it in the long run, but they're willing to take that chance for the pleasure and thrill of the moment. Women do it, too. For the wealthy upper crust, pretty much everybody else is from the wrong side of the tracks, but some rich guys like to go as far off the tracks as they can get. There was a very wealthy business executive, and for reasons that will soon become obvious his name is better left unsaid. This man was from a moneyed, blue-blood family, but he really had a thing for rough and trashy women. His own wife was very genteel, well mannered, and proper. She was very pretty, and he had no real reason to go looking for fun and adventure somewhere else, but like I said that attraction to the dark side is very strong.

By day he worked in a high-rise office in the Denver Tech Center, and in the evening after work he would drive over to the shady side of town and go trolling the seedy strip clubs. An exotic dancer in one of them caught his eye, and he made arrangements to meet her. Slipping twenties into her panties while she danced on stage while everyone else was giving her singles got her attention. This girl could spot a rich, easy mark with her eyes closed. They met and talked, and he started taking her to places where they wouldn't have let her in the front door without him. She liked the sex rough, and he was thoroughly enjoying his excursions to the wrong side of town. Except that his wife began to get suspicious; he was "working late" an awful lot, he seemed distracted when he was at home, and he had a lot of "meetings" on the weekends. They started having some fights about it, and the guy began to get worried his wife was going to hire a private investigator and find out what he had been doing, followed by an expensive divorce. He'd had his fun with this bad girl for a while, and so he decided it was time to go back to his nice wife. Until the next bad girl.

He met up with his stripper girlfriend and told her *Hey, this has been great and a lot of fun, but it's time to break it off. You understand, right?* She shrugged and said yeah, it was fun for a while *so just give me fifty thousand dollars and there'll be no hard feelings. Come back again sometime!* Rich Guy balked at that and said there was no way he was going to pay her fifty grand. The stripper said okay, that's fine. She would just stop by his house sometime while he was at work and have a chat with his wife and tell her where he's been spending his evenings. She even had pictures to show the wife. Now Rich Guy began to realize just how bad his bad girl was. She had been running a little game of her own. The divorce would ruin him financially, and the scandal would ruin his reputation, so in a panic he told her maybe he was being a little hasty. There was no need to break up after all, and they could just keep seeing each other. *No*, she said, she was getting tired of him. She wanted the money and to go back to her own kind of people. He reluctantly told her he would pay her, and he left her run-down little apartment on the wrong side of the tracks and went back to his own side, wondering what he was going to do and how he was going to untangle himself from this mess he had gotten into.

He mulled it over for a few days, and decided that even if he paid her the fifty thousand what was to stop her from coming back later and demanding more? *Oh, what a tangled web he had weaved!* The only way out was to come clean. He decided to just tell his wife and hope she would forgive him. The stripper called and demanded to know when he was going to bring her the money, and they set up a meeting. When they met the next day, back at her apartment, he told her that he wasn't going to pay her. He was just going to tell his wife, she was a good woman and although she would be mad she would probably forgive him. So, Blackmailing Vixen, you can go pound sand because you're not getting a penny from me! he said triumphantly. *The poor fool.* In his world of multi-million dollars business deals and contracts he was accustomed to dealing with people who, although ruthless and cutthroat, still played by a certain set of rules and now for the first time in his life he found himself trying to negotiate a deal with people who played by a quite different set of rules, people who gave "cutthroat" a very literal meaning. Vixen laid it out for him; you pay me fifty thousand dollars, or the same people who had taken pictures of the two of them together, and tracked down his home address, would make his wife disappear, permanently. As in cement overshoes, anchored to the bottom of Chatfield Reservoir, and evidence implicating *him* would be sent anonymously to the police.

Now Rich Guy was really scared, because he was starting to realize that this Bad Girl, the one that he had once lusted for so badly, had some Really Bad People for friends. He believed they just might kill his lovely, unsuspecting wife. He agreed to pay, and left her apartment with his head spinning; does he go home and warn his wife? Does he just pay and hope it's over? And just how would he begin that conversation? "Honey, I've been having a torrid affair with a trashy stripper, then I tried to break up with her because I still love you, but now she says if I don't pay her fifty thousand dollars her gang member friends are going to kill you. Do you forgive me?"

He decided he couldn't tell his wife so in desperation he came to us. We arranged for the rich guy to call the stripper and tell her he had the money, and to come to his house to get it. But the trick was to get her to *say* "Pay me fifty thousand dollars or I'll have your wife killed" or words to that effect. He called her up, and the meet was set. He was upstairs wearing a wire while the police were downstairs, listening and waiting to come up and make the collar on our entrepreneurial Jezebel. At last the doorbell rang, and he invited her in. The detective told him to act like he was vacillating, maybe changing his mind, getting cold feet about the whole deal, so she would repeat her threat. He did just what he was supposed to, and the consensus was he did a pretty fair acting job. The stripper became outraged and right on cue made the threat. The cops all rushed upstairs and we had her. That was one surprised little exotic dancer/extortionist.

The rich guy was all smiles. He had won all the way around. He got to have his fun, he didn't have to pay her, and his wife was blissfully ignorant. She *was* going to remain blissfully ignorant, right? he queried of us. When he learned that to make this case stick he was going to have to go to court and testify against the stripper, his face turned pale. It was a sure bet that his wife would be subpoenaed and most thoroughly examined by both the prosecution and defense. On top of that, this story was just too juicy for the media not to get wind of it. They would be ringing his doorbell as soon as they got the first delicious whiff. *Rich socialite, trashy stripper, sleazy sex, blackmail, murder. This was better than Jerry Springer!* Maybe they were there at his house already...The poor guy turned pale. He could just picture his wife's face as she answered the door to be confronted with news cameras and a bubblehead blonde reporter shoving a microphone in her face and asking "So how does it feel to know your husband's slutty girlfriend tried to have you killed?" He really didn't have a choice because without his testimony there was no case. No victim, no crime. If he wouldn't testify, then his wife would be the only conceivable victim remaining, and then the prosecution would call her in. Even if they didn't, the defense sure as hell would call her. He realized this was a no-win situation. He knew what he had to do.

With a heavy heart, he went home that evening and sat his wife down and told her everything, the whole sordid affair from the beginning watching her dancing on the stage, to sex in cheap motel rooms and her apartment, to taking her with him on business trips, to it all falling apart and up to now as we prepared to take the case to trial. I wish I could have been a fly on the wall for *that* conversation! A lot of men have affairs, and for that matter a lot of women do too, but this had gone way beyond your typical office fling, or helping the neighbor lady move a table and ending up in the bedroom moving her. The wife did not take it well. She left him, hired a wicked divorce attorney, and cleaned him out. He didn't contest anything, because he wanted as little media exposure as possible. And the upshot of it all? He refused to testify against the stripper. "What's the point?" he said. "I already lost my wife, lost my house, lost most of my money, what difference does it make now if some tramp stripper goes to jail?" So in the end, the only one who came out of it as good as she came in was the stripper. Everyone else's lives were ruined, and all because some rich guy just had to have a piece of ass from the wrong side of the tracks.

TWENTY

DISTRICT SIX WAS THE BUSIEST, roughest, most adrenalin-pumping district in Denver. Patrol staffing for weekend nights in District Six centered around the need to keep a lid on the powder keg of Lower Downtown. LoDo was an area of several blocks near Coors Field (home of the Colorado Rockies - the "Blake Street Bombers") centered around Market and Blake streets and lined with bars; The Bash, the LoDo Bar and Grill, the Celtic Tavern, and a number of other watering holes. At least having them all right next to each other meant the good citizens could stagger from one bar to the next on foot without having to endanger the public by driving. The city officials of Denver put on a great media campaign to portray Lower Downtown as a model of urban renewal, an oasis of art and culture. I saw a lot of people on their hands and knees in the alleys puking all over themselves, if you want to call that culture. Or art. Denver itself contained only about a quarter of the population of the metro area, and on the weekends thousands of people from all of the outlying cities and suburbs would flood into downtown to party, blow off steam, and hook up.

Most of the suburbanites came here just to have a good time, and most of the local criminals came here to prey on the suburbanites. Still others were like the soccer hooligans in England, and came down here for no other purpose than raising hell and getting into fights. Finally, there was the hard-core criminal element that came here to rape, rob, and occasionally murder people. Denver averages about 60 homicides a year, and it seemed to me like they all happened on Saturday nights in District Six. We maintained a strong police presence in LoDo, and when out-of-towners would pass a group of four or five of us patrolling together they would sniff derisively and ask "Why do you have to have so many cops down here?" I would always tell them "Stick around and you'll see."

Every night at roll call the Lieutenant would assign people to work the bars, and even the other districts had to send people down because Six couldn't handle LoDo plus the nightly mayhem of the district with the staffing we had. Around midnight the officers assigned to LoDo would start breaking off from their precincts and start streaming into downtown like herd animals in the Serengeti moving to a water hole. We would park our cars along Market Street and gather into groups of four or five officers and start casually moving down the blocks, letting our presence be seen, mingling with the crowd.

Typically, things would go pretty smooth for a while and we would break up a few fights, toss a few drunks into the Detox van, and move on to the next block and the next bar. There was a club called The Bash, right at the corner of 19th and Blake, that was the source of a good percentage of our troubles. It was a hip-hop club, and there was a big parking lot across the street where the clubbers would gather after closing, and that one club and that one parking lot accounted for so much trouble and so many of our calls that we finally just started gathering outside at closing time to wait for it.

Arguments between rival gangs that started in the club would spill out to the parking lot, with the big difference being that a lot of people had weapons in their cars, and they would go get them and then the Wild West shootouts would start. We put spotter teams on rooftops with binoculars to use their birds-eye view of events on the ground to steer us to the trouble spots before somebody got killed. *"Okay, heads up!* West side of The Bash, black Escalade! We got a fight starting! Four males, the guy in the red jacket, *grab him!* He's the instigator! Yeah, that's him, that's him, you got him!" And so the night's festivities would begin. The crowd outside The Bash didn't like us raining on their parade and would frequently turn hostile. One night I had a rookie in my group and like a lot of rookies he was too eager for his own good. He saw somebody in the crowd heave a bottle, and he bulled in after him. I grabbed him by the back of his duty belt and hauled him back, saying *"Whoa son!* You go in there by yourself and you might not come back! Sometimes you just gotta let it go." You definitely did not want to get separated from your group. Have you seen those nature shows where the lone lion gets caught and surrounded by the hyenas? You get the idea.

Another night a big brawl broke out near Coors Field, and there were probably a dozen people flailing and pummeling each other. We were down the street a bit and people were yelling for us to come break it up. One of the rookies started to run toward them but we yelled for him to slow down, hold your horses boot; let those guys get some of the piss and vinegar out of their system and get tired a bit before we start dealing with them. I made my own stupid rookie mistake one night soon after I started. I was on patrol and was making a pass through LoDo when I saw a group of girls fighting in a parking lot. I find girl fights more disturbing than fights between guys. It's just not natural, and goes against everything I feel about womankind. A crowd was forming around the combatants and I didn't want to step in without somebody to watch my back, so I tried to get on the radio to call it in, but the radio was so busy that night that I just couldn't get on. Every time I keyed the mike some other joker would beat me to it and start squawking about his own problems. Finally I caught a one-second break in the traffic and said "623 fight." Dispatch asked "623 what's your 20?" I told her and cars started calling in from all over the district that they were en route, and blue and whites started screeching in from all directions with sirens wailing. *Man, these guys are sure on the ball tonight with the backup! That's nice of them.*

Guys were jumping out of their cars and running up to me and asking me if I was okay and where the perps were. By now the fight had broken up and everybody started running when they heard all the sirens, so I told the guys it was over and thanks for the cover. "You dumb jackass! We thought *you* were in a fight!" one of them said to me. "Don't you know the radio procedure!?" One by one the guys came up and chewed me out for pulling them off their details to come running downtown for nothing. *Oops! Sorry my brothers and sisters in blue!* Still, even though they chewed my butt for it, when I climbed back into my car I couldn't help but have a smile on my face. It was great knowing that if any cop needed help, all of his fellow officers would come through hell or high water to rescue him. It was things like that that made me love police work, that band-of-brothers camaraderie that's shared by cops everywhere. If you're wearing a badge, I'll risk my life for you even if I don't even know you, and I know you'll do the same for me.

One particularly bad Friday night we arrested several people for everything from brandishing weapons to starting fights to throwing glass bottles at passing cars. The crowd didn't like the po-po hauling all their friends away and got downright hostile, and we ended up pepper-spraying them to drive them back. Alcohol combined with stupidity has a wonderful effect on pain tolerance, however, so I ran my can dry and grabbed a spare and sprayed some more, and the Lieutenant produced a big fire-extinguisher sized can from somewhere and started hosing the whole front rank down. That worked.

The next night, Saturday, tensions were high right from the start of the evening so somebody (I heard it was the SWAT guys - though they deny it) decided the best way to avoid more trouble was to prevent people from congregating in that big parking lot, and they came up with an ingenious solution. If you have ever played paintball you know that those little plastic balls can sting and make you yelp when they're fired with some velocity behind them. In the PD we had something called Pepperball, which is like a souped-up paintball with a wicked little twist. It was fired from a high-velocity gun that looks like something from *Star Wars* and when it hit a rioter it not only left a welt but it would pop and let out a puff of pepper gas. If you've never been pepper-gassed, I'll tell you that it's like tear gas or Mace only several times more potent. It makes your eyes feel like they're on fire and makes you cough and choke. I've sprayed combative drunks with Mace and had them lick it off their fingers. I've never had one do it with pepper spray.

Somebody took handfuls of Pepperballs and scattered them around on the ground in the parking lot next to The Bash, and when closing time came and the crowds poured out into the lot they started stepping on the Pepperballs or running them over with their car tires and popping them. Every time one popped it let out a little flatulent puff of gas, and in just minutes the gas was wafting in little clouds through the air. People started coughing a little, then their eyes started watering and stinging, and it was catching some of the cops too, because like I said not everybody was in the know. In just minutes all the clubbers had gone to their cars and cleared out the lot, and we had no shootings or stabbings or fights that night. I did notice that none of the SWAT guys were down there, though, and there were always a few of them around. Somebody else said it was the Downtown Motorcycle Unit that did it. Regardless of who was responsible, some complaints were called in to Chief Whitman's office at Headquarters the next day and the word quickly came back down that if it happened again there would be some IA investigations coming down. They tell you to think outside the box, come up with some creative solutions to the LoDo problem, then when you do you get in trouble for it. Whoever thought of it, I'll buy you a beer.

* * *

We had a prisoner transport unit, a van with what was basically a big metal box mounted on the back like a small moving truck, with benches on three sides and rings on the benches to cuff people to. We called it Paddy 6, and two officers got tasked to drive the wagon every Friday and Saturday night. We would park Paddy 6 on Market Street, and as the cops on foot patrol would round people up they would bring them back to the wagon and cuff them in. When it got full we would have the Detox van from Denver Cares (*yeah, sure they do!*) come by and haul the drunks away, which would free up more space in the paddy wagon for arrestees with criminal charges.

Sometimes we would get so many collars lined up at the wagon that we couldn't keep track of which guy was charged with what or even who anybody was. When you arrested someone they would go in the cuffs and all their belongings would go in a plastic bag; their wallets, belts, keys, drugs, knives, ID's, and the ticket charging them. The patrol guys were supposed to give the Paddy 6 crew the bag and tell them who went with what bag, but if it was busy they would just toss the perp in the back and the bag in the front and go back out to make some more collars. Then the crew of the wagon would be left to figure it out; *"Hey! Green shirt!* Are you the Drunk and Disorderly?" And he would say "No, man, I'm Public Intoxication! *He's* Drunk and Disorderly!" pointing to the guy across from him, and then *that* guy would protest and say "Hell no! I ain't no Drunk and Disorderly! I'm Indecent Exposure!"

I was driving down Larimer Street when a drunk tried to beat my patrol car across the road. He was standing on the sidewalk and looked down the street and saw me coming. I was going under the speed limit, just cruising and watching the crowds, and his alcohol-fogged brain convinced him he could make it. He was like those squirrels that wait until your car is *almost* up to them, then they make the mad dash across the street. He took off at a run determined to make it to the beckoning far sidewalk, and I was only about ten feet away from him when he suddenly ran out in front of my patrol car. As he crossed my hood I hit the brakes to avoid running him over, then hit the air horn to wake this idiot up, but that had a completely unexpected effect. Have you ever seen children running on the playground, where their legs start moving faster than their brain can keep up with and then their arms start flailing and they go out of control and do a faceplant? That's what this guy did, and as he put on a final burst of speed his legs went out of his control and he started windmilling his arms in a vain attempt to keep his balance, and ran headfirst into a metal light pole with a resounding *GOONNNGGG!* before collapsing in a heap on the sidewalk like he'd just been pole-axed. I stopped my patrol car and ran to check him over, only to discover he had knocked himself out cold. Chuck "The Iceman" Liddell couldn't have KO'd him any better. I called for the bus to take him away. I figured that with the headache he was going to wake up with, there was no need for any public intoxication or jaywalking charges.

I was partnered up with Mike Morelock one night and we were walking through The Bash parking lot after the bar let-out, working our way through the crowd and getting looks of challenge from the guys and looks of flirtation from the girls when a distraught woman came up to us asking for help. She was here with her boyfriend and her brother, and her brother got drunk and was trying to pick a fight with her boyfriend. We walked back to the car with her and met the boyfriend. He was sober and so was she, and they were just trying to get her brother calmed down and into the car so they could take him home. The brother was your typical drunk asshole, full of fight and attitude, and he was telling us his sister's boyfriend was a pussy and a faggot and he was going to kick his ass. I told him he wasn't going to kick anybody's ass tonight, and he'd better calm down or we were going to toss him into the Detox van and he'd spend the night there.

He was swaying and slurring and had beer spilled down the front of his shirt, and if it wasn't for his sister being so nice we would have just hooked his drunk slobbering ass up, but because of her pleading with us to just try to get him calmed down and into the car we didn't. He was not making things any easier for himself, however. I would ask him if he was going to calm down and go home nicely and he would get cocky and say "I don't know, am I?", and this circular argument went on for about five minutes.

I was really starting to lose my patience with this guy, nice sister or no, but he finally agreed to calm down and just go home and sleep it off. He climbed into the back seat on the passenger side, and Morelock was on the other side talking to the sister. It looked like we finally had this under control. I was leaning in a little bit to talk to Drunk Asshole when he leaned forward and tapped my badge with his finger and slurred "You see this? This doesn't mean *shit* to me!" *That's it! Game over!* You don't touch my badge. I reached in and got one hand on his shirt and the other on his belt and heaved him out of the car. Morelock said afterward that here he was thinking everything was cool and we were wrapping this up when all of a sudden he looks over and the brother is airborne, with arms and legs outstretched and landing in a heap on the asphalt, and right behind him was me leaping onto him like WWF wrestling. We cuffed him up and started leading him away, and the sister was wringing her hands and begging us "Please don't take him to jail!" and right behind her was the boyfriend nodding to us and silently mouthing *"Take his ass to jail!"* We took him to Paddy 6 and he was mouthing off the whole way so we were none too gentle with him. When we got him to the van he didn't want to get in. He put his feet up on the doors to brace himself, so we all grabbed an arm or a leg and tossed him headfirst into the wagon. I bet the next morning he woke up wondering what happened, why his face hurt, and why he was in jail.

One summer night I had just finished working the rush when the bars let out downtown and I had broken up a couple of fights, mediated a few arguments, and tossed a few troublemakers into the paddy wagon. It had been a busy night and I was tired but feeling pretty good when I left LoDo, after the last stragglers had stumbled away to sleep it off. I was headed down 19th street away from downtown when I saw something up ahead that caught my eye. It was a splash of bright color in the bleak urban jungle, and I couldn't make out what it was, but it was definitely in my lane and it was definitely not a car. I slowed down, and as I eased up on it my eyes widened in surprise. It was an elderly black woman, dressed up in a white blouse, a bright pink jacket and a big swooping white hat, looking for all the world like she was off to church on a Sunday morning. Except that she was in a wheelchair and pushing herself along in the middle of the street at three a.m. *Good Lord!* Some drunken fool is going to come along and run this sweet old woman right over.

I stopped my car in the traffic lane in front of her and got out and walked up to the old woman. She was still pushing herself along with her head down, so I figured she just didn't see me. I wondered where on earth she came from and where was supposed to be, so I called out to her "Ma'am? I'm Officer Miller with the Denver Police Department. Can I ask you what you're doing out here in the street at three o'clock in the morning?" She stopped the chair and slowly raised her head, and do you know what that sweet old lady said to me? She said "I'm mindin' my own *God-damn* business, and I don't need no God-damn *po-lice* fuckin' with me!" You know, sometimes you do your damndest to be a good guy and do the right thing, and nobody gives a shit. I had been feeling pretty good up until now, and felt like I was sort of doing my Boy Scout good deed by helping this vulnerable little old lady out, but all that went away now. "Okay lady" I said "so that's how this is gonna be, huh? You need to get yourself and your wheelchair out of the street before some drunk yuppie runs you over." She ignored me and just started pushing past me. I told her to stop but she just kept her head down and kept slowly rolling her way down the street. Just then another squad car rolled by, no doubt because they had seen my overhead lights. The car slowed down and Ricky Nixon's head popped out the driver's side window, but when they saw what I was dealing with he hit the gas and they drove away laughing at me over the PA. *Thanks assholes.*

Now I was starting to get a little perturbed at the old lady, and I ran to catch up with her. I grabbed the handles on the back of the chair and pulled her to a stop. She half turned in her seat and let out a blue streak of curses aimed at me that would make a sailor proud. She called me every dirty name in the book plus a few I never heard before, and I said "Lady, I'm pulling your ass out of the street right now to keep you from getting flattened under a Suburban!" I pulled back on the chair to take her over to the sidewalk but she clamped her hands down on the wheels so they wouldn't turn, and just like that away we went with me dragging the chair and yelling at her to let go and her holding on for dear life and cussing me out. I finally wrestled her up onto the sidewalk and we both stopped to catch our breath. During our brief truce I asked her where she lived, but she wouldn't answer. I asked her if there was someone I could call to come get her or if there was somewhere I could take her, but she just straightened her big billowing hat and glared at me. Technically I couldn't really do anything with her except ticket her for jaywalking. She was a free woman and had already amply demonstrated that she was in complete control of her mental faculties, so if she wanted to roll around in a dangerous part of town at three a.m., well that was her business. I told her if I caught her in the street again I'd throw her in the pokey (which was all bluffing) and she told me to go to hell and with that we parted company.

* * *

We were so busy on the weekend nights that I would literally be running call to call all night long, for ten solid hours. I didn't even have time to run through a drive-up window to get something to eat. Finally Todd Ondrak pulled me aside one night and said "Listen, rookie. I've been listening to you on the radio and you're runnin' yourself ragged. Do you hear any of the old hands doing that?" *Well, as a matter of fact I didn't...* Todd explained it to me; you can run yourself into the ground trying to put out little fires all over the city, clearing one and rushing off to the next one, but you'll never get them all. As soon as you extinguish one, two more pop up on the other side of the district. So relax a little bit, and just take them as they come. Don't scramble to finish a call so you can jump the next one. Take time to eat. Drive slower. Don't burn yourself out. The city will wait.

On the subject of eating, there were only a couple of places in the neighborhood that were open all night. There was Pete's Cafe on one end of Colfax and The Denver Diner on the other end. When I was in District One the place to go was McCoy's. Some of the cops dated the waitresses at The Diner or McCoy's, but not from Pete's. There was aDelectable Egg restaurant that opened at 5:00 a.m., and I once suggested we go there for breakfast. The guys all looked at me like I sprouted another head, and said "Miller, I don't know what you guys did in Cherry Hills, but Denver cops do NOT eat at any place that has the word *Delectable* in its name!" I often brought my own dinner and would just pull over in a quiet spot in my precinct and eat, while for ambience I listened to the city self-destructing over the radio; a family fight here, a stick-up there, shots fired down by the tracks. Mealtimes are important to cops; it's when we get to relax for a few minutes, socialize and catch up on what was going on with each other, and talk about the craziest calls we had that night.

One night I got a phone call from a Westminster PD officer. It seems he had a warrant for the arrest of one of the cooks at Pete's, for domestic violence. *Oooh, this was not good.* I told the Westy cop "Okay, we'll go get him with you, but you *can't* arrest him inside the restaurant. And you gotta make it clear that it's *Westy's* warrant, not Denver's." We took the Westminster cop down to Pete's and told him to wait outside while we went in to talk to the cook. We brought him outside so he wouldn't have to get arrested in front of his coworkers and customers. The Westy officer took him away, but he was back at work a couple of days later. He was very thankful to us for handling it that way, and I never heard any of the guys complain about their food after that. Still, I made sure I didn't eat there for awhile.

When I was still in Cherry Hills we used to sneak out of the city to eat at a Perkins restaurant on Colorado Boulevard. I would go with the guys but I steadfastly refused to eat anything there. It made Pete's look like fine dining. One night there were ants crawling all over our table. Another night Matt was drinking a cup of coffee when he suddenly choked and coughed. He said he just swallowed a chunk of something. He looked into his cup and there was a layer of something white and solid at the bottom of it. Coffee isn't supposed to be solid, or have chunks. On a different night we were sitting around a table and a filthy, bearded homeless guy staggered in the front door, wrapped in an old dirty yellow blanket. This guy looked like he had been sleeping in a ditch for a week and hadn't showered in twice that long. I nudged Matt and said "Hey, look at this guy. These are your dining companions." I was wrong, though. He wasn't there to eat. He staggered through the front door and right into the kitchen, where he put on an apron and started cooking.

We weren't supposed to be at Perkins, because it was against policy for us to eat together, but we figured what the hell, there ain't no way the Captain is going to drag his butt out of his soft bed in the middle of the night to come check on us.

One night we got a hot call in our city, so we all ran to our cars and started racing back. On the way we passed a stalled car and a guy standing in the roadway trying to flag us down. First one black and white flew past him, then another, and another. As each car passed he would frantically wave his arms in the air trying to get us to stop. *Sorry pal, but you didn't see us because we were never here.* As the last car passed his wave changed to flipping us the bird. Can't say I blame him.

* * *

What do you suppose is the scariest call a police officer can face? A man with a gun? A physical domestic? A bank robbery in progress? None of the above. What makes a cop's blood run cold is a call of a naked man acting strange. When people get jacked up on cocaine or PCP, it sends their heart rate racing and their core temperature rises. They start sweating profusely and take off their clothes to cool down. When an officer rolls up on that call, he knows he's about to go up against a monster with superhuman strength and who is impervious to pain, and that there will be no good end to this call.

One night a couple of District Six officers named Scott and Ray got a call of a naked man wandering around the halls of an apartment complex. They responded and located him in a stairwell, and as soon as he saw Scott come around the corner he screamed like a wild animal and rushed for him, grabbed him in a bear hug around the body, and tried to throw him down the stairs. Ray jumped on him, and then the three of them were punching, kicking, and rolling around in a furball on the stair landing. Scott and Ray are pummeling this guy with everything they've got, and it's not even fazing him. Scott whipped out his baton and started hitting him with it, but the guy wasn't even reacting to the blows. They called out they were in a fight and needed cover, and units started rolling in Code 10 to cover them.

Ray pulled out his Taser and repeatedly contact stunned the guy with no effect whatsoever. Then they shoved him off and Ray shot him with the prongs. The suspect grunted and stopped fighting for all of three seconds, then he ripped the cords out of his chest and lunged back into the officers. He grabbed Scott's baton and tried to wrench it out of his hand. By now the fight had been going on for some time, and Scott and Ray had run out of gas. They had nothing left in them, and the guy was still charging in like a wild animal. So they just picked the guy up and threw him over the railing and down a flight of stairs. That finally stopped the fight. They had already decided that if he got up and started coming back up the stairs after them, they were just going to shoot him.

On another day a naked man was wandering around down on the Sixteenth Street Mall. People wandering around naked in public might not draw much attention in California, but it does here. Several cops responded and tried to take the guy into custody, but he started fighting with them. Cops were getting thrown around like rag dolls, and one of the officers pulls out his Taser and shoots the guy in the chest. He might as well have shot him with a squirt gun for all the effect it had. The guy just reached down and ripped the prongs out of his chest and plunged back into the fight. My buddy Benny carried the OPNs, the police nunchakus, and he whipped them out and gave them a spin over his head to build up velocity and cracks the guy right across the face so hard it breaks the chuck right in two. That blow would have dropped a horse, but the guy just stands there and screams at Benny "IS THAT ALL YOU GOT!!?" *Well yes, actually, that is all I've got.* The guy is five eight and 150 pounds.

Same kinda call, different night. Now it's Lieutenant Henning's turn. Henning was one of the best command officers I ever worked with. He still got out there and shagged calls, even though he didn't have to. This time, instead of fighting with the police the guy runs away. The police are chasing him, and he comes to a fence but instead of climbing over it he does a strange thing. He puts his arms up and does a Superman launch that carries him right over the fence, six feet in the air. Henning's never seen anything like it. This guy could have won the gold hands down in the Olympics for the high jump. Henning goes over the fence after him, by the more normal method of climbing over it, and next the running drug addict comes to a stairwell with a railing about waist high around it. Again the guy puts his arms up and Superman's over the rail head first, disappearing down the stairwell. Henning and the other cops think the guy's probably dead, going headfirst down the deep stairwell like that. They walk up to the rail and to their surprise here he comes, charging out of the stairwell like a bull, with blood all over his head. The cops all jump on him and by sheer weight of numbers get him down on the ground and get him cuffed. They stood him up and then he starts hyperventilating and shaking like an engine winding up to the redline, and just as suddenly the guy stops shaking and falls over dead. His heart just exploded. When people OD on a stimulant drug, they get crazier and stronger and more pain resistant every second until they just die.

TWENTY ONE

MAKING DETECTIVE IS THE HOLY GRAIL OF POLICE WORK. Every cop out there worth his badge wants to be a detective, unless they're already doing something equally cool and macho like SWAT or the Motor Unit. All the cop movies and television shows are about the detectives; Kojak, Crockett and Tubbs, Dirty Harry, Riggs and Murtaugh. Even James Bond is a detective of sorts, because being a spy is like being the ultimate detective, plus he drove really cool cars and got all the exotic secret agent women, too. Matt had been working patrol out in District Five, and I rarely saw him at work though we still got together every other week for dinner and to get the families together. I think Matt set some kind of record for making detective at DPD, because he got his gold shield after less than three years at the Department. We thought back to how Captain Charlie Bates said Matt would make detective over his dead body. That guy couldn't tell a good detective from a jelly doughnut. As his detective car they gave him a Toyota Prius, a bright red one that we called The Red Skittle, after the little coated candies. No Aston Martin with machine guns behind the headlights, no Lotus that could go underwater, and no dusky-eyed Bond girls either.

In District Six, the patrol officer who worked Precinct 617 got his detective's shield too, which suddenly created an opening for a permanent precinct assignment. Getting your own precinct was a feather in your cap, a sign that the brass considered you a top cop, and on the rare occasions when a slot opened the competition was fierce to get it. I put in for 617 along with a lot of other officers, and to my surprise they gave me the nod, even though I had less than two years on. Precinct 617 was over on the southwest side of the District and was more generally known simply as Lincoln Park. The Lincoln Park Housing Projects were actually only one neighborhood in the Precinct, but it was the area that kept us the busiest.

The projects were called simply "the jets" by all the patrol officers, and here they consisted of several blocks of red brick two-story buildings arranged in rows, with parking areas on each end and a kind of central courtyard between the buildings. Out front there was a sign that read YOU ARE NOW ENTERING A DRUG FREE ZONE. *Glad to see City Hall still has a sense of humor.* On the north end was a large park with green grass, trees, and a community center with a swimming pool. The racial makeup was mainly a mix of black and Hispanic families, with a scattering of whites and Asians. The surrounding area was a blend of industrial and residential, with little clapboard houses and roach motel apartments, with a few liquor stores and bars thrown in as standard furnishings of all such neighborhoods. There was a strong gang presence here, and you could see the war of words reflected in the graffiti on the walls of businesses and apartment buildings, and on the underpass of the 8th Avenue bridge as the Inca Boys and the GKI's (which variously stood for Gangster Killers of Incas, or Gangster Killers Insane, or Gallant Knights Insane, depending on who you asked) staked out their turf. Yeah, it was a bad neighborhood but hey, it was home.

When a rookie first clears Field Training, and his FTO's sign off that he sort of knows what he's doing and probably won't get himself or anybody else killed right away, they get assigned to whatever beat needs bodies that night, so you could end up working around the yuppie suburbanites in the bars in LoDo, busting crack dealers in Capitol Hill, or chasing the seemingly endless shots fired calls in Five Points. But once you were assigned to a precinct, you owned it. It was yours, and you were expected to get to know every street, alley, and dark corner. You'd know who the local bad guys were and where they lived, where the flophouses and crackhouses were, know the hookers by name and how much they charged, and you were supposed to get to know the decent people too, while you were at it, and build trust with them, because without at least some of the people on your side you were swimming upstream. When you got your own precinct you became so closely identified with it that your precinct number almost became a part of your name.

When I rolled into my new beat that first night, I cruised around with the windows down and a cocky attitude. There was a new sheriff in town, and I meant to let everybody know it. That first night I did something I had never done before; I parked my squad car and started walking around in the courtyards between the buildings. The people sitting on their porches rocking their babies and talking to their neighbors were dumbfounded when they saw me coming down the sidewalk. I don't think they would have been more shocked if a polar bear was strolling between the buildings. Cops always drove around the streets that formed a sort of square perimeter around the projects, but they *never* came inside, unless there was something going on or they were there to take someone. All the talking stopped and the people just watched me, wondering who I had come for. I just walked among them, pleasantly tipping my hat and saying hello and good evening. My polite small talk did nothing to ease the puzzled looks on their faces; if anything it made them even more suspicious. There were a couple of young men who eyed me warily, ready to either run or fight. I ignored them and finished my walk-through and headed for the park. I had a plan, and today was just the beginning. Cops get a bit lazy like everybody else and they don't want to get out of their cars if they don't have to, but I made a habit of walking the projects every night, and the people got used to seeing me. Some of them didn't like me being there, intruding into their turf, but I figured they were the ones that needed to know I was going to be there, all the time. The rest of the people were slow to warm up to me, and I knew this was going to take some time, but when the mommas on their porches started to smile and say hello when I came by I knew I was getting there.

A lot of guys go to work, answer their calls, do their job, and go home. That's fine, but if you want to be really effective, if you want to be feel the pulse of what's going on in your precinct, you can't just work the street, you've got to engage it, you've got to get down into the heart of it. That means seeking trouble out instead of waiting for it to come to you over the radio. Some cops who come from a middle or upper class background do not like to mingle and talk with the people from the jets, both because the difference in backgrounds makes it hard to relate to them, and because the fact is that a lot of the people in the jets are drug addicts and they have needles on them, or body bugs, or they're just plain dirty. They're dirty, their houses are dirty, and their kids are dirty. TV has it all wrong when it comes to how cops talk to perps. If you try the tough guy approach, shoving them up against the wall and threatening them, you're not going to get anywhere. Some of them will cower and lie to you, and the hardened "street soldiers" will laugh in your face. When a guy has already been shot and stabbed three or four times and lives in mortal danger every week, you think tossing him up against a wall is going to scare him? You know how you get people to tell you things? You be nice to them. Chester the Molester is not going to tell you he perped on the little girl next door if he thinks you're going to kick his ass for it. But he will tell you, if he thinks you'll understand. So you listen, you nod your head, and you encourage him to go on, go on and guide you through the sick and twisted maze of thoughts running through his head. I had a guy tell me that the little girl he molested seduced him, led him on, and that's why he did it, so it wasn't really his fault, see? The little girl was three. So you listen, he spills his guts, then you hook him up and fry the sick son of a bitch.

When we would go see someone for a chat at their apartment, if we didn't have a warrant but we wanted to talk to them about something we thought they were involved in, we called it a "knock and talk." If we saw a guy on the street we wanted to talk to we called it "bumping him up." Most of the public and even a few baby DA's and defense attorneys have got it all wrong about when the police can talk to someone. I blame Hollywood. *Round up the usual suspects! We're bringing you in for questioning! Put 'em in the chair and turn on the spotlight!* All of that is wrong. Nobody has to talk to the police if they really don't want to. On the other hand, the police can talk to anybody they want to talk to, without a warrant, without Probable Cause, or even Reasonable Suspicion. It's just like you in the grocery store; you can just walk up and talk to anybody you see. All they have to do is say no, they don't want to talk to us, and keep on walking but surprisingly few of them do that. Most of them think they can outsmart us, baffle us with a line of bullshit, and the funny thing is that it doesn't matter if they're a Colfax junkie or a high powered business executive, they all think they can outsmart us. Prisons are full of people who thought they were smarter than the police. Some of them feel guilty, nervous, or scared about what they've done and can't keep their mouth shut. If you're polite but firm, they start talking. Even when you're being friendly to these guys, you always have to maintain a certain distance, let them know that yeah, you're talking to them, but you're not one of them. If you're too distant, they won't talk to you. If you get too close, they lose respect for you. It's a fine line to walk, but when you do it right it's magic.

The young males drifted in and out of the projects, moving from one hidey-hole to another to stay a step ahead of the law or a rival gang or the people they owed money to. The women and their babies stayed in one spot, and that was how we usually found the guys we were looking for. When I got a call in the projects of a domestic or a fight or shots fired and showed up on scene, people knew me. I could grab someone and pull him or her aside and tell them to cut the bullshit and tell me what happened, and they would. I got to know my precinct like the back of my hand, but there was one important thing that I kept forgetting. All the roads in the neighborhood were good, but running right along Ninth Street the road dipped down sharply, for water drainage or something, I can't even tell you how many times I would be running hot down Mariposa or Navajo with lights and sirens wailing and come up on Ninth and suddenly remember THE DIP! SHIT!! and jam on the brakes, but it was too late and my car would bang down into it with a shower of sparks and slew around like a bucking bronco when I came out of it, and I'd hit the gas again and speed away as much out of embarrassment and not wanting anyone to see what I had just done as much as getting to the call. Once I crashed into it and when I came out the other side my car was making a squealing noise and the front end was shimmying. Later on it went away and I breathed a sigh of relief. Along with seniority came a regular car assignment, and my car was Unit 0475, or as I called it, "The Antichrist".

The cars were supposed to go in for regular maintenance, but at Denver we just drove 'em until they dropped, then they'd be towed out to the big Vehicle Maintenance facility on I-70, from which they apparently never returned. 0475 had some evil spirit in its electrical system. Headlights would turn off and on at random, the overhead rotating lights would cut in and out so that sometimes only one or two of them would work, and sometimes my siren would get sick and emit a long, drawn-out wail that sounded like a dying moose. It was just plain embarrassing. Sometimes the whole system would just shut down at the most inopportune times. I pulled over a carload of gangbangers late one night and lit them up with my takedowns and spotlights and approached. Right away when I contacted them the hairs on the back of my neck started tingling. There was something just not right about these guys, especially one fidgety guy in the back seat. I had my hand on my gun and I told the guys in back to show me their hands, nice and slow. They had just started pulling their hands out of their jacket pockets and right then my car chose to die behind me, and all the overheads, takedown lights, and spotlights went out with it, plunging us all into sudden darkness. I backed out fast, expecting to see flames of gunfire stabbing towards me. Instead the driver gunned the engine and took off, and of course I couldn't follow because my car was KO'd, and I just had to stand there and watch them screeching away.

On another occasion I was running to an Officer Needs Help call and I was really flying, hitting triple digits. All of a sudden I thought *That's funny...My steering feels kinda heavy.* That's when I realized the car had died and I was flying along at 110 miles per hour in an unguided missile. You want to talk about pucker factor? I broke out in a sweat and managed to ease the heavy Crown Vic, with no power steering and no power brakes, mind you, over to the shoulder and got her brought down to a stop. I thought I was driving some blue and white Christine, except *that* car killed her owner's enemies and my car was only trying to kill *me.*

Speaking of gunfire, I will never forget the first time I got shot at. I was on a traffic stop in the early evening, in the Five Points neighborhood. In this neighborhood there was a Cold War going on between the cops and the gang members. Like the Cold War between America and the Russians, which I was also a part of, there was a lot of blustering, posturing, and threatening, but not much real violence. If a carload of gang members would drive past the cops out on a call, as they turned the corner and right before they passed out of sight they would fire their guns in the air then take off. This was to show the cops that they were not afraid of us, and that they owned this neighborhood.

On this particular night, I had pulled over a motorist for a traffic violation and I climbed out of my patrol car and walked up to the driver's window. I never saw the carload of gangbangers cruising up behind me, but as they turned the corner I suddenly heard the whine of a bullet go right past my head then the *Boom!* of the pistol shot. I instantly sprinted for cover around the back of the car I had stopped, only to have him gun the engine and take off, leaving me standing there like an idiot, with my heart rate pegging out at around 200.

I ran for my car to take cover, and called it out on the radio, but the 'bangers were long gone, and though we searched the area we never found them.

* * *

Right at the end of shift one morning I got a call. Every cop hates getting calls at the end of shift. When you've been in the saddle for ten hours chasing down calls all over the city, you just want to go home. I had already turned the nose of my patrol car toward the stable of the north lot of the District Six station, and I was looking forward to my soft bed at the end of my weary drive home. For those who work nights, sleep is a precious commodity, and you just never know when the most innocuous sounding call will turn into a major headache. I once had to tow a car that was stalled out and blocking traffic, at the end of my shift. No big deal. I called the tow truck and while the driver is hooking up the car he backs into it and crunches up the front end. *Oh Great!* Now I have an accident report to do, too. While doing the accident report and taking the tow driver's license information I discover the tow jockey has a warrant. *Wonderful!* Now I have to take him to jail, *after* I finish the accident report, then I have to find someone to come get his tow truck, and call yet another tow truck to still pick up the stalled car that started all of this. By the time this mess was all cleaned up I was four hours late getting off, and had to be back to work that night just nine hours later, and I hadn't even left the station yet. So you see why the cops dread the last minute calls? Can't crime have the decency to wait just a few more minutes to let a working man get off on time?

In this case a man got up in the morning and showered and shaved, and put on his tie and jacket and got ready for his day at the office. He grabbed his cup of coffee and his briefcase and rushed outside, only to discover thieves had broken into his car and stolen everything that wasn't nailed down. Just the locals' way of saying good morning. When I pulled up in front of the house, with Todd Ondrak pulling in behind me to assist on the call, the guy was standing there dejectedly staring at the broken glass from his passenger side window littering the ground. His wife was in her bathrobe standing next to him and looking equally forlorn. They were really nice people, and they sadly told us they had moved into their new house just last night. They were from California and had wanted to get away from the crowds and the crime and the traffic, and thought Colorado sounded just like heaven, with its Rocky Mountains and open spaces and friendly Western people.

They hired a local realtor to find a house for them, and when he told them he found a perfect place in a nice neighborhood called Lincoln Park, they got so excited they bought the house sight unseen. They packed up their things and hit the road, and they didn't arrive until yesterday evening. They had been busy unpacking until late in the night and decided to just leave all the stuff in the Jeep until the next day. It would be safe for one night, right? I said "Your realtor told you this was a nice neighborhood?" "Yeah", they guy said. "Does this sort of thing happen a lot? Is this a high crime area?" I hesitated to break the bad news to the guy, but Todd cheerfully chimed in "The highest! Your realtor really screwed you over, pal." The poor guy looked even more forlorn as he digested this news, and looked around the neighborhood, seeing it for the first time in daylight. He said "What should I do?" Todd said "Move. Move now. Don't even finish unpacking!" After I took the report and was driving away, I felt really bad for these people. They were a nice young couple, looking for a decent place to start a family and this is what they got. First their realtor robs them, then the locals rob them. Welcome to the neighborhood, pal.

* * *

My precinct was residential on the east side, and industrial on the west. There was a rail yard and a big scrap metal recycling plant that brought to mind the old black and white movies of smoggy, dirty, Industrial Revolution factories filled with clusters of grim-faced unsmiling workers with dark smudges of soot on their faces. There was also a meat packing plant that had such an awful, horrible charnel-house smell that whenever I drove by it I would speed through the area with the windows up, my hand over my face and holding my breath, while the illegal immigrant workers would stand on the dock and impassively watch me fly past. They could have run a stolen car chop shop, a whorehouse, and an illegal gambling operation all under one roof in complete safety.

There was a meat packing plant of a decidedly different nature in my Precinct. Denver General Hospital was over on Bannock Street, and I was there at least two or three times a week. They have since changed their name to the fancy sounding Denver Health Medical Center, but to every cop in the city it was always known simply as "DG." It was a trauma hospital, and the medical colleges would send their interns here for an in-your-face baptism of fire into what we called "the knife and gun club" that was the DG Emergency Room. Some of the students couldn't handle it, and we'd pass them in the halls, leaning against the wall with ashen faces and queasy stomachs. The ER doctors and nurses at DG were miracle workers. Many was the time we would bring in a victim of a gunshot or a stabbing and I would be making the sign of the cross as the crew worked feverishly on him and I would be checking the "Deceased" box on my report, and they would somehow bring him back. If not for those incredible men and women, the homicide rate in Denver would be double what it is now.

DG was the best around, so when any of the other hospitals in the metro area got a really bad one they would often AirLife them or run them by ambulance to DG. On busy Saturday nights it was a macabre scene, with the wounded flowing in like a river until all the operating rooms were filled, and then they would just start lining them up in the hallways and as you would walk past the rows of gurneys they would be reaching up to you with bloodied arms and begging you for help or for water. It reminded me of "The Fall of Atlanta" scene in *Gone With The Wind* where Scarlett O'Hara is walking among the sea of wounded soldiers being off-loaded at the train station. Ambulance crews would be running the gurneys down the hall with the ones who were on the verge of death, and police officers with notebooks in hand would be maneuvering among the paramedics and doctors and shouting "What did he look like? What was he wearing?" trying desperately to get scraps of information before the victim died.

Since DG was in my precinct this constant parade of injuries made a lot of extra work for me, and I would get called down to the ER for one thing or another two or three times a week. Todd and I went down on a report of a domestic. We went into the ER and met our victim, a pretty white female whose boyfriend had assaulted her. I took one look at her and let out a low exclamation. This guy had really worked her over. Her left eye was swollen almost shut and had a big ugly purple and black bruise on it, from where he clobbered her with a right. Her lip was busted and swollen and had dried blood crusted over it. When I worked in Cherry Hills, we didn't have domestics like this. Often we would go to a scene and look both parties over and ask "Okay, who hit who?" Out here, there was no doubt. These people beat the hell out of each other.

Todd and I stood over this poor girl and asked her what happened. As she fought back tears and described to us how he had shoved her head against the wall, then kicked her and held her down and punched her repeatedly, Todd and I were looking across the bed at each other. No words were necessary. Men who beat women were only a step above child abusers, and we were going to find this guy and beat the crap out of him for resisting arrest, whether he resisted or not. I finally asked her how she ever hooked up with this guy, and she brightened up and said "Oh, we use the same meth dealer!"

You know, you just can't save people from themselves. When people go out of their way to put themselves into dangerous situations, there is only so much that can be done to protect them. We filed the report and went on our way. As I drove away thinking about that girl, a line from a James Bond movie popped into my head. As 007 is putting his Walther PPK into its shoulder holster and getting ready to go out and do his thing, the supporting character says to him "Remember, Mr. Bond, before you go out and try to save the world, that the world...it doesn't *want* to be saved."

* * *

Some poor unfortunate souls are just born to suffer. Like the comic strip characters who always have a rain cloud over their head, drizzling on them wherever they go, I've met some unlucky people that life just craps on repeatedly. I went to a call of an assault, and my victim was a white female who had just been dumped by her boyfriend. He drove that night and after the breakup he left her at the restaurant, so she went out to catch a cab. She couldn't find one, so she had to make the long walk home. She started walking back to her apartment when she got jumped and beat up by two other girls, who stole her purse. She got worked over pretty good, with a black eye and a busted lip to go with her broken heart, so I went down to the hospital with her to take the report. I felt really sorry for this girl and tried to cheer her up before I left. Ninety minutes later I get a call of an auto-ped right outside the hospital. I pull up on scene, and it's her. She's lying there in the middle of the street with a busted leg. She had just had her injuries treated and was released from the hospital, and she goes out the door and starts walking across the street when she gets nailed in the crosswalk by a hit and run driver. Poor kid. I wanted to just take her home and make her some hot cocoa and tell her it'll all work out somehow.

I almost ended up in DG myself one night. I was running hot to a burglary in progress, with a possible sexual assault. I was flying down Park Avenue controlling the wheel with one hand and talking into the radio mike with the other when I felt something crawling on my neck. I was in full adrenaline mode and just ignored it and continued talking into the radio when suddenly my transmission was cut off in mid-sentence as I felt something like a red-hot drill boring into my neck. The pain was excruciating, and my radio transmission went something like "617 I'm en route from YEEOOWW!!"

An astonishingly big and mean-looking hornet had lined up a bulls-eye on my neck and plunged his stinger in to the hilt. *Now where did he come from? And what did I do to piss him off?* I ignored the pain and continued to the call, and we caught the burglars while they were trying to break in. There was no sex assault - the girl was his accomplice, not his victim. After we got them loaded into a car and off to jail, Nixon turned to me and his eyes got real big and he said "Jesus! What happened to you?! Your face is all red and puffy!" I told him a hornet stung me and it was no big deal, I was fine. Then the other guys started asking me "Are you breathing okay? Do you feel faint? Is your throat closing up?" and another one piped up "You know you can go into anaphylactic shock and die within minutes from hornet stings." I *had* felt fine, but now with all these guys telling me my throat was going to close up and I was going to stop breathing and die, all of a sudden I wasn't so sure. Maybe I *was* having a little trouble breathing...I shook it off and got back in my car and got the hell out of there. But for the next hour I was very aware of every breath.

One night I went to DG and who should be there but Matt. I was so used to seeing him in uniform that I almost passed him without recognizing him in his suit and tie. He looked like a real cop-show detective, looking very suave with his Detective shield and perfect hair and gun peeking out from his behind his jacket. He was following up on one of his cases, and as it turned out his brother Robert came in the ER doors a short time later. Robert was a deputy sheriff working for Arapahoe County and he was here to pick up a wanted person. Matt and Robert got to talking of course, and suddenly Matt got a curious look on his face and reached out and pressed his finger into Robert's chest. "Where the hell is your vest, you dumb shit?!" Matt said. "It's summertime, and it's hotter than hell out there!" Robert protested. Matt started giving Robert an earful about his officer safety, but Robert was just waving him off when suddenly Matt said "I'm telling Mom." Robert got a panicked look on his face and said "You wouldn't!" Matt replied "Oh yeah! I'm telling her!" Robert begged him not to, but Matt was as good as his word and a few days later he got an angry phone call from Robert, who had just finished getting chewed out by their mother for not wearing his body armor vest.

On another occasion I got dispatched to go to the DG ER to pick up a wanted party, on a felony warrant with a no-bond hold. No bond holds usually meant a homicide suspect or some other dangerous felon, so I picked up Todd and Jose Juarez to go with me. The reporting party said he was in room 8, so we double checked his name and description and went there to check his condition and see if he was in any shape to be moved. If he wasn't, we would make arrangements with hospital security to put a hold on him and notify us immediately when he was ready to be released. The hospital security people were very professional and we had a good working relationship with them.

We got to room 8 only to find a large gathering of people in the room. A woman was lying on the hospital bed being given her last rites by a Catholic priest, dying from who knows what. The wanted party was her husband, kneeling by her bedside in tears. All the information we had showed that he had been brought in as a patient. I felt like a complete ass handcuffing him and taking him into custody there, under those circumstances. Everyone was looking at us with pure venom in their eyes, even the priest and the hospital staff. But somebody in that room had dropped a dime on him and called us. If he had not been a dangerous felon, I would have just let him go and caught him another day. Even a bad man deserves to say goodbye to his wife in peace.

* * *

Right after roll call one weekend night I got called out to help the Watch 3 guys with an apparent suicide, a jumper. I drove to the scene, a high rise apartment building downtown, and around the back I saw the red and blue lights flashing and the police tape blocking the entrance to the parking lot. I parked the Antichrist and got out and walked toward a cluster of cops gathered around and looking at something on the ground. I walked up to Sergeant Spielmann and said "Whaddaya got?" Spielmann grunted "Dead guy" and moved aside so I could see. There indeed was a dead guy, a young black man, body and arms and legs all sprawled out at completely unnatural angles, with his face looking up at the sky, eyes wide open and white, as if he still couldn't believe he was falling. There was a large, drying crimson stain on the asphalt under his head. I looked up, and

Spielmann followed my gaze. "He lives on the seventh floor. Looks like he took a header off the balcony." From down here, the seventh floor looked *waaay* up there. Spielmann told a few of us to start knocking on doors, see if anybody heard or saw anything. He would stay with the body until the Crime Lab guys got there, and a couple of detectives had been called in and were already up checking the deceased's room for clues about what happened to him and how he ended up in his present pitiful state.

I took the sixth floor, one down from where the victim lived. I started at one end of the hallway, knocking on every door, asking the people inside if they had heard or seen anything unusual, or if they knew the jumper. This was a low-rent apartment building, not one of the upscale yuppie lofts that were springing up all over LoDo. This was government subsidized housing, mostly minority folks living here and a sprinkling of disabled people. Most of them said they didn't see or hear anything and quickly closed the door. One guy, however, brightened up just as soon as he saw me at the door. He said *"Come on in!"* and stood back and held the door open wider. I was a little suspicious of his enthusiasm, especially after the cold reception I had been getting so far. But I went in and started asking him questions. He was a middle-aged white guy, with some wild shaggy hair, but his apartment looked clean and orderly. He offered me a drink, which I declined (not knowing what was in it) but he was eager to listen and answer my questions. I think he was just a lonely guy who was happy to have somebody, anybody, to talk to.

No, he didn't know the guy, he said. But, he said he did see *something*. A few hours ago he was sitting on his couch watching TV, he said while gesturing to his couch for emphasis, and the patio door was open because it was summer and it got hot in the apartment. He was sitting on the couch and he heard some shouting from down below. He went out on the balcony and saw a black male running across the parking lot. He remembered the guy was wearing a red hoodie and had a backpack on his back. No, he didn't see the guy's face real good because the hood was up. *Why was he running?* I asked. Because another guy was chasing him and firing shots at him, he replied. I was surprised, because there had been no reports of this passed on at roll call, and none of the cops from Watch 3 said anything about shots being fired. I pressed him for more details, but he couldn't tell me much more, except that he was quite sure about the red hoodie and the backpack, which he remembered had some yellow on it. He couldn't remember much about the guy who was chasing him except that he had a gun and shot at him, and he said he just closed the patio door and went back to watching television. I asked him why on earth he didn't call the police and he shrugged his shoulders and said he just didn't think of it.

I thanked him and moved on, continuing my canvassing of the rest of the floor. I figured the guy was full of crap, just eager to talk to someone and tell a good story, knowing if he said he saw nothing I would just move on. *Why yes Officer, I did see a spaceship piloted by green aliens!* Nobody else heard any shots or saw anyone chasing anyone, and even in this neighborhood that gets people's attention, and *somebody* surely would have called the police. I finished my floor and went up to the seventh where the jumper lived. The detectives told me to stay out until they were done processing the room, and to take a post down the hall to keep the curious away. I told the detective at the door what the guy on the sixth floor said. The detective, thinking what I was thinking, said there had been no reports of shots fired, and no one else in the building reported anything like what Shaggy Man had said. I took up my post and waited, along with another officer.

Not long after that, an elderly black gentleman came out of the elevator and started walking down the hall. He looked puzzled when he saw all the police activity, and he stopped and asked us what was going on. He said he lived right next door and he knew the man in the apartment the detectives were processing. He said the young man's name was Jamal, and they were supposed to get together and play cards tonight. How was Jamal anyway, was he okay? I hated doing death notifications. People scream and cry, and fall down, and it's just so emotional and tough to watch people hearing for the first time that a loved one had been killed. I started to speak, but the officer who was with me cut me off. I didn't really know this guy very well, but I already didn't like him. He was a cocky, swaggering young punk. He said "Oh you won't be playing cards with Jamal tonight!" "Why not?" The old man asked, puzzled. "Well, he's been transported down to Denver General." A look of concern crossed the old man's face, and he said "I better get down there and see how he is" and he started to turn around. "Don't bother" the young cop said. "How come?" asked the old man, turning back around. "Because he's dead" the cop said matter-of-factly. I looked at the young cop in disbelief. What an incredible jerk. The old man was stunned, and in shock. The young cop just shrugged his shoulders and walked away. I took the old man to a chair and sat him down, and explained everything that we knew about what had happened. The old man said there was just no way Jamal would commit suicide. He was happy, he had a new girlfriend, they played poker every week. He owed a guy some money, but who didn't owe money to somebody? I left the old man sitting in the chair and went down the hall to see the detectives.

The detectives were almost done. In fact, one of them had already left and the other guy was just finishing up. He told me there was no evidence of foul play and they were officially calling it a suicide, and he was just getting ready to clear the scene himself. I walked in to have a look around, just out of curiosity. I peered over the balcony he had jumped off, and it was a *looong* way down. The cars and the people down below looked tiny, like ants and toy cars moving around. I imagined someone looking down at that, then jumping off and free-falling through the air, until impact. I'm not good with heights anyway, so the sight gave me the willies and I backed off and went back into the apartment. As I did so I looked into the kitchen, and to my astonishment there was a red hoodie and a yellow backpack on the kitchen table. I excitedly told the detective again what the guy on the sixth floor had said, and pointed to the hoodie and backpack. I told him what the old man said about Jamal owing a guy money. The detective sighed and looked at me. He was tired, their investigation was done, the verdict was in, and why was I coming in here now and making his life hard? He looked at the backpack and hoodie, looked up at the ceiling pondering for a minute, then he looked back at me and said "Suicide!" and walked out. He went down the hall, and the young cop fell in beside him. They didn't even look at the old man when they walked by, and they got in the elevator and left.

I took a last look around the apartment. It just seemed *unfinished*, was the best way I could describe it, like maybe there were still questions that needed to be answered. I turned the lock and shut the door. I went back to the old man in the hall and talked to him for another minute. He said he would be okay. Jamal had a sister who would look after his things, and he would call her. I didn't really have anything more to do, and I was the only official person left on the scene. I put my hand on the old man's shoulder and told him I was sorry, then I turned and left. Whatever had happened here, suicide or murder or tragic accident, it was a closed case now.

* * *

We had another jumper call, on another night and off another apartment building. I suppose there comes a point for some people when dying is easier than living. A few seconds of free fall and it's all over, compared to the struggle and pain of drug addiction, disease, alcoholism, loneliness and despair.

The citizen who called it in thought the guy took a dive off the west side of the building. Three of us responded and looked on the west side and didn't see anything, so we split up and walked around all four sides of the building. *Nothing.* It was like he fell right through the earth itself and was swallowed up. Then Ryan Phillips walked by a deep window well and shouted out "He's in here!"

We walked over to where Phillips was pointing, and down in the deep window well a guy was lying all crumpled up in the bottom. We tried to get him out, but he was too far down. Even lying on our stomachs and reaching down we couldn't get to him. Somebody was going to have to go down in there and get him. He looked dead alright, but you gotta go down there and check his pulse and breathing to make sure, just in case he's still alive. People have survived some pretty amazing stuff; plane crashes, falls, gunshots, so we had to go check him out to make sure he was really dead. Nobody wanted to go down there, so we played a quick game of rock-paper-scissors. Phillips lost, and had to climb down into the window well. He's a very big boy, built like a linebacker, and it took a little huffing and puffing to get his big frame down in there. He picked the body up and threw it over his shoulder and started climbing out with him, and when he got him up over the edge of the window well we each grabbed an arm and hauled him up. We checked his pulse. *Nada.* This was the last ride for this fella. The guy must have broken every bone in his body when he hit because it was like lifting a rag doll full of broken sticks.

* * *

Vicki Ferrari (who was built like a Ferrari) was out on a traffic stop one night in Capitol Hill and called for backup. I was right around the corner, so I radioed that I would cover and she told me to call her on the phone for the particulars. I thought that was unusual, so I was curious as to what she had that she couldn't tell air over the air, so I dialed her up and got the story. She had stopped a car on Logan right in front of an apartment complex, and no sooner had she contacted the driver when some jackass steps out the front door of the apartments and starts yelling to the driver *"Don't talk to her! You don't have to say shit, man! Don't even give her your name!"* Vicki ignored him at first but he kept it up, leaving the doorway and coming out onto the front lawn. She didn't like having him close to her and behind her, so she told him to shut up and go back inside, but he flipped her the bird and started cussing at her. She told him if he didn't go back inside he'd be arrested for interference. He kept up the chatter and she came after him, but he ran back to the apartment complex and scuttled inside the foyer and shut the front door.

Like all the apartment buildings in Capitol Hill this door automatically locks when it closes, to keep the riff-raff out. Well, I should the say the riff-raff that doesn't already live there. So this guy is standing in the foyer leering at Vicki and taunting her. She went back to the traffic stop and sure enough, The Mouth came right back outside and again started yelling to the driver not to talk to her. That's when she called for another car, and she wanted me to sneak around the back of the apartment complex and get between The Mouth and the safety of the front door. This was starting to sound like it could be fun, so I eased my car around the back and got out. Just then a young cop named Konigsfeld, a boot just out of the Academy but a good kid, pulled up alongside and asked what was going on. I told him to come along and briefed him on what we had, then we sneaked around the north side of the building.

As I eased up to the edge of the building I could hear Genius running off at the mouth, yelling at the driver and yelling at Vicki. I peeked around the corner and saw him; he was a white male, early twenties, medium build, wearing a t-shirt with a peace sign on it and shorts and sandals, and clearly drunk. He looked like a frat boy from nearby Metro State, with his wispy attempt at a beard and his man-bun. While he was focused on harassing Vicki I started to ease up behind him, smiling at the prospect of catching this completely oblivious moron by surprise when from behind me the boot suddenly yelled "STOP! IN THE NAME OF THE LAW!" I turned around in disbelief and the boot was standing there with his arm extended and his hand out in the classic palm-forward stop gesture. *Did he really just say that?* Nobody says that, except in old movies. Maybe Genius had seen the old movies because he actually stopped, if only to stare in befuddlement at the boot. Suddenly he saw me easing up on him by a big juniper bush, a lot closer and a lot more threatening than the boot, and his eyes got as big around as saucers and he turned and started to run. He looked first to the safety of the door but he knew he would never make it back there, so he bolted for the alley around back. I ran after him as he went around the far corner of the building and into the alley. Somewhere along the way the boot slipped and fell down, ripping his pants and skinning his knees and palms. *Aye yi yi, those damn boots! They'd be dangerous if they weren't so comical!*

Now right here you need to know something about me. I tipped the scales at around 200 pounds and was built on the stocky side, so sometimes perps give me a glance and think they can outrun me. My younger brother Dan was a national-caliber track star (3rd in the nation in the 400 meter), and I used to train with him so I was very fast in a sprint. I ran down the alley after Genius and after a short chase I easily caught up to him. My first thought was to do a flying tackle and bring him down in a tumble of arms and legs like a cheetah nailing a gazelle on the Serengeti, but here is where experience and maturity come into play. My flash second thought was that if I tackle this guy on the concrete I'm going to get my uniform all dirty, scuff up my leather gear, and maybe even scratch the beautiful cocobolo wood grips on my Para-Ordnance SSP .45, so I came up with a new plan. He was kind of a slow runner, or maybe the alcohol was affecting his coordination, but I closed up behind him and planted my right hand firmly between his shoulder blades and gave him a real hard shove. He went flying forward and did a faceplant into the hard surface of the alley. He skidded for several feet on his hands and his chin before coasting to a stop, and as I was cuffing him up he was moaning *"Oooh, that really hurt!"*

I searched his back then rolled him up on his side to search his front when the boot came walking up, looking dejected with his torn pant legs and scuffed up knees and hands. I said to him "Stop in the name of the law? Really?" He shrugged his shoulders and said "It just came out!" I said "Look at yourself! No self-respecting cop falls down on a foot chase! Now go clean yourself up!" I marched The Mouth back around front to where Vicki was waiting. She lit into him, chewing him out while he just hung his head and said "I'm sorry! I'm sorry!" When she was done I released him with a ticket and he was still apologizing as he closed the apartment door. And just for the record, the boot became a fine police officer and even made detective.

* * *

Some male officers don't like working with women, but I think that attitude is retiring along with the old-timer cops. Besides, women tend to have a beneficial civilizing effect on groups of men. When females are around, men try not to belch, fart, and cuss as much, which makes the station house a lot more pleasant for everyone. Despite what the feminists say, it is an incontrovertible fact that women don't brawl as well as men (except Ronda Rousey, God bless her), especially the kind of men that are willing to take on the police, and the best female police officers I knew did not even bother to try to act like small men. Ever see a woman step into the ring with Chuck "The Iceman" Liddell? No, and you never will. Still, Vicki was a tough little fireplug and despite weighing about ninety pounds soaking wet she never hesitated to jump right into a fight. She was even a contestant on the TV show *American Gladiators* and she did the Department proud. Probably the best female officer I ever worked with was another District Six officer named Dani. She was a blonde-haired German immigrant who still spoke with a touch of an accent, like a feminine Arnold Schwarzenegger, but she was one of the most competent, professional cops I ever knew. We got a call of a huge fight in a bar downtown, a real Wild West saloon brawl with chairs flying, bottles breaking, and people being thrown through windows. The first officer on scene quickly got embroiled in the fight before realizing just how far in over his head he was. He got on the radio and yelled "I NEED COVER! SEND ME MEN, NO WOMEN!" He got a day off without pay and a trip to Sensitivity Training for that one.

* * *

Marriage can be a wonderful thing. It can bring two people together, to walk hand in hand down life's road toward a brighter future together, to raise children, to get that dream house with the white picket fence. And when the kids move away to college, it's time to travel and see the world, and grow old together, to always have that someone with you that you can count on. There are marriages made in heaven, and then there are the other kind. A newly engaged couple were celebrating at one of the bars in Six, and began immediately making their wedding plans, their honeymoon plans, for their wonderful new life together. Unfortunately, the blissful moment convoluted into an argument over the wedding plans and his family and her mother. The argument continued in the car and got more heated. She tried to jump out of the moving car, and he tried to stop her by grabbing her arm. The bride-to-be grabbed his hand and bit down on it until she drew blood and he let go. Then she jumps out of the moving car right onto Seventeenth Street. She went to the hospital and he went to Detox. That's love.

When a relationship reaches the point where it just becomes toxic, there is really only one thing to do. Let's face it, we've all been dumped at one time or another and it sucks, but we deal with it and move on. Some people, however, have a little more trouble letting go, and the following remarkable episode of just such a situation is one hundred percent true. In District Six there are several very exclusive, very expensive apartment complexes with names like The Beauvallon and The Prado, high-rent places full of high-rent people, mostly successful young to middle aged yuppies living beyond their means, determined to party until the money runs out. In one of these lived a basketball star for the Denver Nuggets. Women flock to star athletes and this man was no exception. He would pick them up in the clubs, use them for sex and entertainment for a few days, then toss them out when the next one caught his eye. When that happens, the woman who got jilted often cannot comprehend that she's been dumped and simply refuses to accept the ugly truth. They call incessantly, start showing up at the door at all hours of the day and night, and start the whole stalking thing. That's when we get involved.

This basketball player dumped his girlfriend of the week, a tall athletic brunette, and replaced her with a petite blonde. Not to be so easily dismissed, this jilted girl took stalking to a whole new level. Literally. She wasn't satisfied with calling fifty times a day and leaving messages alternately pleading for him to take her back and threatening to kill him or herself if he didn't. She wasn't satisfied with showing up at the door and being turned away by the doorman at all hours of the day and night. Oh no, she did *much* better! The way he told it to me, the basketball player was reclining on his couch with his new squeeze one evening watching TV when he heard a noise like a thump on his balcony. He glanced over toward the open sliding glass door but didn't see anything so he thought nothing of it. After all, he lived up on the sixth floor and there was no way to access the balcony from below, right? Well, he just wasn't thinking outside the box. After being turned away again by the doorman, Jilted Stalker prowled around the outside of the building seeking another way in. There's nothing like looking if you want to find something, as my Dad used to say, and she found something. She climbed *up* a big drain pipe, the kind that has cross-braces every few feet to attach the pipe to the brick wall. Six stories high she went, kicking off her shoes for better grip on the cross-braces and going hand over hand like some insane spider, and landed on her ex-lover's balcony.

The basketball star had just turned his attention back to the TV when the patio door suddenly flew open and The Stalker was standing there, clothes wet and dirty and torn, with sweaty face and wild hair from the exertion, like some nightmare hag. She saw the new girl on the couch and screamed and ran across the living room and leaped on her, clawing and biting and cursing. The new girl was so startled she couldn't even defend herself and just curled up in a ball on the floor while the psycho hag rained down blows on her. The basketball player pulled The Stalker off and threw her in the bathroom and wedged a chair under the doorknob to keep her in there. Then he called 9-1-1, and the dispatcher said she could hear screaming and pounding on the door in the background. The call was aired to us as an unwanted party. I think that's an understatement.

When I arrived with a couple of other officers she was still in the bathroom, screaming she was going to kill that little bitch, and kill him, and kill herself. In the next breath she would pleadingly tell him how much she loved him and she was so sorry for all this, and if he would only take her back she would be good. I looked at him with raised eyebrows and said "This was your girlfriend?" He just spread his hands in a helpless gesture, and the three of us lined up by the door in preparation for letting the wildcat out. I gave a three-count to the other guys and pulled the chair out. The door flew open and out she came, with claws up and screaming like a banshee. As soon as she crossed the threshold of the door we jumped her and dog-piled her to the floor. Crazy people are enormously strong, and coupled with us just getting in each other's way we had some difficulty getting the cuffs on her. When that was done we sat on her to take a breather, then hoisted her up. As we were half-dragging, half-walking her out the door she was looking back at him with pleading eyes and saying *"I love you! I love you so much! Please call me…"* Yeah, lady. He'll get right on that.

TWENTY TWO

THE BEAT I WORKED was officially labeled Precinct 617 on all the Department maps, but everybody just called it Lincoln Park. To the east of me was 616, where Todd Ondrak worked, and to the west was 618, where Jose Juarez was the precinct officer. The three of us covered each other on calls regularly, and one night Jose was transporting a prisoner when I rolled up on a big fight in the jets and called for cover. He diverted from his transport and came down to help me out, but when we got it sorted out and he went back to his car the back seat was empty. The doors were locked, windows up, but his prisoner was gone. Vanished. *Poof.* He got on the air and nervously said "Ahh, if anyone sees a Hispanic male walking around the area of 9th and Mariposa with handcuffs on, grab him." Personally, I think I might have just quietly let that one go, preserving my dignity and sparing myself the endless ribbing for the price of a pair of lost handcuffs.

The park was just one part of the precinct of course, but as it was centrally located and everyone knew it, the name stuck. The park itself was actually deceptively nice, having tall trees with squirrels rustling around in the branches, green grass, picnic tables, and a swimming pool. A casual passerby, a good citizen traveling through from somewhere else would think *"Oh, what a nice area!"*, but a look at the surrounding neighborhood would quickly dispel that sentiment. Surrounding the park on two sides were the Lincoln Park Projects, long single and double story red brick apartments with concrete walkways running like spider webs between the buildings.

The city had originally planted grass between the buildings but it had died long ago, like the hopes and dreams of the people who lived here. Now there was only dirt and blowing trash and debris, and clotheslines strung between the buildings, and kids would run around with bare feet and rags covering their bodies. During the day families played in the park, kids splashed in the pool, and couples walked the paths holding hands. Once night fell all the decent people cleared out, as the gang members, crack heads, prowlers, and an assortment of homeless and crazy people took over the park, despite the 11 o'clock curfew that ordered everybody out.

There was one old black woman, probably sixty-something but I couldn't be sure, who could be found in the park every night like clockwork, curfew or no curfew. Everyone called her Martha, but I don't know if that was her real name or just one that stuck. Many homeless and mentally ill people have recurring habitual behaviors. I've seen some who walk in circles and talk to themselves, others who have rhythmic hand motions waving in the air like a symphony conductor directing an imaginary orchestra, and Martha's was cleaning. God only knows where she stayed during the daylight hours, but every night she would clean up the park. She would walk along picking up trash at a feverish pace, all the while muttering and carrying on some low conversation with herself or someone only she could see. All of us cops left her alone, and none of the other night people ever seemed to bother her either. Yeah, technically she was violating curfew by being in the park, but as she was doing a public service we left her alone to do it. I tried to talk to her a couple of times but she would usually just keep walking and muttering and picking up trash like I wasn't even there. So after those failed attempts to communicate, when I would do my walk-throughs of the park and see her I would just say "Hi Martha! How you doin' tonight?" Sometimes she would stop and stand completely still, with her head down and avoiding looking at me, and as soon as

I would tell her "Good night Martha!" she would immediately go back to her work.

One night Todd and I were having dinner at Pete's when we heard one of the rookies just out of the Academy call out that he was with a suspicious black female in Lincoln Park after curfew. Todd and I looked at each other as we realized he was out with Martha. We got him on the radio and told him to meet us after he cleared the call. He met us, and told us he had written her a curfew ticket. *Damn FNG's!* They were so eager to enforce the law they would write their own mothers a ticket. We told him to give us the ticket and get out of here, and leave Martha alone, damn it! We tore up the ticket, but I didn't see Martha in the park the next night, or the next. I wanted to kick that rookie's butt. The one person actually doing something good in Lincoln Park and he busts her.

The third night I was walking through the park again and saw the familiar form, bending and walking and bending again as she cleaned up the refuse and debris. It was with more than usual enthusiasm that I greeted her, but now she seemed very nervous and scared. I talked to her for a minute just making small talk to try and reassure her that it was okay and build some trust back, and I left her two oatmeal raisin cookies (my favorite) from my lunchbox as a penance. I don't know if she ate them or not. She probably just threw them away and I wonder if her muttering was now all about us, and whether she has joined the rest of the precinct in hating the police.

* * *

Under the streets of Denver are big steam tunnels, and spaced along the streets at regular intervals are grates and manhole covers from which clouds of steam roll and boil out, and particularly on cold nights they form a spooky white fog that blankets the ground, so that the streets of my precinct looked eerily like the streets of London in an old werewolf movie. Homeless people often lie on these grates and manhole covers, trying to capture some warmth from the rising steam. Occasionally they fall asleep on them and get run over by cars. One early morning a federal agent on his way to work downtown ran over and killed a homeless man sleeping in the street, and because of the darkness and the mist no charges were filed against the agent, although he felt just awful about it. Standing there at the scene my mind went back to a time in Cherry Hills;

A doctor was out jogging, pushing her baby in front of her in one of those big-wheeled super-duty baby carriages made for running. She had just about cleared an intersection when a passing car didn't stop and clipped her, knocking her down. Luckily the baby carriage was well clear, and the doctor was not seriously injured. However, the story rocked our little community and stirred public outrage. The local newspaper, *The Villager,* was flooded with angry letters to the editor. *How dare someone hit a doctor?!* It was discussed at City Council meetings, and at Police Department staff meetings. The detectives were ordered to clear their desks to work on the "Doctor Jogger" case full time. The outrage was not confined to Cherry Hills, however. Television news stations picked it up, and tip hotlines were set up to look for a blue Mustang. A video recreation of the accident was even produced and aired on TV, with Beth starring as the Doctor Jogger. She would have made a great Hollywood stunt girl.

The manhunt was ultimately successful, and the detectives tracked down and charged the driver, a young white female, and found the car stashed in a garage with the front end damage still unrepaired. During that same time period while the hunt was going on, two people were struck and killed in Denver by hit and run drivers. There were no manhunts, no tip lines, and no video recreations. Those people were killed, and the Doctor Jogger was hardly injured. Thomas Jefferson wrote that we hold these truths to be self-evident, that all men are created equal. We may be *created* equal, but it sure doesn't stay that way. I guess some of us are more equal than others.

* * *

I don't know if half the stuff that went on out on the street ever made it back to the ears of Headquarters. Street cops will say that police administrators are not real cops, and from what I've seen working in four different agencies, I'd generally have to agree with that, though the brass at DPD were better than most. Something happens to people when they pin little gold and silver bars, or even worse, stars, on their collars. It's like they switched teams or something. In many larger police departments the brass themselves seek to perpetuate this; they wear different hats, or white shirts instead of blue shirts, they have "scrambled eggs" gold embroidery on their hat brims and shirt cuffs, and most of them have a coffee cup permanently welded to one hand. You see them show up at big crime scenes; they walk around, steaming cup of coffee in hand, looking grim and serious and wise. They'll ask a few gruff questions of the detective or the patrol officer standing guard outside the crime scene tape, then they'll nod their head gravely a few times at the answer and take a sip from their cup.

The brass like to be "on the inside", to show they're on top of things, part of the inner circle investigating this murder, robbery, drive-by shooting, or what have you. It makes them feel mighty important to walk up to the scene and duck under that yellow crime scene tape, especially if there are news cameras rolling nearby. The problem is that they're mucking up the crime scene by walking around in it, and bothering the people who are trying to investigate it and put all the pieces together and figure out who did what dastardly deed and to whom. Some of the brass hats know this and try to be decent about it and stay out of our way, so at DPD we hit on an idea that would make everybody happy; the Brass Corral. When we have a major crime scene, a big one where we know the press is going to be all over it, we started setting up *two* crime scene perimeters. We'd string the yellow tape around the actual crime scene, then we'd string *another* one a little farther out. That way the Captains and Commanders and their entourages can arrive on the scene, duck under that tape like they love to do, and walk around looking Captainly and Commander-ish, and still stay out of the dicks' way. It's perfect. Everybody's happy.

* * *

I keep myself in good shape and I'm a decent looking guy, and while on the Job I would get hit on all the time by women. Sometimes they were just trying to get themselves out of trouble. I had stopped a girl for weaving on a Friday night, and I could smell some alcohol on her breath, not strong but it was there. She admitted she had a drink or two, and I asked her to step out of the car to do the roadside maneuvers. She opened the door and stuck a long, tanned leg out, and then the rest of her emerged wearing a short skirt with a low-cut top. As soon as she got out she stepped right up so her face was next to mine and she purred "Sergeant Miller, I'll do *anything* to get out of this ticket!" But just then Beth pulled up, and being a woman she knew in an instant what the Pretty Purring Girl was trying to do and walked right up and took over from me without even asking. She hated when hot girls used their looks to get what they wanted, and I knew better than to argue with Beth when she was mad. Pat Weathers used to ticket all the hot girls and let the ugly ones go with a warning, his philosophy being that the hot girls had been getting breaks all their life and nobody gave an ugly girl a break. I couldn't argue with that logic. At other times girls weren't trying to get out of trouble, they just wanted to hook up with a cop. One girl explained to me that police officers were considered a good catch because they made decent pay and didn't have criminal records. The background check had already been done for them. Smart girl. I had another girl ask me out right after I arrested her boyfriend. When I say *right after* I mean while he was still handcuffed in the back seat of my car. The back window was partly down and the boyfriend could hear us talking, and he was yelling at her *"You fuckin' bitch!* You whore! I can't believe you're asking him out when he just arrested me! I hope you both get run over by a truck!!"

I don't know what it is about cops and strippers, but they seem to be drawn to each other like moths to a flame, like two magnets pulling irresistibly toward each other. Maybe it's because strippers are bad girls who aren't really all bad, and cops are supposed to be good guys but have a little badness in them. Maybe it's because girls love a man in uniform. Or maybe it's because they both work at night and always seem to end up around each other. Whatever the reason, they just seem to gravitate to each other. In District Six there was a gentleman's club called La Boheme. It's a two story red building down on Stout Street and we would end up going there every now and then because somebody would be getting drunk and disorderly and would have to be thrown out, or someone would be getting too handsy with the girls. At any rate, around three in the morning you could drive around to the back parking lot and see a line of several police cars, as cops were waiting for their favorite girls to get off work and come out. That back parking lot was the safest place in town.

One night I stopped a guy for running a red light, and he pulled over in the La Boheme parking lot. I contacted him, got his license, registration, and insurance and went back to my car. I cleared him to be sure he wasn't wanted and scratched him out a ticket. I went up to his car and gave him the ticket and sent him on his way. As I turned around to go back to my car, there walking towards me across the lot is one of the girls from inside.

She's a curvy brunette with a nice smile, and she waltzes right up to me and introduces herself. Dominique, she says. See? Like moths to a flame.

On another occasion Matt and I decided to go to breakfast at a Perkins restaurant up on Colorado Blvd. We were working for Cherry Hills at the time, before we both left to go to Denver, and there was a rule that officers were not supposed to go outside the city to eat. As usual, we said the hell with the rules and went out for pancakes and eggs. We had finished off breakfast, and were sitting back with a cup of coffee when a couple of girls came in. They were dressed down in just sweats, but we could spot a stripper a mile away and these were definitely of that species. Shotgun Willie's was just up the road from this Perkins, and sometimes the girls would come in after they got off work. These two made a beeline for us, and as they walked up to our booth they just slid right in next to us. The way they made themselves at home you'd think we were expecting them. The blonde next to me looked tired, but she was pretty. Shotgun Willie's didn't hire just anybody, and they had some racehorses in their stable. They started chatting with us and said that yes, they were from Shotgun's and just got off work. The gal next to me put her hand on my leg. They said they weren't quite ready to go home yet and wanted to party some more. She started rubbing my leg, and they asked what time we got off work. Matt and I were getting a little uncomfortable with this...umm...level of friendliness, from the two girls. We told them thanks for the invite, but we were both married. "Oh, that's okay!" they said cheerily, "We don't mind! You can still come back to our place and party with us!" *Now this was just not fair!* How often is a guy going to be quietly sitting at breakfast and have a hot stripper come in, sit down next to him, and tell him to come home with her? Where were these girls when I was single?!

Matt and I looked across the table at each other. No one would ever know but the two of us. And God. And our consciences. We told the girls sorry, we'd love to but we just can't. They couldn't believe we were turning them down. The girls wrote down their phone numbers and said we should come see them, backstage, any time. Then the girls slid out of our booth and left. Matt and I were left cursing at how unfair life was, and then we decided we had better tear up those phone numbers right now and toss them in the trash. Just in case our will power breaks downs after we separated.

* * *

Despite all the exposure to the worst in human nature, of man's inhumanity to his fellow man, and despite the toll it took on my body and the strain it placed on my family relationships, there were nights that I just loved being a cop. When you were suiting up in the locker room, joking around with your buddies, you were really preparing for The Unknown. You knew that tonight you were going to be a cop, but that's all you knew. When you climbed behind the wheel of your squad car and nosed it out of the gate of the police parking lot, you wondered what the city was going to throw at you tonight. Would it be talking down a person about to commit suicide? Another murder, another life lost because somebody 'dissed somebody else? Would you be forced to kill someone? Or maybe you would be bringing a runaway back home, or helping someone get their car back, their stolen property back, get their dignity and their life back.

I grew up a country boy, and I still love walking the woods and wide open spaces of my little retreat up in Wyoming. I love to sit on my porch at night and look up at a million stars, serenaded by the songs of the coyotes. It brings peace to my soul. But the city has an appeal of its own, an energy and a pulse like a living, breathing thing. The streets are its arteries, the tall buildings its bones, and the people the swarm of cells that give it life. Some nights the city is quiet, relaxed, gentle. Other nights it's a storm of mayhem and violence, and still others you can feel the city holding its breath, tense, waiting, to see if this will be a good night or a very bad one. On such nights I would smile with anticipation, behind the wheel of my patrol car. *Bring it on, City...*

TWENTY THREE

If you could block out of your mind the squalor and graffiti and trash of the surrounding tenements, Lincoln Park was green and peaceful, a tranquil little place of swaying trees and green grass that could have come from a Terry Redlin painting. There was an outdoor pool where during the day kids would splash and play in the water while their parents lounged and chatted. Other families would have picnic lunches under trees and couples would hold hands and go for walks in the park. But each night the park transformed as the decent people retreated indoors as the sun retreated from the sky, and yielded to the night and the creatures of the night, both four-footed and two-footed. The park became a hangout for junkies, the homeless, and groups of young male gang members out and up to no good.

In an effort to control the crime and vagrancy the city of Denver closed all the parks at eleven, and I patrolled the park either by driving the perimeter and spotlighting it if I was having a busy night, just to let everyone know the police were here, or if it was a slow night I would kill the lights and ease up to one end of the park and do a furtive foot patrol and see what I could catch. There was a three-legged fox who lived here. One of the old-timers told me she got one of her back legs cut off trying to beat the light rail train across the tracks. I don't know where she hid during the day but I would see her often at night, with her hopping gait to accommodate her lost leg, prowling around the bushes and the picnic tables looking for mice or if she was lucky some tasty morsel dropped by the day's picnickers. I wondered if she had babies, and I started leaving food out for her in case she did. Life's a bitch sometimes, and harder still with a missing leg and I figured if I could do my part to make life a little better for somebody in this God-forsaken precinct, it might as well be this small creature.

Late one night I was walking silently through the park, long after it had closed, when I heard the distinct sound of people laughing and splashing and having a grand time in the pool. Now I'm not one to begrudge anyone innocently having a good time, but rules are rules and it's not up to me to decide who gets to break the law and who does not. So I walked up to the pool and saw two males and a teenaged girl splashing in the pool. One of the males was just climbing out, and he happened to look over and see me standing by the pool's edge. He took one look at me and yelled "*COPS!*" and turned and ran at full speed to the south, toward the projects. I let him go, partly because he looked young and fast and I didn't feel like chasing him, and partly because I had two other people in the pool that I could collar without even taking a step.

I shined my flashlight on them and told them to get out of the water. They swam to the edge and climbed slowly out, and I told the girl to stay put while I pulled the male aside. He was probably about twenty, a tough-looking kid with gang tattoos covering his chest and shoulders. I asked him who his friend the rabbit was, and he said what they always say "I don't know man. I just met him." I asked him what they were doing out here and he replied "Just havin' a little fun in the pool with my homey and my lady." I let his admission about his "homey" that he supposedly just met slide, and I asked him who the girl was. "She's one of my bitches, man. I got lots of bitches!" he said proudly. I asked him what gang he ran with and he said "GKI, bro! We own this park!" I had seen a lot of GKI and Inca Boys graffiti around the neighborhood. I noticed he had tattooed in large script letters across his back the name Graciela, and I asked him about that. He said "Oh, that's my little girl man, my daughter." I asked where she was and he simply shrugged and said "She stays with her mom." That was street-speak for meaning that he had fathered her and abandoned both her and her mother. It's hard to go bangin' with the homeys when you're pushing a baby stroller.

I cleared him and dispatch came back that he was Six Frank, wanted on a felony warrant, and he was on parole to boot. I turned him around and hooked him up, then sat him down in the grass while I went and talked to the girl. She was about eighteen or nineteen, and she was definitely not from around here. She was a middle class kid from the suburbs, and I asked her what she was doing running around down here with this kind of scum. She got a pouty face and said "I love him!" I told her "You love him, huh? He told me you're just one of his bitches, and one among many at that." She didn't seem to care, and said all that mattered was that she loved him. Well, I informed her, I hope you like long distance relationships because the love of your life has a felony warrant and a parole violation so he's going back to prison.

When I told her that she became very upset and begged me not to take him to jail, as her eyes filled up with tears and her voice became pleading. She said she couldn't live without him. I was disgusted by this whole display, and doubly so that this otherwise decent girl was throwing herself at this dirt bag who was only using her for sex and money until he got tired of her and tossed her aside. She asked how much his bond was and I told her it was five thousand. Her forehead wrinkled up as she did some mental calculations, and she asked me "Do you think I could put up my car for his bond?" Before I could reply she said "My dad bought it for me, so would he have to find out?" Now I started to get mad, and I told her "Open your eyes, girl! This guy doesn't give a damn about you! If you put up your car for his bond I'll tell you what's going to happen. He's going to skip out and the bail bondsman is going to take your car, then you'll be riding a bicycle around and Romeo over there won't give you the time of day after that. Don't you dare do something stupid like that!" She got mad back and said "You sound just like my dad! You guys just don't understand how much I love him!" I turned to Romeo, sitting on the ground with his hands cuffed behind his back and said *"Hey, did you hear that? She loves you! Do you love her?"* He just sat without moving, staring at the ground between his feet. I turned back to the girl "See? You're wasting your time with him." I walked over to my prisoner and got him to his feet, and as I was putting him in the back of my car the girl was following us and tearfully calling out to him "I love you! I'll come to the jail and get you out!" He called back to her not that he loved her in return, but "Come to the jail! Post my bond and get me out of this shit!"

When we got rolling on the way downtown to the jail I was thinking about my own daughter, who granted was only nine at the time, and about the father of that girl. I felt for the guy, even though I didn't know him. What father would want to find out his precious little girl, who he bounced on his knee when she was a toddler, and raised and protected all those years when she was changing from a girl into a young woman, was being used and abused as a sex toy for a scumbag gang member? He was probably using her for money and her car as well. And now she was going to sell the car her father bought her, probably for her sixteenth birthday, to get this dirtball out of jail. For some women anything that is thoroughly bad for them they somehow find irresistible. There are thousands of nice, hard-working guys out there with careers and decency and good hearts who can't get a date to save their lives. And meanwhile the unemployed stringy-haired tattooed small-time criminal and full-time loser has women fighting over him, because he's a "Bad Boy" and so many women find that irresistible. There's a reason that Bad Boys are bad, as the women who date them eventually come to realize, usually after he's spent all their money, slept with their friends, and dumped them. You can think about life and people all you want but you can never understand what makes people do what they do.

* * *

The Job is hard on families. The cop often doesn't realize it because he's so wrapped up in the whole police life that he doesn't see it, until something happens to shake him up and make him see. Sometimes it's his wife walking out on him or having an affair, or his kids getting arrested or pregnant. To the kids, their dad is some guy in a uniform they probably idolize when they actually get to see him. He's like Santa Claus, a mysterious and exciting person who shows up once in a while and gives them presents or a pat on the head and a kiss before bed. For me, I had a revelation that thankfully did not involve my wife having an affair or divorcing me, but it was a shock nonetheless.

We were all going out for dinner one evening, and we were putting our shoes on by the front door when my son Nick, who was five at the time, asks my wife where we're going. She told him "We're going out to dinner, honey" then Nick tugs at her sleeve and leans close to her, and points at me and whispers "Is he going, too?" *From the mouths of babes...*It hit me like a sucker punch in the gut that my own son hardly knew me. I had never realized how much my wife was raising the kids as a single mom. I was going out every night getting into fights and chases, busting bad guys, feeling the adrenaline rush, while she was changing diapers, getting them dressed, taking them to doctor's appointments, day care and school. Then at night she would get them dinner and tuck them into bed.

On the weekends I would be working or sleeping, and she would take them to the zoo or the museum or to get together with family and friends. Most of the family photos from those years do not have me in them, and people were actually surprised when I would show up at family gatherings. Even when I was off duty I hung out with my cop friends and we talked about work. I didn't often talk to my wife about work, because it's hard to make someone understand it unless they've done it. It's like a pilot could talk all day to someone about flying, but if the person you're talking to has never been off the ground, it's all just words. Another reason is that she often didn't want to hear stories about hookers or fights with drunks or shootings. I don't blame her, I guess. She sometimes told me that she felt like I had a whole other life, that she and the kids were not a part of. And she was right.

It was after these things happened that I began to think seriously about leaving police work. After all, I had given more than a decade of my life to serving the public, and along with it my blood, sweat, tears, and my sanity. I wanted to be home now, sitting around the kitchen table for dinner with my wife and kids, like a normal family, instead of in the squad room night after night with some microwave mush served on a paper plate. It wasn't just how hard the Job was on my family. It was also the Job itself. The vast majority of cops really do want to help people. You come out of the Academy with your shiny new gear and pressed uniform and head full of dreams of saving the world, but the daily grind of the Job just beats it out of you. You soon learn that when you roll up on a scene nobody there is happy to see you, not even the people who called you. It doesn't take too many times of cruising through the neighborhoods and waving at the kids only to have a nine-year old flip you the bird before you're driving around muttering to yourself and thinking dark thoughts. That's why all the old-timer cops are bitter at the world. A group of us were at a buddy's house for a backyard barbeque and one of the old vets was grousing about everything, and he was looking down at the lawn and said "I hate grass. Grows everywhere you don't want it to, looks like hell if you don't water it all the time, have to pick weeds out of it. I hate that damn grass!" I was still young and idealistic and excited about being a cop, and I wondered if that's what police work did to a guy. Man, if you can find hate in your heart for grass, you gotta get out of this line of work.

One weekend night I was cruising around my precinct when we got a call of shots fired down on the 16th Street Mall, a brightly lit pedestrian area of shops, restaurants, festive lighting, and street performers playing for money. It wasn't my call but when dispatch updated that one person was down and possibly DOA all the available cars started rolling, hoping to intercept the shooters. When I arrived on scene I parked my squad car and joined up with two other cops walking down the Mall to where we could see a large crowd of people gathered. We pushed our way through the crowd to where a hysterical young woman was kneeling over a young man down on the street and not moving. He had been shot in the chest at least twice, and his shirt was red with blood and it was running off into little rivulets down his side and onto the concrete sidewalk. It looked bad.

The girl was crying and screaming hysterically, and when she saw us she turned on us in a fury. "It's about fucking time you got here!" she screamed and then her tone abruptly changed to pleading "Please save him! Help him!" I pulled on latex gloves and started applying pressure on his wounds, using his shirt. All the while the girl was alternately screaming at us in anger and imploring us to please help him. "This is *your* fault!" she raged. "If you were here this would never have happened!" The bystanders picked up on her anger and I could hear it go rippling through the crowd *"Yeah! Fuckin' cops! Never here when you need 'em!"* and someone else said "Fuck the pigs!" and just like that we became the bad guys, and somehow to blame for the whole thing. The other two officers were trying to talk to witnesses, to get a description of the shooters, but all they got was "Fuckin' pigs! Brother gets shot and *now* they want to talk!" and no one would tell us anything. I tried to get the girlfriend to calm down and tell us who shot her boyfriend. Did she know them? What did they look like? But she refused to tell us anything about them and just screamed at us that it was our fault.

The paramedics were trying to reach us, but the now-hostile crowd wouldn't let them through. The paramedics were being shoved and punched by the people in the crowd, and they started calling for us to come and help them. We pushed and bulled our way back through the crowd and pulled the paramedics behind us back to the injured male. They started taking his vitals, and one of them looked up at me and shook his head. The girlfriend saw it and screamed *"You killed him! You killed him!"* I looked at her in disbelief. She hangs out with gang members, her boyfriend gets shot by another gang member, she refuses to cooperate with the police, he dies, and somehow in her twisted mind all those things are the fault of the police. And the crowd was behind her completely. Why do I bother? Just put up a big wall, block the exits, and let them all kill each other.

* * *

I was cruising 11th Avenue, which flanks the north side of the projects, one summer evening not long after the shooting on the Mall. My shift had just started and so far the city was fairly quiet for a weekend night. Off to my left I could see people hanging out in the park, and off to my right I could see others hanging out on their porches with their ever-present "40s" of cheap beer, and still others were strolling along the concrete pathways that spider-webbed between the two story apartment buildings, on errands of their own, either legitimate or mischievous. I got a few waves from some of the people and got flipped off by others, and I returned the waves and ignored the fingers. As I passed by taking in the feel of my precinct, its mood for the evening that would help me gauge how the night was going to go, I saw something dark on the sidewalk, up ahead on my right. It was a dark motionless blob, like an old duffel bag someone had dropped and left. As I got closer the blob took on human form and I stopped my patrol car and walked over to it.

It was a woman. She was Asian, early twenties I guessed, a little well dressed for this neighborhood, and she was in bad shape. She had multiple stab wounds and her blouse was covered in blood. Her hair was caked in blood so she probably had head wounds as well, and she was unconscious. I radioed it in and requested an ambulance Code 10, then ran back to my car. I popped the trunk and pulled out the first aid kit, pulled on my latex gloves, and ran back to her. I felt for a carotid pulse, and I detected a faint heartbeat. *She was still alive.* Somehow, some way, she was hanging on. I started cleaning off some of the blood, trying to find where the stab wounds were, and peeling off rolls of gauze bandages and applying direct pressure to the worst of them to try and stem the bleeding. All the while that I was feverishly trying to save her life there were people walking by on the sidewalk, people sitting on their porches in plain view of it all, and they were watching me with the detached unconcern of people watching the weather report on the TV news. I kept working on her until the ambulance arrived and took over. The paramedics took one look at her and quickly scooped her onto a gurney and rushed her off to Denver General with lights flashing and siren wailing, trying to get her to the ER before she bled out.

I asked another officer to go with her to the hospital while I talked to the people in the neighborhood to try to figure out who she was, how she got here, and what happened to her. As soon as the people saw me walking towards them they got up from their porches and went back inside, and wouldn't answer their doors. The ones I did talk to nonchalantly said they didn't know who she was, they didn't see anything, they had nothing to say. The people in the projects present a united front against the police; nobody saw anything, nobody heard anything, and nobody is talking. They take it as a point of pride, without seeing that this stiff-necked resistance is the very thing that keeps their neighborhoods full of crime and gangs and drugs, then they complain loud and long that the police aren't doing anything about the crime in their neighborhood.

I went to the hospital afterward and she was still in surgery. A while later a doctor came out and reported to us that she didn't make it. The wounds were too deep and too many, and she had lost too much blood. Homicide took over the investigation. As I drove out of the parking lot of DG I was seething with fury. That young woman had lain there for God knows how long, in full view of dozens of people, with her life's blood running out of her and onto the sidewalk. She was laying right across the main walkway leading from the street to the project houses, so people had to have been stepping over her or walking around her. Nobody helped her, nobody got off their porches, nobody even lifted a phone to dial 9-1-1. Nobody cared at all. Just then I hated the people in the projects. It was a madhouse of depraved lunatics who had lost all humanity and reason, a place where all that mattered was the next fix, the next bottle, the next government check, and where they were willing to kill if someone "dissed" them, as if they were worthy of respect.

As I drove in silence ruminating over these dark thoughts I remembered the story of Kitty Genovese, the young woman who was raped, stabbed and murdered on a public street in New York, in two separate attacks that spanned more than half an hour. While she bled and screamed for help, and while her attacker repeatedly beat and stabbed her, not one person tried to help or even called the police. Reports over the exact number of people who actually witnessed the attacks vary from a dozen to more than three dozen, but the number is not the point. The utter indifference is the point. On the side of my patrol car it said "To Serve and Protect." I wondered if society was worth it.

PART FIVE

TWENTY Four

"It's a madhouse!! A madhouse!!"
 - Charlton Heston, *Planet of the Apes*

Nut Jobs

I'm sitting in Five Guys having a burger and fries for lunch, looking through the big storefront windows out over the big parking lot of the Marketplace shopping center, thinking about nothing in particular. Then something caught my eye. Or rather I should say, someone. Spiderman, to be precise. Yes Spidey, the superhero, the web guy. Some nut job in a complete Spiderman costume was standing in the parking lot, pretending to shoot webs at the people walking by. He was also throwing karate kicks in the direction of the passersby, who were studiously ignoring him. *Sigh... I guess I better go out there.* This was a damn good burger, too.

I started to wrap up my bacon cheeseburger preparatory to going out to meet Spidey, then another thought suddenly occurred to me. The thought that I should just pretend I don't see him, keep eating my burger, and then go about my business. Because I could already see in my mind how this was going to go; I would approach Spiderman, he would pretend to shoot webs at me, then start doing karate kicks at me, whereupon I would Taser him, and all the passersby who had been avoiding him would suddenly be writing detailed witness statements saying poor old Spiderman wasn't hurting anyone, then the mean policeman came along and Tasered him for no reason. So I just kept eating my cheeseburger and watching Spidey continuing to shoot webs at people, until my lunch was over. And you know what? We didn't get a single call about him.

We have a term in police work – BSC. It stands for "Bat Shit Crazy", and it seems to apply to an increasing number of people that I encounter in my work. I figure it's something in the water. After all, way back when modern cities were first built they dug the trenches and laid the water pipes, filled the dirt back in, and turned on the pumps. And for decades since then the water that flows out of our faucets has been running through those same pipes and who knows what has accumulated in them over all this time? Buildups of heavy metals, mold, assorted gunk, dead bodies, lots of rats, garbage, alligators that people flushed down the toilet when they were babies and now they've grown huge in the dank darkness. The point is, I am sure you have noticed as well as I have that we now have an abundance of crazy people out there; the BSC zombies are growing and spreading.

Case in point: I get a frantic call from two women who say that these creepy guys are following them. The girls are now in their motel room but the guys are still waiting outside in the parking lot. I go over there with another officer, take the elevator up to their room, and contact these two girls. They open the door and invite us in, and we are presented with two very normal looking suburban white girls, dressed like every girl you see at the mall on the weekends. They both start jabbering at us and telling the story of how they were driving downtown and were at a stoplight when a carload of guys pulls up next to them. They roll down the windows and start talking to the guys, but decide these guys are a little creepy and not really their sort, so they roll up the windows and drive away, but the guys follow them.

They start driving around downtown trying to lose the guys, but the guys stick to them like glue. So they come back to their hotel and run upstairs and call the police. We had gotten a description of the car from dispatch and an officer checked the lot and the car was not there. But the girls insist the car is still down there. I reassured them that an officer checked the lot and the car was gone, and then one of the girls says "I know they're down there because I can feel their brain waves scanning me right now." *Huh? Come again?* She says "Yeah, can't you feel them? They're scanning the whole room right now with brain waves." I look around the room, half expecting to see squiggly waves in the air. Nothin'. Nut jobs.

I met another woman in a motel – okay, I probably could have phrased that better – I responded to another call at a motel involving a female acting strangely. The desk clerk had called us because he went up to the room to investigate some thumping noises. He opened the door and all was dark inside, so he flips the wall switch to turn on the light. Nothin'. No light. Suddenly a voice shrieks at him from the darkness of the room "GET OUT DEVIL!!" The clerk about jumped out of his skin and beat a hasty retreat from the room, wondering what to do next. And when in doubt what does everyone do? Call the cops.

I went up to the room and knocked on the door, before gently easing it open and identifying myself as a police officer, so as not to be mistaken for the ruler of the underworld like the poor desk clerk was. A voice spoke to me from the darkness, but it was actually quite a pleasant voice, inviting me in. I shined my flashlight in there and beheld a very ordinary looking woman, probably in her early forties, just standing there in the dark. I struck up a conversation with her and we got around to discussing why she was hanging out in a dark room, and she explained it to me. The room was dark because she had unscrewed and removed all the light bulbs. *And why, pray tell, would you do that?* She leaned in close, like they always do, and whispered conspiratorially that *they* have planted tiny cameras in all the light bulbs, so they can *watch* you! She beckoned me into the room and I followed with some trepidation, not sure what I was being led to. She took me to a cardboard box. It was a big box, one of those 24-count rolls of paper towels sized boxes, and it was filled to the brim with light bulbs.

Now don't go thinking that the girls have the market cornered on crazy. Same motel, different night, different nut. The night clerk calls and says the guy in 236 keeps calling down to the desk and complaining about the guy in the next room doing something to him. The guy seemed a little freaky and she didn't want to go up there, so she called us, because freaky people are our specialty, our nightly fare. We go up there and knock; "*Hey, open up it's the police!*" The door opens a sliver and a round blue eye peers out at us. Then the door opens wide and the wild-haired Charles Manson look-alike beckons us in quickly, then shuts the door.

He has a half-crazed look to him and his eyes are rapidly darting back and forth as he explains that the guy in the room next door is reading his mind. "And how is he doing that, sir?" I ask dubiously, but Charles lowers his voice and scoots close to me, like they always do, and points downward towards the wall, whispering "He's sending in his brain waves *there,* through the outlets!" I look at the electrical outlet, and it's pretty innocuous looking, no more sinister than any other outlet. But I do notice there's a blob of something gooey on this one, and I ask Charles about it. He grins and scoots even closer to me, and says in a low, conspiratorial voice "I *fixed* him, so he can't read my mind anymore!" I look closer at the outlet and discover that Charles had peeled some bananas and squished them into all the electrical outlets. I was unaware up until then of the brainwave-absorbing qualities of bananas, but I will tuck that little tidbit away in case I ever need it in the future.

Crazy crosses all ethnic, racial, and social divides. I went to a sprawling magnificent mansion in the snootiest, bluest-blooded enclave in the city, on a report of a burglary. Makes sense; if I was a burglar this neighborhood would be my playground. Why burglarize the ghetto when you can sneak and peek in a multi-million-dollar estate? I meet a middle-aged woman at the front door who escorts me inside. She is well-dressed, as rich matronly women are, and she leads me to the garage. She says she found her passport lying on the floor in the garage, while it is usually kept in a drawer in the bedroom. I'm taking notes while she's talking, and then she leads me into the parlor. My house doesn't have a parlor, does yours? I have a living room, but a parlor is apparently an *extra* living room, that nobody actually ever lives in. Sometimes they come equipped with a butler, who looks down his nose at you and sneers *"Wait in the parlor while I inform the Lord and Lady that you are here."*

Anyway, she shows me a stack of books and a picture on an end table, and says that when she left the picture was facing *that* way, and now it's facing *this* way. And the books have been rearranged. The book on New England seaside colonial homes was on top when she left, and *now* the book on fine wines of Napa Valley is on top. I stopped taking notes about then. Then she led me upstairs toward her bedroom, and I have to tell you that as I ascended the stairs I was becoming a little concerned about what she wanted to show me in there. My concern heightened when she led me straight over to the bed and flipped back the comforter. *Now ma'am I appreciate your support of the police, but this really isn't necessary* I started to say, but then she turned my attention to her pillow. She leaned closer, like the crazy people always do, and whispered that the National Security Agency was sending covert agents into her house at night, and they were spraying a secret substance on her pillowcase so they could steal her memories when she went to sleep. *Aye yi yi*... I'm tellin' ya, it's the water!

Marilyn Monroe is Alive and Well

In case you were wondering, Marilyn Monroe is alive and well. She lives on a quiet little cul-de-sac in a nice but modest brick house. I know this because I talked to her. I went to her house on an alarm call, and I'm walking around the house checking the doors and windows, and I hear this voice behind me; a voice, by the way, that sounds instantly and unmistakably familiar. I turn around and there she is, in the flesh. Much older, of course, but she's got the hair, the voice, the look, the lips, everything. I'm standing there open-mouthed and dumbfounded, and she goes right on talking in that same soft, lilting voice that sang ♪ *Happy Biirthdaaay,, Mister Presidennntt* ♪, to JFK. I remember watching Marilyn Monroe in *The Seven Year Itch* and *Gentlemen Prefer Blondes*, and if that wasn't her I'll eat my leather gun belt. Just to be sure, I ask her for her date of birth. *For the report, ma'am.* She gives it to me. And you know what? The month and day are different but the year matches. Witness Protection Program, baby.

TWENTY FIVE

That's Amore!

As a veteran cop I have by experience and by necessity become a student of human nature. I am not talking about everyday human nature; wake up, get dressed, kiss the wife or hubby goodbye, and go off to work or school, the stuff of normal life. I am talking about human nature when things get decidedly *abnormal,* and I have concluded that pretty much all of the vast range of human activity is motivated by a very short list of needs and desires. Money, sex, and looking for love covers about 90% of all that we do.

I have heard it said that all of modern civilization is just an attempt by men to impress girls. I think whoever said that is on to something, because what do guys do when they want to impress a girl? They get a nice car, flash some money around, take her to nice places. And every invention of modern civilization pretty much fits into one of those three categories; money, sex, and looking for love. We go to college to get high paying jobs so we can have money. Which means we can then get nice cars, flash some money around, and take girls to nice places.

I have worked everywhere from the wealthiest gated millionaire snob neighborhoods to the crack-house ghettos and housing projects, and all socioeconomic levels in between, and if you want to have a happy life here is the secret: Are you ready? Find someone, that special guy or girl for you, and stay focused on the romance. That's 90% of the battle. In fact it sounds so easy that half of you are openly scoffing at it right now. Aren't you? You can admit it.

What matters is that the two of you go down the road of life hand in hand, and don't let all the distractions of societal expectations and careers and kids and money stresses get in the way. I want each of you, singles and couples alike, to ask yourself this one question: When did you have the most fun with your gal or your guy? Chances are it was back when you were dating and didn't have ten bucks between you. It was because back then you were focused on each other and on the romance. Don't let that die.

I know from my own career path and divorce that it is all too easy to lose perspective on what is really important, to get lost in the stresses of your job, child care and paying bills and trying to juggle a dozen different things. We think that what will make us happy is getting that promotion, buying that bigger house, climbing that socio-economic ladder. Let me tell you something people; the higher you climb that ladder just means the farther you have to fall and the farther from solid ground you get. Maybe we are all going the wrong direction, and we should be thinking *simplify* rather than *get more stuff*.

Here is a tip for those of you who have children or are thinking about getting some. When you are married, you still have to keep your spouse as #1. NOT your kids. Ladies, I'm mostly talking to you here. Your husband still has to be #1. I know that sounds counter-intuitive, but trust me on this. I've seen it hundreds of times. It is *soo* easy to forget about the health of your marriage, to neglect your relationship with each other, in the consuming process of taking care of the kids. Then when the kids are older and in school and don't need you so much anymore, you and your spouse are suddenly looking at each other and seeing two strangers.

Guys, this is where you really need to step up. Let's just face it, the women do a lot more with raising the kids than we do. We need to keep the romance alive, to make our wives still feel beautiful and wanted. Those old standby's of flowers, gifts, and romantic dinners really do work. That's how they got to be old standby's. If you keep yourselves focused on having a good marriage, the raising of the kids will fall right into place.

* * *

I have a private theory that much of human behavior can be traced back to the caveman. After all, this modern industrial/ technological society we live in has only existed for a few hundred years. Prior to that we had 10,000 years of caveman. You can't just turn off those instincts and behaviors that quick. I think the cavemen had it so much easier in some ways than we do today. Here is a caveman's Day Planner:
- Get up, put on bearskin tunic, pick up spear
- Find something and kill it
- Eat
- Take a nap until evening
- Play bongo drums
- Build a fire and spread out bearskin
- Eat dinner
- Make love to cave girl
- Sleep

That's it. No quarterly reports, no taxes, no traffic jams, no jerk bosses.

* * *

Sometimes love and romance can be fickle, and hard to find, so you have to make some substitutions. I get a call of a disturbance at one of our local one-star motels. It seems a guy is in the lobby and he's going berserk, tearing the place up and throwing things around. I get there and the place is in shambles, the suspect is now winded from his exertions and resting in the corner, and the desk clerk is hiding and peeking over the counter. I question the clerk and get the story; the guy checks into the hotel and wants to rent a room just for the night. The clerk tells him it'll be fifty bucks and the guy pulls out his wallet and starts to count out some bills. Then the clerk tells him they also need a hundred bucks for the security deposit. And that's when the guy flips out and goes nuts. I talk to the guy and he's nodding his head and agreeing with everything the clerk says. So I ask him "So why did you flip out then?" And he says to me "That hundred bucks was all my hooker money. Whadda you think I wanted the motel room for?"

Same type of call, different night, different place. Guy breaks up with his girlfriend, and she suspects he is seeing someone else. So she sneaks over to his apartment and puts her ear to the door. Sure enough, she can hear him in there and another girl's voice, and they're giggling and laughing and having a good time. So the ex starts pounding on the door and screaming to be let in so she can kick that dirty whore's ass (her choice of words, not mine). Boyfriend is yelling at her to go away, but that only makes her start kicking and pounding on the door even more. Dirty Whore is really starting to freak out now, and the boyfriend calls the cops.

While we are en route the ex is starting to realize that she is not going to break down this door just by sheer physical force. So she starts digging around in her purse and finds a pocket knife, and she uses it to start jimmying the lock. And it works! She pops the lock and comes into the room, and boyfriend and Dirty Whore, now in a panic, lock themselves in the bathroom. She figures *Hey, it worked once I'll try it again!* and starts working on the lock with the pocketknife. That's what she was doing when we entered the apartment. We got her to drop the knife and put her in handcuffs, and as we're leading her away she is pleading "I love you! I love you *sooo* much! Call me!" Nothing says "I Love You" like Breaking & Entering. They could put that on a Hallmark card.

* * *

I used to work with a guy named JD. He was a handsome Italian guy and got lots of girls, but his big thing with women was warmth. We would see one of the rich trophy wives go walking by, with all the equipment in all the right places and her nose in the air, and JD would just shake his head and say "Mikey, she may look good but she's got no *warmth!* Fuhggedaboudit!"

JD is right, of course. We always want the bright hummingbird when maybe a nice sparrow would be a lot easier to live with. Sometimes we have to find warmth wherever we can get it. I found a couple sleeping in a car in a parking lot one night. I'm looking in the window and I see the two of them, such a cute picture all snuggled up together under a blanket. I knock on the window and they flip the blanket back and turn toward me with a panicky look. Turns out they weren't sleeping at all. No indeed, they were engaged in other snuggling-related activities.

I give them a minute to compose themselves and get their clothes on, then they step out of the car to talk to me. It's Tony and Misty, and they explain to me that they have a room upstairs but they just couldn't wait. I appreciate their passion but I run them for wants and warrants anyway. Busted! Not Tony – Misty. Seems that Misty got into some trouble awhile back and skipped out on her court date. So I had to spoil their fun by putting the steel bracelets on Misty and taking her off to jail.

Later in the same night I go out on another call at the same motel. The desk clerk wants the people up in 355 out for not paying rent for the second night. I go up there and knock on the door, and I meet Angie. Angie's only half-dressed, and I run her and she's got a warrant, too. I tell her to step back in the room and put some clothes on, so we go back inside. And lo and behold! Guess who is in the bed with her? It's Tony. He's lying in bed wearing only his underwear, and when he sees me his eyes pop open and he jumps up. I told him to relax, we were there for Angie. As I'm hooking up Angie I say to Tony "I guess you were so upset about Misty getting arrested that you had to find some comfort with Angie, huh?" Tony says nothing, but as I'm leading Angie away she's yelling at Tony "You're doin' Misty too!? She's my best friend, you bastard!" As I was walking her away that old Dean Martin song came into my head " ♪ *When the moon hits your eye like a big pizza pie, that's amore!! ♪*"

* * *

Of course many marriages end up in divorce, which can bring on a whole new set of problems. Don't think that because your divorce was final that your troubles are over. Oh no, sometimes that just opens the door to troubles you never dreamed of!

I got a call one day from a psychologist telling me to come and get her patient. Now we all know that when you go see your shrink or your lawyer that you can tell them pretty much anything, because of the doctor-patient privilege or the attorney-client privilege. You can tell your shrink that you've slept with pretty much every man in town and you know they're not going to tell anyone, just like you can tell your lawyer that Yep, you sure as heck *did* kill that guy! and you know that he is not going to tell the judge what you said. In the medical and legal professions that confidentiality is treated with near reverence. So given the strength of that privilege I was very surprised to hear a shrink telling me to come get her patient. I was wondering just what the heck was going on as I drove over there.

Upon arrival I met first with the shrink in the hallway outside her office. Through the window I could see a very normal looking woman in her early thirties, playing with a little boy and a little girl on the carpet. The psychologist explained to me that this woman came in to see her, saying she had some issues related to her ex-husband she needed to air out to someone. She was not a regular, in fact it was their first visit together. The psychologist asks her what issues she was feeling in relation to her ex-husband. The woman says "I want to kill him." "Come again? What was that?" the shrink replied. The woman clarified the situation; "I want to hunt him down, I want to find him, and I want to kill him very slowly." I imagine that people who see psychologists are often conflicted and confused, and I'll bet the shrink wasn't used to someone expressing their feelings with quite such clarity or depth of feeling.

I told the shrink I would take it from here, and I went into the room to have a friendly chat with the homicidal lunatic. She was quite pleasant to talk to, and while I motioned for another officer to maybe take the kids into the next room and keep them occupied, we sat down to talk. I decided on the direct approach; "So I hear you want to kill your ex-husband?" "Yep" she nodded matter-of-factly, as if I was asking if she liked cream and sugar with her coffee. Now people pay attention, because here is Cop Lesson #34; we have something called an M-1, an Emergency Mental Health Hold. By statute, a police officer (but not a fireman, ha ha ha!) can take someone into custody if they are a danger to themselves or others, or if they are incapable of adequately caring for themselves, you know things like feeding and clothing themselves, taking a bath, seeing little green aliens in the room. Now to ascertain this a good cop tries to determine some very specific points of information; does she have a *plan*, or is this murder just one of those whimsical daydreaming, "someday" kind of things? Does she have a *method*, meaning has she given it a lot of thought, like *I am going to kill Professor Plum, in the library, with the candlestick, at noon.* If they have both a plan and a method, then we need to put the jacket with the funny sleeves on them and take them to see the men in white coats.

So I began asking this woman those things, and she did not disappoint. You see, her ex-husband was in hiding from her (*gee, there's a shock*), and she was going to hire a private detective service to find him, then she was going to sneak into the house and slip a roofie into his drink, then while he was unconscious she was going to handcuff his hands and feet to the bed, gag him, and then slowly carve him up with a knife. *Yeah...I think she's given this a lot of thought.* I asked her if there was anything else she wanted to do to him, just to get the big picture. She said yes, there was (I *knew* she was going to say that!) She said she wanted to gouge out his eyes. I hesitated to ask, but I had to. "And can you tell me why you want to gouge out his eyes?" She laughed and playfully touched my knee and said "Silly, because the eyes are the windows to the *soul*, of course!" *Yes, of course, how silly of me to even ask.*

Now I was ready to scoop her up right there, while carefully searching her for carving knives or eye gougers, but we had the problem of the children. The shrink flatly refused to take responsibility for the children, so we had to play phone roulette with Child Protective Services to arrange for care of the children. Child Protective Services said they had to make a Safety Plan before they could come pick up the children. *Safety plan?* How about we put the homicidal nutcase in a straightjacket and you come take the kids? How's that for a plan? They didn't appreciate my suggestion. Luckily my partner has a cooler head than me and he assumed the role of negotiator. While we were waiting for CPS to get their safety plan together and come over, the little boy wanted to go to the bathroom. Well *I* wasn't about to take him, so we let the mom take him while one of us stood outside the door. Then of course the second the boy gets back the little girl needed to go. So we let her take the girl. All of you armchair quarterbacks out there screaming that we shouldn't have let her do that can just zip your lips right now. I am not going to put up with two small children doing the pee-pee dance and crying to go to the bathroom when we had no idea how long we were going to be there. And I am damn sure not going to go in there with the kids and help them use the bathroom, not in today's accusatory and litigious society.

While we are waiting I got a phone call. I thought it was Child Protective Services and I started to say "Where the hell are you guys?" but it wasn't from them. It was from a cop at Arvada PD. They were looking for a particular girl who was in our city and they wanted some help finding her. I said "Sure we can try to find her for you." The APD cop on the other end said he appreciated it, gave us her name and asked could we just call him when we located her? I said "Okay, I found her. She's sitting right across from me." The cop on the other end was confused and frankly so was I, but as he explained the situation everything became crystal clear. Apparently while she was taking her little ones to the bathroom she took the opportunity to send some choice texts to her ex-husband, graphically describing how she was going to hunt him down like the dog that he is and put a knife in his heart and twist it. Now that takes some *cojones*, folks. To send someone threatening messages *while* the police are questioning you about sending threatening messages.

CPS finally arrived and the ladies were very nice, then we put the bracelets on Lizzie Borden and bundled her off to the mental ward, with the understanding that if and when she was released Arvada PD would be waiting for her. I have an ex-wife, and we get along pretty good, for which I am thankful. After all, it could be worse. Much, much worse...

* * *

As a cop I investigate crimes. All of the crimes I investigate pretty much fall into one of three categories; financial, emotional, and depraved hearts. Most crimes are done for money; identity theft, shoplifting, burglary, robbery, etcetera. A fair number of them are done because emotions get out of control; assault, murder, domestic violence. And thankfully the smallest number are the fruit of a sick and depraved mind; rape, child molestation, premeditated murders. On the subject of murder, I have always believed that money obtained by murdering someone could never bring any satisfaction; the knowledge of how it was obtained would rob any joy or pleasure from the spending of it. Invariably the money will soon be gone, but you will always carry the gnawing guilt of knowing you are a murderer. But so it is with human nature; people often spend so much time plotting and dreaming of a thing, the careful planning and execution, with never a thought of what happens after – how do you live with it after you've done it?

TWENTY SIX

The Curse of Technology

In case you haven't figured it out, I'm old school. I don't do yoga, I don't eat quiche, I'm not politically correct, and I am not in touch with my feminine side. I like guns, steaks on the grill, and classic rock music. And I don't like new technology. These days it seems that every week some new-fangled phone app or piece of technology is coming out that we suddenly just cannot live without. I'm at a home store the other day with my wife, and the young millennial sales guy in the appliance section who is following us around and won't leave us alone is telling me that well of course you just *gotta* have a refrigerator that is connected to the internet! *Duh, Grandpa! Have you been living in a cave?!*

Why does my refrigerator need to be connected to the internet? For fifty years my refrigerator has not been connected to the internet and nevertheless has worked just fine. I don't need my refrigerator to talk to me, and if I want to know if I need milk I will just open the door and look. I don't need my 'fridge to greet me, give me uplifting messages to boost my self-esteem, tell me my salad dressing has gone bad, or have the government and Google spying on me through my ice dispenser.

My view on technology is that most of it is completely unnecessary. Most of the new technology centers around video games with very realistic and gory blood and body parts being blown up, a proliferation of Youtube videos of people doing stupid things, and ever more porn sites. Many millennials seem to believe that before computers and cell phones were invented we all lived in caves and wrote on stone tablets. I would point out that before laptops and smart phones were even invented we managed to build the Empire State building, the Brooklyn Bridge, the Hoover Dam, the Pyramids of Egypt, and put a man on the moon. There is an aqueduct in the city of Jerusalem that carries water from the Jordan River. It was built 3,000 years ago. And it still works. Will your iPhone still work 3,000 years from now?

Most people labor under the false impression that if something is new and high-tech, then it must of course be better. This point of view is completely misguided. I say *if it ain't broke don't fix it!* Case in point: In the first two hundred and forty years of police work in America, if you got arrested by the cops they would take you down to the station for mugshots and fingerprints. *Awwright, hold the little signboard under your chin, face the camera, now the side view shot; now let's roll your fingerprints on the card...* In my police department we have a Chief of Police who is a very good guy, but he is one of those technology geeks and he is forever getting excited about some new piece of gear or some new computer program he saw at a Chief's convention and is now inflicting it on us. We have replaced our old-fashioned fingerprint cards and ink pads with an expensive shiny new glass and steel contraption that *electronically* takes a person's fingerprints. It records a suspect's fingerprints by placing the fingers on a glass platen and scanning the ridges, loops, and whorls of a print. Sounds great, right? Very high tech? Except that the thing is ridiculously complicated, more finicky than a rich lady's Persian cat, and works about one in three times. And that's with people who are *cooperative.* Now imagine trying it with a drunk. It comes with a *134 page* Instruction Manual. One hundred and thirty four pages on how to take fingerprints. That's progress. You know how many pages the old ink and card system had? Zero. It was so simple you didn't need a manual.

We replaced our report writing program, too. The old way was you sat down at the computer, opened a Word document, and started typing; *On such and such a day I observed Dirtbag steal a woman's purse and attempt to abscond with it down an alleyway, whereupon the police K-9 was released and bit the aforementioned Dirtbag in the buttocks region.* We replaced this nice, simple, easy to use program with a brand new one that featured drop-down menus, cool graphics, the ability to import arrest records and link citations, and brew you an espresso while you waited. The Instruction Manual for that one was over *800 pages.* Eight hundred pages on how to write a report. After a year of having it in service, still nobody knows how to use it.

One thing that cops do a lot of is write tickets. I've given out thousands of them over two decades on the Job. *License, registration, and insurance, please...*Well now we have a high-tech new way of writing tickets, too. Gone are the days of whipping out a ticket book and scratching out a citation for speeding, shoplifting, urinating in public, soliciting a prostitute, etc. Now we have this gizmo that looks like a large calculator on steroids, where we have this 2 inch screen with a picture of a keyboard, and you use a stylus to punch the keys to enter the information. Only you can't because the keys are about the size of a BB and you can't read the letters and numbers without a magnifying glass. And that's in the daytime. Try it at night, when your eyes are fifty years old. Then when you're done you have to Send it to a portable printer, which has a shoulder strap and you carry it around like a man-purse. Yeah, that's easier than a piece of paper with check boxes. The first year we had it, the number of tickets written by officers fell through the floor. Give me a gun, a nightstick, and a ticket book, and that's all I need to do police work.

The Job

Cops everywhere call our profession by the simple term "the Job." You can go anywhere in the country, and if you see someone that you think might be a cop you can just say "Hey pal, you on the Job?" and if he is he will welcome you like a long-lost brother. That little phrase sums up all the good, the bad, the ugly, the humorous, and all the bizarre facets of cop life.

We had a bomb threat that got called into an office building by a disgruntled former employee, so we evacuated the place and started going through it floor by floor. I was walking through a suite of offices when I noticed a brand new officer had his baton in his hand. I thought that was a little curious, so I stopped to watch what he was doing. My curiosity turned to alarm as I saw him poking and prodding backpacks and purses with it. I asked him "What are you doing?!" He looked at me like I was an idiot and said "I'm checking for the bomb, of course!" *Of course, because we all know that bombs have a blast radius of only two feet.*

Cops have always had a friendly rivalry with firefighters, and we always razz each other on calls. They get to be the heroes when they pull a cat out of a tree or put a Band-Aid on a skinned knee, and we get compared to Nazis. I can't give them too much grief though, because in the military I was sent to Shipboard Firefighting School and Aircraft Firefighting School, and I was part of an aircraft crash rescue squad. One summer day I got a call of a kid stuck in a piece of playground equipment at a park. I arrived at the park and found a cute little six year old girl who God only knows how had gotten herself wedged between the plastic ship's steering wheel and the side wall of the playset. The kid was crying, the mom was panicking, and there was a crowd of women gathered around, and they were all looking at *me* to fix it.

I tried different ways to twist and turn the little girl to get her out, but every way I turned her she said it hurt. Then I hear the dreaded sound – the fire truck was coming. Then one of the women in the crowd said "Oh, the firemen are coming! *They* will get her out!" and the other women all expectantly turned to look. Oh *Hell* No! No way I'm going to step aside and let the firemen walk in and be the big heroes for all these women. While the women were distracted and looking the other way I turned to the kid and whispered "Suck in your tummy and we go on three!" She sucked her tummy in, I grabbed her under the arms, and we went on three. Straight up and out she came!

Mom and the other women all clapped and cheered, and the little girl was beaming. Now the firemen were out of their truck and walking up, and it was with more than a little pleasure that I said it was all over, nothing to see here. Not to be outdone by a cop, the firemen started handing out little stickers to the kids. I one-upped them by pulling out a little plastic badge that I carry and handed it to the little girl, who broke into a big smile. The other kids threw down their fire department stickers and said "Hey, we want police badges too!" *Sweet victory!*

* * *

Police work is a highly stressful job. Aside from the possibility of death and serious bodily injury every time you suit up and go to work, and the fact that half the public hates you and thinks you get up each morning thinking about whose civil rights you can violate today, we have to put up with the constant doses of crap from the administration. Every cop will tell you that the "admin stress" is far worse than the "street stress", meaning that we would rather get into a foot chase followed by a knock-down drag out fight than have to get called into the sergeant's office and get written up again because some irate citizen called and complained to the commander that you didn't use your turn signal while driving through a grocery store parking lot. That's not a joke, by the way. That letter is still in my file. When I pointed out that a driver is not legally required to use a turn signal in a parking lot I got reprimanded again, for being a smart-ass.

Nearly all police command officers have two lists for their cops: The Golden Boy List and the Shit List. Every cop in America who is reading these words knows *exactly* what I am talking about. The Golden Boys are the ones who kowtow and flatter their bosses, and suck up and do special projects to get noticed, and the Shit Listers are the ones who simply do not have it in them to kiss anyone's rear end. Do I even have to tell you what list I and my buddies are always on?

If you are a Golden Child, you can do no wrong. If you are on that *other* list, you can do no right. Allow me to illustrate; one of our Golden Boys went to a call, an odor investigation at a house. The sewer had backed up and was overflowing into the front yard, and a trail of the effluent was creeping towards the street and a storm drain. The cop threw some dirt on the little trickle to keep it from going into the storm drain. The next day he had a glowing letter of commendation written up and presented to the whole Department, with the Commander praising him for his "quick thinking" and "decisive action." You would have thought he ran into a burning building and carried out some orphans on his back, all while engaging ISIS terrorists in a firefight. All of us just rolled our eyes, and I gave a nudge to Matt Hopkins.

Hopkins and I had not long before saved a guy's life on the light rail train. He was a young man, just twenty five, with a heart condition he was completely unaware of. His girlfriend was standing on the train talking to him and he just collapsed of a sudden cardiac arrest. When Matt and I got there we took one look at him lying motionless and ashen-faced on the floor and I thought *Oh he's a goner. He's done checked out and went to meet his Maker.* I got down and checked his vitals. Not breathing, no pulse. We went to work on him, doing CPR for about ten minutes, cycles of breaths and compressions, hooked him up to the AED, and you know what? We brought him back. The ER doctor said he would never have made it but for us doing CPR for so long. That young man is alive today because of what we did. As a matter of fact, I think every cop out there who has been around for a while can count at least a few people who are alive today because of them.

Our team sergeant put is in for a lifesaving medal. It disappeared immediately into administrative oblivion. For months we didn't even get a *Hey nice job guys* from the brass. One guy throws some dirt on some poop and he's a hero. We bring a guy back from the dead and we are still on the Shit List. Just another day on the Job.

The Sarge would not let it die, though, and when the Mayor heard about it they were forced by political pressure to give me and Hoppy our due, but it took almost a year. They wouldn't even pin the Lifesaving medal on my uniform, just handed it to me in a box. The medal is nice, but what really mattered to me was seeing that kid that was lifeless and dead on the dirty floor of the train, smiling and talking to me from his bed in the Emergency Room.

* * *

One day I went to the gym before going to work, and I wore white socks. When I got to the PD and suited up in my uniform I still had my white socks on. The Policy Manual says you gotta wear black socks. I was sitting in the squad room and the commander was walking by and saw a glint of my white sock under my trouser leg. That simple thing became "The White Sock Scandal" and reverberated around the halls of power upstairs for months. The brass had meetings to discuss what should be done. Memos flew back and forth between the Chief, the Commander and my sergeant. The Commander thought my white socks were a deliberate "F*** You!" directed at him and his authority. Ever notice how some people in power think everyone is plotting against them? It became a standing joke around the entire Department that when someone would screw up and get in trouble everyone would pat him on the back and say *Hey, at least you weren't wearing white socks.* In the end I got written up again and the White Sock Incident was mentioned in my monthly evaluations for the next four months. And again on my Annual Eval.

A Gruesome Tail of Murder

The White Sock Scandal was soon to be overshadowed, however, by an even more nefarious incident, one that ended in *murder.* An old prosecutor once told me that in the courtroom you can never just say "murder" – you have to drag it out a little bit, and give it a melodrama voice. Now which sounds more interesting? "John murdered Jane", or "John *muurrderred* Jane!"

The murder that occurred became known throughout the Department by the very descriptive name of "The Dead Cat Incident." Naturally it was my call, because I am cursed, and "The Incident" would reverberate around the halls of power, split the Department in two, and haunt my evals for months. WARNING: the following account contains graphic descriptions of death, dismemberment, and shocking cruelty. If you are squeamish, if you love cats, if you are a quiche-eating, man-bun and skinny jeans wearing millennial who faints at the sight of blood, I advise you to stop reading right now. You've been warned!

The murder began on a day like any other, on an unassuming typical suburban street in a typical white picket fence neighborhood. A man was out taking his dog for a stroll when he came upon the grisly scene. In the front yard of a house, on the bright green grass of the lawn laid out like a demented artist's macabre canvas for a hellish ritual, lay a dead cat. Not just any cat, a domestic shorthair tabby, that had been torn limb from limb. The front half of the unfortunate cat lay facing the street, while the back half was several feet further into the yard. The innards of the tabby protruded from the anterior thoracic cavity, spread out onto the yard for several feet. Telltale blood spots spattered and stained the grass in mute testimony that cried out for vengeance, for justice.

The man was alarmed at the scene spread out before him, and immediately called 9-1-1 for officers to come investigate and bring the perpetrator to account. It was not in my +d/ istrict, but I got the call anyway, because I seem doomed to be assigned to every call that is bizarre, convoluted, and destined for controversy. I arrived on scene and stood in the front yard, taking in the carnage. I also took in the red fox that was skulking in the undergrowth nearby, watching me from the cover and concealment of a privet bush. With a weathered eye and the perceptive skill that comes with twenty years of investigating crimes I surveyed the scene and rendered my verdict: *Dead cat.*

I knocked on the door of the house, not wanting the kids to come running home from school and find Fluffy in such a state of shocking disrepair, but there was no answer. I debated bundling up the cat into a trash bag and tossing him in a dumpster, but I considered the following factors; the little red fox earned this kill fair and square and was entitled to her meal. It is the way of nature that one creature dies so another can eat, and what if she had hungry kits waiting in a nearby den for Mom to provide for them? Also, if I took this kill from her she would just go down the street and kill another cat somewhere else. Second, the cat was on private property and I had no legal right to take the carcass. Third, in the upscale area where I was now working it was entirely possible that I and the Department would get sued if I took the cat and ignominiously gave it the last rites by simply tossing it out with the garbage when the owner intended to erect a statue and a stone monument to Fluffy and bury him in a place of honor. So, after pondering the variables, ramifications, and eventualities I left the cat as it was. And thus my nightmare began. *O what tribulations arise from such simple decisions of expediency!* This seemingly minor incident blew up overnight into a scandal of epic proportions; the Trump-Russia Collusion Special Investigation was as nothing compared to it, and this is how it happened…

The owner of the house came home an hour later. He was, as it turns out, an odd fellow in an odd circumstance. He was divorced from his wife but he still lived with her, her having the upper floors and he dwelling in the basement. Now I don't know about you, but I don't know *anyone* who would go through the pain and drama of a divorce, child custody fights, alimony acrimony, and all that unpleasantry and still want to live with their ex. After my divorce I would sooner have lived under a bridge in a cardboard refrigerator box than move back in with my ex. As it turns out the wife loved this cat deeply, and the husband quickly saw this as an opportunity to somehow win her back. If he could show his support and dedication to her in her hour of need, could be her shining knight fighting this battle for her, she might suddenly fall in love with him all over again. Or so his thinking went. So he immediately called the police department to report his precious cat had been the victim of a heinous and deliberate killing.

The police dispatcher informed him that an officer (yours truly) had already been out there and determined it was animal predation. He flew into an immediate rage and angrily denounced me and my slipshod investigation and vowed to "Get to the bottom of this!" He cleaned up the mess and staged the cat, posed it if you will, with the two halves put neatly back together and separated by a mere whisker, as it were, and took photographs showing the cat cleanly sliced in two, as if by some passing samurai who took a fancy to testing the sharpness of his sword. Then he collected the body of the cat and *froze* it and transported it to a local veterinarian. There, the unfortunate cat may have become the first house cat in history to have an actual autopsy done to determine the cause of death. Then after dropping off the cat with the vet he stormed down to the police station, staged photographs in hand, to wave them about and harangue and harass the Command Staff about what kind of half-assed investigations do they do around here, and what was the world coming to when a cat can't even walk down the street in safety anymore in this town?

The brass, never ones to follow my personal mantra of "seek first to understand", immediately believed every word of what the man said, and flew into action. Then things took a turn to the *really* bizarre. One of the girls at the local high school was talking to another girl about how this weird loner kid at school liked to torture cats, and the School Resource Officer caught wind of it. The connection was immediately made (based on no evidence whatsoever) that this weird kid *must* have killed this unfortunate cat, and was even now surely on the verge of planning the next school massacre. *And how in the world did Officer Miller miss all of this!?* the brass demanded.

Like the Special Prosecutor and the team that was assembled to investigate Donald Trump's alleged Russian collusion, so a similar team was hastily assembled to investigate this equally weighty matter. Like the team investigating Trump, getting to the truth of the matter, finding facts, was never the goal; nailing your target, finding some trace evidence of malfeasance, some "t" that wasn't crossed or some "i" that wasn't dotted, was the real mission. Donald, I feel your pain brother.

The Task Force Kitty prosecutorial team that was assembled consisted of a senior patrol officer, the Animal Control Officer, the School Resource Unit's sergeant, and a senior detective. The team set to work, visiting the scene of the crime, examining the dead cat's frozen body, interrogating the weird kid, poring over the autopsy results, interviewing the veterinarian. They even obtained X-rays of the deceased. *X-rays*. Of a dead cat. I, in the meantime, was on vacation while all this was going on, splashing around in the warm Caribbean waters, enjoying poolside margaritas, and blissfully unaware of the brewing storm back home. As soon as I came back to work I was quickly pulled aside into my sergeant's office and quietly warned that The Powers That Be had me in their sights, accusing me of doing a slipshod investigation, of not connecting the dots, of utterly failing to recognize that this death was plainly the work, not of a fox as I foolishly claimed, but rather of a homicidal lunatic, a modern Jack the Ripper stalking our quiet little town.

In the end, the first autopsy was inconclusive. You heard me right, dear Reader. I said the *first* autopsy. Like Michael Brown of Ferguson, Missouri, this cat was destined to receive far more official attention in death than it ever had in life. The cat was packaged up, refrozen, and shipped a hundred miles to the Colorado State University Veterinary Lab. While everyone was breathlessly awaiting the results of the second autopsy the special investigation pressed forward, but a split developed in the investigative team. The Animal Control Officer stated flatly that this was an animal kill and she had seen enough of them to know it when she saw it. The detective, Sarah, who was well respected by one and all in the Department, said the man who owned the cat was a fruitcake and frankly she didn't believe a word he said.

Even so, just as with the Trump special investigation that came to one dead end after another, a faction within the Department remained committed to the Jack The Ripper Theory and doggedly clung to the belief that I, like Trump, had botched the job, mucked it up, and simply had to be guilty of *something*. Then the second autopsy report came in: I was not privy to the resultant meeting, having been told that I was *persona non grata*, but I can only imagine the brass standing before the assembled team and eagerly ripping open the envelope, only to read the crushing Final Report: *Cause of Death: Natural Predation.* The deceased was clearly the victim of a coyote or fox kill, the State Lab concluded. They must have been so disappointed to see their Special Prosecution, like the Trump investigation, fizzle away to mere shadows and speculation. And me? How did I come out in the end? Thanks to the report of the veterinarian, the detective, and the Animal Control Officer, I was saved from anything other than a mild rebuke and dark glances from the brass that I had somehow once again evaded my just desserts. Sarah, I owe you a beer.

* * *

The brass set ticket quotas for us. They didn't want to use the term "quotas" because the public hates that, so they called it "data." As in "Does Officer Miller have enough data this month to offset his white socks?" A cop could solve the kidnapping of the Lindbergh baby *and* the assassination of JFK in one shift and the brass would say "Yeah that's great but did you write your two tickets today?" Well quite frankly my data was never that great because police work is not about numbers. It's about people. I get letters, phone calls, and emails all the time from people thanking me for everything from finding their lost dog to changing a flat tire on the highway to helping them get through the death of a loved one. That is the unmeasurable, unquantifiable heart of police work that the bean counters don't understand.

* * *

One Wednesday we received a BOLO at the station concerning a missing soldier. The soldier was stationed at Fort Benning, Georgia, and had not shown up for work. The BOLO (Be On The Lookout) said he was a sergeant, and his superiors considered him a model NCO. They did not think he had gone AWOL as that would be highly out of character for him and they suspected there might be some foul play at work.

Now he was from Georgia, and with all the vast United States of America before him, he ends up in my little city in Colorado. On Friday we got a call from the Army. They said the soldier had sent his wife a suicide note, and that he had a gun and was going to kill himself. The Army investigators pinged his cell phone and the signal was coming from a motel in our city. Nick, Steve, and I went to the hotel. We checked with the desk clerk, and sure enough he was registered here, in room 245. On the drive over I had taken the opportunity to call the soldier's commanding officer, who relayed to me that he was a combat veteran and a highly trained infantryman. *I've got Rambo holed up in our hotel. Great!* We went up to the hotel room and tried to make contact by calling to him through the door. No response. We called his cell phone, and we could hear it ringing in the hotel room. No answer. This was not looking good. As a precaution we evacuated the nearby motel rooms, and those people were not happy about being rousted out of bed at 6 a.m. They wanted to know what was going on, and we said we couldn't discuss it at this time, but the sight of the three of us with guns drawn, and Nick with his AR-15, was enough to convince them to evac the area in a hurry. By this time Brian had arrived, so we sent him downstairs to get a hotel key card. He came back up and I slid the key into the reader on the door, and Steve pushed the door open. The door opened but only an inch. It was latched from the inside. He was in there.

We called to him again for the next five minutes, trying to get him to talk to us. Nothing. We suspected he had probably already shot himself in there. I had previously called our Commander to brief him on the situation, and I called him back to give him a sitrep. Now began a conversation that was almost surreal. I told him that we were outside the door, he was almost certainly in there, and we had no communication with him thus far. It was my opinion that either he had already shot himself and was dead or dying in there, or he was waiting for us to make entry and shoot it out with us. A discussion of the Fourth Amendment now developed between all of us at the scene and the Commander on the phone. Nick and Steve were of the opinion that we did not have enough probable cause to make a warrantless entry, as suicide is not technically a crime. If we did force entry and ended up shooting him, we would have a lawsuit on our hands. Not to mention that if we forced entry one or more of us would also certainly be shot. Myself and the Commander were of the opinion that this had nothing to do with probable cause, that one of the exceptions to the Fourth Amendment warrant requirement was the emergency aid exception, to render medical aid if he had in fact shot himself as we believed. He was also a potential threat to the other guests, if he was mentally unstable and armed, thus creating another exigency. We couldn't just walk away and leave him there like that.

You see what cops have to deal with, because of lawsuits and ACLU lawyers? All we wanted to do was keep anyone, including the soldier, from getting hurt or killed, and instead we have to engage in a lengthy round table discussion about the fine points of the Fourth Amendment in the middle of a volatile tactical situation. In the end the Commander's opinion won out, because he's the Commander. He told us to make entry. *Boot the door.* I was uncomfortable with that idea, and so was Steve. If this trained soldier was in there, playing possum and just waiting for us to come in, we would be in a very bad position, in the "fatal funnel" of the doorway. Now Steve was a former Army soldier himself, Special Forces no less, a Green Beret, and he said he would not make entry without a ballistic shield. The Commander said no, Steve hadn't been to the training course on the ballistic shield, wasn't signed off as being qualified on it, so he couldn't use it. Steve correctly replied that it has a handle, you hold it up in front of you, and it stops bullets. *No, you're not trained. You're not on SWAT. It's a liability.* We had kind of a "SWAT mafia" at my PD, where if you were not on SWAT you were presumed to be an incompetent bumbling fool as likely to shoot yourself as the bad guy. Here was Steve, a former Special Forces weapons expert, and me, another military veteran and a firearms instructor who could outshoot pretty much anybody on SWAT, and we were being treated like we didn't know which end of the gun the bullet came out of. This discussion went back and forth for a few more minutes, and ended with Steve being denied the use of the ballistic shield, and Steve adamantly refusing to make entry without it.

I thought this whole situation was just ridiculous. Because we were not on SWAT, because we hadn't had the right boxes checked on some administrative forms, we were going to have to do the much more dangerous entry without a ballistic shield. To resolve the impasse the Commander made the call-out for the SWAT team, which was fine with me because I wanted SWAT called out from the moment we opened the door and discovered it was latched from the inside. I wanted SWAT and the Crisis Negotiator Team.   So, the page went out to the Team and we settled in to wait in the hallway. In the movies, you call out SWAT, the van comes screeching up to the building, and lots of guys in black BDU's and carrying submachine guns come bounding out and race into the building. In the real world, the page goes out, the guys who worked the night shift roll out of bed scratching themselves and yawning, the guys who are awake have to come down from the mall or fishing or whatever they're doing, and they all meet at the station and suit up, somebody goes out and starts the truck, and then about an hour later they all show up at the scene. Most hot calls are resolved by the regular patrol guys long before SWAT gets on scene, and when you see footage on the evening news of all those guys walking around a scene in black armor and armored vehicles rolling around, it's what I call "Tactical Theater" because it was all over before they got there, but it sure looks cool on the television news.

If you are a patrolman and you have a dynamic situation like a school shooter, a bank robbery that turns into a running gun battle, or a terrorist attack, the cavalry will not be riding over the hill to save you. Everybody in the public, your commanding officers, the victims and the bystanders, the news cameras, literally everyone will be looking to just one person to resolve this situation; they are all looking at *you*. No pressure, patrolman.

Nick and Steve were on the left of the door as you were facing it, and I was on the right. We had been standing there about ten minutes when suddenly we heard a rattle at the motel room door. Our guns came up and out the soldier stepped into the hallway. His hands were in the air and we ordered him to the floor. I cuffed him and searched him, and we got him up. Nick searched the room, and there on the nightstand was a loaded Glock handgun with a loaded spare magazine next to it. We sat the soldier down on the bed and asked him what was going on. He was a big boy and very muscular. I was very glad he didn't fight with us. He said he had been sitting quietly in his room just listening to us talk, and trying to decide if he wanted to commit suicide or come out with the gun and have us kill him.

He was very emotional, very upset and crying and said he just didn't care anymore, that he just wanted to die. We sat with him and talked for about twenty minutes, and he told us that he just found out his wife had been having an affair and had filed for divorce, and it was so devastating to him that he just didn't want to go on living. I felt bad for the guy. He had been described by his commanding officer as an exemplary soldier.

After we cleared the scene, I thought a lot about that soldier and what had happened to him. Trained for everything an enemy could throw at him but devastated by something he never saw coming. The only thing I could figure was that most people have certain anchors, some thing or someone that serves as the rock they build their life on. When that is taken away, it can be such a shock that a person does not know how to handle it. Now this is just one man's opinion, but I believe that it can be a big mistake to make that anchor another person. People are just too fickle, too unreliable. Particularly a love interest. We all know that those come and go like the seasons. If you have people that are your anchor, make it your blood family, your parents, your siblings, your kids. Or your anchor can be the principles by which you live your life; duty, honor, country. Or your anchor can be your God. For me, my wife walked out on me after we had been together for over twenty years. It was shocking and difficult, but it didn't rattle me to the point that I considered suicide. I spent a lot of time after my divorce sitting in my little apartment alone, reflecting on how the hell I got to where I was. In those moments of reflection I realized that my ex-wife had never been my anchor. I suppose my father had been one of my anchors, along with my faith, and my own internal core values. I had already been through enough adversity in my life that I looked at this as just one more kick in the teeth that Fate was giving me. But Fate was never going to beat me. This soldier was a perfect example of how that kind of dependence can go so wrong. *Godspeed, soldier…*

Special Operations… *Very* Special…

Police departments love special teams, even more than the military does. They create SWAT teams and dress them up in black uniforms and armor, they assemble Crisis Negotiation Teams and give them tan slacks and green polo shirts that say CNT on the back in big letters. The Motor Unit officers (of which I was a part – *vroom!)* swagger around looking cool in our leather jackets, aviator sunglasses, and Barbie boots. The Bicycle Unit guys think they look cool in their shorts and bike helmets – but they don't. Then you have the hardest working special unit, the

K-9 officers with black utilities that are eternally covered in dog fur, and in which the dogs are the stars not the officers. We also had my beloved Firearms Training Unit, with our red polo shirts, black BDU trousers, steely-eyed gaze and deadly gun skills that would have made Clint Eastwood's various characters of Dirty Harry Callahan, Josey Wales, and The Man With No Name proud.

My department was no exception. The command staff created all of the above units, but that wasn't enough. They also created a haphazard unit with a vague mission to suppress crime around the city. They needed a name for the new unit and were asking for suggestions, so I suggested calling it the Summer High Impact Team. The brass loved it and the name was formally adopted, until they realized with anger what the acronym for the team would be, formed by the first letter of each word. I thought it was hilarious – them, not so much.

In my younger days I was kind of a badass. At least that's how I remember it, as I stand on the precipice of fifty years old. All cops think of themselves that way, just a notch or two below Navy SEAL status. In my police department we did have a few guys who were actual badasses, combat vets who really were just a notch below Delta or SEAL Teams. We had a Green Beret, a couple of MARSOC operators, and one heroic fellow who is one of the most decorated combat Marines alive today.

Age has a way of creeping up on you, in such a subtle way that you don't even notice it until it gets driven home, usually by painful methods. It started for me with little things, like climbing up from the ground floor onto a second floor balcony. It seemed to take a lot more effort than it used to, and people who ran from me seemed to take a little longer to catch, and longer for me to recover. How come when I was in my 20's I was chasing teenagers, in my 30's I was chasing teenagers, and even at 50 I am *still* chasing teenagers?

One night we had a chilling call; a frantic woman dialed 9-1-1 and said her adult son had called her on the phone and said he was going to kill his wife and then himself. The mother told us he had many rifles in the house and was an avid shooter. There were only three of us on duty; Me, the team sergeant Tracy, and Curtis. We couldn't wait for a SWAT call-out, because the Team takes an hour to assemble and we didn't have that kind of time. We needed to do something *now*. We drove to the area and set up an ad hoc command post in a school parking lot a short distance from the target house. We pulled out our maps and looked at the layout of the property, then we got on Google Earth and looked at aerial photos of the location, and we made a plan. We all had our "war bags" in our cars, complete with black Kevlar helmets, tactical body armor with heavy ceramic rifle plates in them, Oakley goggles, lip mikes – we called it our "ninja turtle gear" and man did we look cool when we had it all on! But it's bulky and heavy as hell, so we decided to leave it in the trunk for this op, choosing stealth and mobility over maximum ballistic protection.

Before we go on with the story you need to get a picture of the scene. The house was a rural estate set on several acres, with a high brick wall on the west and on the south. On the west it faced the main street, and there was a very large, very stout double wooden gate set in the brick wall that literally looked like the entrance to a castle. The rear of the estate was to the east, abutting the back of another large estate. To the north the property was bounded by a wooded area surrounding a large irrigation canal.

The plan was that I would recon the house from the canal, and Tracy and Curtis would go to the front gate and attempt contact with the son, via an intercom set into the wall. If things went hot, we would have him in the classic L ambush. Now we didn't have the SWAT team, and there were only three of us, but I had a great deal of confidence in our little team. Tracy had been a cop for over thirty years and had been in a couple of shootings and was still alive to talk about it, and he always had his Tactical Brain engaged, and Curtis was our SWAT Sniper. He was into Crossfit and was training all the time, and if you were within a thousand meters of him he owned you. I had a great deal of confidence in myself and my own abilities, as well. Remember way back at the beginning of this book when I was in boot camp, and talked about having an "excess of self-confidence"? I still had that, perhaps a little too much, as it turned out.

It was dark, with only the light of a full moon to guide me as I started stealthing down the canal. When on an op of any kind, I was always very careful of noise and light discipline and would not be using my flashlight, relying instead on the friendly light of Mr. Moon to help me. I was walking quietly on the gravel service road that ran next to the canal, and when I got abreast of the house I stopped to take stock of the tactical situation. The house faced to the west, a large ranch style home, and across the front yard and closer to the canal was a horse stable and a big barn. I could see a couple of horses and I hoped they wouldn't whinny when they caught scent of me. I was looking particularly for dogs and geese. Geese will scream and honk and set up an awful racket when they see a coyote, or anything they perceive as a potential threat – like a cop sneaking up on them through the canal. Then the nut job in the house with all the guns would start shooting, recon by fire. There was a fence on the north side but it was a simple affair, wooden posts with wire stretched across to keep the animals in, no problem. I called Tracy on my phone and quietly told him it was all clear here, and I would be moving through the canal and take up a position on the north side of the house. Tracy acknowledged and I moved out.

The service road was a narrow gravel road about the width of one car, designed for the water department's use to service the various pumps and valves that controlled the flow of water in the canal. Luckily the canal was dry this night, or that would have added a whole new set of problems for me. The bed of the canal itself sat about eight feet below the service road, and the bank turned out to be unexpectedly steep, and I slipped and slithered half on my rear end down into the bed of the canal. Now I started to move across the bed itself, which turned out to be covered in drifts of cottonwood and poplar leaves several inches deep. Because it was a cold winter night the leaves were brittle, and crackled and broke with every step I took. Sound carries particularly well on cold still night air, and I winced inwardly at all the noise I was making, but there was no other way to do it, so I shuffled my feet through the leaves rather than stepping on them.

I reached the far bank. Now here, folks, is Tactical Lesson #1. The best laid plans of mice and men oft go astray. Aerial maps and color photos don't tell you jack about what conditions are like on the ground. And so it was tonight. The far bank of the canal was almost vertical, eight feet straight up, and completely choked with brush, bushes, thorns, and tree branches of every description. I walked along the canal looking for a space that was free of undergrowth, and I found a clear spot. I tried to climb up, but my feet simply could not get a purchase on the dirt wall, and there was such a drift of leaves on the bank that my hands kept just scooping up leaves. I would get halfway up and slide back down, grabbing for handholds to stop my descent but only coming up with handfuls of dirt and the crackling leaves.

After several efforts I gave up that approach and went back up the canal to find another way. I found a likely looking spot and started to climb back up the bank, using the branches of bushes as handholds. In uniform with my body armor and duty belt on, I tip the scales at about 230. I was grabbing handholds but the brittle branches kept snapping off in my hands. I was puffing and struggling, climbing in the dark, getting whipped in the face by branches snapping back, poked in the eye, cut by thorns, and finding my way blocked time and time again by the impenetrable jungle in front of me. Finally, after making enough noise and racket for a herd of rhinoceroses, and by sheer dogged persistence and lying flat on my belly and slithering like a snake up the bank, I cleared the undergrowth and reached the fence. Hallelujah!

From my initial vantage point standing across the canal, the fence had looked to be an easy barrier to cross. It was only six feet high, and even had a handy two by four top rail that I could use to climb over. Problem was, the fence was constructed right up to the edge of the bank of the canal. The ground was so steeply sloped here that I literally could not even stand up. I was half lying, half crouching and trying not to fall down the bank and looking up at the top of the fence, which now seemed like the Great Wall of China. I gathered myself, and made a mighty leap upwards. My feet instantly slid out from under me and I fell flat on my face in the dirt. My hands managed to grab the wire, and using that I pulled myself up. I have a pretty good bench press and I'm a strong guy, and by going hand over hand I pulled myself up the wire until I was standing.

I moved my hands to the top rail and hoisted myself up. I tried to throw my left leg up and over the top rail, intent on performing a very tacti-cool roll over the fence to minimize my outline, but my damn radio was stopping me. I carried my pack-set on my left hip, and it was preventing my left leg from going up and over. I struggled for a moment, hanging there on the top of the fence like some sumo wrestler trying to do a hurdle, and finally swung my leg over. *A ha! Now we're getting there!*

I had just swung my left leg over when *ZAP!!* I got hit with a teeth-rattling sharp jolt. Turns out there was a hot electric wire running along the inside of the fence, no doubt to keep the livestock in. Another thing Google Earth doesn't tell you. I involuntarily jerked, twitched, and fell head over heels. Luckily, I fell on the *inside* of the fence, and not back down the bank. I lay there for a moment, flat on my back, recovering my breath and my dignity, thankful that no one else could see me in the dark and thinking *just turned fifty and still trying to be a ninja - I'm too old for this shit...*

I rolled over onto my stomach and got up. I started walking toward the house, just in time to hear Tracy call out they were Code 4, situation under control. I reached the house, and Tracy and Curtis both turned to me and said "Where the hell have you been?! And why are you covered in dirt and leaves?"

The upshot of it was that after we got everything sorted out I went back to my car – and realized I did not have my phone. I had lost it somewhere out there in all the slithering, crawling, jumping, and getting electrocuted. I sighed and thought *Can't I just leave it there and get another one?* But I knew I would get written up for misuse of equipment, so with great reluctance I picked up my personal phone and went back down the canal, stopping every few feet to dial the number to my work phone. At last I saw the glow and heard the musical ♪ *deedle-dee-dee* ♪ of my phone, lying in a pile of leaves. It was, of course, at the top of the bank, on the other side of the fence, right where I had been shocked. So I got to do it all over again.

My dad did two tours in Vietnam, and after my brief excursion I gained a whole new respect for the Old Man. And for all those guys who had to fight a war in that kind of terrain.

Not four days later, I'm on midnight shift patrol when I get a burglar alarm at a house under construction. I kill the lights as I enter the neighborhood, park the car and quietly push the squad car door closed and sneak up the street to the house. It's dark as pitch, and I paused for a minute to watch and listen (you can learn a lot by pausing to listen, in a whole lot of areas of life), then started sneaking and peeking around the house. It had been raining and snowing off and on for the past few days and the ground was just a mud bog, and as I came around the side of the house, looking in the windows, I fell straight down into a pit up to my chest. One second I'm on solid ground and in the next I'm free-falling. I landed with a jolt and bounced between the walls of the narrow pit. Who the hell digs a pit and doesn't cover it? I put my hands on the edge and hoisted myself up with many a grunt and curse, but my knee hurt, my uniform was covered in mud, my gun belt, gun butt, flashlight, radio, and everything was covered in black, stinking mud. *I'm too old for this shit...*

* * *

In the movies operations go off without a hitch; the special operations team HALO jumps in, stealthily breaches the terrorist camp's security, kills all the bad guys, escapes with the hostages and gets back home in time for a cappuccino. In reality things are much more confused. Most of the time the information you get is sketchy and incomplete, you never know all the facts you need to know, such as what does the bad guy look like, how many of them are there, where they are, and the one thing that you can count on is that unexpected things are going to happen. Case in point:

One February night it was an hour before the end of my shift and I am already pointing the nose of my patrol car toward the barn to finish up some paperwork and go home, when dispatch squawks on the radio those four little words that make every cop's heart rate shoot up: *"All cars stand by."* They say this when they are about to hit the Alert Tone for a hot call in progress. She hits the wailing Alert Tone and says we have a Homicidal/Suicidal Subject on Emporia Way. Across the city we all spin the cars around and start heading that way, while dispatch gives us updates en route.

Dispatch says a male caller is on the line saying he is watching his father while he is sleeping, and when his father wakes up he is going to kill him and then kill himself. *Whatever you do Dad, don't wake up...* The caller continued by saying he is an Iraq War combat veteran and under a lot of stress, and he has an AR-15 rifle. *Great…this call is getting better by the minute.* You see, that's the thing about being a cop. One minute you can be getting a cup of coffee from 7-11 and the next minute you are en route to the call that can end your life.

We all met up in the parking lot of a nearby church for a quick powwow and a battle plan. Now here is where my hat is off to my team sergeant, Tracy Thompson. Tracy is a very experienced cop with over thirty years on the Job and he's been in a couple of shootings and is still around to talk about it. But he sought the opinion of one of the youngest and newest officers, Austin Speer. Speer was a combat vet with the 101st Airborne, and had proven himself to be a cool head and a capable operator. Tracy could have just said *"I'm in charge here and this is what I say!"* but he didn't. Not many leaders can do that, because their egos get in the way.

We quickly formed up a plan and broke huddle to go to our positions. My part was to go to the next street to the south and take up a position overlooking the back of the target house. I drove to the area and parked a block away and stealthed my way into position. Now here is where things started to get murky right away. The target house was a white duplex, on a street lined with identical white duplexes. It is one thing to look at a map and say *that's the house* and quite another to stand on the dark street looking at the back of a row of houses with no numbers and say *Was it* this *house? Or is it* that *house?* I picked the one I thought it was and began to sneak through the sprawling back yard of a big brick mansion to get into position.

I moved up on the west side of the house and through the back yard, trying to get a look at the rear of the target house through a belt of trees. I'm standing there in the darkness, feeling pretty sneaky, when all of a sudden the homeowner flips a light on in the house, which paints a beautiful rectangle of light in the back yard, with me standing smack in the middle of it. *Really?! You're going to do that right now?!* I jumped out of the light and circled back around the front of the house and moved to the east side.

I stopped at the corner of the garage and paused to listen for a moment. Dead silence. As we were moving into position dispatch was giving us updates. She said that they were on the line with the soldier, and the dispatcher said she could hear what sounded like a struggle in the background and a dog barking furiously. *A struggle. Is he killing his father right now?...Do we need to go in hot and force entry? Do we wait for more information?* These are the thoughts that go through your mind, as you're standing there in the dark by yourself, and there are no easy answers. You know if you go in hot and a firefight erupts and people get killed, and it turns out what the dispatcher heard was actually just a TV show in the background, your ass is grass. You're going to get sued, probably get fired, and the talking heads on the news who have never experienced greater danger than a paper cut will go on for hours about how you royally screwed this up, and they will have their guest expert/armchair quarterback on to tell everyone what you *should* have done was wait. On the other hand, if you don't go in and he really is killing his father while you're holding a perimeter position, your ass is grass again, and the same talking heads and Monday morning quarterbacks will tell everyone why you should have immediately gone in.

I didn't care much about all of that, but what I did care about is that none of my fellow officers got hurt or killed by blindly rushing in too soon. The dispatcher had said she heard a dog barking furiously. As I listened carefully in the darkness I didn't hear a thing. It was as quiet as a cemetery. That didn't seem right. Then the dreaded thought hits you; *are we at the wrong house?* Now the dispatcher was talking to the soldier's mom, who was at a house several miles away. It began to sound like the soldier was actually there with the mom, and not here at all. *That makes more sense.* We all began to mentally relax a little.

Then the Sergeant gets on and tells dispatch he doesn't think so, and to ping both phones. A moment later dispatch comes back on and says Mom is at the house several miles away, but the soldier is *here*, in our target house. *Pucker factor goes back up.*

I am standing at the corner of the garage, hidden in total darkness, peeking around the corner at the target house just a scant few yards to the northwest of me, but I cannot see very well because there is a stand of pine trees in the way. Several feet away there are two parked cars, and I could get a better vantage point if I moved to the nearest one and around the passenger side, up to the front. Problem was, I would have to cross several feet of open ground, partially lit up by a streetlight. *I can cross it in two seconds!* half of my brain said. *He can put a dozen rounds in you in two seconds* replied the other half. I had a quick debate with myself, and in the end I moved quietly back down the side of the house and swung a wide circle and snuck in by the second car. Never did I make a better decision!

I eased up alongside the second car and then moved around the trunk in a low crouch/crawl. I have seen what rifle rounds can do to human bodies and it's not pretty. I had my Go-Bag in the patrol car with my helmet and my heavy rifle plate carrier inside, and some of the guys had already put theirs on, but I opted out of it. The gear is heavy, bulky, it's hot, it restricts your hearing and vision, it's noisy with the nylon and Velcro, and the chances of me taking the round in my twelve inch rifle plate rather than anywhere else on my tender body was slim. It looks very tacti-cool, and if I was charging through a front door I would absolutely have it on, but for playing ninja in the dark the best place for it is in the trunk of my squad car.

Dispatch was still on the line with the guy and had been giving us updates, but the line had now gone quiet for several minutes. I was flat on the concrete now, and low-crawled and eased up around the passenger side of the car, and peeked my head around the front tire to get a better look at the back of the house. *And there he was.* He was standing in the darkness of the yard on the east side of the house, quietly smoking a cigarette not five yards from the driver's side of the car, and I was crouching on the passenger side of the same car. *Pucker factor goes up another notch.* I could hardly make him out in the darkness, but I could see the glow of his cigarette, and I could hear him softly exhaling. If I had sprinted from the corner of the garage to the trunk of the car a few minutes ago, he would have had me cold.

Now I was in a pickle. Everyone thought he was still contained in the house, and I needed to let them know ASAP that he was outside and mobile. But my portable radio makes a quick three-chirp little electronic noise every time I keyed the mike to talk, and the little *beep-beep-beep* would sound like gongs in the still darkness, and could have brought on a hail of 5.56mm fire. *You better do something Mikey, before he just strolls away down the street.* I suddenly had an idea. I couldn't transmit on the radio but I could call. I could call dispatch on the phone and whisper the information to them and they could air it to all the other units. *Sometimes I even amaze myself!* I thought as I eased my phone out, punched in the number and hit the Send button. And waited. And waited. The phone kept ringing and I silently sent my brain waves over space and time to dispatch – *pick up the phone...pick up the damn phone...*I guess my brain wasn't on the right frequency, or more likely didn't have the wattage to reach dispatch, because they never answered.

I thought briefly about trying to take him down myself; pop around the car, light him up with my flashlight and gun drawn and order him to the ground. I quickly discarded the idea, because if he was suicidal anyway he might just decide to go out in a blaze of glory and gunfire, and with him being a combat vet and better armed he just might win that fight. Aside from that Crystal, our Hostage Negotiator, was on the scene and trying to establish contact with him and I needed to give her time to do her work. If we could get everybody out alive - especially me - that would be the best of all possible outcomes.

Since dispatch wasn't answering, I had to transmit on the radio. I had no choice, because I had to let everyone else know that he was not where everyone thought he was. He had somehow sneaked out without anybody seeing him and was roaming free. I covered the microphone with both of my gloved hands (it was February, after all) and quietly muffled the sound of the chirps, then I whispered into the mike *222 the suspect is not in the house! He is* outside *on the east side of the house, and I have a visual on him. Repeat, he is* not *in the house!!* No sooner had I finished transmitting than some jackass, who will remain nameless, starts shouting into the radio WHAT WAS THAT 22??!! DID YOU SAY HE IS ON THE EAST SIDE OF THE HOUSE??!! YOU CAN SEE HIM?! Un. Fricking. Believable. Did he think I was whispering just for dramatic effect?

Luckily, I had anticipated that exact reaction from said jackass, and after transmitting I had immediately covered the mike with both hands. The suspect did not hear any part of it, and just then his cell phone rang. It was Crystal. I laid there in the dark next to the car tire and listened while she did her thing and talked to him, with my pistol trained on him and ready to ventilate him if tried anything sneaky. Austin got on the phone with him, and veteran to veteran they talked for a while about the war and how hard it was to come back to normal life. He said he never intended to kill his father, he was just crying out for someone to help him. He surrendered peacefully to Austin and they took him in for a mental health evaluation.

Turns out he was a Green Beret, on a Special Forces A-team and had seen some heavy duty combat, had suffered a traumatic brain injury, and had been sent home only to be tossed aside and forgotten by the VA system like yesterday's news. The last thing you remember was hunting Taliban with your team in the mountains of the Hindu Kush, then you wake up and you're sitting alone in the recovery lounge at a hospital, watching TV, nobody is talking to you, and you're wondering how you got here. Now he was suffering from PTSD compounded by alcoholism. Sometimes things just aren't black and white, you know. We want things to be black and white, good guys and bad guys, right and wrong, because that makes the world easier to understand. But there's a lot of gray out there, folks. A whole lot of gray.

TWENTY SEVEN

Human Frailty

Humans are frail creatures. We have weaknesses of spirit, of body, of faith. We have desires – for material things, for power, for love, for sex, for something and somewhere better than where we are, and that frailty and weakness can lead us to some pretty dark places.

One late summer day I found myself seated outside an examination room in a hospital ER. I was there because the police department had received a frantic phone call from a man in Nebraska, and this man told us that a female friend of his was sending him desperate text messages pleading for him to come get her, before it was too late. She texted him that she was at a motel, being held against her will and forced to be a sex slave. She got the motel address from the stationery in the motel room and gave it to him, begging him to hurry before they found out she had texted him and moved her again.

As soon as we got the information we swarmed the motel, putting people in the back in case anyone tried to bail out the ground floor windows. We made contact at the door to the room, having almost no idea what was going on or who we were even looking for. At our knock on the door, an adult man and woman met us, careful not to open the door more than a few inches. They told us no, there was no one else here, just the two of them, a nice normal couple on vacation here in beautiful Colorado. *Do you mind if we check the room then?* Nervous glances back and forth. They didn't want us to check the room, but we already had the legal basis, we had exigent circumstances, so we pushed our way in and began checking the rooms.

We found a young girl, in her late teens, hidden in the bathroom, down on the floor with wide and fearful eyes, looking for all the world like a small frightened animal in a trap. We got her up and brought her out into the main room, and the man and woman at the door shot dagger glances of warning at her. We separated everyone, and suddenly the nice normal couple just vacationing in Colorado became very sullen and angry, and demanded to see their lawyers. But the girl told us everything.

I was in the hospital with her for eight hours. Eight hours while she got medical treatment, some food, examinations, and a rape kit. During the down times when the doctors and nurses were in and out of her room, she told me her story. And what a tragic and sad story it was. At first she acted hard and brash, cussing like a sailor, acting like she didn't care. But I've been around the block enough to know that this was all a front, a brave façade she had put up to protect herself from what she had been through. As she talked more about it and realized that at last she was in a safe place with safe people, the brave front came crashing down and she began to sob uncontrollably. I sat next to her with a hand on her shoulder, and let her get it all out.

Her name was Vladilena, and she had been born in Russia. She had never had a family, because her mother died when she was just a small child, and her father was sent to prison, for what reason she did not know. In Russia, these things happen. You can go to prison for saying the wrong thing to the wrong person. So she grew up in an orphanage, surrounded by other children but always feeling terribly alone. She spent her childhood years there, growing up into a teenager. She was a beautiful young girl, slender with dark hair and dark eyes, and a pleasing figure. The matronly women of the orphanage hated her for it and treated her cruelly. The men who worked there lusted after her and pawed at her and tried to force themselves on her. Her existence became even more miserable and lonely, and in her misery she began to fight back, to grow a layer of hardness.

The day came when the staff called her into the office, and she wondered what she had done and in what way she would be punished. But instead they told her to pack her things. She was going to a foster home, with an American family. Her hopes soared to the heavens. *America!!* Everyone in the orphanage dreamed of America, a magical place that almost didn't really exist, a place of plenty where people were never hungry, where people could be happy. Where she could be happy. Over the next few weeks she went around the orphanage with her feet barely touching the ground, imagining her new life in America.

She was fourteen years old when the plane touched down in the United States. She did not want to talk to me much about the family that fostered her, and I could sense this was something she did not want to delve into. She said the family had other kids, and the mom quickly grew to not like her. I don't know what happened there, but I suspect the mom saw her as some kind of competition, a younger and prettier woman in the household. Maybe the father saw her that way, too. So she left the family, ran away and struck out on her own before she reached her seventeenth birthday. She liked America, and even though it wasn't quite what she had dreamed of it was much better than Russia, and she learned to speak the language and drifted between minimum wage jobs and living with boyfriends.

She was working at a McDonald's in Nebraska, taking orders at the front counter and cleaning tables, when a woman came into the restaurant that made her sit up and take notice. The woman was about ten years older than Vladilena, and she was dressed in fashionable clothes and jewelry that made her envious, things that so far she could only dream of. The woman struck up a conversation with her, so nice to talk to, so interested in her. No one like this woman had ever paid the slightest attention to her, so she warmed to her immediately and they struck up a friendship. This pretty woman who drove a nice car and wore fancy clothes represented to Vladilena the America she had dreamed of back in Russia.

This woman, Jessica, took Vladilena under her wing like a big sister. She took her out clothes shopping, got her hair and nails done, bought her pretty jewelry. As she looked in the mirror Vladilena's breath was taken away as she saw herself. Could that girl in the mirror really be *her?*

Jessica was what human traffickers call a "recruiter." They find vulnerable young girls, girls who have no connections, no close family, no one to miss them if they disappear. Lost souls. Jessica played Vladilena like a musician plays an instrument; feigning friendship, the close relationship these girls are longing for, someone who cares about them. Maybe a combination of mother figure and big sister that they never had. They take the girls out shopping, make them feel pretty and wanted. Then they move in for the kill. Jessica told Vladilena she was an escort, dating doctors and lawyers and handsome rich men who gave her gifts and money. Lots of money. She made the life sound so glamorous, and all Vladilena had to do was come with her to California and it was all hers.

So she went with Jessica. Jessica introduced her to a male friend of hers, Frank. Frank handled the money and set up dates for them. Frank was a pimp, but Jessica called him a "manager." He seemed very nice. They were going to L.A., but they had to stop in Denver first. That was when the reality hit her like a ton of bricks.

Frank and Jessica put Vladilena up in cheap motels and pimped her out with internet ads. There were no handsome doctors and lawyers taking her out to parties and buying her gifts; just dirty smelly motel beds and being pawed and held down and raped by filthy, disgusting men with bad breath who paid $200 bucks a turn with her. There were five or six men coming to her every night, and Frank and Jessica were making $5000 a week off of her. She got a venereal disease. One man drugged her and she did not remember what he did to her. Another man put his hands around her neck and choked her until she blacked out. They would move her to a different motel every two or three nights and start it all over again. They took her phone, they watched her day and night. She didn't even know where she was.

She tried to commit suicide, by hanging herself in the bathroom with the shower curtain, but Frank burst into the room and stopped her. Then he beat her. When she finally spotted her chance, when Jessica was out and Frank went down to the front desk, she frantically searched Jessica's suitcase and found her phone and texted her friend back in Nebraska for help. *Please please come get me!!* If he couldn't, she would find a way to kill herself.

* * *

Some people live their whole lives never experiencing any human compassion, the kindness of a mom hugging them when they are little girls, or a father to tuck them in and kiss them goodnight. We who have this just take it for granted that this is normal, that everybody grows up like that. For some people, childhood is a constant state of fear, hunger, trying to hide. After Vladilena was released from the hospital I took her to a Wendy's to get something to eat. She wanted chicken nuggets. I have a teenaged daughter, and as I watched her eat, amazingly calm now after all that she had been through, I couldn't help but think about my precious little girl and what would I do if something happened to her like what had happened to this girl. I don't think I will ever look at my daughter the same way again.

The police department put Vladilena up in a decent hotel while the case against Frank and Jessica was being put together.

As I was driving her to the hotel she told me that after all the terrible things that had happened to her, the rapes, the beatings, the one thing that made her really sad was that she didn't have a mom and dad to run to.

* * *

That poor girl had no one, living in a cold and empty world. Yet some people have everything and because of simple human weakness lose it all. I had just settled into a break room chair one Sunday summer evening, to take my Code 7 and watch the Denver Broncos and the Detroit Lions duel it out on the gridiron. The radio squawked as dispatch gave me a welfare check. We get these all the time, maybe someone hasn't heard from Mom in a couple of days, or a brother or sister, and they just want us to go check on them, reassure themselves that their loved ones are okay.

This request was from a woman who was in the hospital, asking us to go check on her husband. She was eight months pregnant, and there were complications with the pregnancy that caused the doctors enough concern to keep her there in the prenatal unit. The woman said she hadn't heard from her husband since yesterday and she was worried something was wrong. I believe quite firmly in woman's intuition, and I could sense the unspoken fear behind her words.

Scott and I drove to the house and saw nothing amiss from a cursory check of the outside. We rang the doorbell, knocked on the door. No response. There was a big picture window on the front of the house and a patio on the west side. The blinds were drawn on the front window and we could see nothing, so we hopped the knee-high brick wall enclosing the patio and looked through the sliding glass door. The vertical blinds were only partly closed here, and we could just make out what looked like a person lying face down on the floor. We knocked on the patio door. No response, no stirring of movement from the person on the floor.

A police officer can enter a home without a warrant in certain circumstances without running afoul of the Fourth Amendment, and to render emergency aid is one of them. We slid open the patio door and entered the house, and we went to the man on the floor. He was dead, and had been for several hours. We checked the rest of the house for other people and found another man sprawled on his back in another room. We checked him too, wondering just what the hell we had stumbled into. Murder-suicide? Double murder?

The man in the other room was alive, but just barely. We called an ambulance for him, and we were able to get him revived enough to talk to us. While we were waiting for the ambulance we gathered the story. This man did not know the guy in the other room. They had met downtown earlier that day. People in the drug culture can spot another user from a mile away, and these two immediately got together and decided to go back to this house and shoot up some heroin.

The guy on the living room floor had died of a heroin overdose. I don't know if he injected too much, if he got some bad stuff laced with fentanyl, accident or homicide, but either way it did him in. This was the husband of the woman who called us. We checked the pockets of the other guy and found drugs, money, and the birth certificates and driver's licenses of the family who lived here. The man who died had invited this guy to come back to his house, and he thanked him by stealing from him.

This house was now considered a potential crime scene, and we started stringing up the yellow police barrier tape. As I was looking around the house I saw a small kid-sized chair with Mickey Mouse on it, a red wagon, a teddy bear and toys scattered around the room. This guy had two young kids. *What were you thinking*...Now I had to go to the hospital and tell this woman her husband was dead. I arrived at Presbyterian St. Luke's and made my way up to Labor & Delivery, dreading each step of the way.

I found her room and paused outside the door for a minute. I hated this part of my job. I hated being the one to tell people that someone they loved – a mom, a dad, a spouse, a child – would not be coming home ever again. This one was going to be bad one, because on the other side of this door was a woman who already had two kids and was pregnant with another, and worried because there were complications with the pregnancy. I turned the handle and went in.

The woman lying on the bed was in her mid-thirties, blonde hair pulled back in a ponytail, with a very large belly with some kind of leads attached to her, wires running back to a monitor next to the bed. As soon as she saw me come in she sat up in bed, with an expectant eager look on her face. *"Did you find him? Is he okay?"* There is no good way to tell someone these things, so I have learned to be compassionate yet direct. If you say things like "I'm sorry but he's gone" people don't get what you mean. They refuse to accept it and say things like "Gone where?" So I told her that I was sorry to have to tell her that her husband was dead. She screamed and cried out, and I let her get it out. It's human nature to want to reassure people, to comfort people and tell them that things will be okay. But sometimes things are just not going to be okay. She kept saying *Not my Mikey! Please not my Mikey!*

She asked if I was sure that it was him, sure that he was dead. People want to hope that maybe we made a mistake, maybe we got the wrong person, maybe he's just hurt. I told her the facts of what we had found, that there was no doubt, and was there someone I could call for her? I called her father, and I sat with her while we waited for him to arrive. There was little that I could do for her, except pull up a chair next to her bed and be there with her until her family arrived, and listen to her and answer her questions. In the midst of her grief I think the enormity of raising three children by herself began to set in. She kept softly repeating *How could he do this to us? How could he do this to us?*

Afterward, as I was walking down the halls of the hospital back to my car I was thinking about what a selfish sonofabitch this guy was. When you have a family to take care of, a wife who was pregnant, two other kids who need their Dad, you don't screw around with drugs. After twenty years of doing this job I don't want to say that I have lost my faith in mankind, but I have come to not expect much from people. So much of human nature is selfish and petty and weak, and it takes some inner strength to rise above that, to be a better person, a better wife or a better husband, a better parent. It seems there are so many who just don't have it in them to do that.

* * *

One of the bitter ironies of modern society is that while we have more ways to communicate than ever, we seem to do less of it on any meaningful level. When I was growing up if you wanted to communicate with someone you called their home phone, you wrote them a letter, or you went to their house to see them. Three ways. That was it. Nowadays we have all that *plus* cell phones, texting, tweeting, Facebooking, Instagramming, Tweeting, chat rooms, and I don't even know what else. Add to it that our population has grown by millions, and who can explain why we have more people than ever who feel isolated and lonely even in the middle of a crowded room?

I went to the station to take an ordinary-sounding call, a man complaining of having seen someone suspicious near his house a couple of evenings ago. We get those all the time, someone sees a shadow, hears a cat rattling around in the trash cans outside, gets a little spooked, and calls the police. I went into the lobby and found awaiting me perhaps the most innocuous-looking man I have ever encountered. He was of indeterminate age, somewhere between forty and fifty five, brown hair, average height, a little flabby, a man you could look directly at and as soon as you turn away forget what he looked like. He would have been a perfect spy.

He started off by explaining that when he came home from work a couple of evenings ago he saw someone on the walking path that looked suspicious to him. No, he wasn't *doing* anything suspicious, he just *looked* suspicious. In my mind I was already formulating my plan to reassure him that it was probably nothing and that we would do some extra patrols in his neighborhood, but then the man continued by saying he did not like where the bus stop was on his street, and could we get the school to move it please? I told him that was something he could bring up at a school board meeting. Then he turned to the stoplight at Quebec and Belleview and could a couple of police officers be stationed there? After that the conversation turned to the homeless people panhandling, the dangers of carjacking in Rio De Janiero, assault rifles, the epidemic of crime in South Africa, and I forget what else. All the while this fellow was very polite and well spoken, but clearly the elevator was not going to the top. Like the old saying says, *lights are on, nobody's home.* A lot of police officers would have just ended the conversation at this point, but I just let him go on until he had said all he wanted to say, and he thanked me and left happy. I figured this guy was one of those people who live in the undercurrent of our society, living alone, dutifully going to work each morning, coming home to an empty house each evening, except maybe a cat or two, eating dinner for one night after night, one of the lonely people who just desperately want someone to listen to them. There are a lot more of them than you think.

Among the daily doses of crap and human misery that cops have to deal with, one of the bright spots for me is talking to kids. I mean the little guys and girls about six or seven years old. They are so bright-eyed and hopeful and innocent of all the evil in the world. I have seen kids in Third World squalor with not enough to eat or clothes on their backs, and they are laughing and running and playing in the dirt alleys next to the shacks they live in. We had a lockdown of area schools when we had an active shooter threat. Some twisted kid who idolized the Columbine killers called in and said he was going to randomly shoot up a school today. I went to a nearby elementary school to stand guard and I was looking forward to the opportunity to give the SOB the lead suppository he deserved if he showed up.

While I was standing by the front doors I saw a girl, cute as a button in her little dress and pigtails, and I struck up a conversation with her. She said she was six years old and was waiting for her mom to come get her, and we talked about her pesky little brother and her dog and her cat, and her teachers, and what she wanted for Christmas. We talked about all these things while I was there to stop someone from shooting up her school. The world will never be as good and as innocent as it is through their eyes.

In the hustle and bustle of modern society it is easy to feel like you're twisting in the wind, getting blown about by forces beyond your control. Here you are, a good person just trying to make ends meet now and build a future for yourself down the road, and life keeps throwing roadblocks in your way so that you feel like it's one step forward and two steps back. I know how you feel, and sometimes it really is not your fault.

I met such a fellow one night on patrol. I got called to one of our local motels on a report of a suicidal male. I went to his room and did not find him. I walked around the lobby, the restaurant, the pool – no dice. I walked around the motel grounds and found him at last, sitting on the grass and staring out to the west at our magnificent Rockies. I have noticed that in times of trouble and soul-searching people find comfort and solace in the majesty of nature, in the soaring mountains or the restless sea. I think it is a reminder of how small we are in the universe, and our search for our place in it.

I could see at a glance he had been crying and had a heavy heart and a troubled soul, so after giving him a quick visual inspection for weapons I sat down in the grass next to him and told him to tell me all about it. He said he was an engineer, for a big energy company. He was not from here, he lived in California with his wife and kids, but his company had sent him out here to manage a project that had bogged down. It was supposed to be a short-term deal – fly in for a few weeks, get things turned around, and fly home. But one thing after another kept him out here, and the company wouldn't let him go home.

He had now been out here for two years. Two long years with hardly ever seeing his wife. Two long years of his childrens' lives that he was missing and would never get back. He had begged his company to let him go home, at least for a while. The reply was always *Sure, just as soon as we get things up and running here you can go back home.* Today he had been served divorce papers.

He turned to me with tears in his eyes and said he just didn't know what to do. If he stays here, his wife will divorce him. If he leaves, his company will fire him and his career is over. *What do I do, Officer?* he pleaded. He was lost in the wilderness and needed help, needed a guide to show him the way out. So I showed him. I told him this: Go home to your family. Go upstairs and pack your suitcase and head for DIA. Tonight. Right now. On your way to the airport call your boss and tell him to kiss your ass. When you get home, take your wife out on a romantic getaway, just the two of you. Hug your kids, go to their school events, and get back to being their Dad.

There is an old saying that when you're up to your ass in alligators it can be hard to remember that you went there to drain the swamp. Meaning that in the pressures of careers and schedules and family and just getting by, it can be easy to lose sight of what you're doing it all for. In modern times so many of us get sucked in so deep into our careers and trying to make money and get promotions and not get fired, that a career path can turn into quicksand. Sometimes you just have to get out.

I helped this guy go back upstairs and pack his stuff. He seemed happy, like the weight of the world had been lifted from his shoulders. Sometimes you know what you need to do, it's just so hard to bring yourself to do it. Sometimes you need a push. Take my word for it, folks. Your family is more important than your career. Don't lose sight of that.

You know it's funny to me, that with all the technological advances we have made in the span of my lifetime, for all the time and effort we spend in college and career to get ahead, still the one thing we all want the most is that basic human need just to be appreciated, valued, and loved by someone else.

Sometimes I was not successful in talking people out of suicide. A wife called 9-1-1 to report that her husband was sending suicidal text messages to her. He was in his late 50's and had just been to the doctor, who broke the news to him that he had an aggressive terminal disease, and that he would deteriorate rapidly over the next few years, until he finally died when his respiratory muscles ceased to function. He texted his wife that he loved her and that he would not put her through this. I found him at a local motel. He was holding a pistol to his head, and as I was trying to talk him into putting the gun down he pulled the trigger.

* * *

There were times when I could save people, reach out a hand to them and pull them up out of the muck and misery, and those times made it all worthwhile. I have personally seen more lives destroyed by alcohol and drug addiction than from any other cause. Maybe I am just being insensitive, maybe it's because I have seen it too often, but I have a hard time feeling sorry for them, because nobody held a gun to their head and made them drink, or shoot up, or toke up. But I do feel sorry for the families, the friends, the innocent people in the public, who also pay the price for the addiction. And sometimes in spite of myself I do feel sorry for the addicts.

I was dispatched to a call at a cheap motel - unknown situation. A woman staying at the motel was talking to her son on the phone, she was crying and all he could get out of her was that she said she needed help. Then the line disconnected. With this bare bones information from dispatch I went to the motel, took the elevator up and went down the hall to the room. Whenever we get a call at a motel room we don't just walk up and knock on the door. You can learn a lot by just taking a minute to pause and listen.

I stopped and put my ear close to the door and listened. I could hear a woman crying and a phone ringing incessantly, and no other sound. I knocked on the door, and knocked again, with no response. I knew from the son that her name was Jill, so I said "Jill, this is Officer Miller, can you come to the door and talk to me?" This went on for a couple of minutes, with no sound from inside but the woman's broken sobs. We don't usually force entry into homes, because despite what the liberal media tells you we really do respect people's rights, but I didn't know if she was in there cutting her wrists or downing a bottle of pills or what, so I called another officer to get a key from the front desk so I could go in.

While I was waiting for the key I kept talking to her through the door, saying I just needed to check on her and make sure she was okay. I heard the bed creak and footsteps across the floor, then the door opened. One of the most haggard and disheveled looking people I have ever seen was standing in front of me, in pajama shorts and top, rat's nest hair that had not been brushed in days, and a face with red-rimmed eyes and tear stains old and fresh running down it. This was a woman who had plainly been going through Hell, for some time.

She went to the rumpled bed and dropped onto it, curling herself into a sort of seated fetal position with her arms around her knees, drawn up to her chest. I could see at a glance that this was a girl who was far gone down the road to ruin. Still, I could see that she had at one time been a pretty woman, with a slender figure and a nice, friendly-looking face.

The room reeked of stale whiskey, with empty bottles on the floor and pills from a container were spilled on the countertop. I did a quick sweep of the room for other occupants and weapons, then I sat down on the bed next to her. Cops are accustomed to being in charge, and when they talk to people they usually take a commanding stance and voice, what we call "officer presence." There is a time and place for it, but that time and place was not now. When you want someone who is in distress to open up to you, you have to get down on their level, like with kids. When people are in distress they revert back to those basic emotional needs of childhood; love, understanding, acceptance, and an offer of help.

Jill told me that she had been battling alcoholism for years, while trying to carry on a normal life. She had two grown kids, a son and a daughter. She had been a registered nurse, working in the ER, but she lost her job because of her drinking. She had been in and out of rehab a few times, but she just couldn't kick it. And now here she was, on her last legs. She had been sitting in this room for three days, popping painkillers and drinking herself to death.

As I was listening to her I couldn't help but have my heart go out to her. I think that call to her son was her last cry for help, and that if he had not picked up the phone I would have in a couple of days been responding to this room on a DOA subject;

white female, forty years old, cause of death: alcohol poisoning. Tag her and bag her.

I was determined to get this girl the help that she needed, to give her one last shot at saving her life. I got her up and into her shoes, and walked her out to my patrol car to take her to a nearby hospital that we all felt had the best alcohol and drug rehab program. As I was helping her get her shoes on and gather her things, she grabbed on to my arm with both of her hands and would not let go. As we went down the hall I had to help her walk straight, and she was holding on tight to my arm like a rope to a drowning person. Even as we were walking into the ER at the hospital she would not let go. I think for her, she felt that hanging on tight to me was like hanging on to her last hope on Earth.

TWENTY EIGHT

Class Warfare

The city where I work is mostly upscale residential, a patchwork of million dollar homes interspersed with higher-end retail shopping centers. Even so, we have occasional homeless people drift in, and we always know when a new one arrives because we get a deluge of phone calls from scared citizens and irate business owners who want them "moved along" immediately.

We had one old homeless man who had been living in the city for so many years he had become a fixture around the place. His home, such as it was, was the shade of a particular large pine tree with spreading boughs to provide a roof. His name was Robert, and he could regularly be found in the southern quarter of our city. Interestingly, everyone always called him Robert. Never Rob, or Bob, and cops are famous for giving nicknames to everyone; each other, suspects, hookers, the brass, the citizens who call us repeatedly, but we always called him Robert. Somehow it just seemed fitting.

He would approach people and ask them for food or money, and they would take one look at him and get scared and call the police. He had a shaggy Grizzly Adams beard, wild hair, and perpetually wore a set of headphones. He could always be seen walking around boppin' his head to the music. Trouble was, the headphones weren't connected to anything, the cord was always just dangling. Robert was just jammin' to the music in his head.

One of our officers, Alden Langert, took it upon himself to get all the paperwork together, talk to the government people, and get everything filled out and processed to get Robert onto Social Security disability payments. I admire Alden for that, because he didn't have to do it. For the first time in years, Robert had his own money and then he stopped scaring people. Alden even got him set up with an apartment but Robert never went there. He liked his pine tree. When Robert died, several of the officers went to his funeral.

We had a new homeless guy move in. I got a call one afternoon of a homeless man in one of the retail shopping centers. It seems the huffy manager of a ritzy day spa was calling because her customers did not like this man hanging around and wanted him moved along. I went up there and picked him out of the crowd instantly; long hair, beard, rags for clothes, and filthy. I mean dirty, grungy, smelly, filthy. His face and hands were black with dirt. He hadn't seen the inside of a shower stall in years. However, he was surprisingly articulate, soft-spoken, not a drug addict, and gentle in speech and manner. Over the next few days we kept getting calls on him, in different areas of the city, and each time the description was the same. I started calling him "dirty Jesus", and the name stuck.

The merchants in the retail shops did not like it when I refused to order him to move along, and they did not like it at all when I told them that dirty Jesus had just as much right to be in the public shopping center as they did. They would get all huffy and ask *What are we paying you for?!* To which I would reply that I was there to protect the rights of *all* the citizens, not just the ones who had money. Besides, I figured it this way; if Jesus were to come back from time to time to walk among us, and to measure how much compassion and goodness we have in our hearts, He is not going to do it wearing flowing white robes and a halo around his head, nor is He going to do it looking like a Hollywood movie star – He would do it looking just like dirty Jesus.

* * *

After I had been in law enforcement for twelve years, I left the profession. It was the culmination of a lot of things coming together. My kids were getting older and I felt like they needed me around more, my marriage was on the rocks, and on top of that I was getting soul-weary at the day to day exposure to rapes, assaults, child abuse, domestics, murders, and the parade of human suffering and inhumanity that I saw every week on patrol.

So I left police work. I wanted to strike out in an entirely new direction, turn over a new leaf, embark on a fresh new career path. I went to law school, graduated, and passed the bar exam, and became a licensed attorney. You want to talk about pressure? Try being a junior associate in a law firm. Forbes magazine did a survey of the unhappiest jobs in America. You want to know what the number one unhappiest job in America is? Being a junior associate lawyer in a law firm. The bosses are constantly on your ass to make your billable hours, draft this, file that, bill more hours. Always bill more hours. And they dangle in front of you the carrot of approval from your bosses, promotions, the corner office, the shiny BMW and the six-figure salary. And all you have to do is give them your soul.

I enjoyed some of my work as a lawyer. I like the courtroom drama, the battle of strategy, the war of wits and wills. But police work just gets in the blood, and when the bug bites you it sinks its sharp little fangs in and doesn't let go. So, after being away from police work for more than five years I came back. I can't articulate very well exactly what drew me back, but I have a personal habit of stepping back at times and examining my life from the aerial perspective of an alien coming down in a spaceship. I call it "the view from 30,000 feet." It is a very helpful and healthy exercise that keeps me grounded. From that perspective I think that I came back for two reasons; the camaraderie of cops and the certainty that I am doing something worthwhile. Sure I'll never make the money I could have made being a lawyer, but I got out of that rat race and I have my peace of mind. I like my job. I like my life.

On a small team, whether in the military or in police work, the shared danger, hardship, and experiences creates a bond that simply has no equal in civilian life. I am not denigrating in any way the work of anyone in civilian life. I know very well the challenges of working together on a big project or a big case, and the thrill of accomplishment that comes when you win the case or pull off a big success. I've done that and it's a great feeling, and well-deserved. What I am talking about is lying on the ground next to your buddy in the pouring rain, in the dark of night, drenched to the bone and miserable, aiming your rifle at a house where someone is holding a hostage, waiting for them to show themselves so you can take the shot. I've done that too, and it's just on a whole different level. Combat has been called the ultimate human experience, and was expressed so eloquently by Ernest Hemingway; *There is no hunting like the hunting of man, and those who have hunted armed men long enough and liked it never care for anything else.* I am not saying I am bloodthirsty by any means, but there is simply nothing like it in the civilian world and once you've lived it, everything else seems tame and mundane.

The other reason I came back to police work is the certainty of knowing that I am doing something really meaningful and valuable. When I would win a case as a lawyer, I felt the thrill of victory and I scored a win for my client, not to mention my bank account, but sometimes my clients were people who I didn't like very much. Sometimes I don't want my client to win, but I have a duty to zealously advocate for them. I had a case, a terrible criminal case, where when I learned the full details of what my client had done I tried to withdraw from the case, but the judge denied my motion. So I was stuck with the case, and I did my duty. I did it well, and some very serious felony charges were dismissed or acquitted at the trial. He still went to prison, but not for as long as he deserved. After the trial I was congratulated by my fellow attorneys, but I didn't feel much like celebrating. I felt like a needed a shower.

As a police officer I know that every day I will help someone, even in some small way. Making arrests and putting bad guys in jail is very satisfying, but in truth it is only a small part of what we do. We have probably all heard the expression "the thin blue line", and what those words mean is that thin line of steel between law and anarchy, safety and fear, freedom and oppression. Americans sleep safely in their beds at night because we are out there, risking our own lives to protect yours and your family's. We are hunters, and those who would do evil flee from us. We are guardians, and those in distress run to us. We are protectors, and when we drive down your neighborhood street you know that all is well.

* * *

When I was in my twenties, I thought being a cop was literally the greatest job in the world. I was so excited to suit up in the locker room every night that I couldn't wait to get out there and hit the streets. Foot pursuits, fights, car chases, danger and excitement and adrenaline every night – there was no other job in society like it, not even the military unless we were at war. Every other job seemed boring and ho-hum by comparison.

When I was in my thirties, and especially after my children were born, the fights and foot chases were still kind of fun but not as much as they used to be. Now I looked at my job with a more measured eye; my paycheck was decent and it was dependable, the benefits were pretty good, the health care plan was better than most, and I had unbeatable job security. By the time I was in my forties I started thinking *How many more years do I have to do this before I can retire?*

* * *

Still, there are some days that I wonder why I stay a cop. These gloomy thoughts usually enter my head after I have just finished getting chewed out in the Chief's office because some citizen made a complaint about me, or because it's Christmas or Thanksgiving and instead of being home around the dinner table with my family eating turkey and pie and watching the Lions/ Bears game, I'm out here driving around by myself pushing this patrol car around the city, watching other happy families through their living room windows.

Sometimes I get these thoughts when I have just left an accident scene, and had to help pull one more bloodied person out of the wreckage, or gone to another domestic, another child abuse, another drug overdose. It wears on you, year after year of seeing man's inhumanity to his fellow man.

It's not the big things that keep you going. Those are very satisfying when they happen, like when we tracked down and caught a serial rapist that had been terrorizing the neighborhoods and making every woman live in fear in her own home. But the big things are too few and far between. It's the little things that keep you going.

I got a call one night of a stray dog. A couple had been out for a walk and were two blocks from home when this old dog fell in with them and walked with them back to their house. He had a collar on but no tags. They didn't recognize him from the neighborhood and didn't know what to do with him, and it was getting dark. So they called the police and I came to pick up the dog. Now our standard procedure when we pick up stray dogs is to take them to the station, enter them in the Found Animal Log up in dispatch, and put them in the kennel until someone calls to report their dog is missing. If no one has claimed the dog within 48 hours we take it to the animal shelter. And you know what happens there to dogs no one claims.

Now I led this dog out to my patrol car and was getting ready to put him in the back and take him to the station like our policy says, but I could see he was an old fella and not moving too fast, so I figured he had to live close by, I'd bet no more than a quarter mile from where I was standing. He was looking at me with his grizzled old face and his tail slowly wagging, and I just couldn't take him to that cold dark kennel out behind the station. So I put him in the car and I started driving around the neighborhood. I know what it's like to lose your dog, and I figured somebody has gotta be out here looking for this fella. Sure enough, a couple blocks away I see the beam of a flashlight shining into the front yards of the houses.

I drove over to the light and saw a distraught man and two kids about seven or eight years old walking down the street. The kids were very upset, with sniffling noses and tracks of tears running down their cheeks. When I pulled up the man anxiously asked if I had seen a brown dog, and when I got out and opened the back door of the patrol car and that dog bounded out and ran to the kids, well it was a reunion that would warm the heart of the Grinch himself.

Relief flooded the dad's face and he said I had no idea how much this meant. They had plane tickets and hotel reservations and were leaving first thing in the morning to spend a week at Disney World. But the kids refused to go if they couldn't find the dog. Now their dog was back, the kids were happy, and their vacation was saved. Yeah, in the grand scheme of things that was a little thing, but it wasn't little to them.

* * *

I was driving along a busy stretch of four-lane road when I saw a man in a wheelchair on the sidewalk. He wasn't moving, just sitting and watching the traffic. About half an hour later I drive by and there he is, still sitting there. I spun around and went back to check on him, make sure he was okay. When I walked up to him, relief flooded his face. He said his wheelchair was broken, and he had been sitting out here for over an hour, trying to flag someone down, but the cars just kept zipping by. The man was a military veteran, paralyzed from the waist down, and his left arm did not function well. Despite that, he was not bitter. He was a cheerful and independent minded guy, and he did not want anyone taking care of him.

Being a military veteran myself, we hit if off instantly. I took a look under the hood, so to speak, of his wheelchair to see if I could figure out why it wasn't working. The motor was running, but the wheels weren't moving, so I figured it was a transmission or driveline problem. I've done a lot of tinkering around with cars, and I got down on my belly and looked underneath with my flashlight. I could see that it was a chain-drive motor, and the chain had come off. I reached up under there, and largely by feel, went to work on it. After about twenty minutes of fiddling with the chain, pushing the wheelchair back or forward a few inches as needed, I got the chain back on. The vet was underway again, and we shook hands and parted company, him motoring off home and me covered in grease and dirt, and both of us happy to have met each other. Chad, wherever you are, good luck to you my friend.

I went back to the station to clean up and change uniforms, and people in the office looked disapprovingly at my dirty uniform. I know I will never get so much as a "Hey, nice job" from the Command Staff, but that's not why we do what we do.

Sometimes it can be difficult to find meaning in what we do. When I worked in the wealthy blueblood neighborhoods, the people would look down on us like we were no better than the hired help, like we were beneath them and they treated us accordingly. When I worked in the public housing projects, it seemed like every call I went on there were no friendly faces, no one happy to see us. Not the victims, not the suspects, not their family members, not the bystanders. Nine out of ten calls was one dirtbag did something to another dirtbag, and today's victim was just as likely to be tomorrow's perpetrator, and vice versa.

That was a tough environment to work in, to find meaning behind what I was doing. Cops don't do the Job just for the money. Lord knows there are easier ways to make money. Hell, I'm a licensed attorney. I could sit in an air-conditioned office and write briefs and file motions all day, at two hundred bucks an hour. Another cop I work with was a stockbroker, another was an electrical engineer, and still another has a Ph.D in computer science. One even graduated from the Harvard School of Business and worked in a corporate management position at a company whose name you would instantly know. Like all of us, one day he heard the call of the wild and just chucked his suit and briefcase to strap on a badge and gun. We don't do this job for the money.

When I reflect back on my two decades in law enforcement I realize what the cost has been to my body, my psyche, and my relationships. Long term sleep deprivation caused by shift work. Social isolation because of the work schedule and the nature of the work itself. The psychological trauma of seeing people die in horrible ways. Broken bones, sprains, strains, dog bites, and plenty of bruises. But you know what? I wouldn't have traded it for any corporate job in the world.

In my long police career I have always been getting chewed out by my bosses because I don't write enough traffic tickets. Truth is I really don't care much if someone is going 48 in a 40 on their way to work in the morning. I like the neighborhood patrols. I make it a point to drive every street and little side road in my district, every shift. I like seeing the people, especially on a sunny Sunday afternoon when I see a dad teaching a kid to ride a bike, families playing in the yard, couples taking walks and holding hands. This is why I do it. Because this is what I value. This is what I will serve and protect.

THE END

Epilogue

When I was a kid I was shocked to discover that my Dad slept with a bayonet and a pistol under his pillow every night. Mind you, this was ten years after he left Vietnam, but a part of his mind had never left the rice paddies and helicopters and firefights. And it never would. Post Traumatic Stress Disorder, or PTSD, is not a disorder at all, in my opinion. It is the natural human response to repeated exposure to unnatural situations.

I see faces at times. Faces of the dead. People that come back to me when I am about to go to sleep, or when I am at a restaurant eating a hamburger, or out for a walk with my dog. The little boy that I tried to save from drowning. The beautiful young woman who was murdered in a parking garage. The criminal thug whose eyes were locked with mine as he died from a gunshot wound that we gave him. They ask me why I did not save them. Fellow officers who were killed and seriously wounded in the line of duty. All these years later I still remember their names and faces. And there are others. It took me many years to make peace with them, these ghosts. I don't mind now when they come around to see me.

To all the military veterans, the law enforcement officers, and others who have had to look death in the face, or who have had to kill others in the line of duty, I know what you are going through. Don't try to bury it. Do what you have to do to learn to make peace with it. Knowing that you did all that you could, that you were on the side of right, goes a long way. See someone if you need to. Join a support group. Talk to your family. Turn to God, talk to your pastor. Just don't try to bury it, because believe me the ghosts will come back to visit you. You will never get rid of them, so accept them and make peace with them, and you can be at peace with yourself.

Made in United States
North Haven, CT
26 September 2023

41989460R00286